P9-DHC-996

CALLIOPE'S SISTERS

A Comparative Study of Philosophies of Art

Second Edition

Richard L. Anderson

Kansas City Art Institute

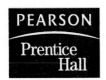
PEARSON

Prentice Hall

Upper Saddle River, NJ 07458

Library of Congress Cataloging-in-Publication Data

Anderson, Richard L.
   Calliope's sisters : a comparative study of philosophies of art   /
Richard Anderson.—2nd ed.
      p.   cm.
   ISBN 0-13-093609-X
   1. Aesthetics—Comparative studies.   I. Title.
BH39 .A57   2004
700′.1—dc22

2003023687

Publisher: Nancy Roberts
Editorial Assistant: Lee Peterson
Production Liaison: Marianne Peters-Riordan
Manufacturing Buyer: Ben Smith
Permissions Supervisor: Ronald Fox
Marketing Manager: Marissa Feliberty
Marketing Assistant: Adam Laitman
Cover Designer: Bruce Kenselaar
Cover Design Concept: Kim Anderson
Cover Art: African/Democratic Republic of
   the Congo/Lega peoples Face Mask

(muminia), Wood with traces of kaolin
9¼ × 6¾ × 2¾ inches (23.5 × 17.1 × 7.0 cm)
The Nelson-Atkins Museum of Art, Kansas
City, Missouri [Purchase] F83-56 © 2003
The Nelson Gallery Foundation
Image Permission Coordinator: Cynthia
   Vincenti
Photo Researcher: Francelle Carapetyan
Composition/Full-Service Project
   Management: Patty Donovan/Pine Tree
   Composition

Credits and acknowledgments borrowed from other sources and reproduced, with permission, in this textbook appear on appropriate page within text.

Copyright © 2004, 1990 by Pearson Education Inc., Upper Saddle River, New Jersey 07458.
Pearson Prentice Hall. All rights reserved. Printed in the United States of America. This publication is protected by Copyright and permission should be obtained from the publisher prior to any prohibited reproduction, storage in a retrieval system, or transmission in any form or by any means, electronic, mechanical, photocopying, recording, or likewise. For information regarding permission(s), write to: Rights and Permissions Department.

Pearson Prentice Hall™ is a trademark of Pearson Education, Inc.
Pearson® is a trademark of Pearson plc
Prentice Hall® is a registered trademark of Pearson Education, Inc.

Pearson Education LTD., London
Pearson Education Singapore, Pte. Ltd
Pearson Education Canada, Ltd.
Pearson Education—Japan
Pearson Education Australia PTY, Limited

Pearson Education North Asia Ltd
Pearson Educación de Mexico, S.A. de C.V.
Pearson Education Malaysia, Pte. Ltd
Pearson Education, Upper Saddle River, New Jersey

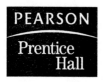

ISBN 0-13-093609-X

CONTENTS

3

ABORIGINAL AUSTRALIAN AESTHETICS: Sacramental Union with the Eternal Dreamtime   63

4

AESTHETICS OF THE SEPIK: Powerful Spirits and Phallic Aggression in New Guinea   86

5

NAVAJO AESTHETICS: A Unity of Art and Life   115

6

YORUBA AESTHETICS: Goodness and Beauty in West Africa 138

7

AZTEC AESTHETICS: Flower and Song 169

8

AESTHETICS IN EARLY INDIA: *Rasa* and the Theory of Transcendental Enjoyment 191

9

JAPANESE AESTHETICS: An Exultation of Beauty and Bliss 206

10

WESTERN AESTHETICS: A Quartet of Traditions   231

PART TWO

11

INTRODUCTION TO PART TWO   253

12

COMPARATIVE AESTHETICS: The Many Faces of the Muse   255

13

ART AS CULTURALLY SIGNIFICANT MEANING   277

14

STYLE, FEELING, AND SKILL 304

15

WESTERN AESTHETICS IN CROSS-CULTURAL PERSPECTIVE 323

REFERENCES 329

INDEX 359

LIST OF ILLUSTRATIONS

PREFACE

The idea for the first edition of this book was born as I was putting the finishing touches on another book, a textbook that surveyed the major issues in the anthropological study of art, with chapters on such topics as "The Functions of Art," "The Artist's Life and Work," and so on. The last professional colleague to review the manuscript before it went to press was Warren d'Azevedo, whose careful reading caught a number of errors and omissions—mostly minor, but some embarrassingly important. Generally, Warren's critique was encouraging and supportive, but at one point he remarked that until anthropologists get out of their habit of studying art exclusively as the handmaiden of other subjects and begin taking art on its own terms, we can never hope to gain a fundamental understanding of art *per se*.

I teach at the Kansas City Art Institute, a college where, far from being a "handmaiden" of anything, art is the central focus of concern. Perhaps because of that, d'Azevedo's remark struck me as being absolutely on target. Art does, admittedly, play an important role in other realms of human life, but what is the core of art itself? Wouldn't it be worthwhile to examine that question in a number of different societies? From previous reading, I knew that sufficient information was available to undertake such a study. After toying with the idea for a while, a couple hours of jotting down ideas produced a rough outline for this book: I would describe philosophies of art in several diverse, non-Western societies and then examine the similarities and differences among them.

Turning the outline into a book has been a protracted (though satisfying) experience; nevertheless, its results remain tentative for two reasons. First, the body of research and writing about non-Western art has increased so dramatically in recent years that no one can claim total familiarity with all of it, and second, the extant literature continues to have numerous gaps, tantalizing lacunae that only future research will fill. But despite these limitations, there is enough information at hand to undertake a synthetic, cross-cultural study of philosophies of art, and that is what this book attempts to do.

There are three principal changes in this, the second edition of *Calliope's Sisters*. First, I have modified the existing material in the book to bring it in line with developments in the field in the last decade or so. Second, for the chapters in Part One that describe traditional aesthetics in recent non-Western societies, I have added substantial epilogues describing changes in art in the colonial and post-colonial eras. In light of these additions, I have also broadened Chapter 12's discussion of "intercultural influences" to include remarks on the globalization of art and aesthetics in the contemporary world. Third, Chapter 10, on aesthetics in the West, has been expanded to include some of the findings of *American Muse: Anthropological Excursions into Art and Aesthetics* (2000), a book written between the first and second editions of *Calliope's Sisters*. These changes have also necessitated some modification of the chapters of Part Two. In addition, I have attempted to improve the clarity of the writing throughout the text.

The book's inevitable flaws and shortcomings would have been far greater had it not been for the assistance and support of many individuals and institutions. Extensive and detailed critical suggestions came from Joann W. Keali'inohomoku, to whose scholarship and good judgment I am greatly indebted. Others who read and provided valuable comments on part or all of the manuscript were Valerie Alexander, Elizabeth Anderson, Jack Cashell, Anne Devaney, Evelyn Hatcher, Harvey Hix, Briggita Hauser Schäublin, John Messenger, Marcella Nesom, Rachel Pennabecker, Paul D. Schaefer, Suzanne Gott, Susan Feagin, Lea McChesney, Joyce Youmans, and Robert Farris Thompson. Countless valuable ideas, corrections, and clarifications have been prompted by students in my classes at the Kansas City Art Institute, and I heartily thank them for their help.

I also stand in debt to the staffs of the libraries (and especially the inter-library loan personnel) at the Kansas City Art Institute, the University of Missouri at Kansas City, Johnson County (Kansas) Public Library, and the Kansas City Public Library. Mimi Pettigrew and Teddy Graham gave able secretarial assistance, and helpful financial support was provided by numerous grants from the Andrew W. Mellon Fund and the Association of Independent Colleges of Art. At Prentice Hall, the ever-competent Nancy Roberts, Marianne Peters-Riordan, and Lee Peterson have all been a pleasure to work with.

Finally, I give my heartfelt thanks to Kim Anderson for her sympathetic support, for her discerning insights into art and the human soul, for the many editorial suggestions she made toward clarifying my presentation, and for being an ever-stimulating participant in the artist–scientist dialogue that this book represents.

R.L.A.
Kansas City Art Institute

ACKNOWLEDGMENTS

Grateful acknowledgment is also made to the following for permission to quote from copyrighted material:

From Laurens Van der Post, 1958, *The Lost World of the Kalahari*, p. 247. Reprinted by permission of William Morrow and Company, Inc.

From Knut Rasmussen, 1931, *The Netsilik Eskimos: Social Life and Spiritual Culture*. Fifth Thule, Vol. 8. Reprinted by permission of AMS Press.

From Ronald M. Berndt, 1964, *The World of the First Australians*. Reprinted by permission of the University of Chicago Press and Ure Smith.

From Carl August Schmitz, 1963, *Wantoat: Art and Religion of the Northeast New Guinea Papuans*. Reprinted by permission of Mouton de Gruyter.

From Gary Witherspoon, 1977, *Language and Art in the Navajo Universe*. Reprinted by permission of University of Michigan Press.

From Robert Farris Thompson, 1983, *Flash of the Spirit: African and Afro-American Art and Philosophy*. Reprinted by permission of Random House.

From Miguel León-Portilla, 1971, "Philosophy in Ancient Mexico," in Volume 10 of *The Handbook of Middle American Indians*. Reprinted by permission of University of Texas Press.

From Masaharu Anesaki, 1933, *Art, Life and Nature in Japan*. Reprinted by permission of Marshall Jones.

From Tom Wolfe, 1975, *The Painted Word*. Reprinted by permission of Farrar, Strauss, & Giroux.

From Eliot Deutsch, 1975, *Studies in Comparative Aesthetics*. (Monograph of the Society for Asian and Comparative Philosophy, No. 2.) Reprinted by permission of University Press of Hawaii.

From Richard Selzer, 1979, *Confessions of a Knife*, p. 196. Reprinted by permission of William Morrow & Company and Hogarth Press.

From George Devereux, 1961, "Art and Mythology," in Bert Kaplan, ed., *Studying Personality Cross-culturally*. Reprinted by permission of Harper and Row.

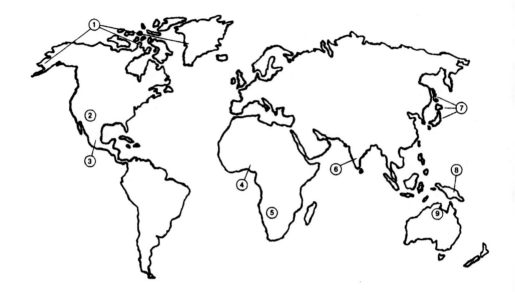

LOCATIONS OF THE NON-WESTERN SOCIETIES
DISCUSSED IN PART ONE

1. Eskimos   4. Yoruba   7. Japan
2. Navajos   5. San   8. Sepik River, New Guinea
3. Aztecs   6. India   9. Arnhem Land, Australia

INTRODUCTION: CALLIOPE'S SISTERS

When the early Greeks speculated about the fundamental nature of art, they initially thought the matter was fairly simple. The goddess Mnemosyne (memory) bore a daughter of the great god Zeus. The child was called Calliope. When she was grown, she gave to human beings the gift of art, a benefaction that was particularly fitting from one who joined the genius of past experience, as represented by memory, with the awesome and immediate power over the present moment that was Zeus's. But this mythical account of the origin of art soon seemed inadequate. How could a single goddess foster such diverse activities as comedy and tragedy, music and dance, sacred poetry and the lyrics of love? By the eighth century B.C., Hesiod was describing Calliope's enlarged family. Now she was the foremost member of a group of nine sisters, the Muses, each associated with a specific art. Or were the nine led by a tenth Muse, Apollo, the god of light? Other accounts assigned still different duties, names, and numbers to these Olympian patrons of the arts.

But mythology's chief value lies in its ability to give humans an unambiguous understanding of their seemingly contradictory and chaotic lives. The classical poets must have realized this because Calliope's family was soon simplified again by attributing all art to "The Muse." This usage generally remains with us today, reflecting our common assumption that all art derives from a single source, that it is possessed of a unitary nature and purpose, and that it can be evaluated by a single principle of criticism. Of course, on closer reflection, most Westerners concede (as did Hesiod) that things may not be so simple; and even a passing acquaintance with non-Western art complicates the picture even further. But despite such problems, this assumption continues to inform much of our thinking about art.

Thus, we still have the ancient dilemma of Calliope's sisters. Are they, and the arts they represent, distinctly different personages with no more than a slight familial resemblance to each other? Or does the Muse have a single identity, capable of donning superficially differing guises depending on time, place, and medium? These questions are at the core of this book, but before we address them some methodological issues must be discussed. We can start by asking why Calliope's family should interest us in the first place.

The Role of Art and Aesthetics

The instrumental concerns of our day-to-day lives, such as making a living, the humdrum business of economics, and the practical matters of politics, provide for our needs as biological organisms. Simply put, they keep us alive. But why live at all? For what reason do we exert our minds and bodies so that we may be sustained? One answer lies not in the instrumentalities of our bodily existence but in the affective realm of our minds. We live to perpetuate our own spiritual existence and the lives of our loved ones; we live because of the symbolic value we attach to life itself; and we live to experience the joys and passions of today and tomorrow. Life's gratifications range from the private to the public, the idiosyncratic to the societal, and the sensuous to the intellectual. It is unclear where practical activities leave off and expressive culture begins, but it *is* clear that the Muse makes a very important contribution to the latter. In a word, art can make life worthwhile. And, as Herbert Read has observed, the alienation that plagues the modern Western world can only benefit from a renewed interest in the blessed Muse.

The apparent neglect of the arts in popular Western culture is paralleled by the scant attention they have received from scholars. While everything from moon rocks to Oedipal urges have been examined in minute detail, art has often been ignored. And when art has inspired study, the most common approach has been merely to describe and categorize it according to stylistic features or else to examine it as an adjunct to more concrete activities such as art's economic functions or the training of artists. What has received far less attention is the issue that constitutes the very core of art, namely aesthetics.

Of course *aesthetics,* as the branch of Western philosophy that focuses on the fundamental nature and value of art, has spawned a substantial literature, and the main currents of Western aesthetics will be described in a later chapter. However, a basic assumption of this book is that the Western world does not have a monopoly on wisdom and insight regarding art. To the contrary, an important means to a deeper understanding of any particular endeavor is to examine it in other human cultures in the hope of ferreting out the components that are shared and pan-human.

From this broader, cross-cultural perspective, let us return to Calliope and her family. The question now becomes this: Looking at the world around us, is there a single motivation that prompts works of art in all human cultures; or, if the essence of art is multiple, does Calliope have only a finite number of sisters; or is the situation one of total relativism, with a unique Muse inspiring every culture's characteristic art?

Progress often results from asking questions that are just difficult enough, neither too easy as to be trivial nor too difficult as to produce only frustration. Questions about Calliope's sisters most assuredly will not prove to be too easy. The danger, rather, is that the questions are too difficult to be conclusively studied at the present time. However, thanks to work carried out in recent years by scholars interested in non-Western art, I believe that the search for Calliope's sisters may now be undertaken with a hope of some real success. Certainly the current state of our knowledge is such that we may begin to get glimpses of some of the sisters and of the fundamental nature of art.

The Cultural Anthropological Approach

Although I will also draw on the work of art historians, art critics, and philosophers, the prevailing perspective throughout this book is that of cultural anthropology. In contrast to *archaeologists*, who learn about societies that no longer exist by examining the materials they left behind, *cultural anthropologists* usually focus their attention on societies that can be studied via the statements of living members of the society. Occasionally, these are cultures of the past. The main outlines of early sixteenth-century Aztec society, for example, are known today largely because the Aztecs and their Spanish conquerors left many written descriptions of Aztec life ways. But far more often a cultural anthropologist's goal is to learn about a contemporary culture by living in it for a year or more, learning the language of its people, and participating in their daily activities. The observations and impressions of such fieldwork serve as a basis for the anthropologist's written account of the society, called an *ethnography*.

The ethnographer may focus on any of a number of subjects, but an important distinction that must be made at this point is between "emic" and "etic" culture, either or both of which the anthropologist may describe. Things that have an observable existence and that can be studied through methods that are applicable in any human population have come to be called *etic*. The average number of people in a native household or the number of calories of food they consume daily are examples of etic data.

By contrast, *emic* culture exists only in the minds of the culture's members, having meaning only in the context of the native conceptual system. Thus, whereas family size is etic, the way family members conceptualize kinship relations is emic.

The distinction between etic and emic culture will arise continually in this book, and it will be important that the reader appreciate that different kinds of information are conveyed by etic statements (e.g., "masks are carved out of wood from two species of trees") and emic statements (e.g., "native critics generally feel that masks carved from one type of wood are more desirable than those carved from the other"). The difference between such statements can be seen, for example, in the fact that they are verified or refuted in different ways. To confirm the etic statement about two kinds of wood being used in masks, one would consult a botanist; to confirm the emic statement about the relative beauty of the woods, a native art connoisseur. *Information about emic aesthetics in ten societies constitutes the primary data upon which this book is based.*

Cultural anthropologists have traditionally spent less time examining the cultures of complex societies such as the United States, China, and India than they have studying small-scale societies such as those of Native American Indians, the societies of sub-Saharan Africa, and the native peoples of the Pacific islands. The first cultural anthropologists, writing only a little more than a century ago, viewed small-scale societies as being altogether simpler, less developed, and generally inferior to contemporary Western society. However, after rigorous methods of fieldwork were adopted, this viewpoint, which would now be called *ethnocentric,* was discarded for both empirical and ethical reasons. It was largely replaced by the concept of *cultural relativism,* the belief that every traditional society, regardless of the size of its population and the complexity of its technology, can best be understood by seeing it as an integrated whole, possessed of institutions and beliefs that are typically suited to the needs of the society's members.[1]

The Concerns of Aesthetics

As the term is used here and in much other scholarly writing, *aesthetics* refers to theories about the fundamental nature and value of art. This definition is of course logically contingent upon a definition of *art,* a thorny matter that reflective people in the West have failed to satisfactorily resolve after 2,500 years of continual debate.

Indeed, the American philosopher Morris Weitz (1967; see also Ladd 1973:417–421) has argued that we can never hope to isolate a single quality that is the definitive feature of all art. Rather, Weitz suggests, art can have only what Wittgenstein called an "open definition." That is, the best we can ever do is note the several traits that commonly give a "family resemblance" to those things that we think of as art. When we meet things with which we are unfamiliar, either because they are new or because they come from other cultures, they are judged to be art according to the degree to which they share these familial similarities—or else the repertoire of family resemblances will itself evolve.

The tentativeness and unwieldiness of Weitz's approach to defining art may be frustrating, but I feel it to be realistic, if for no other reason than that

---

[1]Thus when cultural anthropologists use the term *primitive* to refer to small-scale societies, they only mean ones that (a) have a relatively small and sparse population, (b) rely upon a relatively simple technology that lacks metallurgy, ceramics, writing, and such, and (c) display a relatively low degree of economic specialization. The term is absolutely *not* meant to suggest that these societies or their members are backward, crude, or otherwise inferior to other societies. The intellectual sophistication of the aesthetic systems described in this book should provide convincing evidence on this score. Inasmuch as many people nevertheless associate "primitive" with generally negative qualities, it now seems best to avoid use of the word altogether.

Also, cultural relativism itself has limitations. For one thing, totally objective relativism is never possible inasmuch as the study of any phenomenon is inevitably colored by the questions one asks, the theoretical approach one adopts, and so on. And even if complete objectivity were possible, thoroughgoing relativism is not always desirable. For example, one should not simply study cultural or biological genocide relativistically; one is morally responsible for evaluating its consequences and acting accordingly.

it does not ignore a pervasive feature in the history of art, namely the unpredictability of art's evolution. The traits that seem to nicely characterize the art of one era always change as artists and their art move creatively into the future. (I have previously discussed [Anderson 1989:8–17] the hazards of attempting to use a closed definition of art cross-culturally, especially if the proffered definitive trait is art's being nonutilitarian or prompting a qualitatively unique affective response in the percipient or person who perceives the art work.)

Aesthetics may also deal with conceptions of beauty, but inasmuch as the grotesque may also play an active role in art, aesthetics is not solely a theory of beauty. On the other hand, although natural things such as sunsets and flowers may also prompt feelings similar to those generated by art, the primary concern here is with art produced by the human mind and body. It is usually the shared beliefs and consistent behaviors of a society that most interest the anthropologist, and the present comparative study of aesthetics will likewise deal primarily with aesthetic values held by a sizable portion of the populace for a significant period of time. However, unanimity of belief is neither expected nor necessary. The aesthetic diversity that exists in all societies is both quantitative (some individuals devote more thought to art than do others) and qualitative (there are differences of opinion as to what art is and isn't).

From the foregoing account of aesthetics, it should be clear that the starting point for the comparative study of aesthetics is ethnographic data. The methods involved in such fieldwork have already been mentioned, but a related factor should be made explicit here, namely that useful information about aesthetics cannot safely be *deduced* simply by looking at another society's art works. Stylistic conventions can be described by examining foreign art works, but since there is no simple, one-to-one correspondence between art work and conceptual motivation, and since aesthetic systems are often complex intellectual constructs, aesthetic values and metaphysical assumptions about art cannot be reconstructed in depth and with certainty based on, say, a carving's appearance or a song's melody.

Organization of the Book

After a few more introductory issues are dealt with in this chapter, the remainder of the book is divided into two sections, the first descriptive and the second analytic. The first, and longer, part delineates aesthetic values in ten societies, supplemented by some brief comments about each society's culture, its art, and the adequacy of the data about these topics.

I have used two criteria for selecting these ten societies. First, and most obviously, information about the society's aesthetic system must be available. The present state of the literature is such that very few societies meet this requirement. The cultural anthropologist who spends one, two, or more years living in a society and who may eventually write hundreds of pages describing it often makes little or no mention of the society's art, much less the philosophical values that underlie the art—even though he or she dutifully informs students that art is an important universal phenomenon. And since studying a society's aesthetics requires a broad knowledge of its culture plus extensive face-to-face questioning of the makers and users of art, preferably in their own language, information about native aesthetics is rarely reported by art historians and museum curators, since their chief interest usually lies in collecting and describing art works. Thus the subject of non-Western aesthetics has often remained in the unexplored territory between cultural anthropology and art history. However, at a slow but steady pace, descriptions of non-Western aesthetics have accumulated, and a comparative study is now possible.

The second criterion for selecting societies for Part One is diversity. Within the constraints of the available literature, I have chosen societies that are distributed across every continent, that create art in many media and with varied styles, and that represent distinctly different parts of the continuum of sociocultural complexity: small-scale, nomadic groups that rely upon hunting, gathering, and fishing (the San, Inuit, and Australian Aboriginal peoples); societies that subsist on various forms of horticulture and herding (the Sepik River tribes, Navajo, and Yoruba); and societies that possess complex technologies and large, heterogeneous populations (the Aztecs, India, Japan, and the West).

If Part One is descriptive, Part Two is analytic. In it, I discuss the similarities and differences among the ten aesthetic systems dealt with in Part One. Or to put it differently, after Part One describes Calliope's incarnation in ten societies, Part Two will reveal the traits she seems to have universally, and it will also note why other traits seem to vary systematically from one place to another.

Obviously, our conclusions can only be tentative. Data remain scant, and available information is biased both by the underrepresentation of the hunter-gatherer pattern of living that was the only human option until the comparatively recent past, as well as by the overrepresentation of the complex societies (and their political and intellectual elites) that politically dominate the modern world.

Besides problems stemming from the limited availability of data, a second type of problem hinders our search for the elusive Calliope. Metals are said to be malleable if they are easily shaped, bent, or hammered into a form that meets the smith's needs, and aesthetic systems are by their nature highly malleable intellectual entities, easily twisted and distorted by the heavy-handed treatment of non-natives, especially in efforts at cross-cultural comparison. I have tried to be faithful to the integrity of the aesthetic systems presented in Part One, attempting to describe each one in and of itself, generally avoiding discussing one society's aesthetics as it compares to another's.

A related problem is even more fundamental: Just what is it that we will be describing as "art" in the following chapters? Clearly, if we tacitly accept the Western belief that art is limited to what is on display in galleries and museums, to what one hears in concert halls, or to what is performed on the ballet stage, then the quest for art in non-Western settings can yield only meager results.

If "our" definition of art does not lead to productive results, then perhaps we should use "theirs." But this approach, too, is immediately ruled out by the well-known fact that most languages do not have a word that means the same thing as the English word "art."[2] This being the case, one of the tasks undertaken in the following chapters is the development of a definition of art that avoids these problems.

One might ask, however, do we have to have an explicit and precise definition of "art" before we even begin our comparative study of aesthetics? Fortunately not. Perhaps this can be best understood by considering the way in which anthropologists have gone about studying one of their favorite topics, kinship. Experience has shown that there are two ways that are *not* very fruitful for studying kinship in non-Western societies. In the first place, it is unproductive to describe and analyze a non-Western kinship system by using terms such as "aunt" or "cousin" that come from our own, Western system of kinship. But it is equally useless to go to another society expecting to find an explicit, native statement of abstract kinship principles: One is likely to find that the people in question do not have a word that can be accurately translated as meaning "kinship," much less "consanguinity" or "patrilineality."

But even though they have had to avoid narrowly using either our or their definitions, scholars have made great strides in understanding the phenomenon of kinship. They have done this by, first, accepting the general and broad assumption that when one speaks of kinship one has in mind patterned social relations within nuclear and extended families, notions of legitimacy regarding offspring, ideas about whom one can or cannot marry, and so on. With this general domain in mind, fieldworkers have gone to other cultures and pursued the question—How do the people in this society think

---

[2]After extensive fieldwork with the Bala (a Basongye people living in Zaire), Alan P. Merriam (1973:273–274) concluded that to the Bala way of thinking, music differs from non-music in three respects: Music is always the product of human activity, it is always created in accord with some preconceived organizational principles, and it is composed of sounds that have a minimal continuity in time.

Several factors to which Westerners attach importance in their definition of music, such as the "manipulation of sound for its own sake" (Merriam 1973:278) are not verbalized in Bala discussions about music. Therefore Merriam concludes that if one confines oneself to only explicit statements about aesthetics, then "problems arise when we find a culture like the Bala in which what *we* call art, even though separable as objects produced by people whose behavior is special, is merely something else that man does" (Merriam 1973:281). (See also Chapter 13 of Merriam's [1964] important *The Anthropology of Music*, as well as Keil's [1979] response to Merriam's approach.)

about such issues? Then, after a considerable amount of descriptive information has been accumulated, one can step back from the data and look for any cross-cultural patterns that might exist.

Similarly with art and aesthetics, the best way to proceed seems to be by recognizing that when we use the word "art," we usually have something in mind that is valued beyond its practical contribution to such instrumentalities as subsistence, that is made so as to have some sort of sensuous appeal, and the production of which reflects skills that are more highly developed in the maker than among other members of the society. Then, having in this very broad and tentative way demarcated the area of our concern, we can go to other societies and look for things and activities that generally fall into this domain, asking How do people here think about their "art"?

And this, in fact, is exactly what the chapters in Part One do: They describe philosophies of art as they look from "inside" cultures. After this has been done in ten different societies, we can move to a broader level of generality by looking for the patterns of similarities and differences that exist in the "arts" of the societies we have surveyed. This is the business of Part Two.

A comparative study of aesthetics allows us to develop a deeper appreciation of the arts of other societies, giving us the means to perceive them in the ways intended by their creators, making them not mere curiosities but sophisticated manifestations of metaphysical, cultural, and emotional meaning.

Also, in learning about non-Western aesthetic systems, we begin to understand the rich diversity of human thought as it relates to art. In a study of Far Eastern aesthetics, Thomas Munro has remarked, "If Western aestheticians wish to go on ignoring Oriental art and theory, they might more accurately entitle their books, 'Western Aesthetics,' instead of seeming to make false claims of universal scope" (Munro 1965:7–8).

Cross-cultural aesthetic understanding may also enrich us by stimulating new perspectives on our own philosophies of art, providing us with new ways of looking at the natural, social, and cultural worlds around us—just as the exposure of early twentieth-century Western artists to art objects from Africa and elsewhere stimulated important new directions in Western art styles.

There is, finally, the matter of Calliope and her elusive family. Accounts of non-Western aesthetic systems provide a starting point for a truly comparative aesthetics. After cataloging the ways in which art is conceptualized in a variety of times and places, we can begin to look for commonalities and patterns of variation in these cultural definitions of art. It is unlikely that we shall gain a certain and intimate knowledge of the cunning Calliope the first time out, but the time is ripe to begin the search.

PART ONE

1

SAN AESTHETICS

The Enhancement of Life

in a Foraging Society

In [Nxou's hands the musical bow] seemed to become a greater kind of bow, hunting meaning in the wasteland of sound. . . . All the men could play the instrument but none like Nxou. The women would sit for hours, the full look of peace upon them, listening to him.

(Van der Post 1958:247)

Thinking about the San, a hunting and gathering society in southwestern Africa, prompts one to ask some fundamental questions about what it means to be human. Are we at one with the San, a people whose material circumstances differ enormously from our own? How much do we share of their conceptions of the natural, social, and spiritual worlds? Ultimately, is San consciousness like your and my own consciousness, so that we feel, think, and exist in terms that are not qualitatively different from each others'? Or do we live in different mental worlds, forever shut off and alienated from each other, at most able only to touch fingertips but never souls, capable of understanding each others' meanings in rare moments of insight that result more from accident than design? Both sides of the argument can be supported to some degree.

On the one hand, an unbreachable distance seems to separate us from traditional San. They practiced a means of subsistence, hunting and gathering, from which the Western cultural tradition began to diverge some 10,000 years ago with the gradual adoption of agriculture. They made almost all the things they owned, but they possessed no more than they could carry on their backs and in their arms from one temporary encampment to another. They lived in groups of twenty to fifty men, women, and children, tendering allegiance to no larger polity and maintaining only a bare minimum of internal political organization and economic specialization within the band.

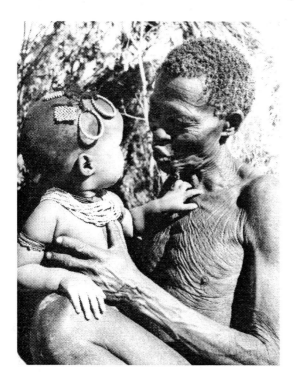

FIGURE 1-1   San man and child.
*(Photo courtesy John K. Marshall,
Documentary Educational
Resources, Watertown,
Massachusetts.)*

On the other hand, personal accounts of San daily life tell us of individuals who experienced the same emotions and concerns that engage us. They displayed courage and extreme ingenuity in the face of adversity and hardship. They put much effort into finding a good mate, providing for their families, and maintaining supportive and harmonious interactions with relatives and friends. They dearly wanted others to think well of them, and they accomplished this not through braggadocio but by being both amiable and responsible. They had a vast capacity for playfulness and good humor (see Figure 1–1).

One way of trying to resolve this dilemma is by examining the San's ideas about art. As we shall see, the satisfactions that traditional San derived from their art strongly resemble those that inform popular culture in the contemporary Western world. But before making comparisons, we must look at San culture, art, and aesthetics on their own terms.

The !Kung San

For perhaps 10,000 years, southern Africa has been the home of a genetically, linguistically, and culturally distinctive people (see map, p. xvi). Europeans long knew one major group as "Bushmen," a term that has strongly derogatory connotations in Africa today and that has largely been replaced by "San."[1] Even before Europeans began arriving in southern Africa by sea, invasions by other Africans had forced the San's ancestors to withdraw from most of the region. These African newcomers were taller, had darker skin, and spoke Bantu languages. By contrast, the San were short in stature, yellow-brown of skin, and spoke Khoisan languages, distinctive for their use of several "click" sounds.[2] The San did not adopt the invaders' horticultural practices and settle into permanent villages but continued their nomadic lives based on gathering undomesticated plants and hunting wild animals.

In so doing, the San were making a virtue of necessity because the only land not taken from them, first by the Bantu-speakers and later by Europeans, was the Kalahari Desert, an area too dry to support very much agriculture by the San or anyone else. During the twentieth century, the San drastically diminished in numbers so that only about 100,000 remain in Botswana, Namibia, and Angola. Most of these survivors have abandoned traditional life ways and now work for White or Bantu farmers. Only a group of northern San, known as the !Kung and numbering about 6,500 individuals, continued to live as hunter-gatherers recently enough for us to accumulate in-depth, fieldwork-based accounts of their culture. Unless otherwise indicated, subsequent references to the "San" will refer only to the !Kung San who lived during the 1950s and 1960s in the Dobe and Nyae Nyae areas, near the Namibia-Botswana border. The chapter closes with an Epilog that discusses some of the developments since then.

The Kalahari conforms to Western preconceptions of a desert in that there is little surface water, and summer temperatures rise as high as 120 degrees Fahrenheit (50 degrees Celsius), but it is not a land of barren dunes. Grasses, shrubs, vines, and scattered trees cover much of the Kalahari; it is this vegetation, along with the wildlife it supports, that allows the San to survive there. Although their existence is somewhat precarious and food is often the major topic of conversation, San rarely die from lack of food or water, a feat that illustrates the San's practical ingenuity. Most of the San's caloric intake and water are provided by the women, who know more than fifty species of edible plants. Men, for their part, hunt with bows and poisoned arrows to kill both small game as well as antelopes and other large animals. The San

---

[1]Although the names "San" and "!Kung" appear most often in the literature, Lee and Biesele (1994:3) have reported "*Ju/'hoansi* (real or genuine people) is the term !Kung have always called themselves, and they would like others to do the same."

[2]English speakers occasionally use "clicks." Sometimes we show mild displeasure or reproof by using a dental click (spelled "tsk tsk," but linguistically indicated by a single slash mark, /), and a lateral click (//) is used to make horses start moving or go faster. In Khoisan languages, however, instead of being "special purpose" sounds, these clicks and three others (an alveolar click,!; a palatal click, ≠; and a bilabial click, ☉.) are normal parts of many words (cf. Marshall 1965:244–245).

consume every part of the animal, down (we are told) to the "mucous lining of the nostrils and the gristle inside the ears" (Thomas 1959:9).

The San's use of ostrich eggs reveals the economy and elegance of their response to the challenges of the environment. A small hole is pecked in one end of the egg and its contents are poured out, providing an amount of food equivalent to about two dozen chicken eggs. After being rinsed, the shell makes an ideal container for drinking water. Its hole plugged with grass, such a canteen is sturdy enough to last for years, always keeping its contents deliciously cool as water slowly soaks through the eggshell walls and evaporates. When it finally does break (or when broken shells are found), it provides the raw material for the most prized San jewelry—ostrich eggshell beads.

Social organization of the San is loosely structured, with only a slight emphasis on the male line. In practice, bands are composed of several polygamous and monogamous families that are compatible with each other and that can hunt and gather effectively together. Usually an older man serves as the minimal leader of the band, but he lacks the authority to compel action. (The !Kung word for "chief," //kai, is used for headmen of the neighboring Bantu— or, in a derisive manner, to the rare San with pretensions of prominence.)

Elizabeth Marshall Thomas (1959) entitled her excellent popular book about the San *The Harmless People,* a phrase that accurately captures the quality of traditional San lifestyle. But the "harmless" San, like many other small-scale, non-Western peoples, have suffered great harm indeed at the hands of those who possess more powerful technologies. With the arrival of the horticultural Bantu-speakers, many San were reduced to serf status, and eighteenth-century Dutch settlers organized vigilante groups called *commandos* that killed San men and carried the women and children into slavery on White farms (Lee 1979:32). Forced labor has continued into the present, and the few remaining San live near the uneasy borders between Namibia, which only became an independent nation in 1989, following a century of rule by European and South African Whites; Botswana, an independent republic whose Black leaders have tried to stay on friendly terms with South Africa; and Angola, where Black guerrilla groups have been active since the early 1960s.

Although more has been written about the San than the other nomadic hunter-gatherers of Africa, the literature is uneven. We understand the San's subsistence activities well; their kinship, social structure, and religion, less well; and their art and aesthetics in only piecemeal fashion. Miscellaneous comments on art may be gleaned from early explorers, but the richest source of information derives from a series of expeditions by individuals associated with Harvard University. This research was not initiated by Harvard anthropologists with academic interests but by Lawrence Marshall, a retired business executive. With the sponsorship of Harvard's Peabody Museum, Marshall and his family lived with !Kung San for several years in the 1950s and 1960s, spending most of their time in the Nyae Nyae area. Lorna Marshall and her daughter, Elizabeth Marshall Thomas, systematically collected ethnographic data, the former publishing several scholarly works on San culture and society and the latter writing a more informal (although highly informative) account of !Kung and Gikwe San life. Meanwhile, John Marshall, a son, has made many movies of San activities, including the classic feature-length film, *The Hunters*. The Marshalls also introduced other scholars to the region, and a growing anthropological interest in the ecological adaptations of hunter-gatherers prompted Richard B. Lee and Irven DeVore to launch the Harvard Bushman (San) Research Project in 1963. Lee's writing, like that of the Marshalls, is exemplary for its clarity and rigor.

Body Decoration and Other Art Activities

The San literature allows us to address a difficult question—namely, in what sense do the San even *have* art? To pursue the issue, we may begin by considering the artifacts and activities that potentially are art: ornamentation of the body and of household items, music and dance, and a few other miscellaneous activities.

Although an early second-hand report claimed that unacculturated San had no clothes (Bleek 1928:8), traditional adult !Kung are much concerned with what they wear. The minimal essentials are made of leather: a loincloth for men, and for women an apron and a "kaross," or large cape held at the waist by a cord that creates a pouch on the women's backs in which everything from babies to firewood may be carried. Karosses are sometimes decorated with colors, and men's loincloths may be worked and fringed, but the greatest decorative effort goes into the younger women's aprons, which may be elaborately decorated with ostrich eggshell beads.

San, old and young, wear many kinds of jewelry. Leather bracelets are made from strips of hide cut from antelope heads; beaded necklaces are common; leather or wooden rings are worn around arms, waists, and legs; and hair ornaments are made of flowers, fur, and, most commonly, beads. Manufactured beads, acquired through trade, are sometimes used, as are beads made of native aromatic wood, nuts, and animal teeth. By far the most cherished beads, however, are those made from ostrich eggshells (Figure 1–2). Lorna Marshall, who is not prone to exaggeration, says that these are "the most prized possessions of the !Kung" (Marshall 1965:257). The beads, which were worn by the San's ancestors throughout southern Africa before they were pushed back into the Kalahari, are made by women. Schapera, paraphrasing Bleek (1928:9), describes the elaborate technique used to produce the beads:

> The eggshell is broken into small pieces, which are softened in water and pierced with a small stone or iron borer. They are then threaded on to a strip of

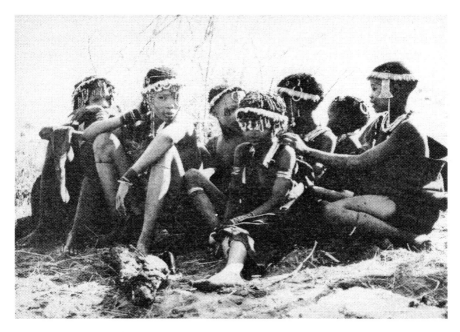

FIGURE 1-2   A group of San girls wearing ostrich eggshell beads. *(Photo courtesy John K. Marshall, Documentary Educational Resources, Watertown, Massachusetts.)*

sinew and the rough edges chipped off with a horn. Soft bark fibre is next twisted between the beads, making the chain very taut, and the edges are finally rubbed smooth with a soft stone. (Schapera 1930:66)

San can never have too many ostrich eggshell beads. Besides their being used to decorate women's pubic aprons, beads are worn in the hair and used to make single or multiple-stranded necklaces, headbands, bracelets, and armlets (Figure 1–2).

San body decoration does not end with clothing and jewelry. Traditional San also often paint their bodies, using fat, clay, soot, or powdered aromatic herbs (Bleek 1928:12; Kaufmann 1910:140; Marshall 1961:242–243; Theal 1910:41).[3] In some San groups, young men powder their hair with pulverized //hara, a sparkling black stone.

A pervasive desire to appear beautiful in the eyes of other San prompts most such adornment. The San create some body decoration for religious purposes, but even then the rationale usually is more sensuous than supernatural. For example, Thomas describes a young girl's preparation for her

---

[3]Prehistoric rock paintings and engravings indicate that body decoration has a long history in southern Africa.

wedding in these terms: "The bride's mother adorned the bride, washing her, hanging white bead ornaments from her hair, rubbing her clothing with red, sweet-smelling powder, a symbol to Bushmen of beauty" (Thomas 1959:158). As in the West, being beautifully dressed does not make the marriage bond more hallowed, but using the occasion to show off one's finery seems as fitting to the San as it does to Americans.

Tattooing serves as another means of body decoration among the San. Girls receive their first scars when they are 7 or 8, and later additions may leave them with decorated legs, buttocks, and faces (Marshall 1965:267). In at least some groups, young men also wear tattoos and scars, typically on their faces, arms, and legs. Sometimes small pieces of animal flesh are placed in the boy's incisions (Fourie 1960/1928; Werner 1906:256). Haircutting provides a final means of body ornamentation. The hair of the San grows into small, tight tufts that eventually break off, but many younger San cut off some of the tufts to make fanciful patterns. The designs (Figure 1–3) are only for decoration and have no particular meaning (Marshall 1976:82).

Although body decoration is by far the most important expressive visual medium among the San, other graphic endeavors include the following:

FIGURE 1–3 San boy with facial tattoos and decorative haircut. *(Photo courtesy John K. Marshall, Documentary Educational Resources, Watertown, Massachusetts.)*

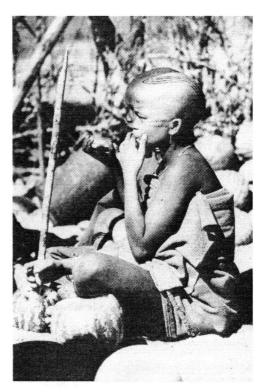

- Ostrich eggshell canteens are sometimes marked or engraved with designs. In some places such decorations help the owners identify their own canteens, but elsewhere beauty is their sole purpose (cf. Lee 1979:122; Marshall 1976:77).
- Stone and bone pipes and wooden utensils are occasionally decorated, the geometric patterns being incised with a heated iron needle. Kaufmann remarks that "the hairline precision of the lines is particularly striking" (1910:194; see also ibid.:152; Bleek 1928:10; Schapera 1930:207).
- San women and youths sometimes make elaborate string figures (Marshall 1976:351), although it is unclear whether the motives are aesthetic, recreational, or both.
- Young women sometimes draw geometric designs on the bark of mangetti and baobab trees (Marshall 1965:275).
- Although Europe's ancient cave paintings at sites such as Lascaux and Altamira are better known to Westerners, the rock paintings and engravings found in southern Africa (Figure 1–4) match the European sites in aesthetic interest and far outstrip them in number. Hundreds of decorated rock shelters and caves are known in southern Africa, and Pager (1975:9) has estimated that 150,000 individual figures probably exist, the most ancient being thousands of years old. It is likely that ancestors of the San created most or all of the paintings and engravings. In fact, rock painting continued into the nineteenth century, when the last known rock painter was shot in a raid by white *commandos*, probably in the 1860s. He was found wearing a belt with ten small horns attached, each containing a different color of paint (Stow 1905). Humans, their artifacts, and the animals they hunt are the most common subjects of rock art; and although their purpose is unclear, the paintings are interesting for their accuracy (Lewis-Williams 1981; Pager 1975). Modern San typically have several characteristic anatomical traits that are visible in the rock art including an inward curvature of the lower back (lumbar lordosis) for both men and women, permanently semi-erect penis for men, and very fatty buttocks (steatopygia) for some women (Dart 1937:1960–166).
- Lorna Marshall observes, "The !Kung are a music-loving people. Most of the time someone in a !Kung encampment is making music. People sing to the babies to soothe or entertain them. They sing to enliven their tasks and their games. They sing at the waterhole and in leisure hours by their fire. Everyone sings, almost everyone plays an instrument" (Marshall 1976:363). Dance, which often accompanies music, is also common in San encampments.

The technology of San music is minimal (Figure 1–5), being produced by four instruments: (a) a one-stringed bow, which may be either the unmodified bow that men use for hunting, with the player's open mouth serving as a

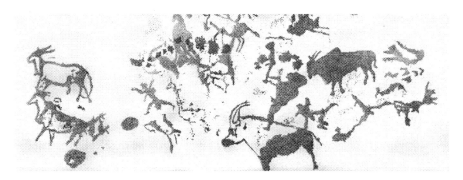

FIGURE 1-4 Tracing of figures engraved on rock surface. *(Source: pages 10-11 of Thomas Dowson's Rock Engravings of Southern Africa, 1992, Johannesburg, South Africa: University of Witwatersand Press.)*

resonator at one end of the bow, or else a bow with an attached gourd or tin can resonator; (b) a one-stringed violin played with a three-inch bow; (c) ankle-rattles worn by dancers; and (d) a four- or five-string lyre-like instrument called *//gwashi* (Figure 1–6). According to Thomas, the sound of the *//gwashi* is

FIGURE 1-5 Group of San boys playing a musical instrument called a *//gwashi*. *(Photo courtesy John K. Marshall, Documentary Educational Resources, Watertown, Massachusetts.)*

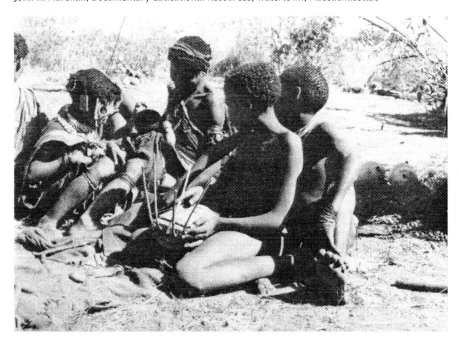

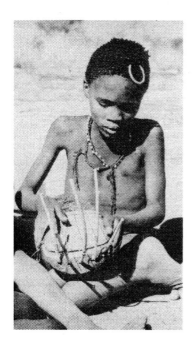

FIGURE 1–6 San boy playing a //gwashi. (Photo courtesy John K. Marshall, Documentary Educational Resources, Watertown, Massachusetts.)

beautiful, sometimes full, sometimes thin, and makes very deep and various music, for Bushmen, their music being by far their greatest art, are not given to whistles or clear, shrill sounds—all their instruments make blurred and vibrant music with a richness in every note. Their compositions, too, are never simple, not even the music of their musical games, but always mixed, always subtle, partly gay but partly sad. (Thomas 1959:223)

San music is often individualistic and spontaneous, and this is particularly true of "mood songs," whose chief function is the expression of intimate feelings and the personal experiences of the composer-singer (Thomas 1959:119).

Music also occurs as part of the Ritual Healing Dance. This dance begins at nightfall and continues at least until dawn. Its purpose is both to protect the healthy and to cure the sick. As women clap and sing, dancers move in a circle around a fire, and the experienced among them begin to feel their spiritual energy, *num* (or *n/um*), begin to warm up. With intense concentration, aided by the rhythm of the music and dance as well as the fire's smoke and heat, their *num* begins to boil, causing a few dancers to go into a trance-like state of enhanced consciousness called *kia*. A healer in *kia* experiences a heightened sense of reality and can see the otherwise invisible arrows that bring people bad luck, disease, or even death. By interceding with the spirits that send the arrows, the healer protects everybody present at the dance from misfortune (Katz 1982; Shostak 1981:291–303).

Do the San Have "Art"?

Compared to other cultures, the San philosophy of art is unusual for two reasons. As the following chapters will show, in many societies aesthetics is intimately linked to ideas about the realm of the supernatural. By contrast, a large portion of San art is made for secular purposes. This alone makes San aesthetics worth studying. But in addition to that, the San philosophy of art is somewhat less complex than its counterpart in the other groups we will discuss. Using the San as our first case study, then, permits us to raise issues that are fundamental to a comparative study of aesthetics and that could easily get lost in a denser context.

Anthropologists often claim that all societies have art, but this is generally presented as an article of faith, not a proven fact. Of course, sweeping generalizations of the sort "All societies have X" can only be conclusively substantiated by examining every single society and finding each one to possess X, a task that, for art, lies far beyond our capabilities. An easier, if less conclusive, alternative is to examine the least likely cases—cultures about which one might say that if any society is without art, it surely must be this one.

San society is a good candidate for such a statement. If the only evidence on the question were to come from the galleries of non-Western art in Western museums, the answer would be perfectly clear: The San have no art. Moreover, Western Africanists generally believe that !Kung visual arts have a low degree of development (Wolfe 1969:5).

Ultimately, of course, the question hinges on one's definition of art. As noted earlier, Morris Weitz (1967) has argued convincingly that we should not expect to find a single trait that, once and for all, distinguishes art from non-art. Rather, we can only recognize that those things we have come to call art usually share several characteristics, like the traits that constitute a "family resemblance" among siblings. Other objects are "art" to the degree that they share the traits that we associate with the rest of the "family" of art. A central goal of Part Two will be to identify and examine the recognition criteria that would constitute a cross-culturally usable definition of art. For now, however, it is illuminating to consider the previously discussed San objects and activities, not as a list of characteristics defined by academics but rather in light of three traits that are often associated with "art" in popular Western thought, namely, beauty, skill, and the idea that art is immanently nonutilitarian. Each of these traits is complex and will merit in-depth analysis in Part Two, but for now it is interesting to ask, If many (albeit far from all) Western art works are held by the public at large to be beautiful, skillfully made, and nonutilitarian, to what extent does San "art" possess these same qualities?[4]

---

[4]As will be apparent later, the San produce art not only by the informal definition used here but also by the more rigorous list of traits discussed in Part Two. I am grateful to John Adams [personal communication] for suggesting this clarification.

Although most contemporary Western artists and aestheticians agree that it is not necessarily present in art, *beauty* has often been associated with art in earlier eras of the Western tradition, and the idea remains popular today. For their part, the San clearly recognize and value beauty. The preceding description of San body decoration clearly shows that they are much concerned with personal appearance, and a closer look reveals that there are several dimensions to native conceptions of 'beauty' as it applies to the human body.

First, it is possible to cull from the literature several bodily attributes that San find beautiful. For example, part of a song recorded by P.R. Kirby (1936:431) says:

> The Bushman girl with the "pepper corn" head,
> The lice are playing in her hair,
> But she has lovely legs!

Judging from other references (Marshall 1959:349, 1976:39; Thomas 1959:184, 227), a woman's legs are considered "lovely" if they are neither long nor thin.[5]

Besides not being too thin, a beautiful San woman should have light skin, good teeth, youth, and should stand about five feet tall. For men, the criteria of attractiveness are somewhat different. A group of San young women told Lorna Marshall that a man should be "a good hunter like /Gunda; and they like handsome teeth and a wide smile like Tsamgo's, and straight, slender legs like //Ao's and a fluid, swift walk like /Gao's, and they hate a big black belly" (Marshall 1959:349). (Thomas [1959:86–87, 168–171] recounts two occasions on which young San women humiliated and rejected men with this last trait.)

But "art" and "aesthetics" usually bring to mind not the gifts of nature but the products of human activity, and instead of people's physical attributes, it is the ways in which they decorate their bodies that are most often mentioned in San discussions of beauty. From the accounts of those who have lived with the San, there is no doubt that a desire to improve one's looks and enhance one's beauty is the chief motivation for the San's making and wearing jewelry, tattooing and painting their bodies, decorating their clothes, and cutting their hair. When Bleek asked an old San woman why women tattoo themselves, the answer was, "That the men may see us pretty" (1928:11), and

---

[5]Tobias (1961) has hypothesized that the characteristically large buttocks and thighs of many San women may have resulted from an interplay between natural and sexual selection. Like the camel's hump, the fat helps the women of the desert sustain themselves and nurse their children through periods of scarce food and water. The development of the trait might have been accelerated by the San's great admiration of steatopygia, thus making a virtue of necessity.

when Elizabeth Marshall Thomas wondered if Gikwe San women really felt that being tattooed was justified, a woman said that "in her case it had been worth the pain and trouble because she was extremely ugly and had been made more beautiful" (Thomas 1959:52–53). Also, at least some of the men's tattoos are made for ornamental purposes. As will be noted below, supernatural beliefs do prompt some of the San's tattoos and perhaps some San body painting as well, but undoubtedly the most important motivation is the desire to be beautiful. The San clearly go to great lengths to cultivate beauty through decorating their bodies.[6]

The San also enjoy the beauty of music and dance. Mood songs give pleasure not only to the performer but also to the audience. The songs of the Ritual Healing Dance are believed to be potentially powerful because, like healers themselves, they contain *num*. However, according to Richard Katz, who has studied the Ritual Healing Dance in depth, "The *num* songs are both spiritual vehicles and beautiful music. The !Kung can appreciate their beauty without the danger of releasing their *num* because they believe that *num* is activated only during the dance, especially when it interacts with the dancers' *num*" (Katz 1982:124).

Another feature of the "family resemblance" of art (at least, as it is commonly thought of in the West) is that it is made with *skill*. Indeed, throughout the 800 years of its recorded history in the English language, "art" has consistently been used to refer to "skill, its display or application" (*Oxford English Dictionary* 1971:467). Only in the last 300 years has it come to be used more narrowly to apply to "the application of skill to the arts of imitation and design, Painting, Engraving, Sculpture, Architecture" (ibid.).

The skills involved in the creation of art may be manual or conceptual; but in any case, to play a role in art, the skill must be differentially distributed. In essence, if everyone does it equally well (whatever "it" may be), the activity is probably not considered to be art. As Sieber (1971) pointed out regarding other African societies, the artist's special skills set him or her apart from non-artists, leading to that hallmark trait of large-scale societies, specialization—and also leading, one might add, to connoisseurship.

To what extent does this apply to San culture, where social homogeneity is exceptionally high and where specialization is nearly nonexistent? If art is thought of as those activities in which some people have noticeably greater skill than others, do the San have art?

---

[6]Interestingly, although the San literature frequently mentions personal beauty, the San rarely apply the concept of beauty to things other than people. When they do, it is often by means of allusions to the desirable qualities found in men and women. For example, Marshall reports that the !Kung distinguish between "male rain," which is violent and destructive, and "female rain," which "beautifies the trees and grasses" and makes wild plant foods grow (1959:232).

Regarding music and dance, the answer is an unequivocal "yes." Although the San lack full-time singers, players, or dancers, Marshall states that some San "are more talented as musicians than others, and some take more interest in playing and singing well" (Marshall 1976:363; cf. also ibid.:373; England 1968; Kaufmann 1910:151). Further, other San definitely appreciate and admire the more accomplished performers. Van der Post describes the playing of the hunting bow by a man named Nxou: "In his hands it seemed to become a greater kind of bow, hunting meaning in the wasteland of sound not with arrows of flint and iron but with . . . ordered notes flying out of the silence. All the men could play the instrument but none like Nxou. The women would sit for hours, the full look of peace upon them, listening to him" (Van der Post 1958:247; cf. also Thomas 1959:73, 131; Marshall 1962:148).

Differential skill among the San is less well documented outside the performing arts. Almost all old people among the San are storytellers, but some are applauded for giving more rousing renderings of folktales than others are capable of (Biesele 1976:307, 310). Indeed, it appears that as long as one is not boastful about it, creative energies may be displayed in any expressive medium (Shostak 1984).

Lastly, art is often defined as being *non-utilitarian*. In popular thought, art is highly valued despite its making little or no material contribution to the practical maintenance of life. The San's ostrich eggshell beads fit this pattern well, being important for reasons not directly necessary for day-to-day life. For instance, Thomas (1959:156–157) tells of a "tragedy" in which an old couple's hut accidentally caught fire and burned to the ground, injuring no one but destroying all the hut's contents. The greatest cause of the distress felt by the couple and their neighbors was that the old woman had been a prolific beadmaker, and all her beads were destroyed by the fire.

San love ostrich eggshell beads because they make the wearer attractive, but we might ask, what is it that makes them more beautiful—and more valuable—than beads made from other materials? Inasmuch as the supply of raw material—ostrich eggs—barely meets the needs of the beadmakers, scarcity may be a factor. Also, because beadmaking is a long, tedious process, the several thousand beads of a typical ornament represent an enormous investment of labor, causing the San to attribute special value to them. Gift-giving plays an important role in San culture, not only at rites of passage, such as betrothals and weddings, but also when items are exchanged spontaneously to reaffirm the reciprocity that ties members of a San band into a tightly woven social fabric. On such occasions, ostrich eggshell beads, with their intrinsic attractiveness and labor-intensive nature, are perfect gifts, symbolizing the bonds that hold people together.

In summary, if art is tentatively conceived as referring to things or activities that either are of outstanding beauty, are skillfully produced, or are nonutilitarian, then the San do have art. San certainly love the beauty of personal appearance and adornment as well as the beauty of the songs of the Ritual Healing Dance. And at least for singing "mood songs," some San cultivate special skill, and others appreciate their abilities. Further, the San value ostrich eggshell beads beyond their overt contributions to material well-being.

If, however, art is defined as existing in a single medium that is beautiful, skillfully produced, *and* non-utilitarian, then the situation is less clear. Whereas each of these qualities exists in different San media, we do not know if any one medium has all three. Regarding San mood music, for example, differences in skill are recognized, and it seems clear that San often make music for the sheer enjoyment of it, rather than for any overtly practical purpose. But although Western visitors among the San have often reported that they found great beauty in San music, we can only speculate about the Sans' own feelings about the music they make. It seems extremely likely that, if asked, a !Kung individual would say, yes, mood songs are indeed beautiful. But the issue cannot be settled until we have more information.

San Aesthetics

No explicit philosophy of art has been reported for the San. For example, Bleek and Lloyd (1911) left us with an enormous compendium of San folklore and mythology, but references to art rarely occur in it, and no theory of San aesthetics, latent or explicit, is to be found in its stories.

This is not to say that the San give no thought to art. Clearly, the San spend much time making and enjoying art, especially in the forms of body decoration and music-making. But in the absence of individuals who are full- or part-time specialists in formalizing and verbalizing abstract concepts (that is, lacking professional philosophers), San aesthetic values are not available to us as an overt, integrated system of thought. Therefore, we must reexamine San art and its uses to discover the ideas that are implicit in San culture regarding the fundamental nature and value of art.

First, we may dismiss as inapplicable several aesthetic theories that have had some currency in Western culture. Although a founder of formalism, Roger Fry (1910), praised the aesthetic qualities of southern African rock paintings, nothing in the literature indicates that the San themselves make art in accordance with explicit, formal principles of composition, color usage, and so on. It is also alien to San thought to use art as a status symbol: The San are egalitarian in the extreme, and even if they were inclined to one-upmanship, their nomadic way of life obviously rules out the accumulation of property as a means of displaying one's elevated status. Thomas (1959:22) remarks that "a Bushman will go to any lengths to avoid making other Bushmen jealous of him. No one cares to keep a particularly good knife too long, even though he may want it desperately, because he will become the object of envy." The San take pride in having a handsome appearance, but it is inconceivable that art would be used as a symbol of elevated status in such a society.

To a limited extent, San aesthetics is linked to religion, although the relationship is not a simple one. !Kung do not pray to deities associated with sun, moon, or stars; they do not systematically beseach the spirit world for rain or food; and they do not believe that animals, trees, water, or other natural phenomena are inhabited by spirit beings (Marshall 1962). They do believe in the existence of two gods—one greater, one lesser, each with a wife and children. The great god ≠ Gao!la created all things including people and human knowledge, and he is believed to be all-powerful in controlling both nature and humans, often using the spirits of the dead, or //gauwasi, as his agents. The //gauwasi are not, however, identified with specific ancestors, and there are no San "witches" who try to further their personal interests by influencing the //gauwasi.

The San also keep ethics and religion separate. They abhor unacceptable conduct, of course, but they believe that after death the bad people as well as the good go to the east to live with ≠ Gao!la. Preventing or avenging a mortal's wrongdoing is the responsibility of other mortals. There are no priests, but individuals may pray spontaneously and quietly for favors—perhaps that Khwova!na, the wife of the great god and mother of the bees, will give men good luck as they hunt for honey.

The Ritual Healing Dance is the most significant religious ceremony among the San. During its lengthy performance, one or more individuals enter a trance state. The dance, along with the rites of passage performed for young men and women, is intended to induce the supernaturals to look favorably on the participants and aid their well-being.

The visual arts play a limited role in San religion. The San do make oracle discs of antelope hide (Figure 1–7), and Lee's research shows that some scarification is religiously motivated.[7] For example, after scarifying a young man, an older !Kung told Lee, "I cut his chest and put in medicine—to lift up his heart and make him want to seek meat; I put [medicine] in his arm and wrist to make his arm soft and his aim correct" (Lee 1979:239; cf. also Marshall 1976:41; Werner 1906:255; Lebzelter 1934:41; Schapera 1930:304). But these activities bear only a tenuous relationship to art. For example, applying the three criteria mentioned above, we find that the accouterments of religion are not esteemed for their beauty, require no special skill in their production, and are considered to be purely of utilitarian value.

---

[7]Sometimes the relative importance of vanity and religion is unclear. For example, the linguist Bleek noted that it was difficult to know if her informants were saying that facial tattoos enhance the wearer's ability to "see well," or that they enhance beauty and make one "look nice" (1928:11).

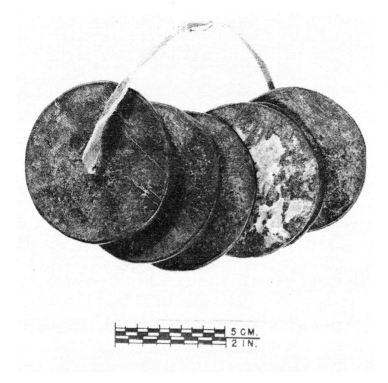

FIGURE 1–7 San oracle discs. *(Smithsonian Institution, Department of Anthropology, catalogue no. 407191.)*

It is interesting, however, to examine the role of the performing arts in San religion. Music and dance are essential parts of the Ritual Healing Dance—and, for that matter, of female rites of passage as well (Figure 1–8). A healer named Nisa told Marjorie Shostak, "When the drum[8] starts sounding 'dong . . . dong . . . dong . . . dong,' my *n/um* grabs me. That's when I can cure people and make them better" (Shostak 1981:302); and another healer told Richard Katz, "Rapid shallow breathing draws *num* up. What I do in my upper body with breathing, I also do in my legs with the dancing. You don't stomp harder, you just keep steady. Then *num* enters every part of your body" (Katz 1982:42).

But as this quotation suggests, it is *num*, not the aesthetic qualities of the music or dance, that is the activating agent. It is interesting to quote Katz again in this regard:

---

[8]A drum, played by a man, distinguishes the women's dance, to which Nisa here refers, from the Ritual Healing Dance, in which most of the dancers are men. Women are less likely than men to be healers, but some women do go into the trance state of *kia.*

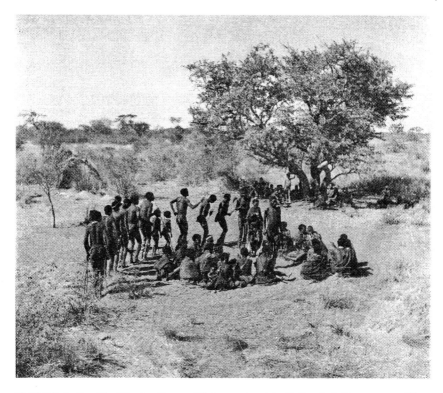

FIGURE 1-8 San Ritual Healing Dance. *(Photo courtesy John K. Marshall, Documentary Educational Resources, Watertown, Massachusetts.)*

"If many persons *kia* at a dance," I ask, "is it because the singing is strong?"

"When the healers fall into *kia*," Nai says, "it is because of *num*. We don't congratulate anyone. It is the *num* which does it."

In the dancing, emphasis is not on style or aesthetics, though the dance is a beautiful, sensitive art form, which becomes more exciting when the individual dancers imbue it with their own expressive manners. As with the singing, the emphasis is on dancing as a vehicle to allow *num* to boil.

If dancers are too intent on perfecting fancy steps or too concerned with how they appear to others, their dancing remains in the foreground and obstructs their ability to let their *num* boil. The male adolescents who typically dominate the beginning stages of a dance are examples. (Katz 1982:127–128)

Further evidence that the religious efficacy of the Ritual Healing Dance lies more in *num* than in the performing arts is seen in the fact that the music and dance are not themselves sacred. On the one hand, the Ritual Healing Dance provides an occasion not only for curing the sick but also for ribald joking and flirting. On the other hand, the same music is commonly used in distinctly secular settings such as lullabies and the melodies that people hum or sing spontaneously and for simple enjoyment.[9]

But if the sacredness of San music and dance are questionable, the aesthetics of San performing arts may have a deeper religious motivation in that these activities provide a means of unifying the San and their collective spirit. In Marshall's words, San dance "brings people into such unison that they become like an organic being" (Marshall 1965:271); and Katz observes that the Ritual Healing Dance "is, quite simply, an orienting and integrating event of unique importance" (Katz 1982:36). These remarks, taken with other observations by Marshall and corroborated by various other fieldworkers, indicate that ceremonial music and dance do constitute religious art for the San, directed not toward specific, tangible ends but intended as a means of enhancing the morale and spirit of the performers and their community.

To take stock of the picture of San aesthetics thus far: There is no ethnographic evidence that the San conceptualize their art in formal terms. Equally absent is a native theory that sets the aesthetic response apart from other affective states. Lastly, the role of art in San religion is limited in that it is not used for didactic purposes, nor is art believed to have supernatural efficacy. Some body decorations occur in ritual contexts, although this has no more religious significance than, say, a Western bride's efforts to look her prettiest. Some scarification is believed to bring good fortune, although the aesthetic qualities of the scars seem to be of little importance. Only music and dance appear to make a significant aesthetic contribution to religion by providing a feeling of community that is characteristic of San cooperative life.

But having factored out these considerations, we are left with a great amount of art activity, practiced primarily in the secular domains of body decoration, music, and dance, that is motivated solely by the simple pleasure and gratification it brings. The San—especially young adult San, and most of all young San women—are walking art objects, proud of their beauty and pleased by any satisfaction their beauty gives to others (Figure 1–9). Music and dance, for their part, are intrinsic components of day-to-day life in a San encampment, providing a continual source of pleasure for performers and audience alike.

The fundamental aesthetic principle of the San is that *art brings pleasure*, whether by augmenting one's natural appearance or by providing enjoyable pastimes to make daily life happier. In religious contexts, San art enhances the sense of community among the living members of San encampments, but

___

[9]There is no clear consensus regarding the distinction between "sacred" versus "secular" beliefs. Most scholars, however, would emphasize that the difference lies in the subjective state of the believer rather than the content of the belief. The realm of the supernatural, the sacred, or of religion and magic generally has a potential for provoking mystical, awe-inspiring feelings that are qualitatively unlike natural phenomena. In some ethnographic contexts, however, the line between the sacred and the secular is so blurred as to disappear.

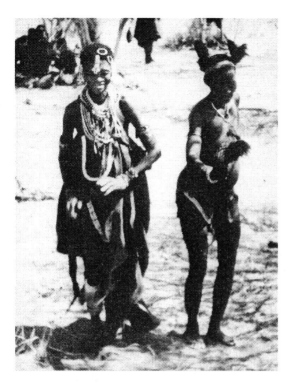

FIGURE 1-9 San women with many types of jewelry, including ostrich eggshell beads in their hair. *(Photo courtesy John K. Marshall, Documentary Educational Resources, Watertown, Massachusetts.)*

San art is justified primarily by the gratification it gives. The satisfactions of art are, for the San, not extreme—no aesthetic ecstasies or flights of imaginative passion. However, art is a continuous, reliable source of pleasure during every waking hour of San life. Just as the San make optimal use of the sparse resources of the Kalahari Desert, they also seem to get the greatest possible satisfaction from the aesthetic activities that their lifeways afford.

Conclusion

Although at first glance one might think that the San have no art, closer scrutiny has produced several interesting findings. The San treasure beauty, and they go to great lengths to cultivate it—certainly in body decoration but also in music and dance. In addition, they appreciate the skills of individuals who are particularly capable in music-making. So if art entails beauty or skill, the San do indeed have art. Further, their ostrich eggshell beads, like Western "fine" arts, have a cultural significance that far exceeds their overt contribution to physical well-being. So although the San are not well known for their art, they do not contradict the widely accepted premise that all societies have art.

It is also interesting to note what San art is not. First, San visual art is almost entirely confined to the medium of body decoration; about the only other things that receive any measure of adornment are utilitarian items such as their ostrich eggshell canteens and their pipes. Clearly, this should not be ascribed to a lack of San creativity or imagination but represents a good solution to the problems of living a nomadic life. Moving from one encampment to another and lacking beasts of burden, they obviously benefit by concentrating on music and dance (which weigh nothing in themselves and require only minimal instruments) and by decorating the things they must carry with them anyway—their tools, their clothes, and their own bodies. Earlier generations of San had one additional answer to the question of art-making in a nomadic society—rock painting. Although they could not take the parietal art with them, they could leave the designs behind with the assurance that the decorations would be awaiting them the next time they visited the site.

Traditional San visual art is not representational, nor does it carry a great weight of symbolism. Again, though, this should not be attributed to a lack of artistic ability. The highly sensitive rendering of people and animals found in the rock art of the past proves that the San's ancestors could make lifelike drawings if they so desired. Instead, it may be due to the media in which San art is created. Body ornamentation everywhere tends to call more attention to the decorated person than to some other subject matter.

As for music and dance, the San do have some program music in which melody and rhythm are used to convey specific emotions or subjects. San songs are not narrative, and although traditional mood songs and the songs of the Ritual Healing Dance do have titles, they have few, if any, words. Also, several San dances effectively mimic certain animals or activities. However, San art, like art elsewhere, does symbolically represent the deeper cultural predispositions and values of the people. For example, Nicholas England, who carried out ethnomusicological fieldwork in the Nyae Nyae area, has observed that when a San man who is singing or playing a musical bow is joined by other men,

> they will also draw upon [the same] melodic phrases, choosing whichever they desire at the moment and perhaps adding their individual embellishments and variations to the basic phrase designs. This interchanging of melodic phrases is a common method of music making in Bushmanland, and it is a principle that, to my mind, epitomizes the Bushman way in general: It clearly reflects the Bushman desire to remain independent (in this case, of the other voices) at the same time that he is contributing vitally to the community life (in this case, the musical complex). (England 1967:60)

Lastly, it is noteworthy that although the San do have art, their aesthetic values are not set out as an explicit theory. This reflects, of course, the absence of full-time philosophers among the San. But this is only part of the story, because it is abundantly clear that the general absence of philosophical speculation in San culture is not due to their being so busy providing for the material necessities that they have no time left to philosophize. Systematic study by Lee (1979) reveals that there is in fact an abundance of leisure time in San life.

This raises a second possibility. The San simply may not to *need* an explicit theory of aesthetics, and this could be true for two reasons. First, San aesthetic values are not conceptually complex. In comparison to the systems of aesthetics found, say, among the Aztecs (Chapter 7), the precepts of San aesthetics are so self-evident that they can be summed up quite succinctly: To bring happiness and well-being to yourself and your people you should sing, dance, and adorn yourself and your possessions. An aesthetic system as straightforward as this can be handed down from generation to generation as part of the normal process of socialization. The San do not need special teachers of art appreciation or aesthetics.

But recalling again the cultural homogeneity of San society, we see another reason why the San do not need an explicit aesthetic system. In complex societies such as the West, art creators and art consumers are usually distinctly separate groups. In such settings, one job for aestheticians and art critics is to mediate between these two groups, explaining the artist's works to patrons of the arts and commenting on the artist's role in the larger context of culture. Such mediation is not needed in a classless society such as the San's. Among the San, where no great gulf exists between maker and user, art is created not just for the patron's sake but for everybody's sake.

Having described the life-enhancing aesthetics of the San, we can return to the question that was raised at the beginning of this chapter—namely, to what degree do we, as products of the Western tradition, live in the same conceptual and emotional world as the San, whose material circumstances are as distant from our own as any people on earth?

San feelings about their art are actually very similar to our ideas about popular art in our society. In religion we generally believe that art objects, though a traditional and desirable adjunct to religious ritual, do not by themselves have a supernatural efficacy, although art in general, and music in particular, may provide a sense of oneness among the faithful. But that aside, Western popular arts such as clothing, fashions, and home decoration are largely justified in the public mind by the sensuous pleasure they bring. If we add to this the popularity of commercially recorded music so omnipresent at home and at work, the aesthetic parallels between San art and Western popular art become striking indeed. And there is one further similarity. In both cases the arts spring not from explicit aesthetic theories but from a tacit consensus that the "natives" generally feel is too obvious to require elaboration—namely, that art makes life richer and more enjoyable.[10]

---

[10]In Chapter 10 we will find that such superficial appearances notwithstanding, Western popular art does rest upon a complex aesthetic system.

This postulated parallel between popular culture in the West and traditional culture of the San should not, I feel, be written off as a finding that is too abstract and academic to have any relevance for us. Admittedly, there is a wide range of variation among members of Western society, with Western fine art finding no counterpart in San culture; and the amount of cross-cultural variation is greater still. Thus, we cannot claim to have shown that all humans inhabit the same conceptual world and experience existence in the same way. But we *can* conclude that the San are kindred spirits to us. They are people who view art in terms similar to our own, a folk whose imaginative and psychic worlds are much in tune with ours. I, for one, find this a reassuring conclusion.

Epilogue: The San Today

As noted at the beginning of the chapter, the foregoing picture of San art and culture is based largely on fieldwork reports that date from the 1950s and 1960s. During the last half century, however, many aspects of life have changed for the approximately 90,000 San who live in southern Africa. Very few remain in their traditional territories, and rather than hunting and gathering, today

> most San live in conditions of marginalization and poverty on the periphery of the global capitalist and state systems. The majority of San now are farm workers and domestic servants on Afrikaner-owned cattle ranches or are casual laborers on the cattle posts of Bantu-speaking pastoralists. . . . The San are widely recognized as the most impoverished, disempowered, and stigmatized ethnic group in southern Africa. (Sylvain 2002:1074)

Moreover, intense political upheaval and reform have swept southern Africa in recent decades, and the San were not unaffected by the resultant turmoil. In the 1970s the South West Africa People's Organization, or SWAPO, recruited San men in their ultimately successful fight for Namibian independence from South Africa, and Namibian San remain actively engaged in governmental processes (Figure 1–10). Likewise, San political participation has steadily increased in neighboring Botswana since that former British colony gained independence in 1966, with San winning seats in District Councils and the House of Chiefs. One cause of activism in Botswana was the government's attempt to remove San from the Central Kalahari Game Reserve. The resultant national park, touted as the second largest protected area in the world, has been a boon to tourists and safari operators,[11]

---

[11]In addition to the tourism, the Botswana government justified moving San out of the Central Kalahari Game Reserve, which had been created in the 1960s as a haven for them, on grounds that a severe drought in the 1980s had diminished wildlife resources for the San who relied on hunting and gathering. However, skeptics have also noted that the land beneath the Reserve holds rich diamond deposits.

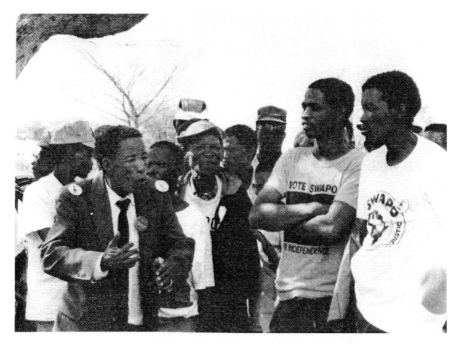

FIGURE 1–10 1989 political rally of San in support of the South West African Peoples Organiza-tion (SWAPO). (Most whites supported a different party, backed by the then aparteid regime of South Africa.) Tsmake has said, "If I work for the Boorasi (whites), I am the owner of nothing; if I have cattle, I work for myself on my own land." *(Photo courtesy John K. Marshall, Documentary Educational Resources, Watertown, Massachusetts.)*

but the resettlement of hundreds of San removed them from the land that long provided their livelihood and has forced them to adopt different forms of subsistence. In 1998, Botswana's Vice President Festus Mogae told the press, "The only solution, as I see it, is that they must come out of the park and engage in what other Basarwa [i.e., San] are engaged in—rearing don-keys, cattle and goats" ([South African] Dispatch Online, Thursday, April 9, 1998). In addition to threats to their land and resources, the San face life-and culture-threatening problems caused by and discriminatory health and education policies (cf. www.kalaharipeoples.org/documents/San-pol.htm).

Several visitors to the Kalahari in the 1960s and 1970s commented on the resilience and adaptability of San culture (cf. Lee 1993:177). For exam-ple, in 1986 Richard B. Lee (ibid:177-181) followed the progress of a group of schoolchildren in the Dobe village of /Xai/xai who called themselves the /Gwihaba Dancers, as they ascended through the ranks of a national dance competition. Although their choreography included both old elements (a dramatic imitation of a lion hunt) with new ones (the hunters carrying a wooden gun), and even though the troupe's teacher and some of the children were Bantu rather than San, the group ultimately won first prize. The young people's accomplishment brought tremendous pride to the people of /Xai/xai, but we cannot ignore the fact that it took place in the new cultural context of a state-sponsored competition, rather than solely for the entertainment of the children themselves. Lee concludes his account of the episode thus:

> In a landscape (and not just in Botswana) strewn with the debris of racism and intolerance, the story of the /Gwihaba Dancers offered a counter-example of hope; Tswana teachers, working with Ju/'hoansi parents, and teaching Herero and Ju/'hoansi children—creating a tradition of harmonious cultural relationships. Or, it could be just a brief moment with no portent—whose larger meaning will be lost in the sand without a trace. (Lee 1993:181)

Another effort to address the issue of culture in transition was initiated in the 1990s in western Botswana by the Dutch Reformed Church in the remote farming village of D'Kar with the establishment of the Kuru Development Trust. After a group of Naro San from D'Kar were taken to see the rock paintings in the Tsodilo Hills of northern Botswana, they began producing graphic art that combined the old with the new. Since then they have supplemented long-established San art media (earth pigments, charcoal, and plant juices) with introduced materials and techniques including oil paints and silkscreen. The subject matter of the Kuru artists is equally diverse. Some paintings portray traditional stories, but others address topical concerns such as HIV/AIDS. As in the old petroglyphs, in contemporary paintings the portrayals of the plants and animals of the veldt outnumber those of people. On the other hand, when people do appear, now they are sometimes shown wearing Western-style clothes.

The twelve to seventeen artists at D'Kar work in the community-owned Kuru Art Centre, which has painting and printing studios, a photographic darkroom, a storage room, and is staffed by a full-time art coordinator and two assistants. Their work has been exhibited, sold, and won awards not only in southern Africa but also Europe, North America, and Australia. The global interplay of cultures is dramatically seen in the fact that in 1988 British Airways used a painting by one of the group, C'goise, to decorate a Boeing 747, as well as airline tickets and stationery (http://www.africaserver.nl/kuru/english/index2.html).

On the Kuru Kalahari web page, a woman artist named Dada says,

> I am always thinking about my art. I am thinking and planning new paintings all day. It won't leave me, even when I lay down to sleep at night, the colours and images keep on coming back. . . . My prints and paintings are depicting facets of my culture and my world. I like to depict the things that bring me joy, like the plants from the Kalahari that can fill an empty stomach when you are hungry or can satisfy your thirst when there is no water to be found. . . .

Our lives are changing: Old traditions do not count any more and money is getting more important. My painting "woman and her husband" depicts the sad fate of many women whose husbands do not want to be responsible for their children. . . .

Yes, the main reason for me to paint is to show the world the things that my people and I love. It is a way of making a living, but more than that—it is to show other people who we are and how we live. It is also a way of learning. Through art you learn about new techniques, about other cultures, about how other people think and live. It lifts you out from the darkness. (ibid.)

Dada's words deftly weave together many themes of this chapter—the intimate connection between the San and their physical environment, the ways in which art is used to negotiate complex relations between people, and the importance of the arts in individuals' lives: "It lifts you out from the darkness." But it also unequivocally and irretrievably situates the San and their art in the contemporary world, a world in which Self inevitably confronts Other and where art can be, and often is, asked to provide some measure of mutual understanding.

Further Reading

As one of the few hunter/gatherer cultures that remained viable well into the twentieth century, traditional San have been the subject of a rich body of ethnographic information, much of it written in an engaging style that emphasizes the human and personal dimensions of both the San and those Westerners who lived with them.

Richard B. Lee's *The Dobe Ju/'hoansi* (2002) provides a excellent, concise overview of Dobe San, with chapters on the ways in which traditional San survived the semi-arid conditions of the Kalahari, San social structure and cultural beliefs, as well as some of the more recent changes in long-established San lifeways. Accounts that give an intimate picture of traditional San life are Elizabeth Marshall Thomas' classic, *The Harmless People* (1959) and Marjorie Shostak's *Nisa: The Life and Words of a !Kung Woman* (1981; see also Shostak 2000). By documenting the seldom-described Hai‖om of Namibia, Thomas Widlok's *Living on Mangetti* (1999) reveals the range of variation among the peoples of southern Africa while at the same time providing an account of their integration into a modern nation state.

Of the various media that the San have used for artistic expression, only the performances of the Ritual Healing Dance have received focused attention by Western scholars. A comprehensive treatment is *Healing Makes Our Hearts Happy* (Katz et al., 1997), which describes both traditional practices as well as the continuing popularity of the dance among contemporary San. Indeed, because of the rise in incidence of diseases due to poverty and contact with non-San, trance dancing has increased in importance, with some dancers becoming famous not only for healing but also for embodying a vital indigenous practice of which the San are proud.

There is also ongoing scholarly interest in the paintings and engravings that the San's ancestors left on many rock faces in southern Africa. Two frequently cited recent studies are David Lewis-Williams' *Believing and Seeing: Symbolic Meaning in Southern San Rock Paintings* (1981) and Thomas Dawson's *Rock Engravings of Southern Africa* (1992).

2

INUIT AESTHETICS

Art as Transformer of Realities

"My Breath"

This is what I call this song,
for it is just as necessary to me to sing
as it is to breathe.

I will sing a song,
A song that is strong.
Unaya—unaya.

Sick I have lain since autumn,
Helpless I lay, as were I
My own child.

Sad, I would that my woman
Were away to another house,
To a husband
Who can be her refuge,
Safe and secure as winter ice.
Unaya—unaya. . . .

Dost thou know thyself?
So little thou knowest of thyself.
Feeble I lie here on my bench
And only my memories are strong!
Unaya—unaya.

(From a song told to
Knut Rasmussen [1931:321]
by the Netsilik, Orpingalik)

A life of traveling nomadically from one location to another, accompanied by fewer than thirty relatives and friends, and providing for the material necessities of life with a technology not of iron and fossil fuels but primarily of wood, stone, and human muscle—such was the sole life way of humans for almost all our history. Only during the last 10,000 years have the primeval techniques of hunting and gathering been supplanted in some locales by a sedentary existence based on farming; by clusters of population numbering hundreds, thousands, and even millions of people; and by a technology dramatically different from the flint knife and spear-thrower of the past.

Of course, compared to one person's life, 10,000 years is still a long time, so it is natural that we often take for granted these innovations (which were the basis for the "Neolithic Revolution") and that we view as exotic aberrations the few stone-age peoples that survived into the modern era. But we should remember that such an assumption is as temptingly comfortable as it is dangerously wrong: In the true long-term picture of the human race, we are the aberrant ones, and nomadic hunter-gatherers are the norm.

This being the case, we are lucky that a handful of small-scale societies did survive into recent times and, wonder of wonders, that a few individuals had the foresight to study and record their lifeways in as much detail as possible. One such nomadic culture, well known in the ethnographic literature, is that of the Inuit, or Eskimos,[1] of the North American Arctic.

Admittedly, the Inuit of the twentieth century differed markedly from most peoples of the pre-neolithic past. Fish, sea mammals, and meat in general have always been more prominent in arctic diets than in those of most hunter-gatherers, vegetable foods being relatively less important. We must also bear in mind that for many decades the effects of Western culture have been increasingly apparent in the Arctic, due both to the colonial policies of Western nations and to the Inuits' own adoption of Western technology.

But compared to other areas of the New World, most natives of the Arctic were still relatively unacculturated when Knut Rasmussen organized the Fifth Thule Expedition in the 1920s. Born in Greenland with Inuit ancestry on his mother's side, Rasmussen spoke the Inuit language fluently, and he and his colleagues' research led to the publication of extensive accounts of traditional Inuit "intellectual culture" (by which Rasmussen meant religion and mythology) and "material culture" (i.e., artifacts and technology). Taken together with the field reports of many others, this literature gives us a good picture of traditional Inuit life.

---

[1]Although the Native Americans of the Arctic were once all referred to in the English language literature as "Eskimos," many of those now living in Canada and Greenland call themselves "Inuit"—and greatly prefer to be called that by others. On the other hand, "Eskimo" is still used more often in Alaska. Therefore, in this book I try to use "Inuit" when referring specifically to groups in Canada and Greenland, restricting the use "Eskimo" to the native peoples of Alaska (see Ray 1996:xix). Moreover, inasmuch as even in Alaska the younger generation is taking up the name "Inuit," I will use that term in references to Arctic peoples in general when no specific location is known or intended.

Background: Origins and Art Production

Modern residents of the North American Arctic are the descendents of people who first arrived from northeast Asia about 4,000 years ago (see map,
p. xvi) and who eventually spread across the entire, treeless Arctic region, all
the way to the shores of eastern Greenland. Wherever they wandered, they
took along characteristic cultural adaptations to the Arctic, many of which
they shared with their near relatives in eastern Siberia. The Inuit differ genetically, linguistically, and culturally from the Native American Indians living
south of the tree line, whose ancestors had been in the Western hemisphere
long before the arrival of the Inuit.

Some eras of Inuit prehistory have produced more art than others, but
art of one kind or another has been made in many media.[2] Western collectors
and museums have long prized Inuit ivory carving (Figure 2–1), but Inuit
men also carved figures in bone and wood (Figure 2–2), as well as ephemeral
works in snow and ice. Most such pieces were smoothly molded human and
animal forms, polished to a lustrous sheen, sometimes decorated with incised
patterns of lines and dots. The exigencies of a nomadic life dictated that few,
if any, such items served solely decorative purposes. Some were tools for the
shaman; others, toys for the children. Many utilitarian items, such as bone
tubes for storing women's needles, were carved in such a way as to suggest animal forms. Masks (Figure 2–3) were carved for various uses, and they ranged
in size from 2 to 20 inches (5 to 50 centimeters).

If carving was a man's art, the leather, fur, and sinew used to make arctic
clothing provided a venue for artistic expression for Inuit women (Figure
2–4). The style and amount of decoration on clothing varied from one locale
to another, with especially elaborate parkas being worn for group festivities in
both Alaska and Greenland. In some regions, specially decorated mittens and
fans were made for use in dances. Most patterns were geometric and were
created by the ingenious use of varying colors and textures of furs.

In some places, kayaks, mortuary boards, and dance drums bore
painted and carved designs, but tattooing was the most widespread type of
two-dimensional art (Figure 2–5). Created mostly by women, tattoo patterns
were made either by rubbing ashes into pin pricks or by passing a needle and
thread covered with grease and ash under the skin (Birket-Smith 1959:119), a

---

[2]Robert McGhee (1976) has examined variations in the quantity of art produced in the
arctic from one time and place to another. Interestingly, he found that art production does not
seem to be correlated with the availability of leisure time, nor was there a gradual increase in the
amount of art with the passage of time. Variations were only weakly correlated with the duration
and size of settlements, factors thought to be important in promoting art production elsewhere.
In another study, Taçon (1983) found that art production was particularly prolific during the
Late Dorset period, 800–1500 A.D., and he speculated that this development may have been a result of stress due to adverse changes in the environment or the in-migration from Alaska of Eskimos bearing the new Thule culture.

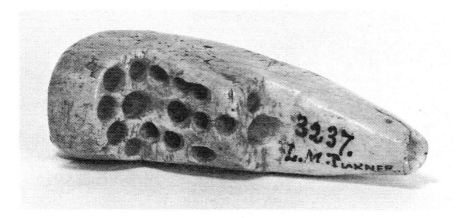

FIGURE 2-1 Eskimo carved ivory gaming device. *(Smithsonian Institution, Department of Anthropology, catalogue no. 90228.)*

method that the Inuit's counterparts in Siberia called *vyshiva*, Russian for "embroidery." Cat's cradle string designs (Figure 2–6), some of which were extremely elaborate, constituted another pan-arctic three-dimensional art form. Eskimos in Alaska made basketry and pottery, but these media had limited importance for aesthetic expression.

FIGURE 2-2 Children of different ages receive varying amounts of help from their elders while playing a Natsilk game. *(Photo courtesy Documentary Resources, Watertown, Massachusetts.)*

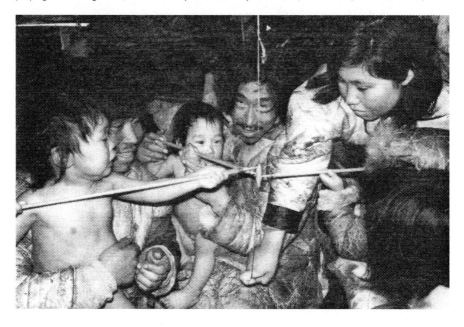

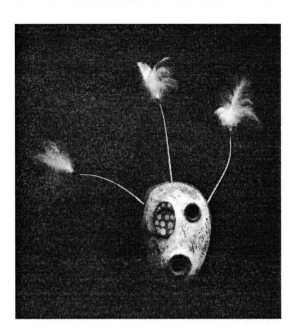

FIGURE 2-3   Asymmetrical Eskimo mask, ca. 1875. Alaska, Lower Yukon area. Wood, paint, feathers; including feathers: 16¼ x 17½ in. (41.3 x 44.5 cm). *The Saint Louis Art Museum, Friends Fund.)*

FIGURE 2-4   Inuit woman in decorated fur parka. *(Photo courtesy National Museums of Canada, Canadian Museum of Civilization, neg. no. 51-571.)*

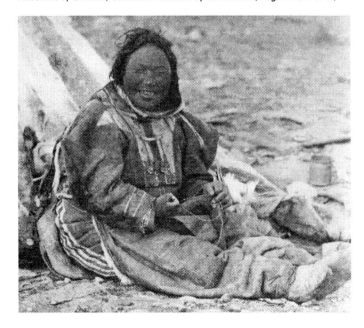

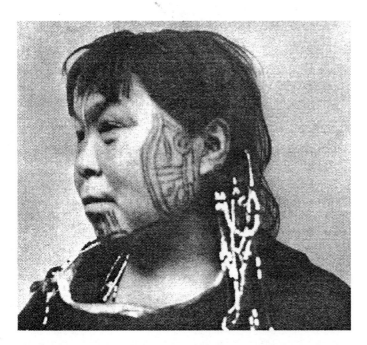

FIGURE 2-5   Aghhaaya, a Gambell, St. Lawrence Island, Yupick woman, with facial tattoos. *(Courtesy of National Archives and Records Administration.)*

FIGURE 2-6   Inuit cat's cradle figure. *(National Archives of Canada/PA11413/Photo by Richard Harrington.)*

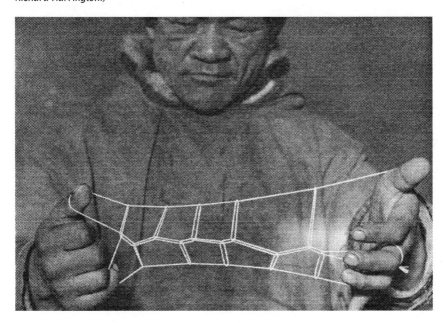

By contrast, the performing arts of dance, music, and song were quite important throughout the arctic, both in ceremonial and recreational settings (Figure 2–7). In traditional times, at any given moment in an Inuit camp the singing of women could be heard (cf. Lutz 1978:43). Except for the songs that were sung to accompany juggling (and whose contents are not well understood), most songs' subject matter focused on hunting, animals and birds, and legendary beings of the mythic past. Inuit dances ranged from highly formalized and rehearsed solos to freestyle, group performances, but even in the latter, dancers' movements came from a traditional repertoire of motions, and the best dancers were those who could combine subtlety with liveliness, not an easy feat. One field study reports that "it is remarkable to see a young dancer spring eagerly to the dance floor, spry, energetic, and enthusiastic, but give a disappointing and awkward performance, while an aging dancer who must be led to the dance floor blind and hobbling is transfigured at the first drumbeat to an angel of grace" (Luttmann and Luttmann 1985:58).

Storytelling was also a well developed art form. Seidelman, Turner, and Swinton remark,

FIGURE 2–7   Dance of residents of Dolphin and Union Strait given at a farewell celebration for members of the Fifth Thule Expedition. The dancer, accompanied by a drum, sings songs he composed and owns. *(Photograph by Leo Hansen, 1924; photo courtesy Nationalmuseet, Copenhagen, Denmark.)*

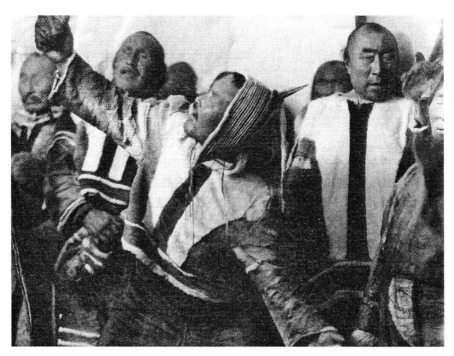

In the Inuit world, the ability to tell stories well was a highly respected accomplishment. A skilled storyteller was always a welcome guest in other communities. Storytelling was a performance art demanding both training and talent. Many stories were recited rhythmically with voice changes, chorus or drum accompaniment, exaggerated physical gestures, animal mimicry, hypnotic repetition and other very dramatic effects. (Seidelman, Turner, and Swinton 1994:22)

Whatever the medium, there is compelling evidence that the Inuit possessed exceptionally high degrees of manual and perceptual skills. Regarding the former, Carpenter (1973:17) remarks, "Aivilik men are first-class mechanics. . . . I have watched them repair instruments which American mechanics, flown into the Arctic for this purpose, have abandoned in despair." As for visual perception and memory, several early explorers asked Inuit to make maps of the land the arctic nomads traversed. Although some drawings portrayed landforms that extended tens of thousands of square miles, they were accurate down to the most minute geographic detail. Clearly, Inuit have no shortage of hand-eye coordination and visual imagery (cf. Rasmussen 1931:93–113; Nelson 1899:197; George Sutton, cited in Carpenter 1973: 10–11).

How Much Can We Know about Inuit Aesthetics?

Presumably, the traditional Inuit had their own good reasons for producing art, but how much can we ourselves know "Inuit aesthetics"? After all, Inuit bands were sparsely scattered over an enormous area of land—well over a million square miles, a territory that was probably larger than that of any indigenous people in the world. We also know that art media, quantity of art production, and skill of construction varied from one arctic region to another. Is it possible, then, to speak of "Inuit aesthetics" as a unitary entity? After all, the distance between the natives of western Alaska and those of eastern Greenland is greater than that from Scandinavia to West Africa, and the arts of *those* divergent areas certainly cannot be forced into a single aesthetic system.

But although variations exist, fieldworkers have found a remarkably uniform Inuit culture throughout the arctic, especially in such conceptual and symbolic areas as language, religion, and myth. For example, Rasmussen was able to speak with Inuit people across the arctic using the language he had learned in Greenland. Or, to give a more relevant example, Colby (1973) constructed a generative grammar to account for formal structures in North Alaskan folktales, and he found that stories from distant Inuit groups in Canada and Greenland fit the same model with only slight modification. Such facts suggest that we can legitimately synthesize an integrated Inuit aesthetic system by using clues from wherever they are reported throughout the vast arctic.

I say "clues" because that is really all we have to go on, and this is a second possible impediment to describing Inuit aesthetics. Although much anthropological fieldwork has been carried out among the Inuit—and despite the existence of many books that lavishly illustrate Inuit artifacts—no one ever thought to systematically and broadly question traditional Inuit themselves about the role of art in their lives.

If the ethnographic literature is examined for references to native ideas about art, however, clues for unveiling a coherent Inuit aesthetic system are indeed found. Myths and creation stories situate art in a metaphysical context; native explanations about the day-to-day uses of art reveal the role of art in the affairs of Inuit life; and ethnographic tidbits, such as the observation that two Inuit bands differ in their ideas about which fur makes a more beautiful parka—these are the primary data of aesthetic style and taste.

Validation of such a synthetic, catch-as-catch-can approach is always illusive. However, when enough scattered and fragmentary observations are put together, a more or less coherent and integrated aesthetic system eventually emerges. Future research will undoubtedly sharpen our focus and give us a more detailed picture of Inuit aesthetics, but the inductive approach I use below produces a first approximation of Inuit aesthetics. It reveals a tripartite system of thought in which art is believed to enhance a person's life today, improve one's prospects for tomorrow, and accomplish this through art's unique capacity to transform reality.

Inuit Aesthetics: The Enhancement of Present Life

In the minds of traditional Inuit, one important rationale of art's existence was that it made today's life more livable. This occurred in several ways, not the least of which was the enjoyment derived from artistic creation itself. For example, one early explorer wrote, "In places where ivory is plentiful the men appeared to delight in occupying their leisure time in making carvings from that material or from bone, sometimes for use, but frequently merely for pastime, and many little images are made as toys for children" (Nelson 1899:196).

But Inuit also realized that the pleasure engendered by art continues after the creative act is finished. That they savored beautiful things is proven in several ways. For one thing, although the Inuit language had no single word for art or aesthetics, there was a term, *takminaktuk*, meaning "it is good to look at or beautiful," and it was applied to a wide range of referents (Graburn 1967:28). For example, the monolingual Pitseolak, who grew up in a traditional setting but who became a very successful printmaker in her later years, once reminisced about her girlhood and "the most beautiful drinking water, the most beautiful water I have ever had" (Eber 1979, unpaginated). Significantly, many art objects were also said to be *takminaktuk*.

Myth, too, confirms the extent to which the Inuit relish sensuous beauty. A major spirit being in the religious beliefs of the Canadian Inuit is a handsome, and sometimes evil, young woman named Sedna, who in one story is courted by a fulmar, a large Arctic sea bird. "Come to me," says the fulmar; "come into the land of the birds, where there is never hunger, where my tent is made of the most beautiful skins." Sedna is won over by the bird's seductive promises but later is disappointed to discover that her new home "was not built of beautiful pelts, but was covered with wretched fishskins, full of holes, that gave free entrance to wind and snow. Instead of soft reindeer skins her bed was made of hard walrus hides"[3] (Boas 1964/1888:175–176).

Inuit most commonly applied the concept of beauty to a person's appearance, where one's natural features could be enhanced in various ways. Eskimos in southern Alaska could choose from lip, cheek, and ear plugs; nose pins; strings of beads suspended from the lower lip; facial tattoos or paint—or they might decorate their black hair with white down. Ornaments were less profuse elsewhere, but Inuit in most regions adorned themselves in one way or another, not for ceremony but for beauty's sake (cf. Birket-Smith 1929:226, 229; Boas 1964/1888:151–153; Hrdlicka 1975:43).

Themes of personal beauty and body decoration also appear in Inuit myths. The "Tale of the Red Bear," for example, tells of the time a group of women met Ta-kū-ka, a woman they had never seen before. They

> admired [Ta-kū-ka's] face and its color, which was lighter than theirs, also several tattooed lines on her face, one up and down between her eyes and three that extended down across the chin from her lower lip; they were pleased also with the shape of her garments, which were very different from theirs. By and by, one of the women said, "You are very handsome with the beautiful lines marked on your face; I would give much if you would teach me how to make my face like yours." "I shall not mind the pain," said the woman, "for I wish to be handsome, as you are, and am ready to bear it." (Nelson 1899:467–470)

As recounted by Nelson, the story ends with Ta-kū-ka tricking the vain woman by drowning her in a pot of hot oil, saying, "There, you will always be beautiful now!" (ibid.).

Like the woman in the myth, mortal Inuit women were willing to bear the discomforts and dangers of tattooing to appear aesthetically, perhaps even erotically, attractive. Among the Copper Eskimo, "tattooing on a woman

---

[3]In an Igloolik telling of the Sedna story, the disillusionment starts even earlier: "One day . . . a kayak arrived and a fine big man called the girl out to go with him; this she did. Stopping by an ice floe en route, the kayaker got out and removed his sun goggles, whereupon the girl burst into tears for the man was puny, having only been sitting tall on a high seat, and had ugly eyes, a northern fulmar in human form" (orig. from Rasmussen; quoted in Seidelman, Turner, and Swinton 1994:73f).

had no religious significance; it was merely a time-honored method of adorn-ment. Just as there were no fixed rules regarding the exact time for the process [of tattooing], so there were no definite ceremonies surrounding it" (Jenness 1946:54; see also Carpenter 1973:160; Ray 1977:23; Hrdlicka 1975:45; Birket-Smith 1933:69).

Thus, visual art enhanced Inuit life by giving pleasure to the creator and by adding sensuous beauty to the environment. But art also lightened the cares and tiresomeness of mundane life through its role in recreation. Children's toys, for example, were often fashioned with aesthetic considera-tions in mind. Most Inuit parents openly expressed love for their children, and they indulged their youngs' wishes when possible. In areas with particu-larly barren environments, natural objects such as small bones had to suffice as children's toys, but elsewhere men often went to great lengths to make in-genious and entertaining playthings. For example, some time in the late nineteenth century a father on St. Michael Island, western Alaska, con-structed the object shown in Figure 2–8 for his son. As Nelson describes the toy, it was

> the image of a woodpecker made of wood fastened to a small wooden spatula by means of a stout quill in place of legs. The surface of the spatula is dotted over

FIGURE 2–8   Eskimo child's toy, St. Michael, western Alaska. *(Smithsonian Institution, Department of Anthropology, catalogue no. 33798.)*

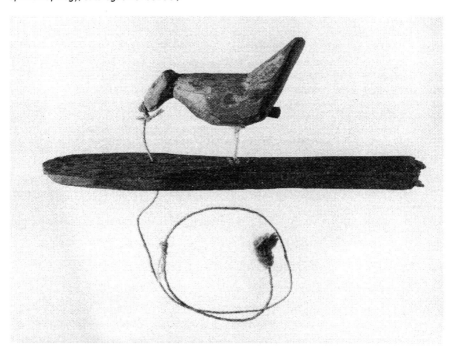

with red paint to represent food. By means of a string fastened to the point of the bird's beak and passing down through a hole in the spatula, the child is enabled to pull the bird's beak down. On releasing it, the elasticity of the quill throws it up again, thus giving a pecking motion and imitating the movements of feeding. (Nelson 1899:341–342)

As in most societies, Inuit children's toys were adjuncts to the socialization process, serving as models that children could use to practice the skills of adult life. Thus, Inuit girls, who would one day become mothers, were given toy dolls, and boys, the future hunters and fishers, played with model animals (cf. Birket-Smith 1929:289; Jenness 1946:146; Nelson 1899:345; Ray 1977:10).

Adult Inuit had their toys, too. During the long arctic winters when the small bands of summer coalesced into larger groups of fifty to a hundred individuals and when daylight lasted a few hours at most, Inuit stayed inside their igloos for extended periods of time. During this period, art, in the service of recreation, helped relieve the boredom of confinement. One game, called *ajegaung*, involved players taking turns with a small object (such as the one shown in Figure 2–1) that was perforated by several holes. The idea was to toss it into the air and then, before it landed, deftly catch it in the proper hole with a slender stick. Sometimes a small animal skull was used, but usually the game was played with an ivory carving shaped like an animal.

A gambling game called *tingmiujang* was also popular. Players would sit around a piece of leather or a wooden board, and one after the other they would take several little figures, shake them, and toss them into the air. The winner was the one whose throw produced the correct number of figures standing upright, rather than lying on their sides or backs.

The performing arts were, if anything, even more important for relieving the tedium of the long winter months. Sometimes there were formal, planned get-togethers. Rasmussen's description captures the atmosphere of such activities in the 1920s:

> The great song festivals at which I have been present during the dark season are the most original and the prettiest kind of pastime I have ever witnessed. Every man and every woman, sometimes also the children, will have his or her own songs, with appropriate melodies, which are sung in the *qag'e,* the great snow hut which is set up in every village where life and good spirits abound. (Rasmussen 1929:228)

A more recent observer noted that in such song "there is no literary, intellectual detachment; the Eskimo is emotionally immersed in immediate experience, including musical experience, for sound is fleeting" (Johnston 1976:6). Like music, there is good evidence that dance also gave great pleasure and enjoyment (Luttmann and Luttmann 1985:57).

Impromptu opportunities for song were also common. Rasmussen again:

> Where all are well and have meat enough, everyone is cheerful and always ready to sing, consequently there is nearly always singing in every hut of an evening, before the family retires to rest. . . . While one of the younger members takes the drum and beats time, all the rest then hum the melodies and try to fix the words in their minds. (Rasmussen 1929:228)

To complete the picture of the Inuit family whiling away a winter evening by singing together, we should remember that the mother's and father's hands may be enjoyably busy making clothes and tools that are as practical as they are aesthetically pleasing.

A Netsilik Inuit named Orpingalik once said to Rasmussen, "How many songs I have I cannot tell you. I keep no count of such things. There are so many occasions in one's life when a joy or a sorrow is felt in such a way that the desire comes to sing; and so I know that I have many songs. All my being is song" (Rasmussen 1931:16). The spontaneous satisfaction of artistic creation; the sensuous pleasure of experiencing beautiful things, actions, and people; and the enjoyment felt by child and adult alike when engaged in song, dance, and play—in each of these ways, traditional Inuit art enhanced life in an environment that gave few other pleasures.

Ensuring Future Well-Being

Art not only enhanced Inuit daily life: In the traditional native view of things, art also improved the likelihood that future life would also be better—safer, healthier, and more prosperous. Art accomplished this through its role in religion.

Traditional Inuit religion had several dimensions. Many taboos prohibited specific activities. For example, if a Netsilik man killed a caribou with a bow and arrow, he was forbidden to eat its meat if he had eaten seal meat previously that day (Balikci 1970:219–220). A second component of Eskimo religion was shamanism. In most regions, shamans could cure illnesses and mitigate crises in the environment; in addition, they could use their supernatural abilities to bring harm to enemies. Also, the world of the Eskimos was inhabited by numerous spirit beings, some dangerous and some benign, some subject to human control and some beyond the realm of human affairs. Such spirits were not abstractions but were conceptualized in very concrete terms. For example, Rasmussen once asked an Iglulik shaman, Anarqâq, to draw the spirits he saw in his vision:

> There was no careless scratching or scribbling; he would sit for hours with closed eyes, solely intent upon getting the vision fixed in his mind, and only when this was done would he attempt to put it into form. Sometimes the recollection of the event affected him to such a degree that he trembled all over and had to give up the attempt. (Rasmussen 1929:44)

Significantly, such spirits could be influenced by art: One of the major festivals among the Inuit of Cumberland Sound included singing by shamans in an effort to marshal the legions of good spirits for protection against Sedna and other evil ones (Lutz 1978:103).

Such religious beliefs influenced Inuit aesthetics on several levels. First, some Eskimo art was made in service to religious belief. For example, although most women's tattoos were made for beauty's sake alone, some were prompted by a desire to supernaturally influence the future. Both Netsilik and Copper Eskimos believed that a woman's tattoos ensured easier childbirth, and Eskimos in southern Alaska believed that tattoos on a woman's chest would increase the amount of milk she could provide her children (Birket-Smith 1933:69; see also Carpenter 1973:160; Rasmussen 1932:plate opposite p. 269).

Tattoos could also influence a person's fate after death. Birkett-Smith quotes one early explorer as quaintly reporting, "If the face be not thus embroidered [i.e., tattooed], the head, they say, becometh a grease tub which shall be placed under the lamp when they come to Heaven or the Land of the Soul" (Egede, quoted in Birket-Smith 1959:119; see also Birket-Smith 1924:215; Rasmussen 1929:148, 1931:313). Birkett-Smith notes, in an interesting reference to the importance of the differential distribution of skill, that one of the several underworlds to which a dead Inuit might go is the "Land of the Crestfallen." It is, he says, inhabited by "unskillful hunters and women whose tattooing has been badly done, [who] sit there, chin on breast, now and then snapping dully after the butterflies which are their only food" (Birket-Smith 1959:162).

If some ivory carvings were simply toys, others served a more serious purpose as amulets—that is, objects with the supernatural power to bring their owners either wished-for things (such as game for the hunter or else the strong shoulders and arms he would need to bring the game down) or desirable abilities (such as the shaman's skill of detecting evil spirits). The Netsilik were particularly amulet-oriented, with Rasmussen (1931:271) telling of a boy who wore a total of eighty amulets sewn inside his parka.

Some amulets were naturally occurring objects. For example, the Iglulik believed that if a bit of excrement from a newborn ermine were placed inside the shoe, one would be a good walker, protected against all types of foot problems. But usually amulets were products of the human hand. For example, "a small doll, made from the extreme hard point of bone in the penis of a walrus, skillfully carved with arms and legs, is sewn into a boy's inner jacket, and he will then, when out alone after caribou, never encounter the dangerous mountain spirits called ijErqät" (Rasmussen 1929:155).

Long ago Sir James Frazer coined the phrase "homeopathic" magic for activities whose supernatural effectiveness derives from their resemblance to the desired end, and many Inuit amulets fall in this category. An old East Greenlander said, for example, that giving a child a doll carved from a straight willow trunk would make its owner grow up with a straight, strong back, "so that he can walk through life erect and fearless" (Meldgaard 1960:7).

The Inuit thought that such items of sympathetic magic are effective because their resemblance to the wished-for quality causes them to attract spirits of their own, spirits with the power to extend their distinctive characteristics into the lives of their mortal owners. But although Inuit had definite ideas about the appearance of spirits, they were not terribly literal-minded about amulets, which were rarely informed by photographic realism. The amulet needed to resemble the desired spirit only enough to convince the spirit to take up residence in it, so most amulets were relatively conventionalized in style.

The Transcendent Dimension of Inuit Art

If we were to end our account of Inuit aesthetics at this point, the result might seem to support the mistaken idea that people in small-scale societies are not capable of serious philosophical insight. Obviously, art's presence can make life more enjoyable, and the use of art in service of sympathetic magic may simply represent wishful thinking.

But Inuit myth, folklore, and art usage convey deeper ideas regarding art's role in the world. The Inuit world view implicitly distinguishes between three realms of existence—the supernatural world, with its out-of-the-ordinary and awe-inspiring qualities; the social world of day-to-day human interaction; and the natural world of animals, plants, and inanimate objects. Many people tacitly accept the existence of these three worlds but ignore the problem of how they are related to each other. How can cold, lifeless matter become warm, living human flesh, and how can the spirit that lives within the flesh transcend its mortal habitation and touch the divine? There is considerable evidence that Inuit conceptualize art as a sort of cultural "philosopher's stone" that makes such transformations possible.

Consider, for example, a creation myth recorded in the late nineteenth century in which First Man, having emerged spontaneously from a pea pod, encounters Raven. Seeing Man, Raven "raised one of its wings, pushed up its beak, like a mask, to the top of its head, and changed at once into a man" (Nelson 1899:451). The superhuman raven/man was astonished to see in First Man a living creature who looked so much like himself. Raven then began creating the things of the world. For example,

> Raven made two animals of clay which he endowed with life . . . but as they were dry only in spots when they were given life, they remained brown and white, and so originated the tame reindeer with mottled coat. . . .
> [Finally, Raven] went to a spot some distance from where he had made the animals, and, looking now and then at Man, made an image very much like him. Then he fastened a lot of fine water grass on the back of the head for hair,

and after the image had dried in his hand, he waved his wings over it as before and a beautiful young woman arose and stood beside Man. (Nelson 1899:454)

Aside from the fact that the myth has males coming spontaneously into existence whereas females are a product of male manufacture, the interesting point in this story is the way transitions occur between the natural, human, and supernatural worlds. First, Raven, a mythic creature with miraculous abilities, removes an art work—a mask—from his face and is thereby transformed into something resembling Man himself. Then, through another act of artistic creativity, the modeling of clay, Raven transforms inert earth into living animals and, ultimately, into Man's companion, Woman.

Another myth from the western arctic reveals the same theme. Once in the ancient past, two men, one from the north and one from the south, fought over a woman, eventually pulling her apart at the waist. Each man returned home with only half a real woman but remedied the situation by carving a wooden model of the missing portion and attaching it to the part of the woman he brought home. Thus, although the upper half of the northern woman was flesh and bone, her lower half was wood; and the southern woman was just the opposite. According to the story, soon the wooden portions became lifelike too, so that the women were able to lead more or less normal lives. Thus in this story too, carving (that is, art) magically changes an inanimate material, wood, into living flesh, thereby making each fragmented woman whole. Or at least nearly whole: The transformation in the tale is not perfect because the woman in the south was never able to excel at sewing inasmuch as her fingers had once been wood; and although the woman in the north was a fine seamstress, the wooden origin of her legs made her a poor dancer. But these consequences are necessary parts of the myth because they explain the belief that down to the present day, women in the south have different talents than those in the north (Nelson 1899:479). Thus the progenitors of two contemporary tribes were created through artifice, and their art-making skills, sewing and dance, are reminders of their origins.[4] In yet another tale, called the Origin of Winds (Nelson 1899:497–498), a childless couple carve and clothe a model doll that, in the middle of the night, turns into a child with extraordinary abilities.

Song, too, is associated with miraculous transformations in some myths: In 1970, Maija Lutz collected a traditional, but enigmatic, song that went in part:

Kayaks down there come on over
You will be my husbands
I am being stuck to this stone
My legs are turning to stone. (Lutz 1978:54)

---

[4]One might conjecture that the myth also sheds light on Inuit conceptions of "women's arts," distinguishing as the story does between domestic skills, as quintessentially represented by sewing, versus the sensual and reproductive dimension that could be associated with dance.

Later Lutz realized that the song referred to a legend that Rasmussen had collected nearly a half-century earlier in which a girl marries a stone; as she sings this song, she begins to turn into stone herself. Interestingly, Lutz (1978:104) also mentions a ritual in which a shaman, in a chant-induced trance, increases the effectiveness of hunters by bringing the soul of a seal into their minds or bodies. Furthermore, when an shaman falls into an altered state of consciousness in order to make contact with the spirit world, those who remain in the quotidian world may sing spirit songs until he comes back into his body (Seidelman, Turner, and Swinton 1994:82). A shaman may also summon the mythic Sedna by use of a special song (ibid.:84).

Of course, all Inuit art made for purposes of sympathetic magic owes its efficacy to art's being able to cross the boundaries between the natural, human, and supernatural realms. For example, cat's cradle string figures, along with their accompanying songs, were believed to entangle the sun and prevent its disappearance. Consequently, the figures were most common in the autumn when the sun's rays were waning (Johnston 1976:5).

Death, too, is a transition that, in the view of the Inuit, requires the soul to forsake its mortal abode for one of several possible realms of afterlife, and art again aids the transitional process. Miniature carvings of tools were often buried with the dead, and the souls of animals received similar treatment, so that in some places the killing of a bear necessitated placing a needle-case beside an adult female and a miniature bow and arrow beside a cub, "that they might not travel empty-handed to the spirit-home of their kind" (Jenness 1928:169; see also Nelson 1899:307, 311; Rasmussen 1929:199).

As with the visual arts, the performing arts could also transcend the boundaries between the three planes of existence. Rasmussen learned that in Iglulik thought,

> no one can become a poet who has not complete faith in the power of words. When I asked Ivaluardjuk about the power of words, he would smile shyly and answer that it was something no one could explain; for the rest, he would refer me to the old magic song I had already learned, and which made difficult things easy. His idea in citing this example was to show that the singer's faith in the power of words should be so enormous that he should be capable of believing that a piece of dry wood could bleed, could shed warm, red blood—wood, the driest thing there is. (Rasmussen 1929:241)

In this case, as in others, art mediates the boundaries between the material, the human, and the superhuman realms.

Other Uses of Art in Inuit Culture

Besides providing symbolic bridges between an Inuit, the material world below, and the spiritual world above, art also helps define social relationships between one Inuit and another. Compared to other societies, Inuit culture is relatively homogeneous, with all families relying on the same subsistence techniques and living nomadic lives that prevent the accumulation of many luxuries. Nevertheless, there are at least a few distinct social roles in Inuit society: Men and women hold noticeably different positions in the culture, as do boys and girls from an early age. Art, in the form of body decoration and clothing, displays these statuses in a highly visible fashion (cf. Ray 1977:23).

Also, Inuit shamans were also somewhat set apart, and occasionally this too was reflected in art. When a young man attained the status of shaman in the central Canadian arctic, he put on a special belt, and his friends and relatives gave him small, carved figures of humans, fishes, and harpoons that he wore hanging from the belt. These ensured his control over powerful spirits (Rasmussen 1929:114).

In a few Inuit groups, art also disseminated noteworthy information by recording the events of the past. The human and animal figures engraved on ivory tools in Alaska—especially on bow drills—depicted hunts and other activities the carver had engaged in (cf. Mason 1927:253, 279; Ray 1961:22–23, 1977:25). Such subject matter was also recorded in song and thereby handed down from one generation to the next.

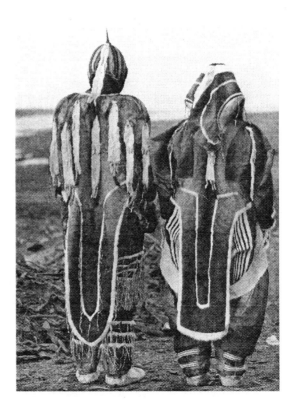

FIGURE 2–9 Inuit decorated parkas. *(Photo courtesy National Museums of Canada, Canadian Museum of Civilization, neg. no. 36–914.)*

Conclusion

Given the technology and environment of the Inuit, one might not expect their culture to be the site of significant art production and serious aesthetic thought. But traditional Inuit produced items that have been held in high aesthetic esteem not only by the Inuit but also by Western art collectors.

There is clear evidence that Inuit recognized the difference between ordinary, run-of-the-mill productions and things that stand out for their special artistic merit. Subtle ivory carvings are reported to have been "tests of the skill of the worker" (Martijn 1964:556); and Carpenter (1973:203), probably inspired by a remark by Leach (1961:29), has compared carving among Inuit to handwriting among members of literate societies. In both instances, most adults possess the skill in question, but a few individuals—called "sculptors" and "calligraphers," respectively—are recognized for their superior abilities.

Our perception of Inuit ideas about aesthetic excellence is obscured somewhat by a native ethos that discourages competitiveness and that seldom overtly rewards an outstanding performance in any endeavor. But the consummate Inuit artist does sometimes get his or her due. Recall, for example, that a woman's well-made tattoos provide a pathway to a superior life after death, whereas poorly made tattoos destined the wearer to a dreary eternity of subsisting on butterflies. Also, it has been pointed out that

> through dance an adolescent could demonstrate acquired knowledge and capabilities in the roles to be played in life, a significant outlet in a culture which censured any form of overt bragging or self-congratulation. [Thus,] a young marriageable woman could demonstrate her desirability as a spouse by miming her talents in dance. (Luttmann and Luttmann 1985:55)

Traditional dress, too, provided a domain for critical evaluation. The aging Pitseolak recalled, "I tried hard to learn how to sew because I envied the women who could sew nicely" (Eber 1979). Moreover, in contemporary Northwest Alaska where almost all men make carvings, only a small fraction are considered to be experts, and every man knows his level of competence relative to all the other carvers (Ray 1961:133).[5]

---

[5]Interestingly, those who are considered to be "experts" by other Inuit carvers are also the ones judged to be "artists" by Western buyers (Ray 1961:132). But before we conclude that Inuit and Western notions of "expertness" are identical, we should take into account the following anecdote recorded by Rasmussen:

> I shall never forget [the Iglulik poet] Ivaluardjuk's astonishment and confusion when I tried to explain to him that in our country, there were people who devoted themselves exclusively to the production of poems and melodies. His first attempt at an explanation of this inconceivable suggestion was that such persons must be great shamans who had perhaps attained to some intimate relationship with the spirits, these then inspiring them continually with utterances of spiritual force. But as soon as he was informed that our poets were not shamans, merely people who handled words, thoughts, and feelings according to the technique of a particular art, the problem appeared altogether beyond him. (Rasmussen 1929:223–234)

Inuit not only create art, but they make it for purposes that are important and profound. Again, the situation is obscured by a trait of Inuit culture, namely the absence of a specific word for art: Some of the objects we have just discussed are simply said to be *sulijuk* (i.e., true or honest), but many others are indicated by the suffix, *-nguaq*, which connotes "diminutive-likeness-imitation-model-play" (Swinton 1978:81). Nevertheless, we must admit that the traditional Inuit philosophy of art was complex and subtle. In the first place, Inuit appreciated the immediate pleasure that artistic production can give to artist and audience alike. The satisfactions of the creative process itself, the sensuous pleasure afforded by artistic beauty, and the enjoyment found in recreations that use artistic paraphernalia—all of these were recognized in traditional Inuit culture. Moreover, Inuit were convinced that art has the power to influence the course of future events, contributing such desirable and important outcomes as health, food, and fertility.

The belief that art can do these things rests upon a fundamental conception of art that is as insightful as any produced by the philosophers of the East and West. Inuit recognize the frightening chasms that separate humans from, on the one hand, the cold, unresponsive material world that surrounds us and, on the other hand, the transcendent supernatural and eternal realm beyond us. Surely reflective people everywhere agonize over these alienating gulfs, instinctively feeling that something should bridge them—but what? The Inuit answer to the dilemma is that a link does indeed exist, and that it is art. This notion is not altogether foreign to the Western student of art who firmly believes, say, that a masterpiece painting is far more than the mere pigment and canvas that constitute its materiality. Inuit know that through art mortals can influence events in the otherwise indifferent realm of nature and that art touches the spirits that stand above both humans and the natural world.

Phrased in these terms, it is easy to see the importance of art's role in Inuit culture and little wonder that the Inuit, despite the simplicity of their material means and the hardships necessitated by their environment, have such conviction in producing art.

Epilog: Inuit Market Art

Small-scale hunting/gathering/fishing societies such as the Inuit may appear to be forever timeless and unchanging, but that image is mistaken. For example, the archaeological record reveals that as century followed century, artifacts called as "winged objects" that were made by the ancestors of modern Inuit gradually changed in shape, in size, and in the decorations that were incised upon them (cf. Anderson 1989:157f). In addition to such slow, evolutionary change, relatively more rapid and dramatic changes also took place in the arctic before the arrival of Europeans, as when Dorset culture, with its distinctive style of art production, was superceded by Thule culture.

Though ever present, the rate of culture change in the arctic has increased exponentially during the last two centuries, paralleling the growing presence of Europeans who came looking for a Northwest Passage to Asia but who instead found fish and fur, souls and gold. For almost all contemporary Inuit, the nomadic life of hunting and fishing in very small bands has been replaced by a sedentary existence in dozens of villages scattered across Alaska, Canada, and Greenland, where every home has a radio, a television, and usually a VCR; where most people are Christians; and where the few remaining dog teams are only kept for recreational purposes (Hessel, Hessel, and Swinton 1998:9).

Predictably, art and ideas about art have also undergone a transformation in the arctic; but equally predictably, their development reflects salient features of traditional Inuit culture. Thus, early European visitors among the Inuit often remarked on their keen perceptual skills, their great manual dexterity in copying items that had proven useful in the past, and their ingenuity in adapting the few available materials to creatively solve new problems. All of these qualities are reflected in recent Inuit art production.

In Alaska, the Gold Rush of the late 1800s brought miners and others from the south, many of whom purchased Eskimo-made items to take home as souvenirs. Soon, Eskimo men were using their traditional ivory-carving skills to turn out thousands of very *non*traditional pieces such as salt and pepper shakers and miniature tools. The card game of cribbage became popular in Nome, and carvers responded by producing countless cribbage boards. For those who wanted something truly exotic, there was an array of what the preeminent scholar of Alaskan Eskimo art, Dorothy Jean Ray, has called "erotic objects," such as men and women in sexual positions and "six-legged bears" (Ray 1977:48).

One of the most interesting innovations in Eskimo "market art" was the "billiken." In 1908 a Kansas City art teacher named Florence Pretz created and patented the design of a plump figure that appears to have been inspired by Asian portrayals of Buddha (Figure 2–10). Said to represent "the god of things as they ought to be" and named for the Billiken Company of Chicago, which began manufacturing them in 1909, billikens were taken up as the symbol of the Alaska-Yukon-Pacific Exposition. By 1910, Eskimo carvers were making hundreds, then thousands, of small ivory billikens. Ray says,

> the billiken has been made in all sizes within the limitations of a walrus tusk, and though departures from the original patented design have been tried—a hat on the head, "millikens" with breasts, milliken-billikens back to back, big ears, bigger legs, seated figures, and hermaphrodites—most of its characteristic elements have been retained: the peaked head, arms straight to the sides, feet indicated by toes or gashes, nipples, navel, broad grin, pudgy cheeks, and a big stomach. (Ray 1977:45)

The popularity of billikens has waxed and waned in proportion with the number of non-Eskimos coming to Alaska, but they remain, in the twenty-first

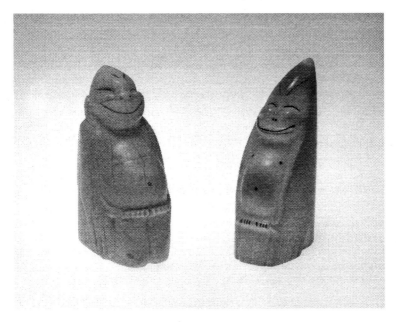

FIGURE 2-10 Billiken, carved out of walrus ivory in the 1920s, probably in Nome, Alaska. 3 1/2 inches high. *(University of Alaska Museum, Dorothy Jean Ray Collection. Photo by Barry J. McWayne.))*

century. Those made by Happy Jack, the very first Eskimo carver of billikens, are sold on the Internet for hundreds of dollars. Billikens continue to survive in other incarnations as well. Saint Louis University uses the billiken as a mascot for its athletic teams, and the presumably Eastern-inspired image has even returned to the Orient: In Japan one can buy billiken ice creams, make a wish before a foot-high billiken in a shrine in Osaka, or perhaps see a 1996 comedy film entitled Birrikin, in which the title character has the power to grant people's wishes.

Besides ivory carvings and engraved walrus tusks, native artists in Alaska have for some time made and sold copies of traditional items, including wooden masks. Paintings and drawings on paper and skin are also produced, and traditional basket making techniques have been adapted to the market.

Native arts in northern Canada have also changed. Since the late 1770s, Inuit have produced decreasing numbers of traditional art forms—amulets, games, and so on—and an increasing amount of market art, primarily for people from the south, who buy objects, traditional or otherwise, that capture their concept of arctic cultures, such as ivory models of tools and figures engaged in daily activities. By the 1920s the Canadian Handicrafts Guild and the Hudson's Bay Company were actively promoting and marketing such pieces.

In 1948, however, a series of events began, the consequences of which continue to reverberate throughout the arctic. In that year, a young Canadian artist named James Houston happened to be in Port Harrison (now Inukjuak) and was given by his Inuit hosts a few small, recently made stone and ivory sculptures in return for some of his drawings. After Houston returned south, the pieces were included in a show in Montreal. As a result of the enthusiastic response to that work, next year the Guild sponsored a return trip by Houston to the arctic to get more Inuit art. Within the first three days of their being exhibited, nearly all of the pieces had been sold.

With the support of James Houston, his wife Alma, the Canadian government, and others, the nascent stone carving industry grew enormously (Figure 2–11). Inuit-owned co-operatives sprang up across the Canadian arctic so that by the end of the twentieth century, most communities had at least a few carvers, the total number of carvers being estimated at about 4,000 (Hessel 1998:78; Swinton 1999:6).

FIGURE 2–11   Soapstone carving attributed to Peesee Oshuitoq, "Mother and Child," 1955, black stone, 33.6 x 21.3 x 22.8 cm. National Gallery of Canada, Ottowa. Gift of M.F. Feheley, Toronto, 1984.
Reproduced with the permission of the West Baffin Eskimo Cooperative, Cape Dorset, Nunavut.

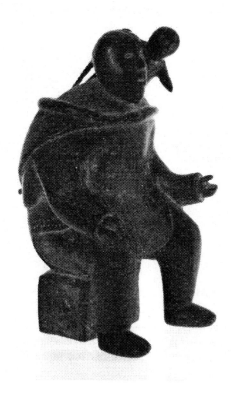

The differences between pre-1948 Inuit carving and contemporary carv-ing are substantial. Soapstone, serpentine, and other relatively soft types of stone previously used only for utilitarian items such as lamps have replaced ivory as the primary sculptural medium, ivory now being reserved for details in mixed media pieces. Also, the commercial carvings have grown in scale from a size that could have been held in the hand of a traditional nomadic, hunter/fisher Inuit to pieces that now are as much as three feet high. Finally, whereas most traditional carving was not figurative, now all of it is, with humans portrayed in clothes and with facial details, often engaged in an activity such as hunting. As Hessel remarks, "Inuit sculpture is always about something. . . . Pure abstraction does not exist" (199:78).[6]

However, stone carving is not the only artistic innovation in the Canadian Arctic. In 1957, James Houston began teaching people in Cape Dorset printing techniques such as stencil, intaglio, and lithography. Today Inuit printmakers in Cape Dorset, Puvurnituq, Holman, Baker Lake, and Pangnirtung produce a great quantity of work, the best known being "stone cuts," in which flat slabs of stone are used to make prints much in the way that wood is used for woodcuts (Figure 2–12) (Hessel 1998:140).[7]

Inuit market art attracts buyers for several reasons, well summarized by Hessel:

> [Post-1948 Inuit sculpture] has the lure of the exotic or "other"; its materials and variety of forms are aesthetically pleasing; much of it has undeniable emotional impact and spiritual content; and most of its subject matter is understandable and universal. In short, unlike much modern [Western] contemporary art, it is accessible . . . . Inuit art has few pretensions—it does not attempt to be intentionally profound; it is made by folks, for folks. . . . Inuit art's initial success was no doubt due largely to its "primitive" look and clever promotion, but its other attributes have maintained its status over five decades.[8] (Hessel 1998:186)

As for the producers of these new art forms in Canada and Alaska, an omnipresent incentive is money. Whether conceived and marketed as "fine art" or as less expensive "tourist art" (and both types of production exist), art production has had a major economic impact in the Arctic. For Canadian

---

[6]Having seen the commercial success afforded by soapstone sculpture in Canada, carvers in Alaska have pursued similar strategies, albeit with their own techniques and styles. There, too, the results were influenced by nontraditional forces, not only with regard to medium but also in the carvers being actively encouraged by outsiders, whether in the government, in craft associations, or in wholesale and retail businesses (Ray 1981:59).

[7]Just as the billikens made by carvers in Alaska had unlikely reciprocal connection with the Far East, the Canadian printmakers adopted production techniques similar to Japanese *ukiyo-e* printmakers, in which artists draw the designs, leaving it to printers to interpret them on stone and to produce the actual prints—one more innovation introduced by James Houston, who had studied *ukiyo-e* in Japan.

[8]Hessel credits Joan Vastokas (1987:16) for making a similar observation prior to his own.

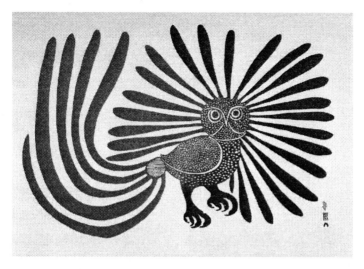

FIGURE 2-12   Kenojuak Ashevak, "Enchanged Owl", 1960, stone cut, 38.5 x 59. Printmaker, Eegyvudluk Pootoogook, 1960. *(Reproduced with the permission of the West Baffin Eskimo Cooperative, Cape Dorset, Nunavet. © Canadian Museum of Civilization, artist Kenojuak Ashevak, printmaker Eegybudluk Pootoogook, 1960. Photo by Harry Foster, image no. 599-14.)*

Inuit, the sale of art works has become largest single source of income (Swinton 1999:188). To place this in its proper context, one must remember the poor economic conditions in which most Inuit live. For example, a careful study at Chesterfield Inlet estimated the unemployment rate to be 72 percent (Irwin 1989). Successful carvers may be accorded the same status as good hunters because both provide well for their families. Predictably, media that proved to be financially *un*rewarding, such as painting, have been abandoned after a brief period of experimentation.

Although it has been popular in the modern West to disparage economic incentives for making art, two facts must be borne in mind regarding Inuit market art. First, it is hypocritical to use a double standard with regard to money and art, damning financial motivations in non-Western settings while congratulating fine artists in the West who, whatever other motives they may have for making art, are successful enough to pay their bills. Second, as Hessel (1998:11) has pointed out, the money gained by Inuit artists actually helps sustain other, more traditional life ways: "The income allows them to buy rifles and ammunition, boats and motors, snowmobiles and gasoline, so that they can continue to fish for food"—rather than emigrate or otherwise seek nontraditional jobs as a source of income.

Whether one hopes to receive economic compensation for making art is one thing; the aesthetic dimensions of the process and product, something else. Therefore, the final question we must ask is Does the financial motivation for Inuit artists affect the way they think about the art they produce? The answer is, yes—in more than one way.

For one thing, forces of the marketplace have caused Inuit artists to strive for well-crafted realism in their work. The carver Kananginak Pootoo-gook has said, "A white man, if he is going to buy a carving, buys it purely by the appearance of the carving. The white people do not consider the meaning of the carving, simply the appearance of the carving" (quoted in Hessel 1998:77). Given this understanding of the market, it is little wonder that Inuit carvers have generally been very concerned with, and themselves take great pride in, their mastery of technique.

Inuit understanding of contemporary Inuit art has, however, another dimension: Like art elsewhere, the visual arts provide a major means of establishing the identity of the community from which they come. Thus, Hessel (1998:75–115) has meticulously described the differences in the materials and techniques in soapstone carving from one region to another, along with the characteristic features of some twenty sculpture-producing villages in Canada. The same inter-village variation also exists in prints, basketry, textiles, and clothing. (So much for the platitude that commercialization brings homogenization!) Despite the traditional egalitarianism of Inuit society, even the identity of individual artists is manifest in the art they produce. In a fascinating survey of Inuit women's footwear, Oakes, Riewe and Riewe conclude, "Skin boots communicate the makers' abilities, strong links to the past, and seasonal changes, as well as the wearer's gender, activities, and political interests" (1996:20).

Even more than individual and village identity, Inuit art makes a statement about Inuit culture *per se*. In a day when ethnic pride is ascendant and the privileged status of Western institutions is widely questioned,[9] Inuit art tells the world—both the world beyond the Arctic and the Inuit themselves—that they have a rich and noble heritage. The Inuit have little access to mass media, but they *do* have artistic media to get their message across. Thus Hessel remarks, "Canada, a young country with an ongoing identity crisis, has adopted Inuit art as its cultural symbol of the north, which plays an important role in the nation's mythology" (Hessel 1998:186). He also quotes Uriash Puqiqnak, of Gjoa Haven, as saying, "We have to keep our language, our stories and our identity alive. . . . The world has to learn about the Inuit" (ibid.:185). This goal is seconded by Baker Lake artist, Ruby Angrnanaaq, who says, "Prints and drawings are our way of sharing our thoughts of the past and present life with the southern people; they are the messages that we are sending out to the rest of the world" (Seidelman, Turner, and Swinton 1994:143).

---

[9]"Some of the younger people have started to look at [Christian] religious services with skepticism. Some of the older people, especially when ill, still believe, at least partially, in the effectiveness of shamans" (Swinton 1999, p. 257).

In recent years, some Inuit carvers have become "artists" in a more Western sense, placing greater emphasis on form than on narrative message (their sculptures and paintings being exhibited in fine art galleries and museums, see Swinton 1999:272–284). But the practice of making market art remains viable and serves important functions for many Inuit people today.

Further Reading

A very accessible ethnography of one Inuit culture is Balikci's *The Netsilik Eskimo* (1970). The classic account of Inuit "intellectual culture," including religion and mythology, is Rasmussen (1929).

Excellent surveys of Inuit art are Swinton (1999) and Hessel (1998); Ray's work (1961, 1977, 1981) is equally comprehensive with regard to the native arts of Alaska. Although they fail to specify the exact sources of the material they quote, Seidelman, Turner, and Swinton (1994) have an interesting discussion of possible parallels between themes found in Inuit mythology and those in Inuit visual art.

Useful bibliographic guides to the literature on Inuit arts are provided by Bradley (1977) and Crandall and Crandall (2002).

3

ABORIGINAL AUSTRALIAN AESTHETICS

Sacramental Union with the Eternal Dreamtime

> [Australian Aboriginal art works] are tangible representations of the sacred mythological past in the present, the bridge that links man with his gods.
>
> (Berndt and Berndt 1964:7)

The senses speak to us of one reality, a world whose palpable immediacy cannot easily be dismissed. But the mind, given an opportunity for reflection, often proclaims another, more significant realm—one that transcends the mundane plane of the senses. Most of us have had presentiments of such a world at one time or another, whether in experiencing the awesomeness of divinity, the ecstasy of love, or even, as in the words of a mathematician and philosopher, "the Pythagorean power by which number holds sway above the flux" (Russell 1967:13). For most Westerners, such epiphanies are the exception rather than the rule, but for the Aboriginal peoples of Australia[1] the world beyond the empirical here-and-now is compellingly genuine and important. Spiritual concerns permeated Aboriginal life, and a careful examination of native Australian aesthetics reveals that, along with ritual, art is the primary means by which mortals may touch this obscure world.

Aboriginals were among the few hunting and gathering cultures to survive into the twentieth century, and their being prolific producers of art makes them all the more interesting for our purposes. Moreover, the spiritual quality of Australian aesthetics compels our attention, forcing us to probe the more remote corners of the heart to search out and examine the voice through which the human soul speaks to the spirit of nature. For Aboriginal Australians, that voice is ritual art.

---

[1]Traditional Aboriginal life, culture, and art have been powerfully affected by the colonial experience. The Epilogue of this chapter will describe some of the resultant changes. Except for that section, however, the rest of the chapter describes the lifeways and beliefs that once existed.

The Cultural Context of Aboriginal Art

The native peoples of Australia have never been numerous. In an island nearly the size of the continental United States, early European explorers encountered only about 300,000 people (fewer than one-third the current population of Rhode Island), and the colonial experience has reduced that small number by about 90 percent. Most of the approximately 500 traditional tribal groups were divided into semi-nomadic bands with less than a hundred members each. The demographic sparseness of the Aboriginals is exemplified by Western Arnhem Land (see map, p. xvi), a region located in northern Australia and the source of much of our information about traditional Australian art and aesthetics, which is now inhabited by fewer than 1,000 people.

But these bands survived remarkably well in the seemingly inhospitable desert and grassland environment found in most of Australia, thanks largely to a technology that was simple but ingenious. Digging sticks and grinding stones allowed women to obtain and prepare food from the earth, and spears, spear throwers, and boomerangs helped men bring down game. (Not all groups had the boomerang; and among those that did, the non-returning type played a far more important role in hunting than did the returning type, which was used primarily for recreation.) The remaining inventory of utilitarian items was small: Aboriginals made shields and clubs for fighting; string, bark, and wood containers; and houses of bark and grass. They cut and worked wood with stone axes, adzes, wedges, and chisels, and they lit fires using fire drills and fire saws.

Compared to the simplicity of their material culture, the intellectual life of Aboriginals was quite complex. Traditional Australian kinship systems, for example, continue to tax the understanding of Western scholars. Australian religion is also a challenging topic for the outsider. Its most fundamental premise is that during some indeterminate period of the past that Aboriginals call the "Eternal Dreamtime," mythic beings wandered through the country-side, their activities creating the notable features of today's landscape, such as waterholes. Also in their travels, the Dreamtime spirits brought into existence a primordial abundance of plant and animal life, human beings, and many human institutions such as ritual, song, and the principles of descent. It was thought that the spirits of the Eternal Dreamtime continued to exist in the time of mortals; and by recounting the stories of their travels (i.e., through myth—see Figure 3–1) and by reenacting their activities (i.e., through ritual), Aboriginals believed that the original harmonious and prosperous state of the world would be perpetuated. Ceremonial practices varied widely and were the responsibility of equally diverse totemic groups—that is, sets of individuals who shared a symbolic identification with a particular species of animal, to which they could trace their origin and with whom they retained a close association.

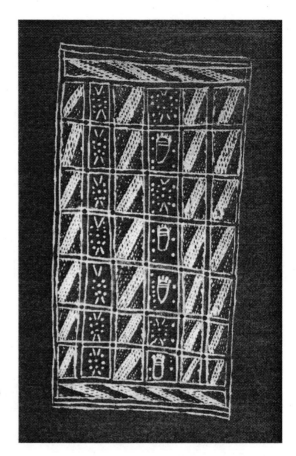

FIGURE 3-1 An Australian Aboriginal bark painting by Banakaka, a member of the Liyagalawumirri, northeast Arnhem Land. It depicts in a traditional style the characters and events that occur in the myth of the Wawilak Sisters, a story "owned" by the artist's clan. *(Courtesy Edward L. Ruhe.)*

Aboriginal Art

Traditionally, the arts of Australia were profuse and varied. Although native languages have no term equivalent to art in general, there are words for specific art media, such as graphic art, carving, singing, storytelling, and ceremonial dance (Berndt and Berndt 1964:306). Like other semi-nomadic peoples, Aboriginal Australians capitalized on the most portable of all media, the human body.[2] They practiced scarification, using both the method of rubbing

---

[2]The majority of Aboriginal art is sacred and its makers felt very strongly that it should be viewed only by initiated individuals. Therefore, most of the styles and media will not be shown here. Some bark paintings may be seen by non-initiates, and three of them appear in Figures 3–4, 3–5, and 3–6. Although they do not exhaust the repertoire of Aboriginal techniques, they give the viewer some idea of the styles common in north-central Australia.

ashes or clay into fresh cuts and also the less common technique of putting ants in the cuts to cause irritation (McCarthy 1957a). The resultant scars served various purposes. Some were made as part of mourning or initiation rituals; others indicated the wearer's social status (male versus female, initiated adult versus uninitiated youth); and still others were created simply to make the wearer's body more attractive.

Many Aboriginal groups used paint to enhance a person's appearance. The people of northeastern Arnhem Land, for example, first greased the body and then applied ochers in complicated patterns (Figure 3–2). The painted designs were "owned" by individuals; in addition to their ceremonial worth, the patterns had economic value in that they could be bartered or sold (Elkin, Berndt, and Berndt 1950: 61–62).

Clothing was minimal or nonexistent throughout aboriginal Australia. Some Aboriginals wore a pubic tassel, but it was meant to decorate, rather than cover, the body. Others wore necklaces and head-, arm-, and waistbands (see Figure 3–3). In some regions the body was painted, and textured designs were created on the body by sticking the fluff from kapok plants onto the

FIGURE 3–2 Bundubundu and Lamilami, residents of Arnhem Land, wearing rarrk body decoration after participating in a traditional ceremony in 1952. *(Axel Poignant / Axel Poignant Archive.)*

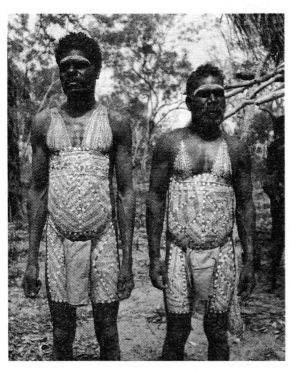

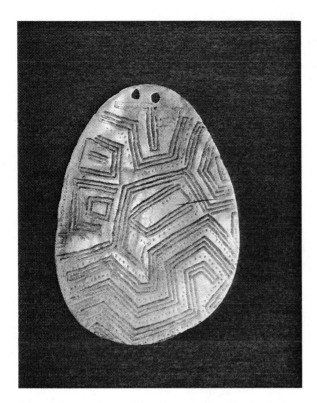

FIGURE 3-3 Australian Aboriginal pendant, with incised figures. *(Courtesy, Field Museum of Natural History, Chicago, neg. no. 272517.)*

body, using blood as an adhesive. Headdresses were perhaps the most elaborate additions to the body. The Arunta of central Australia, for example, pulled their hair together atop their heads, surrounded the resulting bunch of hair with small twigs to form a helmet-like structure as much as two feet high, and sometimes decorated it further by adding several eagle-hawk feathers (Spencer and Gillan 1938:610–612).

But body decoration was not the only medium of Australian visual art. Some groups produced paintings on large, flat sheets of bark from the stringy bark tree (Figure 3–4), and tens of thousands of paintings on rock walls have been documented throughout the continent. In Arnhem Land, some rock paintings portrayed daily life or were "public versions of mythological events," created "to 'make children happy' or were painted 'for fun'. That is, the stories were told in a relaxed atmosphere but served an educational purpose" (Taylor 2000:110). Others served supernatural functions, being made as part of sorcery activity, and were thought to have been made by the trickster-like *mimih* spirits, or again to have been the traces of actual Dreamtime

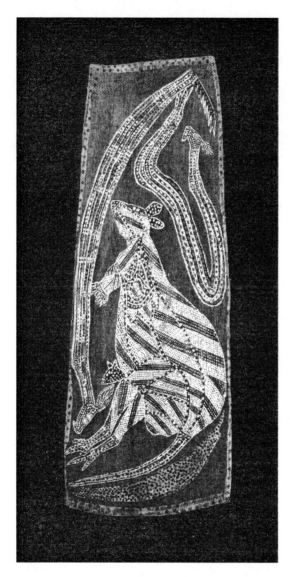

FIGURE 3–4 A bark painting by Mandarrg, of the Dangbon tribe, showing an X-ray kangaroo with the Rainbow Serpent, Borlung, rendered twice and costumed for a corroboree with a false beard and headdress. Note that the kangaroo's gullet, heart, lungs, diaphragm, liver, and spine are all visible, as is the baby in its pouch. A death adder appears above the kangaroo. *(Courtesy Edward L. Ruhe.)*

beings (Taylor 2000: 112). One style of rock art is characterized by "X-ray drawings," which depict not only animals' silhouettes but also their internal organs, painted in an anatomically accurate, polychromatic style (Figure 3–5). The *mimih* drawings monochromatically portray stick-figure humans, and stencil impressions of human hands constitute yet another variety of rock painting.

Many bands of Aboriginals produced three-dimensional art objects, the most important of which were the ritual objects called *tjurungas*—flat, oval, or

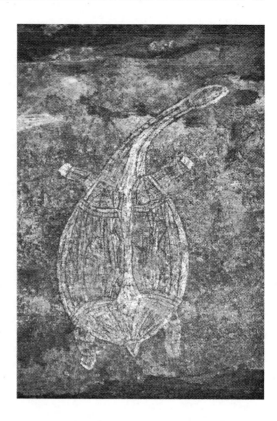

FIGURE 3-5 Spirit figures drawn on stone at the Basin track Ku-ring-gai Chase National Park. *(Alan Keohane / Dorling Kindersley Media Library.)*

circular slabs of wood or stone, from 2 inches to 18 feet in length, often bearing complex painted and incised patterns (Berndt and Berndt 1964:367). Aboriginals also made bullroarers by attaching oval pieces of wood to cords and whirling them in the air to produce an eerie, roaring sound. In some places, such as northeastern Arnhem Land, carvers made wooden heads or full figures of ancestral beings and animals. Elsewhere they cut large designs into live trees for use in initiation rites and as grave posts, and natives of Arnhem Land used earth, sand, and logs to produce huge high-relief sculptures on the ground. Margaret Clunies Ross and L. R. Hiatt (1978) witnessed the construction of five such sand sculptures that eventually covered about 600 square meters. Some tribes made baskets, decorating them with pandanus fiber, red parakeet feathers, white down, fur, and human hair.

The appearance of Australian art varies, both regionally and from one medium to another, but it is always graceful and economical in style. Its makers used a "subjective vision," representing things not as they briefly appear to the eye but as the mind knows them eternally to be (Figure 3–6). Artists also often conventionalized their work, allowing a few characteristic features

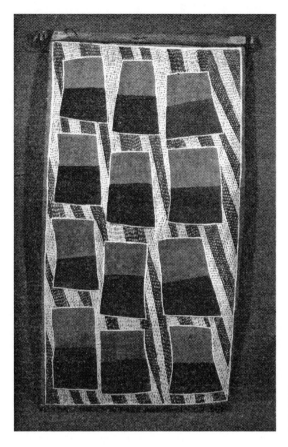

FIGURE 3-6 A bark painting by Midinari of the Galpu, showing the place of the twelve sacred rocks. *(Courtesy Edward L. Ruhe.)*

to represent the whole subject. Kupka describes bark paintings in these terms:

> By stripping down, reorganizing, and recreating natural forms, the Aboriginal painter arrives at a sort of abstraction, as do many "modern" painters, however, abstraction is not at all his aim. On the contrary, every line and every dot in his painting has a real meaning that can be recognized by the initiated. The fact that outsiders cannot interpret them is often an advantage. (Kupka 1965:96)

The performing arts were at least as important in Aboriginal culture as the graphic and plastic arts. Solo and ensemble singing were integral to both sacred and secular life. The songs usually were accompanied by various gongs, rattles, and the *didjeridu,* a drone pipe made from a hollowed-out eucalyptus branch that, when played, produced an eerie and distinctive sound. Some song texts were organized into cycles of up to 300 individual songs, each with densely symbolic meanings (cf. Berndt 1976; Ellis 1985).

The Use of Art in Aboriginal Religion

Aboriginal religion, with its pervasive concern for the Eternal Dreamtime, was the wellspring from which all Australian art flowed, and most Aboriginal religion, with its associated art, fell into two categories. It was either used for increase magic whose purpose was to ensure the availability and growth of food supplies, or it helped initiate young people into the status of adulthood.

The Aboriginal art that functioned as *increase magic* took many forms. Success in hunting, for example, provided a motivation for much cave painting. As Elkin describes it, "A man sees a fine fish in the river; he paints it on the gallery, and then is sure he will see it again and spear it" (Elkin 1964:15). Some eastern Arnhem Land men believed that they could improve their hunting by wearing necklaces with congealed blood pendants (Berndt and Berndt 1964:275). In the Kimberleys, these two agents—paint and blood—were united when men took blood from their arms and smeared it onto sacred paintings. Alternatively, some Aboriginal groups carved wooden poles shaped like animals to insure the fertility and increase of the species they represented; the same was true of some bullroarers.

A Fertility Mother, Kunapipi (or Gunabibi), was the focus of much increase magic, but the purpose of her ceremonies should not be misunderstood. Aboriginals did not expect their rituals to compel Kunapipi to provide food directly to her devotees. More ambitiously, they hoped she would be induced to perpetuate the natural order of *all* things as they were originally created during the Dreamtime, a condition that included the existence of adequate rainfall, the consequent growth of flora, the resultant flourishg of fauna and, ultimately the provision of food to humans (Elkin, Berndt, and Berndt 1950:28).

If increase rituals were meant to perpetuate the world of nature, then *initiation ceremonies* were performed to sustain the realm of humans. Special esoteric knowledge, possessed only by initiated adults, had to be passed down from one generation to the next. This was accomplished by psychologically compelling rituals in which young men (and, to a lesser extent, young women) underwent initiation into the mysteries of the Eternal Dreamtime.

The revelation of some secrets to the initiates was accomplished via song and dance; but the deepest meanings in initiation rituals resided in magically potent carved sticks, strings, wooden poles, ground sculptures and bullroarers—those, and the ubiquitous *tjurungas,* which were believed to actually embody the Dreamtime spirits and were the only items not destroyed after use in initiation ceremonies. The initiators typically altered the appearance of the initiates during these rituals by pulling out some of their teeth or hair, or by scarifying them. Most common, however, were various types of genital mutilation, including, for males, circumcision and subincision (i.e., slitting the urethra along the bottom of the penis) and, for females, ritual defloration.

Increase and initiation rituals were the most important parts of the Aboriginal religio-artistic complex, but they were not the only ones. For example, some bark paintings were made for initiation rituals but most of them served as teaching devices to convey general information to children (and strangers) regarding the non-esoteric aspects of the Dreamtime.

Most Aboriginal Australian art was not only religious but, simultaneously, utilitarian in the sense that it was made in an effort to obtain desired, material results. It was founded on a belief that human well-being depended upon the continuing activities of the Dreamtime spirits. Berndt and Berndt believe that Aboriginal ritual painting and carving "are tangible representations of the sacred mythological past in the present, the bridge that links man with his gods" (Berndt and Berndt 1964:7).[3]

Aboriginal Aesthetics: Transubstantiation via Art

Art clearly played an important role in Aboriginal religion, but two questions remain: What was the basis of art's religious efficacy, and what made art such a necessary adjunct of the Eternal Dreamtime? A clue lies in the Aboriginal conception of the Dreamtime itself. The mythical beings that traveled through the primordial countryside were thought to have never departed from the earth. Being eternal, they remain alive today. However, as supernaturals they can change their outer form, and today they usually have the appearance of natural phenomena such as specific rocks, mountains, and animal species. Despite their current guises, Dreamtime spirits still have close bonds with their human descendants. Indeed, members of a totemic group may not kill or eat their own totemic animal because, for them, doing so would be equivalent to fratricide and cannibalism.

In the view of Aboriginals, the cooperation of the Dreamtime spirits was absolutely necessary for human survival. Elkin, Berndt, and Berndt remark,

> To trail the kangaroo is not enough; it is necessary also to influence it so that it will stand within range. To aim at the fish will not in itself insure accuracy. It must be drawn to the spear of the fisherman. For such purposes, charms, rites,

---

[3]An anecdote recounted by Catherine Ellis illustrates the difference between Western and Aboriginal views regarding the importance of art in society. When she was in secondary school, Ellis participated in a debate in which she had to argue that she herself, as a musician, was at least as important in her (Western) society as a lawyer or a minister. She lost the debate, her fellow British students telling her, "We wanted to vote for you but we couldn't. Why didn't you say you were a teacher, or a nurse, or a doctor? A musician is of no use for anything." Years later in Australia, Ellis learned that in Aboriginal culture "the most knowledgeable person in a tribal community was the person 'knowing many songs.' This individual encompassed within his knowledge of music, the wisdom of his people" (Ellis 1985:1).

paintings and sacred objects are . . . effective because [the hunter] and animals and plants and natural phenomena, both in the past and present, belong to one great moral or social order, each depending on the other—man's duty being ritual, nature's being food-producing. If man is remiss, nature will fail. (1950:2–3)

These observations bring us to the fundamental axiom of Aboriginal aesthetics: Art was a conduit that conveyed the needs and wishes of mortals to the Dreamtime spirits. Every detail of an art work was said to represent

events and situations in the career of the hero of the totemic group or lodge. As the artist engraves and paints he is "impressing" that meaning into it—probably by chant. Later, it is handled reverently as the sacramental link between man and the hero or ancestor, and the creative condition to which the latter belongs. (Elkin, Berndt, and Berndt 1950:7)

To touch a *tjurunga* was to come into direct, physical contact with the realm of the supernatural, and such contact insured the mutual perpetuation of both mortals and Dreamtime spirits.

Thus we see the underlying logic of Aboriginal aesthetics in Aboriginal belief: human welfare requires the blessings of the Dreamtime spirits; these supernaturals are influenced by ritual; and works of art—song, dance, and decorated ceremonial objects—are the effective components of ritual. Since human existence ultimately depends upon art, it is not surprising that native Australians produced art in great quantities and of considerable conceptual sophistication.

Sometimes this central premise of Aboriginal aesthetics was taken one step further. Through art, mortals not only communicated with the Eternal Dreamtime; they actually joined the spirit world themselves. For example, Elkin, Berndt, and Berndt (1950:3) say that a participant in a ritual "becomes the hero or ancestor. . . . By reenacting what the ancestor or great being did, he becomes a life-giver too." The Walbiri believed that Dreamtime spirits were physically embodied *(balga)* in the dancers who impersonated them, decorated as the dancers were with sacred *guruwari* designs (Munn 1973:198).[4] Some evidence suggests that the identity of the dancer in this liminal state may have been more genuine than his normal condition, since the Berndts report that the term, *jimeran,* which refers to men's activities on the sacred ground, may be translated as "making themselves"— that is, becoming their true, spiritual selves (Berndt and Berndt 1970:144). Other components of traditional Australian culture also support the idea that individuals can be

---

[4]Keali'inohomoku (personal communication) has noted that the transformation of mortals into spirits lasts only for the duration of the dance. However, the more often an individual is so transformed, the greater becomes his spiritual power—and the closer he comes (metaphorically) to joining the spirits himself.

united with the world of the Dreamtime. For example, a common belief was that conception occurs when a woman happened to pass by an animal disguised as a Dreamtime spirit. If it entered her body, she became pregnant and the child she later bore was believed to embody a spirit corresponding to the species that was its supernatural father. Thus, a man may have asserted that he was a kangaroo and therefore had a responsibility to join with other individuals who possessed the kangaroo spirit to carry out the rituals appropriate to their totemic father (Berndt and Berndt 1970:200).

Aboriginal aesthetics rested on a religious and philosophical foundation, but it also had a very real psychological basis that imbued traditional Australians' personal lives with a potent spirituality. Formal instruction in Aboriginal religion occurred during initiation ceremonies at the time of adolescence, but much earlier the formative minds of young people came under the sway of the Eternal Dreamtime. Joining in the singing or beating time to accompany the dancers in the great *corroborees* of song and dance that were not restricted to initiated men, even the youngest children must have sensed the power of ritual performance. As the dancing continued into the night and the children drifted asleep surrounded by song and dance, they entered their own, literal "dreamtime" under the influence of the visual and performing arts and their association with the Eternal Dreamtime (Elkin 1964:11). Through the arts, Aboriginals experienced a genuine identity with the spirit world.

Just as the individual's spiritual life began before birth, it was believed to continue after death, a transition after which one continued to lead another life, much like the earthly one. And again, art mediated the transition. The corpse of the deceased was painted with the designs of his or her totemic group, the hair sometimes woven into a string that was revered as sacred (Berndt and Berndt 1964:390, 409).

The concept of the body as a vessel of a Dreamtime spirit underlay many other traditional ritual practices. Because blood is just as vital for the continued life of spirits as it is for continued mortal life, many rituals required the drawing of blood from the celebrants' arms or penises so it could be sprinkled over ceremonial objects or people. (Red ochre was sometimes substituted for blood in such contexts.) In areas where circumcision was practiced, men's sacred baskets may have been decorated with pendants of beeswax that encased the foreskin of the bag's owner or those of his close relatives (ibid.:381).

The role of ritual and art in Aboriginal thought was extremely powerful, coloring all aspects of native life. Any people that could survive the inhospitable semideserts of central Australia for tens of thousands of years by means of a stone-age technology obviously possessed great practical ingenuity; Australians were, after all, the world's sole inventors of the returning boomerang. Moreover, they had confidence in their position in the world and in their time-tested subsistence techniques.[5] But in daily life the mystical and subjective dimension held sway, with far greater importance attached to what they considered to be the spiritual foundation of life, the Eternal Dreamtime, than to the mundane, visible world.

Artistic Ramifications of Aboriginal Aesthetics

The Aboriginal aesthetic system that has just been described did not exist in isolation but had notable implications for creativity and art production, for art's role in male and female initiation ceremonies, for love magic and native standards of beauty, and for secular uses of art. For example, since the mystical efficacy of art was present only in ritual settings, most sacred Aboriginal art had only a brief existence. After use it may have been forgotten, left to disintegrate of its own accord, or deliberately destroyed. A few objects, such as *tjurungas*, which were believed to be the permanent residences of Dreamtime spirits, were exceptions to this rule, as were rock paintings and engravings; but bark paintings, ground sculptures, and, of course, most body decorations and the performing arts were ephemeral, despite the many hours of effort that went into their production.

The transubstantiating capacity of art also limited innovation in Aboriginal art styles. Indeed, traditional Australians believed that the spirits of the Eternal Dreamtime responded only to art that precisely replicated traditional patterns of graphic design or performance. Some groups thought that if the singers' memories momentarily lapsed in the middle of a ritual performance and caused a minor error, the song should be stopped and started again from the beginning to ensure its supernatural efficacy.[6]

The rites of passage that marked the transition from youth to adulthood were highly important in many Australian societies, especially for

---

[5]"An Arnhem Land woman once said in effect, rather patronizingly, as she watched a Fijian missionary working on his mission garden, anxiously concerned because a few of the plants had died: 'You people go to all that trouble, working and planting seeds, but we don't have to do that. All these things are there for us, the Ancestral Beings left them for us. In the end, you depend on the sun and the rain just the same as we do, but the difference is that we just have to go and collect the food when it is ripe. We don't have all this other trouble.'" (Berndt and Berndt 1964:93)

[6]This does not necessarily mean that Aboriginal art is static and unchanging. Sometimes a group would adopt cultural elements from its neighbors, and there are recorded instances in which an individual introduced an entirely new song, dance, or visual design into a group. Among the Yirrkala, such innovations only came into existence through dreams, and once identified they obeyed the laws that constrain all other Aboriginal art works (cf. Waterman and Waterman 1970:107–108).

males; and the blood that flowed from the wounds of circumcision symbolized the severing of a boy's close association with his mother and united his soul with the spirits of older initiates. But on another level, the blood drawn from the penis and arms of the celebrants on these occasions established and validated a sacred bond with the spirits of the Dreamtime. The red blood, like the red ochre used on *tjurungas,* ensured the well-being of the Dreamtime spirits, and this in turn promoted the fertility of humans and the natural species that provide sustenance for humans.

Although female initiations varied from region to region, most combined the themes of sexuality, fertility, and increase in the environment. Three long cycles of love songs collected by Ronald Berndt in Arnhem Land show this linkage clearly. The songs, which poetically reveal Aboriginal views on romance, are particularly illuminating regarding the relationship between spirituality and erotic beauty. For example, one song describes the attractiveness of the breasts of young women as they stand in the cold west wind, fluttering their eyes at men and swaying their buttocks (Berndt 1976:57). Significantly, the text describes the girls as *mareiin,* a term "usually translatable as 'sacred,' [although] here it conveys an extra quality—of being extraordinarily attractive or beautiful" (ibid.).

The conjunction of sexuality, beauty, and fertility appears in other contexts as well. For example, in songs from Goulburn Island, the spirit Yulunggul "symbolizes a penis, and rain [symbolizes] semen; female attributes are blood and clouds. . . . Coitus, symbolic or actual, brings about the desired season of rain which, in turn, promotes fertility" (Berndt 1976:80).

Considerations of fertility and good health also provided the foundation for aboriginal concepts of personal beauty. Aboriginals felt deformities and handicaps to be ugly, and they placed a high premium on a sound body, clear skin, and even a healthy head of hair. They sometimes enhanced the appearance of good health by cosmetic efforts such as rubbing the hair and body with fats. But, we learn, "the greatest stress is on youth. A girl who has just reached puberty is most desirable as a spouse—one with small, rounded breasts, not yet drooping after years of childbearing; so is a young man, newly initiated" (Berndt and Berndt 1964:162).

Love magic can be best understood as being an effort to ensure sexual conquests (and, at the same time, reproduction) by use of objects or actions whose powers depended upon their aesthetic component. Aboriginals believed it is the poetic artistry of a love song that gives it the power to arouse the desired lover's sensuality and draw him or her inexorably into relations with the singer. Also, men sometimes made cave paintings that depicted women with accentuated breasts or elongated vulvas; women making love with men or dancing as semen runs down their legs; or women whose bodies show clear signs of pregnancy. These are instances of imitative magic, with the artists believing that their pictured fantasies would come true.

The Aboriginal aesthetic was pre-eminently sacred in nature, and most Australian art was produced for explicitly religious uses. But some traditional art did occur in nonritual contexts. In northeastern Arnhem Land, for example, various groups made decoratively carved and painted spears, spear throwers, paddles, bobbins, and children's toys. Beautifully crafted baskets, mats, and nets were made for everyday use, and some secular body decorations, such as necklaces and armbands, were produced with great artistry. But even though these items served utilitarian purposes, their aesthetic value derived from the same belief system that prompted sacred art production. Regarding sacred designs on secular objects, Elkin notes,

> *The designs, which are really in themselves symbols of the mythical world—the world of spiritual power—together with the associated songs and chants, impart a 'virtue' to the weapon or other object which they adorn. A weapon so enriched is not only more pleasing, but more powerful.* It is endowed with a power which comes from the heroes of the creative past, a power which, through the medium of myth and ritual, is still available to men. (Elkin 1938:9; emphasis in original)

Although sacred associations informed secular art in traditional Australia, the two realms did differ, and the disparities emphasize the priority of the sacred. Secular art was less strictly tied to tradition than was sacred art so that whereas the creators of sacred art had to copy old designs precisely, the makers of secular art could choose between realistic or symbolic representation, and some innovation was permitted. The sacred/secular distinction also influenced the Aboriginal artist's status. In northeast Arnhem Land, to be able to paint sacred designs was considered a great gift, and only those few who were so blessed were elevated to a high status and paid for their efforts. The maker of secular art, by contrast, gained neither status nor compensation (Elkin, Berndt, and Berndt 1950:110).

Sometimes the sacred associations of secular art emphasized the importance of the message communicated by the art. At Balgo in Western Australia, the Berndts saw men painting boards with maps of the surrounding countryside. Ostensibly, they were recording totemic information about specific locations, but as men traded the boards among themselves, they gained accurate knowledge of local and distant terrain (Berndt and Berndt 1964:114). Likewise, X-ray drawings provided valuable anatomical maps, illustrating information that was useful to anyone wanting to butcher the animal portrayed. Finally, carved and decorated "message sticks" were common. A messenger would carry such a stick, not so much to convey information symbolically but as proof of the importance and accuracy of his verbal communication (McCarthy 1957a:107).

Conclusion

Accounts of the aesthetic systems of hunting and gathering societies prove that the artistic spirit is found even among those peoples who are most distant from the West with regard to technology, population, and specialization of labor. Traditional Aboriginals did make art, and although fieldworkers have often noted that they made no "art for art's sake," Aboriginal artists did experience genuine pleasure in artistic production, a gratification that combined a sensuous satisfaction of the "pretty" with an intellectual appreciation of the spiritually and socially significant (Berndt and Berndt 1964:306, 350, 352; Elkin 1938:10; Elkin, Berndt, and Berndt 1950:10–11; McCarthy 1957a:167; Mountford 1954:9–10, 1961:7–8).

Fieldworkers also consistently report that Aboriginals appreciated differences in levels of skill and that they rewarded exceptionally talented individuals, especially Aboriginal song-men and *didjeridu*-players, who underwent elaborate and prolonged training. But Aboriginal artists, although recognized, were not fulltime specialists who could rely on commissions to provide their subsistence but rather were integrated into the social milieu, performing all the activities appropriate to their sex (cf., e.g., T. Jones 1956/7:28; Elkin, Berndt, and Berndt 1950:110; Mountford 1961:7; McCarthy 1957b:13–14).

But the greatest significance of Aboriginal art was not the social integration of the artist but the cultural integration of the aesthetic system from which art itself derived. Aboriginal aesthetics not only fit into the broader conceptual system of the society; it also played a pivotal role in unifying, explaining, and translating into concrete strategies the belief that through art mortals can come into immediate, intimate, and genuine contact with the all-important spirits of the Eternal Dreamtime. One can hardly imagine art anywhere lacking a spiritual component, but rarely is this motive as important as among the native peoples of Australia. Clearly, if this dimension is taken to be the most rarified aspect of aesthetic creation, then Australian Aboriginals, for all the simplicity of their material culture, produce some of the world's most impressive art.

Epilogue

The roots of traditional Aboriginal culture reach back tens of thousands of years, and in some communities, the long-established practices and ideas described thus far are still to be found. In addition to these continuities, however, a great deal has changed in Australia since it became a British colony over two hundred years ago. For all of the old Aboriginal art forms there are contemporary counterparts that reflect non-Aboriginal influences. At the same time, Aboriginal people have had a marked impact on the world beyond their own.

Fortunately, many specific components of these changes have been studies and described in print (see, especially, Kleinert and Neale 2000).[7]

The changes that occurred in two-dimensional paintings reveal the remarkable interplay of the indigenous with the nontraditional. As noted previously, paintings on rock walls long served a variety of purposes, from instructing young people in the non-esoteric aspects of mythology to being the manifestations of the handiwork of Dreamtime beings. During the wet season, when families' travels took them away from rock shelters, they constructed huts covered with sheets of bark from the stringybark tree, and the figures and designs painted on the bark were congruent with the nonsecret rock paintings.

After Europeans arrived in Australia, some became curious about the rock paintings. One of them, the English biologist and professor at the University of Melbourne, Baldwin Spencer, noticed the similarities between rock paintings and bark paintings—as well as the fact that the latter could be purchased and taken home for study. By 1912 Spencer was commissioning and buying bark paintings in Arnhem Land, paying for them with much-valued tobacco (Taylor 2000:112). As scholarly interest in bark paintings increased, the commercial market for them grew apace. They were sold first through mission shops and later through community art centers funded by the Aboriginal Arts Board of the Australia Council.

That bark paintings have become something of an industry and a significant source of income for their makers should not be taken to mean that the medium has lost its cultural significance among Aboriginal peoples. Vivien Johnson has remarked,

> Now that [central Australian] Kunwinjku do not generally live near rock-art sites, bark painting and painting on paper for the market have come to have an important role in circulating religious knowledge in the secular realm. . . . Paintings now have two uses and two audiences: they are used in a didactic way within Kunwinjku society, and to promote the power of the culture further afield. (Johnson 2000:211)

Some bark paintings now available to non-Aboriginal buyers contain images that were once the sole domain of initiated males, but again, the cultural dynamic is reciprocal: For the Kunwinjku, at least, there has been a conscious decision to share such images as a means of showing outsiders how strong their own culture is (ibid.).

---

[7]As elsewhere in this chapter, the following remarks will focus primarily on the arts of Arnhem Land. The reader is advised to consult other sources (e.g., Sayers 2001:141–145; Megaw and Megaw 2000:197–204) for developments in central Australia, including the important watercolor painters at Hermannsburg, one of whom, Albert Namatjira, "became the best-known Aboriginal person of his day and one of the few Australian artists who was in his own lifetime—and remains—a household name" (Sayers 2001:141).

Aboriginal painting has undergone other permutations, as well. In recent decades, some individuals have entered the world of fine arts. At an early stage, there seemed to be just two options, namely, to reproduce traditional paintings (on bark, paper, or canvas) or to work in the predominantly Eurocentric easel-painting styles of the non-Aboriginal world. Another possibility emerged in 1984, however, with a watershed exhibition held in the Artspace in Surry Hills, Sydney. In that show, entitled "Koori Art '84," twenty-five Aboriginal artists (some from Arnhem Land) presented paintings that were technically sophisticated but were driven in their figurative subject matter by Aboriginal experiences and sensibilities. Social realism and "confrontational imagery" (Neale 2000:267) were the order of the day. "Koori '84" established a precedent, and it has been followed by numerous shows of easel paintings by Aboriginal artists that likewise use the medium of fine art painting to address Aboriginal concerns in a powerful way.

The life of Banduk Marika (b. 1954) illustrates the dramatic changes that painting has undergone in Arnhem Land since the early twentieth century (Marika and Williams 2000:637–639). Marika's father, Mawalan, and her uncle, Mathaman, had long made traditional bark paintings, but when a mission was established at Yirrkala in the 1930s, they were among the first to make paintings for sale (Figure 3–7). (A 1959 painting made by Mathaman was sold in 1996 for $71,250, the highest price ever paid for a bark painting.) Predictably, with the arrival of non-Aboriginal Australians there came not only a market for bark paintings but also threats to Aboriginal culture and land. Inasmuch as bark paintings had traditionally been used for (among other things) validating Aboriginal groups' relationships with the countryside they lived in, it is not surprising that Malawan and other Yolngu leaders were

FIGURE 3–7 Linocut entitled *Minyyapa gaDhanggatiya* by Banduk Marika. 1995, image size: 60.0 x 57.5 cm. (The Australian Art Print Network. © 2004 Artist Rights Society (ARS), New York/VISCOPY, Australia.)

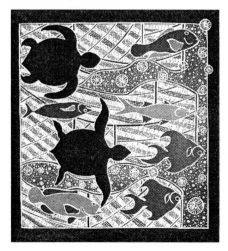 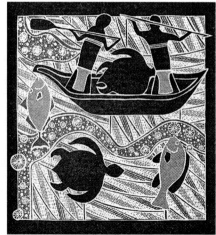

the creators of the 1963 "Bark Petition" in an effort to thwart mining development at Yirrkala.[8]

Mawalan Marika was the first in the area to teach not only his sons but also his daughters, including Banduk, traditional painting techniques. When Banduk Marika was 28, she moved to Sydney, began printmaking, and became artist-in-residence at the Canberra School of Art. In 1993, Banduk used copyright law to stop a carpet company from reproducing her designs without permission. Since then, Banduk has served on the Boards of the National Gallery of Australia and the Museum and Art Gallery of the Northern Territory. Meanwhile, her linocuts and serigraphs have been critically acclaimed, being shown in the United States, India, Egypt, Noumea, and Singapore.

In addition to her work as an artist, Banduk Marika has remained active in causes that link art with traditional culture. In 1990 she spoke at the Iroquois First Nations Convergence of Indigenous People in New York. A statement recognizing her receipt of the 2001 Red Ochre Award from the Australia Council's Aboriginal and Torres Strait Islander Arts Board says in part:

> Her knowledge and expertise in the areas of Indigenous art, copyright, and cultural heritage issues are much appreciated. Being an Elder and artist in her community, Banduk is regularly called upon to advise, negotiate and collaborate between Indigenous and non-Indigenous cultures, as well as between traditional and contemporary practices. Her collaboration with Stephen Page as cultural advisor to the 2000 Sydney Olympic Games Opening Ceremony is an outstanding example.[9] (http://abc.net.au/message/blackarts/visual/banduk_marika.htm)

Thus, in the course of two generations the Marika family has gone from making traditional bark paintings at the small beach camp called Yirrkala to Banduk's involvement in the national and international world of art and art activism. And Banduk Marika is far from the only Aboriginal painter whose career reaches from the traditional to the global. Aboriginal painters have been represented at two Venice Biennales, and in an action that comes full circle with the old paintings on the walls of rock shelters, in 1985 the Aboriginal artist Avril Quaill collaborated on the construction of a large-scale wall mural (Watson 2000:126) in Sydney in 1985.

---

[8] The Bark Petition—a sheet of bark, in the middle of which was a text in Yolngu and in English, bordered by traditional painted figures—was sent to the Australian parliament, fueling an Aboriginal land rights movements that eventually led to the Aboriginal Land Rights (Northern Territory) Act of 1976 (cf. Morphy 2000:100–102).

[9] The statement concludes, "Aware of cultural protocols, before accepting nomination for the Red Ochre Award, Banduk sought and received permission from her community" (http://abc.net.au/message/blackarts/visual/banduk_marika.htm).

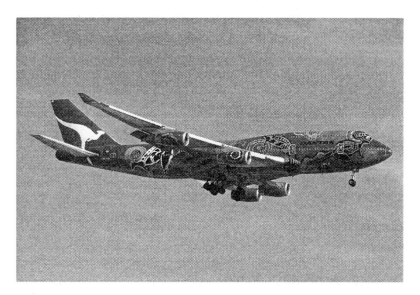

FIGURE 3–8   Using colors taken from the Australian landscape, a team of Aboriginal and non-Aboriginal artists combined traditional and contemporary designs to decorate one of Quantas Airlines' Boeing 774-400's. *(Photo © Ian Moy from Airliners.net.)*

Aboriginal visual arts also have influenced the popular culture of Australia. For example, two 747-400 jets of Qantas, the Australian national airline, have been painted with Aboriginal-derived designs (Figure 3–8); and Aboriginal motifs have appeared on everything from T-shirts to haute couture gowns (cf. Maynard 2000:384–390).

As with visual arts, Aboriginal performing arts have in some contexts remained unchanged while in other ways now reflect two centuries of intimate interaction with the forces of colonialism—sometimes with unexpected outcomes. For example, the *didgeridu,* once found only in northern Australia, has become not only a symbol of Aboriginality throughout Australia but has also traveled beyond the seas to become a popular instrument among Americans and Europeans interested in the New Age movement and World Music —so much so that questions have been raised as to the environmental effects of harvesting so many of the trees that provide the wood from which the instrument is made. In Arnhem Land the Maningrida Arts and Culture art cooperative has even created a website that attempts to educate non-Aboriginal users of the *didgeridu* about its history and complex role in Aboriginal music and culture (Garde 2000:344).

Perhaps more predictably, popular music genres have emerged that combine Aboriginal and non-Aboriginal elements. For example, in 1990 a group from Arnhem Land called Yothu Yindi was the first indigenous rock band to have a recording, *Treaty,* that was on the popular music charts in

Australia. Kathleen Oien notes, "Since then, the band has gained international recognition and produced several albums with a major Australian record label, which has helped to increase awareness and appreciation of Indigenous popular music"— the very thing the band had hoped to accomplish (Oien 2000:335). Another group from Arnhem Land, Blebala Mujik, also resolutely includes contemporary *and* traditional music in its repertoire. Oien says, "When permission was requested for use of one of its traditional songs on an educational CD-ROM, the band granted permission with the proviso that one of its rock songs be included as well, because it wanted to make it clear that it performs both traditional and contemporary music" (ibid.:337). In the same way that most fine art painting by Aboriginal artists since "Koori '84" has tended to be topical in subject matter, Aboriginal popular music often addresses issues of specific concern to the musicians' background. Instead of love songs, "they are more likely to deal with topics important to their communities, such as relationship to the land, community issues, and protest against historical and current injustices" (ibid.:339).

Aboriginal dance has followed a trajectory similar to that of painting and music. For example, both traditional and contemporary dance movements are incorporated in performances by the successful Bangarra Dance Theatre (cf., Meekison 2000:367–369). Djakapurra Munyarryun, who in 2002 retired as principal dancer, has also served as creative consultant for the troupe, providing traditional stories upon which dances can be based, but also ascertaining that the material may be made public, based on the opinions of the elders in his home community of Darlinbuy, in northeast Arnhem Land. Thus, like the printmaker Banduk Marika, mentioned above, Munyarryun serves as a link between localized traditional arts and a contemporary global audience: The Bangarra Dance Theatre has performed from New York to Edinburgh to Johannesburg, and Munyarryun led a group of 1,000 Aboriginal dancers as part of the opening ceremonies of the 2000 Olympics in Sydney.

Aboriginal literature has had a similar course of development. Like painting and dance, oral literature played a vital role in traditional culture, but the old stories are now often dissimenated by means of the written word. Novels, poetry, and drama by Aboriginal writers have all had notable success; the same can be said for radio, cinema, and television. In most cases, the works reflect aspects of both traditional and contemporary culture. For example, Sally Morgan's very successful play, *My Place,* draws upon the theme of relations between individuals of Aboriginal and non-Aboriginal descent as well as the way in which the colonial process unfolded in Australia (cf. Morrissey 2000:316). Paraphrasing the elder and storyteller Maureen Watson, Murri theater artist David Mowaliari has written,

> The traditional role of stories was to provide meaning and shape to the world, to explain why the world is as it is, and what our connection is to it. . . . The coming of new elements to our lives needed new stories. The coming of Christianity, of the horse, of Toyotas, money, AIDS, and alcohol—all needed stories,

dances, painting, and songs. If we cannot tell the story of it, how can we ever get a handle on it? How can we ever accept it, reject it or use it? (quoted in Enoch 2000:349–350)

The hybridization of Aboriginal literature also has a global dimension. The poet and essayist Mundorooroo, for example, was influenced by Franz Fanon, Malcom X, and Bob Marley.

Several themes are apparent in these cases of Aboriginal arts changing as a consequence of European colonialization. Most obviously, the newly emergent styles and genres combine components of traditional culture with elements from abroad, the synthesis producing arts that are unique and important. But in every case, the hybridization between old and new has been conditioned by the unequal social position of Aboriginal and non-Aboriginal peoples, with Aboriginal artists utilizing art media to defend and strengthen themselves and their culture. This battle has not ended. For example, as of the late 1990s there were more than 200 websites with Aboriginal content, about one-third of which were created by Aboriginal organizations or individuals (Nathan 2000:312). But even on the Internet, the identity and heritage of Aboriginal peoples is contested. Thus, the web page of an art cooperative named Maningrida Arts and Culture states, "Each design represents the artist's personal dreamings and is essentially of a sacred nature. The artists have given permission for their work to be presented on the internet for the public to look at and learn from. However, two senior men, George Ganyjibala and Jimmy Angunguna, wish to advise that it is a crime under traditional law to paint someone else's design or copy it without permission. Please respect the spirit in which the work is presented" (http://www.bu.aust. com/~maningrida/gallery/gallery.html).[10]

Another factor that has frequently influenced Aboriginal art is tourism, now Australia's largest industry (Sculthorpe 2000:391). Until the 1980s Australia sought to attract tourists by promoting its natural environment—the recreational atmosphere of its beaches, the dramatic scenery of its interior, and the peculiarity of its unique wildlife. But as international tourists became more sophisticated, it was clear that the marketing of Australia's cultural heritage—that is, its *Aboriginal* cultural heritage—would attract additional visitors as well as revenue.[11] Here, too, Aboriginal identity and control has been

---

[10]David Nathan has pointed out that "the Web has much in common with [Aboriginal] social systems: both consist of networked networks were information transmission is rapid, and an individual's participation depends on his or her identity expressed in terms of the network" (Nathan 2000:312).

[11]A website of the Australian Council for Tourism states, "An official survey of indigenous tourism, conducted in Australia in 1998-99, found that between 85 per cent and 95 per cent of visitors from all countries wanted to experience indigenous tourism on subsequent visits to Australia. This figure is likely to grow, with a worldwide audience of about 3.7 billion people having watched the Olympic opening ceremony" (http://www.aussie.net.au)

and continues to be contested territory, with Aboriginal peoples increasingly involved in guided tours, festivals, and other activities that involve their own people.

By comparison to the unhurried rate of change of Australian Aboriginal art in past millennia, events of the last 200 years have been cataclysmic. But thanks to the extensive documentation and analysis that is available, we can clearly see that the ancient past has not been erased. Rather, it lives on in a multitude of art works, some replicating their earlier counterparts; some in forms that, although dramatically different, are yet viable.

Further Reading

Classic ethnographic texts that provide broad accounts of traditional Aboriginal culture with substantial reference to Aboriginal art are Berndt and Berndt (1964), McCarthy (1957a), and Elkin (1964). Broad studies of Aboriginal art are Ucko (1977) and Caruana (1993). Elkin, Berndt, and Berndt (1950) focus on the art of Arnhem Land, and Berndt's study (1976) of the "love songs" of Arnhem Land is of interest. Luke Taylor (1996) provides a survey of Arnhem Land bark paintings.

Sayers (2001) provides a survey of the history of fine (visual) arts in Australia up to the end of the twentieth century, and he includes a chapter on Aboriginal painting. For colonial and post-colonial developments in Aboriginal arts, the *Oxford Companion to Aboriginal Art and Culture* (Kleinert and Neale 2000) is a monumental work of remarkable breadth, with scholarly treatments of all regions of Australia as well as urban settings. Media include not only the visual arts but also performing arts, literary arts, and architecture. Many essays incorporate discussions of the ways in which recent Aboriginal art reflects traditional culture as well as the political environment in which it has been produced during the last two centuries.

AESTHETICS OF THE SEPIK

Powerful Spirits and Phallic Aggression in New Guinea

> In its own culture, every work of art rouses emotions and appeals to ideas and associations which are not capable of being put into words. Let us never forget that we only know fragments of the culture which has brought forth those foreign works of art. It is impossible for us ever to undergo and enjoy the full effect of these works as they were intended to be—as they really are!
>
> (Carl A. Schmitz 1963:148)

Art is important in many societies of the island Pacific, but perhaps nowhere in Oceania does art production reach such extravagant proportions as in the societies in the vicinity of New Guinea's Sepik River. Consider, for example, the findings of Anthony Forge, who lived with the Abelam of the Sepik for more than two years. Within five-miles of his 1963 base village, he counted over 100 ceremonial houses, each filled with carved and painted art work (Figure 4–1). Moreover, Forge's Abelam neighbors built more than fifteen cult houses, complete with paintings and sculptures, during one six-month ceremonial season (Forge 1970:271). Such an enormous outpouring of art probably puts the Abelam ahead of the "art capitals" of the Western world in sheer quantity of art production.

Although the Sepik people live according to cultural premises that seem distant from our own—some societies practiced headhunting and cannibalism well into the twentieth century—their intellectual capacities are by no means lacking. Gregory Bateson has argued convincingly that in one Sepik tribe, the *Iatmul*, there is an appreciation of such intellectually subtle issues as the difference between emotional and cognitive truth and the potential monism, dualism, or pluralism of the natural and supernatural worlds (Bateson 1958:222, 235). The same Iatmul commonly accomplish feats of memory that we might well be envious of: An individual may have as many as thirty personal names, and Bateson once estimated that a learned Iatmul man knows between ten and twenty thousand such names for his associates.

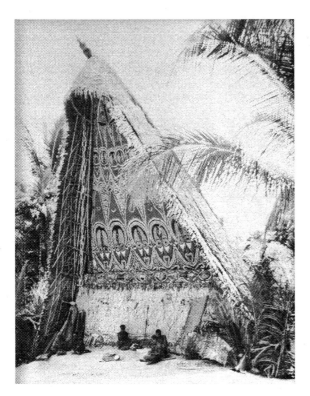

FIGURE 4-1 *Kwarambu*, a tambaran house in the Tagwat-sapu hamlet of Kinbangwa village, northern Abelam. An initiation is in progress, and taboo areas beside the house are closed off with a fence of palm fronds. August 1962. *(Photo courtesy Anthony Forge.)*

But despite this proven intellectual potential, most Sepik peoples seem to have little interest in creating elaborate and integrated philosophical systems to account for the nature of things. Phyllis Kaberry, for example, claims that among the Abelam, "there is no elaborate cosmology such as one finds among the Australian aborigines, and in reply to questions about the origin of the country, natives said matter-of-factly, 'marsalai [i.e., animistic spirits] made it'" (Kaberry 1941:359–360). Similarly, Margaret Mead says that the Mountain Arapesh "have no cosmology and make no attempt to explain the origin of the earth and sky, the sun and the moon" (Mead 1970:239; see also Firth 1936:31). Significantly, there is also a general absence of theorizing about art. As Forge puts it, "we find very little in the nature of indigenous exegesis. . . . Verbalizing about art, in short, is not a feature of New Guinea cultures" (Forge 1979:278–279).

Thus, the societies of the Sepik immediately present us with a seeming paradox. They produce a spectacular profusion of art, but they have no explicit theory of aesthetics that justifies the existence of art, that places the goals of art in a wider philosophical context, or that provides broadly applicable principles of art criticism. However, in the absence of such theories, extensive research in New Guinea by several fieldworkers has revealed that Sepik art is governed by implicit axioms, assumptions that play an important role in the fabric of Sepik society and culture. Uncovering these principles requires an exploration of Sepik religion, personality, and, especially, Sepik conceptions of masculinity and femininity.

Peoples of the Sepik

The vast island of New Guinea (see map, p. xvi), lying north of Australia and southeast of the Philippines, is divided into two political entities, the eastern half being the self-governing country of Papua New Guinea; the western half, the Indonesian province of Irian Jaya. The Sepik region lies in the northwest corner of Papua New Guinea, with a diverse terrain that includes offshore islands, swampy shoreline and riverine environments, and high plains that stretch to the base of the towering Victor Emmanuel Range of mountains.

More than a quarter of a million people live in New Guinea's East Sepik Province and West Sepik Province. Organized into numerous tribes, these groups do not constitute an altogether uniform or homogeneous cultural area—indeed, tribes that are adjacent to each other often speak mutually unintelligible languages. But despite such differences, several fundamental similarities may be found throughout the Sepik district. For thousands of years the residents of the Sepik have been village dwellers who have subsisted on farming, supplemented by hunting and gathering. Taro and sago plants, as well as pigs and dogs, are all long-established domesticates. The larger population, more complex technology, and greater specialization of labor set the Sepik groups—and indeed, all of the cultures discussed in the next six chapters—apart from the nomadic hunter-gatherers of the previous three chapters.

Another commonality through the area is that, at least at first glance, men seem to dominate public and private life. Descent is reckoned through the male line, and men in most Sepik societies have highly competitive dispositions. Men's secret societies, discussed below, constitute perhaps the most distinctive trait of the Sepik District tribes.

Art of the Sepik

Making art is a semispecialized activity in Sepik societies. The more prolific groups recognize the unique standing of some individuals, people we would call "artists," who are commissioned to execute specific carvings and who receive special food for their efforts. But even for these individuals, art is only a part-time occupation. Like everybody else, they and their wives must garden, gather, and hunt for most of their subsistence. The artist's profession does bring prestige, however. In Abelam society, for example, being an artist of repute is one means by which a man can attain an elevated social status, an alternative to the other avenues to success, which are being either a good fighter or a successful yam farmer. In any case, the traditional tools of the visual artist's trade are, in Forge's phrase, "thoroughly neolithic" and include stone adzes; gravers; chisels; awls pointed with pig, dog, and flying fox teeth; lizard skins and rough-surfaced leaves for smoothing; and fire for hollowing large objects (Forge 1967:74).

Most Sepik art serves religious purposes—elaborate decorations of men's ceremonial houses, plus the masks, costumes, songs, and dances that constitute the core of men's cult activities (Figures 4–2 and 4–3). But in addition to wood and wicker masks and the flat and low-relief paintings and carvings that decorate the ceremonial houses, much secular and semisacred art is also made. A list of the utilitarian items that are decorated in one way or another is a virtual inventory of Sepik material culture: neck rests, shields, wooden hooks (used to suspend items from ceilings and walls), canoe prows, toys, clubs, taro pounders, mortars and pestles, and lime containers and spatulae. Portrait masks are made by modeling clay over human skulls (Figure 4–4), and a few groups produce other types of pottery as well. Crocheting and finger-weaving are variously practiced. Extraneous materials such as shells, feathers, and animal teeth often adorn carvings, producing a dramatic, even theatrical, visual effect (Linton and Wingert 1971).

As in many small-scale societies, the human body serves as a major medium of aesthetic expression for the peoples of the Sepik. Hair may be decoratively cut, augmented with a wig, or adorned with feathers, shells, or sprigs of fern. Both men and women are scarified, although the scars usually last only a few years. Traditionally, clothing was minimal or nonexistent, but the clothes that did exist were often decorated by adding fresh flowers or green leaves. Ornaments range from simple shell necklaces to woven arm- and legbands and include the use of bones, shells, dog teeth, feathers, and other items worn through holes pierced in earlobes or the septum of the nose. Body decoration is at its most spectacular during village dances and feasts.

The preceding references to slit-gongs (i.e., long, hollow, percussion instruments) and to flutes suggest the importance of music in New Guinea. Most descriptions of ceremonial activities include references to song and dance, and the music of flutes and slit-gongs is typically supplemented by drums, bullroarers, panpipes, and other instruments.

Intertribal diversity notwithstanding, some traits are common in all Sepik visual art. Sculpture in the round and in high relief is usually painted, red being the principal color. Geometric designs generally tend to be curvi-

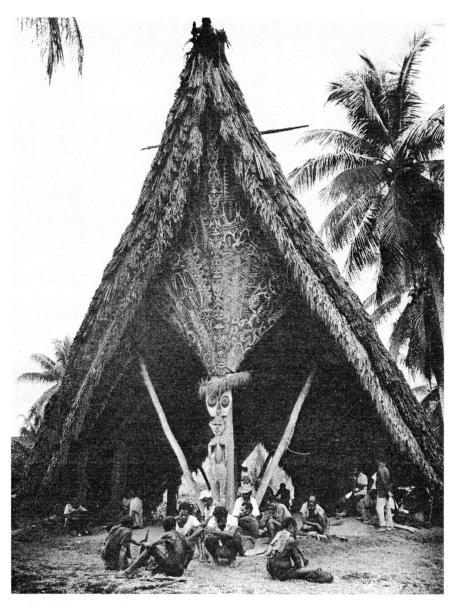

FIGURE 4-2   Waupanal, a men's house in the Kwoma village of Bagwis. December 1973.
(Copyright Ross Bowden. Photo supplied by Dept. of Reprography, La Trobe University, Melbourne.)

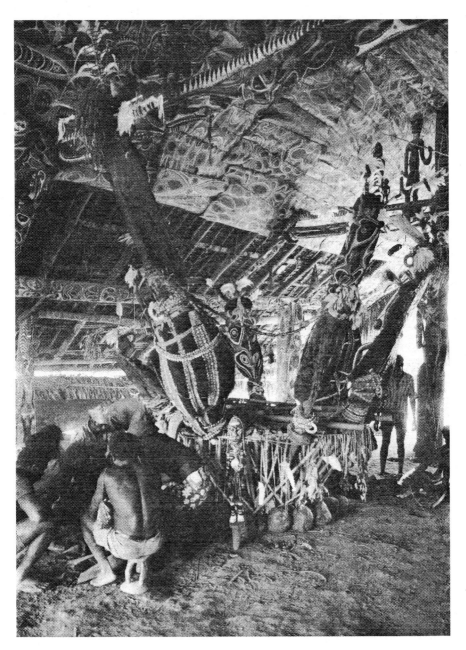

FIGURE 4–3   Inside Waupanal, with *yena* items on display. *(Copyright Ross Bowden. Photo supplied by Dept. of Reprography, La Trobe University, Melbourne.)*

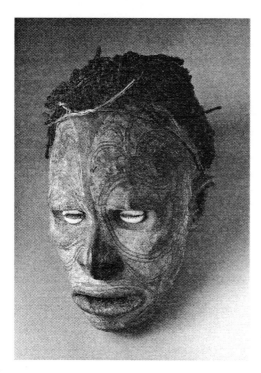

FIGURE 4–4 Iatmul trophy head, Middle Sepik. Human skull and hair, clay and shells, red and white paint. Maximum length, 32 cm. *(Courtesy Saint Louis Art Museum, gift of Morton D. May.)*

linear, with painted, limed, or engraved multiple outlines. Carved and painted figures often represent humans and anthropomorphized animals, usually with extremely long noses. Some seemingly abstract patterns may be stylized figures, as happens in other areas of New Guinea (cf. Gerbrands 1967; Salisbury 1959). Sepik artists integrate these design elements to produce an intense, sensual art (Figure 4–5) (cf. Linton and Wingert 1971:339).

Social Functions

The challenge of Sepik aesthetics is to understand why so much art is produced in the absence of an explicit philosophy of art. Resolving this issue requires some "aesthetic excavation" in that, like the archaeologist, we must start by delving into the most accessible stratum of Sepik culture—in this case, the observable uses of art in day-to-day human affairs—and from there move to successively deeper levels of Sepik thought.

One obvious rationale for art's existence in the Sepik is as a means of displaying social identity. An individual's personal decorations provide a visible indication of his or her age because when a young man or woman is ritually initiated into adulthood, the climax of the ceremony is the giving the

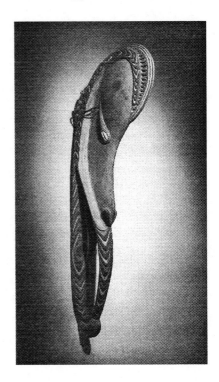

FIGURE 4–5 Mask from the Iatmul village of Kanganaman, Middle Sepik. Wood, shells, and cane; red, black, and white paint; 95 cm high. *(The Saint Louis Art Museum, gift of Morton D. May.)*

initiate decorations befitting the newly attained status—handsome clothes, ornaments, and scars. The information conveyed by such body art is by no means trivial because in the Sepik, to know a person's age is to know his or her potential marriageability and also, for males, their status in the highly important men's society, the tambaran[1] cult. Status *within* one's group also may be conveyed through personal decoration. In traditional Wogeo society, for example, only clan leaders wore boar tusk ornaments. Body decorations display the unity of every village, with each group's characteristic style setting it apart from its rivals. As Marilyn Strathern has written regarding body art found in the not-too-distant Mt. Hagen area, "In using themselves to signify their own achievements, people drape these qualities about their persons" (Strathern 1979:246; cf. also Mead 1963:90; Whiting 1941:63, 106; Hogbin 1934/35:318, 335; Kaberry 1941:360–363; Chenoweth 1979:8–23).

If art, as body decoration, serves to mark boundaries between groups, the trade of aesthetic items can also bring peaceful interaction between

---

[1]The words "tambaran" (i.e., male initiation and the cult houses used by initiated men) and "marsalai" (i.e., spirit beings) are not italicized here because they have been incorporated into both Tok Pisin, the *lingua franca* of the region, and the English-language ethnographic literature.

them. Intertribal trade of art takes several forms in the Sepik, including the tribes of the Wewak coast, who buy and sell entire dance complexes; the Mundugumor, who have little in the way of their own indigenous art style but who trade with their neighbors to get flutes that have fanciful, spirit faces; the Iatmul, who incorporate foreign artistic traits into their own well-integrated style; and the Abelam, Chambri, and Kwoma, who export art objects and whose styles, therefore, influence those of their trading partners (Mead 1963:170, 1970:20; Whiting 1941:119). (So much for the idea that art in small-scale societies is always thoroughly indigenous!)[2]

Implicit Aesthetics

If you ask a Sepik man why he produced a particular art work, he may well give a concrete reply: "This painting was needed for a cult ceremony," "These ornaments must be worn by a man of my age," or "We made these carvings to trade to our neighbors so we can get some of their valuable goods in return." One may gain access to a deeper stratum of Sepik art by asking, "Why does it look as it does?" Although many men might answer, "Because that's the way such things have always looked," abstract ideas about beauty do sometimes appear.

Bateson, for example, quotes an Iatmul man as saying, "I am going to my beautiful dances, to my beautiful ceremonies" (Bateson 1958:141), and in a footnote he elaborates that "the native word for 'beautiful' is *yigun,* a common Iatmul word which is used to describe an admired face or spectacle" (ibid.). Other Sepik groups have taste preferences, too. For example, the Wogeo are avid body decorators, and on one occasion a Wogeo man asked Ian Hogbin for the loan of a mirror to see if it was true that his cockade of red cordyline leaves and white cockatoo feathers clashed with his hair, which he had smeared with a henna-colored vegetable paste. The cockade being found to strike a jarring note, he removed it and pinned a large black and yellow butterfly in its place. Then, after rubbing the red paint from his cheeks, he took a packet of yellow ochre and a stick of charcoal from his handbag. "Black and yellow in the hair demand black and yellow on the face," he explained (Hogbin 1946:196). Sepik peoples also evaluate the performing arts. Chenoweth found, for instance, that when the Usarufa dance, they quickly and bluntly criticize inept dancers (Chenoweth 1979:86).[3]

---

[2]The Mountain Arapesh institutionalized the trading of art to the degree that every man would inherit a path along which he could safely travel from one hamlet to another as he made his rounds, acting as a middleman between the Beach Arapesh and the Plains Arapesh, each of which had incomplete repertoires of art production (Mead 1970:22).

[3]Although the Usarufa can and do criticize individuals for poor performances, Chenoweth found that the songs themselves are not so judged. "Correct rendition is 'good' music. The question was again put to them: 'Is there any bad music?' . . . Both [men] answered unequivocally: 'No, all songs are good'" (Chenoweth 1979:86).

Sepik artists themselves are usually the most astute critics of art works, and Anthony Forge's remarks on the Abelam deserve to be quoted at length:

> [Abelam] artists, particularly when carving, discuss among themselves such things as the shape of a limb and its relation to other parts of the figures, but these things are not appreciated by the non-artist. I have heard carvers reproached for holding up the beginning of the painting [of a new sculpture] by fiddling about, taking a piece off here and there, when the figure already had all the attributes, legs, penis, navel, arms, and head. The artists, although they lack any specific terms, do talk about such things as form and proportion, and derive considerable pleasure from carving and painting things satisfying to their aesthetic sense. They carefully examine and discuss works by other artists and rate one another as more or less talented by criteria that are primarily aesthetic. (Forge 1967:82)

Religious Basis of Sepik Aesthetics

If the Sepik tribes are exceptional for the quantity of art they produce, they are also unusual in the importance of ceremony in the lives of Sepik men. Intertribal variation notwithstanding, most Sepik supernatural beliefs and practices fall into three categories that can be quickly sketched.

At about the time of puberty, Sepik males start being ceremonially initiated into societies known as tambaran cults. Abelam initiation ceremonies show just how complex the tambaran cult can be. They are performed in four installments over an extended period of time. In each one, cult members show initiates (after much fanfare) art objects that are said to be the tambaran spirits themselves. During subsequent installments they learn that the previous carvings were bogus but are shown different art works and *these* are said to be genuine spirits. In the fourth and final ceremony, the initiates see the most sacred carvings of all. Each of the four parts of the cycle occurs only once every few years, so going through the entire initiation requires well over a decade. Moreover, since a man who has just completed the process becomes an initiator of the next generation, he may be actively involved in tambaran activities for more than twenty years of his life.

The details of tambaran activities vary from tribe to tribe, but everywhere women and uninitiated males are strictly banned from the ceremonies. Thus, although Kwoma boys often clandestinely glimpse the "secret" objects, they must feign surprise when they finally see them during initiation. In earlier times, any Kwoma woman who accidentally saw initiation ceremonies would have been summarily killed, shot by an arrow from each initiated man in the village (Chenoweth 1979; Whiting 1941:54).

Long yam cults are the second focus of Sepik religion. These vary even more than tambaran practices (and are altogether absent from some groups), but the usual belief is that a village's welfare is magically related to the growing of yams, especially a variety that commonly reaches a length of eight feet (2.4 meters) and that, in a good season, is as much as twelve feet long. Raising such yams is the responsibility of yam cult members. After harvest, the men parade their longest yams through the village, the yams sometimes being decorated with painted designs and masks (Figure 4–6). Cult members believe that a good yam crop augers prosperity, and this provokes much boasting vis-à-vis other villages (Figure 4–6).

Marsalai are the third focus of Sepik religion. These are spirits through which the supernatural world interacts with mortals. Marsalai live in specific locations, have names, and their appearance is conceptualized in considerable detail. Although they are not thought of as ancestors, individual marsalai are believed to have created all the things of the world as it is now known, including the clans of living mortals.

FIGURE 4–6 Displayed yams awaiting presentation to the exchange partner of the grower. Kwanibandu village, North Wosera, Abelam, Papua New Guinea. January, 1963. *(Photo courtesy of Anthony Forge Collection / Mandeville Special Collections Library, University of California, SanDiego.)*

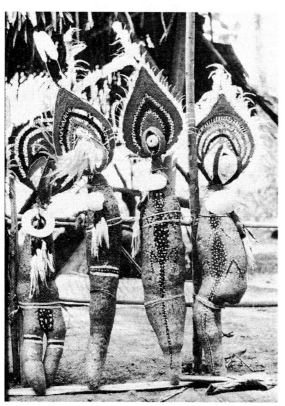

Art as a Home for Sepik Spirits

Most religious activities in the Sepik have aesthetic components, including both the graphic and plastic arts (body decoration, masks, paintings, and architecture) and the performing arts (music, dance, and song). So important is the religious basis of Sepik art that most secular art reflects sacred themes. For example, Forge says of the Abelam, "Decorative art, of course, exists, but its *motifs* are drawn from the art of the tambaran cult; and it carries with it overtones of status from the cult" (Forge 1967:67).

The tambaran house itself illustrates the central position of art in Sepik cultures. In Abelam villages, tambaran houses measure up to a hundred feet (30 meters) in length and have a triangular facade that soars as much as sixty feet (18 meters) into the air, visually dominating the village and literally casting their shadows over the populace. These imposing structures hold the sacred *nggwalndu,* paintings and sculptures of the principal spirits of the village, and their preeminence in the villagescape accurately reflects the importance of the *nggwalndu* in the minds of Sepik men.

Although the relationship between Sepik art and religion is a powerful one, we have yet to specify its exact nature. *Why* are these two realms, which Westerners usually separate, so closely linked in Sepik cultures? The answer lies in this logic: The effectiveness of Sepik ceremonials depends on the active co-participation of representatives of the spirit world; these, in turn, reside in the carvings, paintings, and masks used to depict the spirits during the festivities.

Evidence that Sepik art actually embodies supernatural spirits is found in many tribes. For example, Kaberry learned that when Abelam men build a new tambaran house, they endow it with spirits by performing certain magical rites (Kaberry 1941:358); and Forge says explicitly that the paintings and carvings within the house are also thought to have in-dwelling spirits (Forge 1967:75; 1970:281).

A fieldworker among the Arapesh, Donald Tuzin, discusses this issue at some length. He notes that although all of the paintings inside Arapesh ceremonial houses are "vitalized" by supernatural spirits, some are quite literally the residences of representatives of the spirit world, Nggwal. In the minds of cult members, these "are self-referential; they do not merely represent Nggwal, they *are* Nggwal, they partake directly of the same essence" (Tuzin 1980:190).

Sepik mythology, too, suggests that spirits reside within art works. For example, Newton has recounted creation myths from the upper Sepik in which the first flutes and slit-gongs magically played themselves because they were invested with spirit beings (Newton 1971:34, 52). Thus, art production in the Sepik is motivated by a very powerful aesthetic principle: Artworks provide residences for the members of the spirit world upon whom present and future life depends.

A still deeper component of the Sepik philosophy of art may also be discerned. Some researchers have suggested that there is a sense in which Sepik art serves not only as a vessel for the powerful spirits of the supernatural realm but also for the souls of the men who make and use the art. The most detailed picture of the embodiment of mortal spirits in Sepik art comes from the Kwoma and a study by Bowden of *yena*, the first of three yam ceremonies held each year in traditional Kwoma villages. Of all Kwoma art, *yena* sculptures are believed to be the most powerful, and Bowden presents convincing evidence that "*yena* spirits *are* the men themselves" (Bowden 1983:99). His argument rests partly on the fact that, based on their comments about their own dreams, Kwoma men seem clearly to distinguish the physical body from the spirit that dwells within it. The former is mortal and is subject to the normal processes of the natural world. A person's spirit, by contrast, is supernatural and is identified with *yena* spirits. This spirit resides in one's head, thus leading to the enlargement and iconographic significance of heads in Kwoma art.

The equivalence between Kwoma men's souls, *yena* spirits, and the artworks made for *yena* activities exists only as an unstated axiom of Kwoma metaphysics. If they were explicitly asked about it, Bowden says, the men would deny it. Nevertheless, Bowden cites indirect evidence that the axiom is unconsciously accepted. For example, when men carry out their *yena* ceremonies inside their ceremonial house, they tell the women that the singing and dancing is being done by the spirits. Moreover, Kwoma men clearly believe that *yena* spirits also reside in their yams, a predictable situation inasmuch as the *yena* spirits are first and foremost responsible for the fertility of the all-important yams. But the powerful equivalence between yam and *yena* spirit extends to the yam gardener himself. This is apparent in the Kwoma belief that if a man were to eat the meat of a cassowary bird or of certain types of spiny fish while his yams were growing in the ground, he would later harvest yams with tough, bristly rootlets, similar to the cassowary's quills or fish's spines (Bowden 1983:110).

The congruence between artwork, supernatural spirit, and the soul of the maker appears elsewhere in the Sepik, too. For example, an Arapesh man told Tuzin a myth about how women learned to give birth to children. In this account, husbands once delivered babies by cutting open their wives' stomachs, but this practice inevitably led to the women's death. Then on one occasion, a pregnant woman who had reached full term started having labor pains while her husband was out hunting. A spirit that resided in a carved post of the nearby tambaran house heard her cry out in pain so he came out of the post, found the woman, and taught her how to deliver the child through the birth canal. Later the woman was reluctant to tell her husband about the discovery, thinking he might become jealous of the spirit; but in fact he did not, the reason being that "it was actually the husband's own spirit in the house post, *'for he was the one who had carved it'*" (Tuzin 1980:169). Tuzin also found that vitalized Arapesh paintings are hung inside ceremonial houses in such a way as to constitute a virtual kinship chart of the clan members who made the paintings (Tuzin 1980:177, 180). The same equation between man, art, and spirit has also been reported among the Iatmul (Bateson 1946).[4]

Thus, whereas the peoples of the Sepik do not say so in as many words, their art *is* based on a coherent aesthetic system, and a very compelling one at that. The driving force behind Sepik art production is art's capacity to embody the all-powerful representatives of the spirit world. Moreover, art is an incarnation of the souls of its makers. As such, its importance in Sepik intellectual culture is significant indeed.

Sex and Temperament in Sepik Culture

If Sepik art symbolizes human souls, it must be understood that the souls in question are exclusively those of adult, initiated males. On this point, the men of the Sepik are both conscious and explicit: Art is men's work, and women are systematically isolated, forcibly if necessary, both from artistic production and from most of the religious practice that prompts Sepik art. Although several of the most prolific Western fieldworkers in the Sepik area have been women, neither they nor their male colleagues have described Sepik women's art and ritual as being more than, at most, a shadow of men's activities. Kaberry flatly asserts that Abelam yam ceremonialism "appears to have very little bearing on the life of the women except negatively, in so far as it sets up a barrier against their direct participation" (Kaberry 1941:358). Mead's account of Mountain Arapesh women's situation is particularly illuminating:

> [Girls] learn not to speculate lest misfortune come upon them all. A habit of intellectual passivity falls upon them, a more pronounced lack of intellectual interest than that which characterizes their brothers' minds. . . . This prohibition

---

[4]The foregoing account of Sepik art and aesthetics raises an interesting historical question. Many features of Sepik intellectual culture, including the spirit world's dominance of men's day-to-day lives, the belief that art embodies supernatural spirits and that mortals themselves in some sense enter the spirit world through art, an aversion to artistic innovation because the spirits will come only to art that replicates traditional forms—all of these beliefs of the Sepik are also, as we have seen, present in the traditional culture of Aboriginal Australians. Are these parallels the coincidental result of independent, parallel invention, or do both systems of thought go back to a common ancestor? The land mass of New Guinea plus about 500 miles of ocean separate the Sepik tribes from Arnhem Land, and this would seem to put quite a barrier between the two culture areas. However, genetic and linguistic evidence indicates that although the two peoples are distinctly different from each other, some interaction between New Guinea and Australia has undoubtedly occurred.

cuts them off from speculative thought and likewise from art. . . . Women participating in art . . . would endanger the women themselves, [and] would endanger the order of the universe within which men and women and children live in
safety. (Mead 1963:70)

The aesthetic disenfranchisement of women seems to spring from several factors. First, Sepik men view sexual relations with feelings ranging from
marked ambivalence to high anxiety. Among the Kwoma, for example, the
normal requirements of sexual propriety lapse during the night-long dances
that follow tambaran and yam cult ceremonies, and a generalized license prevails between all men and women except for the young and between closely
related individuals. But the male participants surely must have ambivalent
feelings about the activities inasmuch as many of them have bled their penes
and tongues during the preceding rituals (Whiting 1941).

Among the Wape, ambivalence turns into fear:

A central assumption of any male version of Wape culture is that sexual desire is
dangerous. The sexual act itself is no voluptuous and carefree dalliance under
the tropical moon, but a furtive forest encounter, carefully rationed, with an af-
termath of fear. . . . The sex act is a risky undertaking that drains the male and
places both him and his partner in a position of demonic jeopardy. (Mitchell
1978:162)

Sexual anxiety such as this starts early, at least among the Kwoma. Whiting reports that although no clothing was traditionally worn, Kwoma males
were not supposed to have erections in public, and "any female who observes
a boy with an erect penis is expected to beat the member with a stick" (Whiting 1941:49).

Related to male sexual anxiety, either as cause or effect, is a second pervasive belief, namely, that women themselves are dangerous for adult men
and inimical to their activities. In the origin myths recounted by Newton
from the upper Sepik, women were the first owners of the enchanted flutes
and slit-gongs. The myth notes parenthetically that "now, should women see
[the flutes], their vulvas would close and they would grow testicles" (Newton
1971:34).

As in myth, so in life: While an Abelam man's yam garden is growing, he
is expected to refrain from sexual intercourse; and after a successful harvest
(Figure 4–7) he denigrates his rivals by saying that they do not "know how to
plant yams; they only play with the women," thereby suggesting that the enemies have not refrained from sexual intercourse (Kaberry 1941:355). Women
must stay away from Abelam yam gardens and yam storehouses, because, men
say, "She has a vulva" (ibid.). Kwoma men use the same logic to prohibit
women from watching the construction of the *yena* sculptures that accompany yam ceremonies, arguing that being seen by women would cause the
wooden figures to crack and hence be useless (Bowden 1983:102). Even the

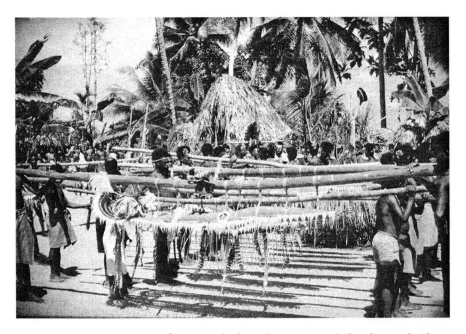

FIGURE 4-7 Bringing long yams for a major display and presentation. Each is decorated with a mask and represents its grower and his ancestral spirit. Wingel Village, East Abalam, Papua New Guinea. July, 1958. *(Photo courtesy of Anthony Forge.)*

planting of yams has sexual connotations inasmuch as the Kwoma word for planting, *chuwa*, refers to any act "in which a long, roughly cylindrical object is thrust into something else, usually a hole" (Bowden 1983:120).

Finally, Sepik men equate the hazards of sex with another threat—that posed by enemies. Like women, foes prompt feelings of vulnerability and fears of defeat, and Sepik males commonly respond to both categories of adversaries with aggression and hostility. The Iatmul, for example, explicitly connect sex and headhunting, believing that both are dangerous ventures that do not necessarily end in successful conquest and that the shame of defeat in warfare is only slightly worse than that of being a passive object of sexual intercourse (Bateson 1958:140).

Phallic Aggression in Sepik Art

Thus, men in New Guinea's Sepik River region share a distinctive constellation of assumptions about sexuality. The sex act itself is dangerous; female sexuality is hazardous and prompts male antagonism toward women; and the aggression against women is comparable to that directed at enemies. These ideas contain the fundamental rationale for Sepik aesthetics: Through their art, Sepik men assert their masculinity and dominance over their adversaries, be the enemy their own women or men of hostile villages. This belief permeates Sepik art, prompting men to make great quantities of art in a distinctively belligerent, masculine style (Figure 4–8). As Forge puts it, "Men [in New Guinea] understand women to be truly creative and naturally powerful. Themselves they conceive to be intrinsically devoid of power but able, through their learned cultural means (that is, ritual and art), to tap some of the power and creativity that is natural and intrinsic to women." (Forge 1979:286)

Although the peoples of the Sepik are not generally inclined to speculate about the philosophical nature of things, they do acknowledge the messages of masculine identity and power conveyed by their art. Consider, for example, the explicit sexual imagery of yam cult art. The iconography of sculptures used in Kwoma *yena* dances, supported as it is by elaborate myths, is too rich to be described here in detail (see Bowden 1983:105–117); but briefly, the enlarged heads of *yena* sculptures symbolize masculine sexuality,

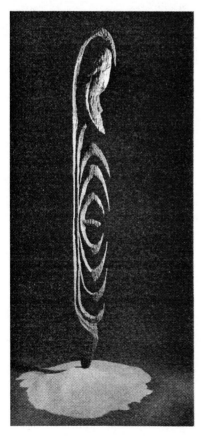

FIGURE 4–8   Carved wooden "Hook Figure," 19th century or earlier. Middle Sepik, upper Karawari Region, Arambak people. Wood and Shells, 225 cm high. *(The Saint Louis Art Museum, gift of Morton D. May.)*

fertility, and aggression. Moreover, if the head symbolizes manhood, the nose serves as its penis (and, sometimes, the eyes as its testicles). There is general agreement that the huge noses of Sepik figurative sculpture are overtly phallic, and in their downward extension they follow the Sepik convention whereby size, rather than upright position, indicates penile erection (Figure 4–9).[5] The association between noses and masculine aggression may be the reason why some Kwoma men wear a boar tusk through the septum of their noses, since the tusk is the deadliest weapon of the most dangerous animal in Kwoma territory. When *yena* sculptures are displayed, they are adorned with the shell and feather decorations of a man who has successfully killed an enemy.

Most *yena* sculptures have extended tongues, and this organ's associations with masculine aggression are also clear:

> During the weekly moots that the Kwoma hold in men's houses, debates are frequently so intense that disputants commonly work themselves up into states in which they become literally speechless with rage. [An enraged man] will adopt a conventional posture that expresses extreme anger and aggression. This involves holding the arms slightly apart from the body and bent inward, hopping slowly from one foot to the other, glaring at the opponent, and extending the tongue out as far as it will go. A man might hold this position for several minutes until he regains his composure or is restrained by clansmen.
>
> Informants interpret the extended tongues of yena sculptures in the same way; they indicate, as men say, that yena spirits are "hard" (*ow katawa*), i.e., that they are quick to anger and will strike a person down for the most trivial of reasons. (Bowden 1983:112)

The phallic association of tongues is also apparent in a Kwoma myth in which the protagonist, Sasap, lifts up two young girls to join him in a tree by extending his tongue down to them. His idea is for them to "stand one behind the other, and for each in turn to hook the end of his tongue into their vaginas" (Bowden 1983:114). The technique works, and the young women become Sasap's wives.

As another example of the pervasiveness of phallicism of Sepik art, consider the iconography found in Abelam paintings of their clan spirits, *nggwalndu*. Standing 10 to 15 feet (3 to 4.5 meters) high, they portray males

---

[5]An anecdote recounted by Forge reveals the importance attached to the nose in the Sepik District:

> A group of Iatmul . . . had found a picture of Thoth, the ibis-headed [hence long-beaked] Egyptian god of wisdom—used as a trademark by an Australian book distributing firm—on the back of a mission school book. This, and the accompanying advertisement, they had copied out and showed to me as conclusive proof that the whites had also sprung from totemic ancestors. My translation of the text, which was irrelevant to the origin of man and the nature of the cosmos, convinced them that I, like the other whites, was determined to deceive them, to deny our common origins, and continue the pretense that whites were a different sort of being from blacks. (Forge 1971a:291)

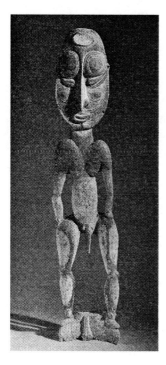

FIGURE 4–9 Iatmul house figure, Middle Sepik. *(The Saint Louis Art Museum, gift of Morton D. May.)*

with impressively oversized heads and large, downward-pointed penes, with a white drop of semen painted at the end. Other paintings show a pig or the clan's totemic bird with its head nearly touching the tip of the penis. Cult members repeatedly told Forge that their clan benefited from such pictures of pigs or totemic birds being nourished.

The architecture of the Abelam tambaran cult houses also links sexual motifs with aggression toward enemies. The men refer to the structure as female, but male imagery permeates its construction. The ridgepole is erected (!) by men who have bled their penes, and, like the men's genitals, the end of the pole is also pierced. Later, a man climbs to the top of the ridgepole to decorate it, finishing his job by shouting out his clan's war cry and throwing a coconut to the ground, where waiting clansmen smash it with slit-gong beaters. Simultaneously, another man drops a rattan decoration containing two skulls—formerly those of killed enemies, although wild pig skulls are now substituted. That these activities symbolize intervillage hostilities is shown by their similarity to a practice, now defunct, whereby one village would repay another for its aid in killing an enemy. In that ceremony, the killed man's testicles were given to the allies, who suspended them above the tambaran dance ground. Sticks would be thrown at them to knock them to the ground, where, Forge says, "they were pounded to pulp, again with slit-gong beaters" (Forge 1971a:304).

Besides Kwoma and Abelam, Sepik men's troubled feelings about women are apparent in the arts and culture of the eastern Iatmul. Silverman reports the belief that, "In the primordial past, women (Figure 4–10) owned all ritual sacra but the bullroarer. One day men used the bullroarer to frighten away women so they could steal the flutes and related paraphernalia" (1999:9). A ritual reenactment of this theft occurs near the conclusion of a long series of activities that follow a death. As part of the final component of the mourning ceremony, called *tshuqukepma,* "men paint the faces of youths who will assume the personae of primordial spirits and participate in the ensuing ritual drama. Their faces are first colored with a wash of red paint, which symbolizes maternal or menstrual blood. When the red coloring dries, men carefully paint swirling lines and patterns in white (Figure 4–11). The

FIGURE 4–10   Eastern Iatmul man decorated as a maternal ancestress. Sepik District, Papua New Guinea. *(Photo courtesy of Eric Kline Silverman.)*

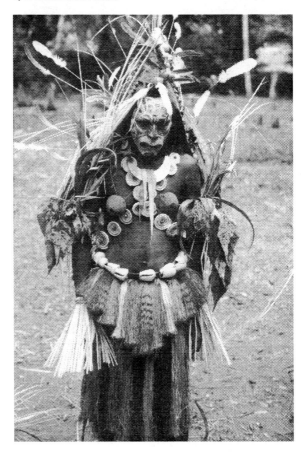

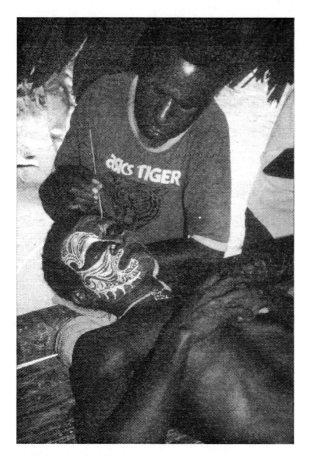

FIGURE 4-11   Ritualized white-on-red face painting inside an
Eastern Iatmal cult house. Sepik District, Papua New Guinea.
(Photo courtesy of Eric Kline Silverman.)

white paint signifies semen and bones" (ibid.:28). Thus, on their very faces, eastern Iatmul men wear the complex and convoluted interplay between male and female principles.

Although the artistically prolific societies of the Sepik have little in the way of an overt philosophy of art, they do have explicit and strongly held views about their own situation in the world. They see themselves as being endangered on two fronts—by female sexuality and by hostile neighbors. In response to their fears, they go to great lengths to claim their own superiority, and art is the primary medium for doing so. Sepik art, significantly, is a statement of the intended dominance of men over women and other adversaries. The urgency of this concern is indicated as much by the symbolism of phallic aggression that permeates the art style as it is by the frequency with which the statement is made. The Sepik stands, after all, as one of the richest regions for art production in the world, a testament to the potential power of male fear and insecurity.

Conclusion: Contradictions in Sepik Aesthetics

A central tenet of Freudian theory deals with men's problematic relationships with their mothers (whom they love but cannot marry) and with women other than their mothers (whom they must marry, whether they love them or not). Finding solutions to these problems, Freud said, are "tasks laid down for every man" (Freud 1956:346); and, he thought, failure in these tasks inevitably leads to serious psychological problems.

Whatever its universality, surely the majority of men in most societies have less apparent sexual anxieties, and handle them with more grace, than do the men of the Sepik region. Men elsewhere have male adversaries too, but an ethos of phallic aggression permeates few societies as thoroughly as among many of the traditional tribes of New Guinea. For example, although the Mundugumor are not a particularly materialistic people, Mundugumor men lavish great attention on their sacred flutes, refer to them by kinship terms, offer them the choicest food, and decorate them with spectacular finery. Mead describes seeing "the sacred flutes with their tall, thin, shell-encrusted standards surmounted by manikin figures with a huge head, bearing a diadem of shell and hundreds of graceful and valuable decorations from the midst of which its mother-of-pearl eyes gleam—this is an experience of major importance" (Mead 1963:213).

What prompts such obsessions? One can only speculate, but several factors may be involved. For one thing, the sexual division of labor in the Sepik is strict and somewhat unusual. Despite their ceremonial preeminence, the contribution of Sepik men to the subsistence prerequisites of life is often limited. Consider these examples:

- Among the Mountain Arapesh, women are responsible for tending the gardens, getting firewood and water, and cooking meals. Men do hunt and carry pigs and heavy logs, but much of their time is spent preparing ceremonial food and tending their special yam gardens. "The women," we are told, "do everything else" (Mead 1963:185).
- For the Iatmul, the division is even more clear: "Men are occupied with the spectacular, dramatic, and violent activities which have their center in the ceremonial house, while the women are occupied with the useful and necessary routines of food-getting, cooking, and rearing children" (Bateson 1958:123).
- The Wogeo simply say, "Men play flutes, women bear infants" (Hogbin 1970:104).

- Although the titular head of a Chambri household is the husband, who claims to "own" one or more wives, the real power lies in the hands of women, who fully realize that through their gardening and trade they hold the purse strings (Mead 1963:255). "Women's attitude towards the men," Mead relates, "is one of kindly tolerance and appreciation. They enjoy the games that the men play, [especially] the theatricals that the men put on for their benefit" (ibid.).

- Despite the heads, noses, and tongues that Kwoma men put on their *yena* sculptures, it is Kwoma women who usually take the initiative in sexual relations, both in premarital courting and after marriage. If a Kwoma boy does want to attract a girl, his only options are either to use love magic or to dress in his finest clothes, decorate his face, and hope for a chance encounter with the girl of his fancy. For their part, Kwoma women in general enjoy a status considerably higher than that implied by the ideology of Kwoma men (Bowden 1984:448).

- Finally, Chenoweth discovered that Usarufa men "feel that women are stronger than they themselves are, pointing out that women live longer, work more consistently, and have hair under their arms rather than their faces, body hair being a measure of strength" (Chenoweth 1979:22).

Thus, Sepik men's fears of being vulnerable to women, so apparent in their arts, have some basis in fact. At home, women are dominant in many activities, leaving men only the symbolic dominance found in their "secret" cult activities, a subject that hardly interests the women. It is illuminating, for example, to contrast the highly serious and self-conscious rituals of the men with women's rituals in those groups where they do occur. For example, the Abelam formally initiate not only young men but also young women. Men are involved in the first stages of girls' initiation rituals, but soon,

> [they] are frozen off their ceremonial ground, and the women perform their own secret ceremonial involving, among other things, transvestite women who magnificently imitate and mock the swaggering of their husbands and brothers. . . . I understand that pantomimes of sexual intercourse and advice on the conduct of love affairs are included, and there is certainly teasing and much riotous laughter. (Forge 1970:274)

Such goings-on may confirm the worst fears of the already threatened Sepik men, prompting them to use every available venue in an effort to legitimize their equivocal positions in Sepik cultures. And, of course, underlying all these details is the most fundamental fact of all: Whereas Sepik men ritually symbolize themselves as the guardians of fertility, the fact of social and biological life is that it is the women who actually provide the vital part of creation by giving birth to the young. Men, in their traditional roles as fighters, are actually the takers of lives.

Some evidence of the insecurity of Sepik men is actually apparent in their art. Sculptures of female figures occur in some ceremonial houses (Hauser-Schaublin, personal communication), and among some groups the houses themselves are thought of as being feminine. Bowden describes several ways in which the theme of feminine fertility occurs in Kwoma art production, such as the requirement that *yena* figures, as they are being painted, "must be placed on pillows made from rolled-up women's net bags *(kow)*, objects which in ordinary social life are not only directly associated with women, but are linguistically equated with wombs, the receptacles in which unborn children are carried" (Bowden 1984:456-457). Perhaps most strikingly, Kwoma men believe that women were the original inventors of all their rituals, as well as the arts associated with them.

Bowden observes that three theories might be suggested to explain the contradiction that is implicit in there being noteworthy themes of femininity within the quintessentially masculine art of the Sepik. It might, for one thing, reflect historical fact, representing a "survival" from a distant time in which women *did* occupy a position of leadership in society, a role now nominally held by men. A second possibility is that the men's art effectively conveys a message of total male dominance, not only in the usual areas of male endeavor but even in those activities and objects (such as bearing children and using net bags) traditionally associated with women. Somewhat hesitantly, Bowden posits a third possibility, namely, that through their inclusion of themes of femininity in their preeminently male ideology, "men may be tacitly acknowledging what, at a conscious level at least, they are denying, namely that it is women, not men, who are the prime creators, for it is only women who can bring forth new human life" (Bowden 1984:457).

In the ideology of Sepik men, male and female principles are diametrically opposed, and although themes of male aggression dominate Sepik aesthetics, female themes are also clearly apparent. I see this as evidence of art's inimitable capacity to embody and express ideas that, to the rational mind, seem altogether contradictory. We will find instances of this phenomenon in some other societies as well, and we must postpone to Part Two a thorough examination of this feature of art. Suffice it here to say that the societies of the Sepik region of New Guinea produce great quantities of highly compelling art. That they do so despite seemingly contradictory underlying principles is as revealing of the nature of art as it is of the complex relations between men and women.

Epilogue

The island of New Guinea was one of the last major land masses on earth to be markedly changed by the forces of modern colonialism. Even as a German, then an Australian, colony, New Guinea was never overwhelmed by foreign peoples and foreign ways. Indeed, some of its interior was not explored by Westerners until well into the twentieth century. Papua New Guinea gained its independence from Australia in 1975, and today it has changed in many ways. Intertribal warfare is largely a thing of the past, a cash economy is pervasive, and the capital, Port Moresby, is a bustling city of several hundred thousand people.

The arts have changed as well. If traditional ceremonies had been the sole destination of Sepik art works in the past, after World War I, more and more of it went to the growing numbers of foreigners—anthropologists and missionaries at first and, later, individuals who came seeking material for museums and private collections. The process is not well documented; but thanks to Eric Silverman's research (1996, 1999), we know that the Iatmul artists who at first traded wood carvings in return for metal tools were, by the 1960s, receiving substantial income from the sale of art. Since 1976, Melanesian Tourist Services has organized excursions up the Sepik River by houseboat, then by steamer, and finally in a large and luxurious catamaran cruiser. Today, tourism is the chief source of income in the Sepik, and the largest part of the money comes from the sale of artwork (Silverman 1996, 1999).

On one level, Sepik market art is unlike the traditional arts of the Sepik. Some of it, such as crocodile-shaped napkin rings, combines local subject matter with foreign design, while other material at most only approximates traditional items. Silverman remarks, "Totemic art is mythically potent and therefore any exchange or sale of this art outside of the village transgresses the mystical potency (*kau*) of the embodied spirit (Silverman 1996:18). Such art has rightly been criticized for its inauthenticity:

> Tourists now descend on the area looking for examples of this art and are readily provided with sculptures that have been made in studios the villagers themselves call "carpentry shops." Usually they have been soaked in mud for several weeks to give them a 'ceremonial' patina. The ancient tools with blades of stone, shell and animal teeth have long since been replaced with metal ones, and synthetic pigments often take the place of the natural earth pigments previously employed. Carving schools have been organized by missionaries and others to bring income to the people, and because they have given up their old beliefs, the motivation for the creation of the art today is wholly commercial." (Wardwell 1989:9–10)

Although Sepik market art is undeniably at variance from traditional work, the effect of market art on Sepik cultures is not simple. For example, Iatmul men told Silverman that if it were not for the income generated by tourism, outmigration of young people would threaten the future of village life (Figure 4–12). Moreover, far from leading to the homogenization of styles, tourist art is substantially more varied than was traditional art. Iatmul artists told Silverman, "If we all carve the same things or just traditional objects, then nobody's objects would stand out; since all men carve, there is

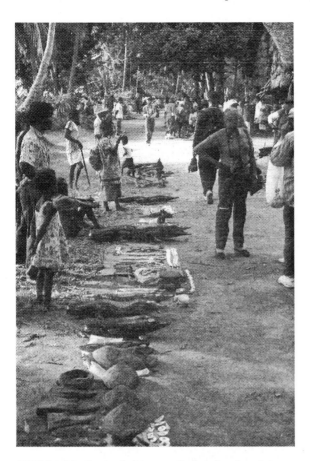

FIGURE 4-12   Tourists looking at a display of art for sale in Tambunum vilage on the Sepik River, Papua New Guinea. *(Photo courtesy Eric Silverman. Copyright Ruth B. Philips and Christopher B. Steiner, Unpacking Culture, University of California Press, 1999.)*

competition to be unique" (Silverman 1996:24).[6] Thus, post-colonial artistic designs and techniques from the Sepik enter the world economy energized by a trait very characteristic of pre-colonial Sepik culture, namely, men's abiding desire to outdo each other.

In various ways, group identity is also a factor in market art of the Iatmul. Insofar as it is consonant with traditional Iatmul art, it sets its makers apart from their neighbors. Moreover, along with other art work from nearby

---

[6]Such artistic innovation is by no means limited to the Sepik. In some areas of Papua New Guinea, traditional war shields are scraped clean of their old paint and repainted with the likes of James Bond and Batman (Cochrane 1997:75).

groups, it plays a role in defining the Sepik area as a distinct and important region in Papua New Guinea as a whole. Finally, inasmuch as work from the Sepik is one of the best known of non-Western art styles in the world, it brings recognition to Papua New Guinea, to the Sepik region, and to the Iatmul themselves (Silverman 1996).

Silverman has also shown that other components of traditional culture are found in Sepik market art. For example, some men from the village of Tambunum buy art works from other villages and sell them to tourists along with ersatz stories of cannibalism and other tales of the exotic. Far from being an altogether new practice, however, it embodies the longstanding pattern in the Sepik of appropriating art motifs from other groups and then creating new uses and meanings for them.

Although the languages native to New Guinea had no word directly translatable into English as "artist," the word "artis" has been taken up in Tok Pisin, the *lingua franca* of Papua New Guinea (Cochrane 1997:45), and it denotes very much the same concept as the English "artist," namely, an individual devoted to creatively expressing him- or herself by means of artistic media such as easel painting and sculpture. The word reflects the emergence of a fine art movement in modern Papua New Guinea, a movement that Susan Cochrane (1997) has usefully summarized from diverse sources of information. Interestingly, however, artists of Sepik background are largely absent from this movement, even though the Sepik region (along with the Asmat region) was one of the most prolific and famous sources of art in traditional New Guinea.

Perhaps this is because the Sepik has long had its own distinctive style of art—in fact, a style that today generates much desired cash income in the area. None the less, some traditional elements of Sepik art have entered the Papuan contemporary art scene. Agatha Waramin, a woman from the village of Wewak (but a long-time resident of Port Moresby) has received attention for her creative modifications of the *bilum,* or women's net bag. Cochran remarks, "She has expanded on the *bilum* repertoire, not only in inventing new combinations of patterns and colours, but by specifically developing her 'exhibition pieces,' larger-scale works which explore the nature and essence of the art of weaving" (Cochrane 1997:101).

Some features of Sepik architecture and architectural details now appear in urban settings. Two of the three wings of the Papua New Guinea Parliament House (Figure 4–13) were designed to resemble the tambaran houses of the Sepik, and the chair of the Speaker is patterned after Sepik orators' tools. Also, carved Sepik house posts have been incorporated into a number of contemporary structures, such as the museum of the Institute of Technology in Lae and the airport terminal in Garoka. In Port Moresby, the design of four police stations includes elements in the shape of Sepik house posts, but are carved to portray "police and rascal (petty criminal) cartoon characters, developed in the late 1970s by the expatriate artist Bob Browne,

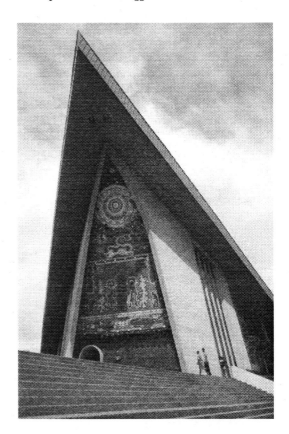

FIGURE 4–13   Papua New Guinea National Parliament House, Port Moresby, Papua New Guinea. *(Photo courtesy of Friedrich Stark / Peter Arnold, Inc.)*

that have become part of the urban mythology of Port Moresby" (Cochrane 1997:117).

The traditional arts of the Sepik are exception for the energy and movement they convey. It is not surprising, then, that they live on today, changed but still vital.

Further Reading

Art historical information (including many illustrations) of Sepik visual art may be found in *Oceanic Art* by Kaeppler et al. (1997); and although now out of print, a brief introduction to the topic was provided by Gloria Stewart (1972). Extensive field-work based research on visual art was carried out by Forge (1967, 1970, 1971a, 1971b, 1974, 1979); and Vida Chenowith (1979) provides a good account of Usarufa music. Donald Tuzin (1971) has written an in-depth account of tambaran performances in the context of Arapesh religion.

Other books that focus on the visual arts, and somewhat more recent than Forge, are Ross Bowden's *Yena Art and Ceremony in a Sepik Society* (1983) and Douglas Newton's *Crocodile and Cassowary: Religious Art of the Upper Sepik River* (1971).

Eric Kline Silverman's exceptional account (1996, 1999) of Iatmul market art avoids the simplistic thesis that all nontraditional art is thoroughgoingly bad, both aesthetically and culturally. Although it contains little about Sepik artists, Susan Cochrane's *Contemporary Art in Papua New Guinea* (1997) is an excellent overview of the post-1969 fine (visual) arts scene, with many striking color illustrations.

5

NAVAJO AESTHETICS

A Unity of Art and Life

With beauty before me, I walk
With beauty behind me, I walk
With beauty above me, I walk
With beauty below me, I walk.

(Navajo prayer, Witherspoon 1977:153)

Many of us go through our lives believing that our view of the world is true and that other people share it. Our grasp on reality usually seems valid enough for us to live from one day to the next. But occasionally this complacency is shaken, and one is confronted with a frightening possibility: What if the "reality" that I usually take for granted is not actually "out there" in the world that my senses seem to tell me about? What if it exists only in my mind and extends only to the limits of my own subjectivity? What if other people (assuming other people exist) live in different realities, traverse different worlds, and believe the universe around them (and within them) is fundamentally different from the one I seem to inhabit?

Cultural anthropologists do not spend much time arguing about which worldviews are right and which are wrong, but we have taken on the job of documenting the worldviews of other cultures. Because they reflect fundamental assumptions about the nature of things, worldviews are often implicit and always abstract, making them more elusive to describe than, say, kinship systems. But we know one thing beyond a doubt: Other people do indeed live in different phenomenal realities. Nowhere is this more clearly the case than among the Navajos of the American Southwest.

Anthropologists have studied Navajo culture intensively for several reasons. The Navajos are geographically accessible—at least by comparison to New Guinea's Sepik District, for instance. Although they have long borrowed various foreign practices from their Indian and Anglo neighbors, they have maintained a highly distinctive and integrated culture. And, in contrast to the nearby Puebloans, they have not been averse to allowing serious, sympathetic outsiders to study their life ways. Due to these practical considerations, hundreds of scholars over the course of five generations have spent much time among the Navajos.

But there is also a compelling theoretical reason for anthropologists' perennial interest in the Navajos that has to do with the nature of Navajo culture itself. Like individuals, some societies seem more prone to speculative thought than others. Every society produces its serious thinkers, but whereas some cultures give short shrift to their potential philosophers, others nurture the reflective life and produce explicit and dense intellectual paradigms regarding the origin and abstract nature of material things, the role of humans in the larger universe, and so on. Navajo is one such culture, disproving once and for all the ethnocentric notion that the West has a monopoly on the search for answers to life's important questions.

The anthropologists who have focused particularly on the religious, philosophical, and intellectual dimensions of Navajo life have revealed a people who view their world with a distinctively aesthetic sensibility. Navajos view both word and thought as being imbued with a spirit that can only be called artistic. An examination of Navajo ideas about art provides us with an excellent opportunity to see just how potent a force ideas about art can be. The Navajos' security in their ecological environment has always been tenuous; their sociopolitical environment, often hostile. Nonetheless, Navajos have increased in numbers and have sustained their distinctive way of life. This may be partially a result of the general philosophy, including the philosophy of art, that underlies their culture.

Navajo Culture and Art

The Navajos, whom the literature sometimes refers to as Nava*h*os and who call themselves Diné (or Dineh), "The People," are relative newcomers to the "Four Corners" region where Arizona, New Mexico, Utah, and Colorado meet (see map, p. xvi). The ancestors of the modern Pueblo Indians had already been there at least 1,000 years when nomadic groups from the northern plains entered the region, probably before the thirteenth century. By the fifteenth century, two major migrant groups had settled in the area, the Navajos themselves and various Apache tribes farther to the south.

The Navajos thrived in the Southwest despite periodic depredations by Anglos, and they have grown in population to become the largest single tribal group of Native Americans, with a population of more than 220,000 inhabiting about 25,000 square miles of land. Sheep herding plays a central role in Navajo life, but Navajos also rely heavily on horticulture, supplemented by some hunting and gathering. Unlike their Pueblo neighbors who have long resided in clusters of multi-family, apartment-like buildings, Navajo families live in individual six- or eight-sided houses called *hogans* that are widely distributed through their territory. Although men are formally the heads of Navajo families, in actual practice women have as much, if not more, importance in social life. Navajos traditionally reckon kinship through the female line; women are the owners of farm and range land, which they pass on to their daughters; and a married couple usually lives in the locale of the wife's family.

Men do generally hold sway in the area of ceremonialism, an important component of Navajo life. The Navajos have an extensive and dense body of mythological stories, and the retelling of parts of this corpus in "Sings" by religious specialists and their assistants provides the basis for the most important ritual activities.

For Navajos, ceremony inevitably entails art. Sings are elaborate performances that last as long as nine days, featuring all-night singing, daytime prayers and chants, and ritual shampooing of the hair with yucca suds. In most (but not all) Sings, much of the chanting reiterates the stories of creation and the activities of the mythic Holy People (Frisbie 1980:171). If a person falls ill, has misfortune, or is jeopardized by some condition beyond their control, the family may hire a singer to carry out a Sing to restore the person's well-being. Other Sings are performed as prophylactic efforts to maintain current health.

At certain junctures in a Sing, the ceremonialists make sandpaintings, illustrating in a richly iconographic style the story's events and personae (Figure 5–1). First the sandpainters smooth an area of the hogan floor so they can work directly on it or else on a buckskin that they spread on the

FIGURE 5-1 Navajo serape, circa 1850–1860. *(Courtesy of Natural History Museum of Los Angeles County, Anthropology Section, William Randolph Hearst Collection.)*

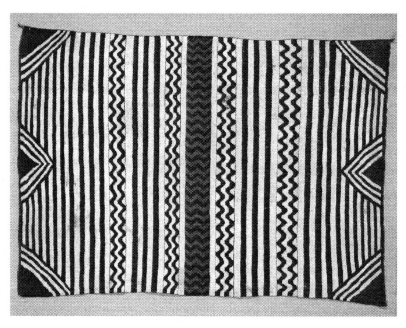

ground. Besides sand, they use colors made from ground minerals, pulverized charcoal, corn pollen and corn meal, and other materials. The intricate paintings are made freehand, with the leader and his assistants producing straight lines and uniformly colored areas by allowing an even stream of dry pigment to run out of the hand between the thumb and forefinger. Sandpaintings vary in size, from ones measuring about 3 feet (1 meter) in width to ones that require a full day's work by the Singer and as many as forty assistants and that measure 25 feet (6 meters) across. When the sandpainting is finished, the person for whom the Sing is being performed is seated in its center and colors from certain parts of the painting are applied to his or her body, further ensuring the efficacy of the ritual (Figure 5–2). Then, having served its purpose, the sandpainting is ceremonially destroyed.

Navajo art is not confined to Sings, however. Navajos probably learned weaving (and, for that matter, sandpainting) from their Pueblo neighbors. Whereas sandpaintings are made by men, women are the chief fiber artists, doing everything from carding and spinning the wool to executing a design on a vertical bar loom. Although the technology of Navajo weaving is relatively simple, the resultant textiles are striking for their sophisticated use of

FIGURE 5–2 Navajo eyedazzler blanket, circa 1870–1875. *(Courtesy of Natural History Museum of Los Angeles County, Anthropology Section, William Randolph Hearst Collection.)*

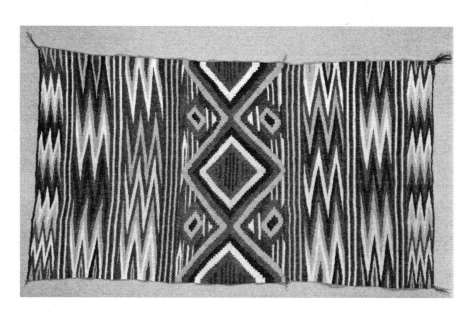

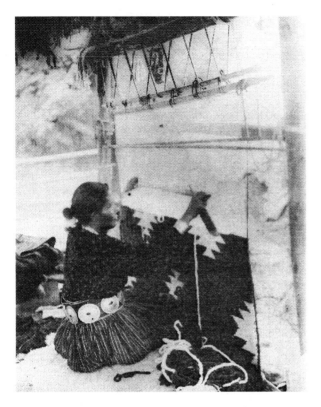

FIGURE 5-3 A Navajo woman working at a vertical loom, weaving a blanket from home-spun, dyed wool. Photographed before 1934. *(Courtesy of the Southwest Museum, Los Angeles, ca. no. 30797.)*

design and color (Figure 5–3). Weaving was initially a utilitarian art for the production of clothing and blankets, but trade goods now fill many of these needs, and today most weavings are sold to non-Navajos.

Silversmithing is a relatively recent Navajo visual art, learned in the late 1800s from Mexican smiths living in the Southwest. Navajo craftsmen began by decorating utilitarian items such as horse bridles, but since 1900 most smiths have produced jewelry, which is in great demand among Anglos and among Navajos themselves (Adair 1944).

We should understand, however, that all these things hold multiple kinds of worth in Navajo culture. Some, such as blankets and silver horse bridles, have an overtly utilitarian use. Many have a cash market value that significantly contributes to family incomes. But, most importantly for our purposes, all are respected as objects that positively embody beauty—or, more precisely, *hózhǫ́*, the central concept of Navajo aesthetics to which we now turn.

Hózhǫ́: The Core of Navajo Philosophy

Shooting Way is an important Navajo Sing, lasting nine days and composed of many songs, prayers, and sandpaintings. At its conclusion, the people sitting in the *hogan* pass around a small leather pouch of pollen. Like the sun's path in the sky, the bag begins with the people sitting along the east side of the hogan, circles person to person around the south, then up the west, and finally across the north. As each one takes a bit of pollen, touching some to the tongue, some to the top of the head, and then scattering some to the world at large, he or she repeats the words,

> *Hózhǫ́ nahasdlį́į́*
> *Hózhǫ́ nahasdlį́į́*

The entire nine-day ceremonial has been successful, and in McAllester's translation (1980:211),

> Conditions of beauty have been restored,
> Conditions of beauty have been restored.

The seminal term, *hózhǫ́*, also appears in many other ritual contexts, often in the phrase *sǫ'a naghái bik'e hózhǫ́* as well as in frequent nonceremonial settings in everyday Navajo life. If we can grasp the meaning of *hózhǫ́*, we will have gone a long way toward understanding the fundamental Navajo philosophy of art.

But explaining *hózhǫ́* is no easy matter. In the late nineteenth century, Washington Matthews carried out the first careful study by Western scholars of Navajo intellectual culture, and he translated the first two words of *sǫ'a naghái bik'e hózhǫ́* as "in old age walking," the second two as "in his trail beautiful" (cited in Witherspoon 1977:24). In a less literal translation, he equated the first phrase with long life and the second with health. Although thousands of pages have been published on Navajo religion and worldview since Matthews's time, scholars continue to debate the precise meaning of *sǫ'a naghdi bik'e hózhǫ́* in general and of *hózhǫ́* in particular (cf. Farella 1984:153–188).

The best approach is to begin, as it were, at the beginning, with the Navajo account of creation. This is a daunting task in itself. Paul G. Zolbrod (1983) has used Matthews's original notes, along with other sources, to produce a complete translation of the story, and the result fills over 300 pages of text, plus another 76 pages of explanatory notes—clear evidence of the richness of Navajo speculative thought.[1] But for our purposes, the most relevant part of the myth cycle is the passage that tells how First Man's medicine bundle, which is itself called *sǫ'a naghdi bik'e hózhǫ*, gave rise to First Boy and First Girl. First Boy is identified with thought and is called *sǫ'a naghái;* First Girl is associated with speech and called *bik'e hózhǫ.* A notable quality of First Boy and First Girl (i.e., of *sǫ'a naghái* and of *bik'e hózhǫ*) is their radiant beauty, both having hair reaching down to their thighs (Witherspoon 1977:17). (Although they came from the same source and share some of the same traits, First Boy and First Girl are not brother and sister.)

The Navajo creation story says that although First Boy and First Girl cannot now be seen in the world, their presence is still felt because they were the parents of Changing Woman, the benevolent Mother who is incarnate as the earth. Changing Woman is the source of all human life, and she controls nature's fertility. We must keep in mind that Changing Woman is the offspring of the primal paragons of beauty, First Boy and First Girl. Thus, the world and all living things are products of *sǫ'a naghdi* and *bik'e hózhǫ.*

We have already learned several meanings of *sǫ'a naghái* and *bik'e hózhǫ.* These phrases refer to First Man's medicine bundle, to two surpassingly beautiful supernaturals who came from that medicine bundle, and to the source of Changing Woman—the earth—and all her procreative power.[2] But nearly a century ago, Washington Matthews translated the phrases as abstract qualities—long life and health—and it is these meanings that give the words greatest significance. The deepest meaning of *sǫ'a naghdi bik'e hózhǫ* is that the world was created in a state of beauty and harmony, happiness and good health—a condition that, by the nature of things, continues today and may persist into the future.

Before turning to *hózhǫ* 's implications for art, one additional component of Navajo philosophy must be considered. The Navajo conception of the world is not permeated solely with everlasting beauty and goodness. Individual Navajos evince a fear of the darker side of reality, as manifest in death, ghosts, and witchcraft. Thus on the philosophical level, *hózhǫ* has a counterpart in *hóchxǫ,* the "evil, the disorderly, and the ugly" (Witherspoon 1977:34). Unlike the West, where evil is distinct from goodness, Navajos think of *hózhǫ*

---

[1]The complexity of Navajo philosophy taxes not only outsiders but Navajos themselves. Denet Tsosie told David McAllester regarding Shootingway, "Fifty-four years ago I began learning some things about this, when I was twelve years old. But though I am always finding out more I will never know it all—and there is much that I have forgotten" (McAllester 1980:200).

[2]*Sǫ'a naghái bik'e hózhǫ* even has a sexual component. After many discussions with John Farella about the meaning of the phrase, a thoughtful older Navajo man named Grey Mustache concluded his "lessons" by focusing on the reproductive dimension of *sǫ'a naghái bik'e hózhǫ,* saying, "The semen of First Man is called *sǫ'a naghái,* and the reproductive fluid of First Woman is *bik'e hózhǫ.* That's what *sǫ'a naghái bik'e hózhǫ* is all about to this day" (Farella 1984:177).

and *hóchxǫ́* as "temporary, although cyclically reappearing, points in an ongoing process" (Farella 1984:36). They are not separate forces, locked in an eternal battle with each other. Their relationship is defined by the phrase, *ałkéé naa'aashii,* meaning that all entities contain within them a vital opposition that insures continuous, dynamic change and that allows them to perpetuate themselves. Day and night exemplify the opposition inherent in *ałkéé naa'aashii,* as do the contrasts between "good" and "bad" deities, the changing of the seasons, birth and death, male and female, and so on.

Only those aspects of Navajo philosophy that are the most fundamental and relevant to Navajo aesthetics have been discussed here; the interested reader is referred to the primary sources, especially Witherspoon (1977) and Farella (1984), for additional information. But one principle should be clear: Navajo philosophy is thoroughly aesthetic in nature. It posits a world of manifest beauty and goodness and of constant change and development.

Hózhǫ́ in Ceremony and Art

The concepts of *sǫ'a naghai bik'e hózhǫ́* and *ałkéé naa'aashii* are not mere abstractions that Navajos discuss as an intellectual exercise. Rather, they have practical and far-reaching implications for Navajo ceremony, art, and daily life.

The non-Navajo can best understand the relationship between theory and practice by recalling that on one level, *sǫ'a naghai* means thought. People in the Western world usually assume that the mind's activities are largely determined by the world outside the mind. Navajos, by contrast, conceive thought to be an active and effective force that can influence the material and spiritual worlds. It was, after all, the union of thought and speech (of *sǫ'a naghai* and *bik'e hózhǫ́,* or of First Boy and First Girl) that brought the world (Changing Woman) into existence. In a parallel fashion, mortals can use thought and speech to bring about change in the material world.[3] That is precisely the purpose of Navajo rituals, where traditional prayers, chants, and sandpaintings repeat the story of the initial creation of *hózhǫ́* and in so doing create it once again. Whether a ceremony is performed to cure the sick or to bring rain during a period of dry weather, it is intended to restore the world

---

[3]The Sapir-Whorf Hypothesis asserts that some aspects of language determine an individual's phenomenal world, rather than the external world determining the nature of language. Although empirical support for the Sapir-Whorf Hypothesis has proven to be elusive, Navajos go about their daily lives assuming that it is true—and presumably were doing so long before Edward Sapir and Benjamin Lee Whorf began to speculate about it. Witherspoon says explicitly, "*in the Navajo view of the world, language is not a mirror of reality; reality is a mirror of language*" (Witherspoon 1977:34, emphasis in original).

to its natural condition of *hózhǫ́*.[4] Thus, the central premises of Navajo aesthetics come down to this: The world was created in beauty and harmony, albeit with the potential for evil and chaos; mortals have the responsibility of sustaining and restore the world's primal beauty. This may be effectively accomplished through the production of art—both in the controlled art of ritual chants and sandpainting, and in the artful living of day-to-day life.

That a non-Western people would equate art, life, and nature might seem to be more the result of a romanticized "noble savage" caricature than ethnographic fact, but Gary Witherspoon, with more than two decades of first-hand experience in Navajo culture, provides ample evidence that the Navajo worldview is indeed based on this equation. Navajos, we are told, "don't admonish one 'to be beautiful' or 'to see beauty' but to 'walk (live) in beauty' and to 'radiate beauty" (Witherspoon 1977:32). A common Navajo prayer says,

> With beauty before me, I walk
> With beauty behind me, I walk
> With beauty above, me, I walk
> With beauty below me, I walk.
>   (Witherspoon 1977:153)

Navajos, we are told,

> . . . do not consider the generation or maintenance of beauty to be particularly elusive. Beauty is in the nature of things, as well as in people. It is the normal state of affairs. The Gods designed this world to be a beautiful, harmonious, happy, and healthy place. To be maintained, beauty needs to be expressed and renewed in ritual, song, art, speech, dress and in daily living. (Witherspoon 1981:32)

Finally,

> The Navajo does not look for beauty; he generates it within himself and projects in onto the universe. The Navajo says *shił hózhǫ́* "with me there is beauty,"

---

[4]Navajos realize that their efforts do not always produce the desired results. For example, Witherspoon witnessed four successive ceremonies that were intended to produce rain. Each time, the previously clear sky became cloudy and rain fell within twelve hours; however, significant rainfall occurred only once. After the less than successful efforts the singers "shrugged their shoulders with a slight sense of humor and not a little dismay and commented, 'How feebleminded we have become'" (Witherspoon 1977:28). It should also be noted that McAllester (1980:231–234) has questioned the concept of the "compulsive word," developed by Reichard (1944) and Witherspoon (1977), suggesting that Navajos do not, in fact, believe that the proper performance of ritual will necessarily lead to the desired results.

shii'hózhǫ́ "in me there is beauty," and *shaa hózhǫ́* "from me beauty radiates."
(Witherspoon 1977:151)

The Aesthetics of Navajo Music

In 1950 David McAllester carried out one of the first empirical studies of non-Western aesthetics among the Navajo, and although he spent only four and a half months in the field, his findings set the stage for extensive later work by himself and others. He initially intended to analyze secular music but soon learned that all Navajo music has religious associations and that the Western distinction between sacred and secular music is not helpful in an analysis of Navajo culture. McAllester focused his study on the chant music used in Enemy Way, a Sing meant to protect Navajos from the ghosts of slain non-Navajos, and one that was widely known and commonly performed in the years following World War II as Navajo servicemen returned to the reservation.

McAllester also discovered that he was naive in assuming that Navajos would have ready answers to questions such as, "What is good tone?" and "What is your favorite instrument?" Eventually, McAllester did discover some Navajo critical values regarding performance style: "Tonality should be consistent [and a song] should not change key while it is being sung" (McAllester 1954:73); and "A good voice is somewhat nasal, the vibrato is rather wide; the voice should be as high as possible, it should be capable of sharp emphases, and there should be an easy and powerful falsetto" (ibid.:74). But Navajos give no more attention to stylistic qualities such as these than to other traits that Westerners would not consider to be strictly aesthetic. A good singer, for example, ought to have a good memory and great endurance—a reasonable expectation inasmuch as the singing that begins at dusk should continue until dawn with minimal repetition and undiminished gusto (Figure 5–4).

Further discussion led McAllester to realize that manner of performance is not very important to Navajos. Their principal concern about music is not, "How does it sound?" but "What is it for?" (McAllester 1954:71). When he asked, "What is it about a song that makes it sound pretty?," the typical answer was, "It's songs like the Lightning Way and some of the songs in the Blessing Way that are most beautiful. It's good for the patient and makes him well. If it's worthwhile it's beautiful" (McAllester 1954:71). Although extracting aesthetic principles from the wider matrix of Navajo philosophy is contrary to their own thinking, this statement—"if it's worthwhile, it's beautiful"—can be taken as one of the central axioms of Navajo aesthetics. In 1950 Navajos even applied this idea to non-Navajo music: When McAllester asked a Navajo woman which Anglo music she preferred, she said, "I like Army songs because they saved the country" (McAllester 1954:71).

Subsequent fieldwork in Navajo culture and an improved understanding of the Navajo language now provide additional insight into these comments about music. Navajos do not conceive music to be a trivial recreation,

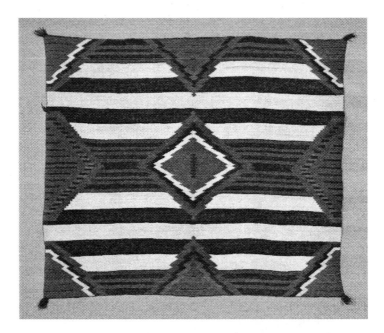

FIGURE 5–4 Navajo third phase chief's blanket, circa 1870–1875. *(Courtesy of Natural History Museum of Los Angeles County, Anthropology Section. William Randolph Hearst Collection.)*

removed from the "important" aspects of "real life." Making music is a serious matter for Navajos, an activity that can make a sick patient well again or help a country win a war. In all cases, music restores the health, harmony, and goodness that the world is potentially heir to. McAllester found that although Navajo music may have varying stylistic qualities and be performed with differing degrees of expertise, first and foremost it must be effective, fostering the *hózhǫ́* that Navajos expect to come from all traditional activities.

Process Orientation versus Product Orientation

Navajo art is based on the premise that the beauty and goodness embodied in *hózhǫ́* are the natural conditions of existence and that every human endeavor can manifest and help perpetuate this state. But besides the harmonious principle derived from *hózhǫ́*, Navajo aesthetics also reflects the processual principle of *ałkéé naa'aashíí. Hózhǫ́*, remember, is not a static state, established at the beginning of the world and unchanged ever after. Instead, *hózhǫ́* is a dynamic process, always interacting with *hóchxǫ*. To describe the situation accurately, the inherent beauty of the world should be spoken of in the present progressive, not the past tense: *Hózhǫ́*, was not "created" but is always "being created." Navajo art and ritual are imbued with a capacity for agency that, McChesney has observed, establishes order "by constantly changing evil to good, stasis to motion" (1978:104). Thus, another basic principle of Navajo aesthetics is that beauty is found in activities, not in things.

Again, Witherspoon's remarks cannot be improved upon:

> A Navajo experiences beauty most poignantly in creating it and in expressing it, not in observing it or preserving it. The experience of beauty is dynamic; it flows to one and from one; it is not in things, but in relationships among things. Beauty is not to be preserved but to be continually renewed in oneself and expressed in one's daily life and activities. To contribute to and be part of this universal *hózhǫ́* is both man's special blessing and his ultimate destiny. (Witherspoon 1977:178)

When this emphasis on process over product is combined with the Navajo belief in the dominance of inner spirit over outer manifestation, the result is an approach to art that emphasizes the internal creation that produce beauty, rather than the external activities involving art media. For the Navajo, "beauty is not so much a perceptual experience as it is a conceptual one" (Witherspoon 1977:151).

These aesthetic premises have a profound influence on Navajo art. For one thing, the performing arts, which are all process and no product, are particularly important components of Navajo culture, an obvious example being the many hours of chanting in Navajo Sings. (A family may spend several thousand dollars in staging a Sing, and over 1,000 people may participate in the event in one way or the other.) Informal singing is also important in Navajo culture. Witherspoon says that daily activities are accompanied by "riding songs, walking songs, grinding songs, planting songs, growing songs and harvesting songs," and a Navajo often "counts his wealth in the songs he knows and especially in the songs he has created" (Witherspoon 1977:155).

The Navajo emphasis on creativity extends beyond the performing arts, however. Besides chanting, Sings require the construction of sandpaintings. After as much as 400 man-hours, however, the sandpainting is used for only a few minutes before it is swept up and ritually disposed of. As with songs, the importance of sandpainting lies in the process of creation, and the finished product has no lasting worth.[5]

---

[5]The difference between the process-oriented aesthetics of Navajos and the product-oriented stance of most Anglos is illustrated by contrasting Navajo versus Anglo attitudes toward sandpaintings. Unlike Navajos, who dispose of sandpaintings soon after they are completed, Western collectors buy thousands of sandpaintings every year as souvenirs, home decorations, and fine art. Commercial sandpaintings, with either novel designs or modified traditional designs, are made on boards covered with glue, so they may hang, forever, on their proud Anglo owners' walls. Nancy Parezo (1982, 1983) has documented the transition of sandpaintings from "religious act to commercial art."

Aesthetics and Art Style

The aesthetics of *hózhǫ* and *ałkéé naa'aashii* provide not only a theoretical basis for Navajo art production; they also inform the stylistic conventions found in the various Navajo art media. Navajos recognize a dichotomy between dynamism and activity on the one hand and stability and conservatism on the other, and they use it to account symbolically for the differences between Navajo women and men.

Navajo men are considered to be static, and this belief is reflected in the stylistic conservatism seen in the sandpaintings men make. For a sandpainting to be effective, it must replicate in almost every detail the designs that have been handed down from previous generations.[6] Also, sandpaintings display a strong impulse toward symmetry, both in total design and in details. But as we have come to expect of the Navajo worldview, although static traits dominate their art, men are not void of the opposite characteristic of dynamism, so sandpainters prefer a rotational symmetry that is far more dynamic than simple, mirror-image symmetry. In Whirling Logs[7] (Figure 5–5), for example, the figures on the right replicate those on the left, but rotated 180°. The sandpainting's symmetry also emphasizes the contrast between the static black cross in the center of the painting and the peripheral figures that move in a sunwise direction to produce a whirling visual effect—all held in check by the elongated figure that encircles the design.

The colors used in Whirling Logs also reflect the static/active opposition. Navajo color symbolism is complex, with any given color's connotations depending upon the other colors it appears with. In this sandpainting, however, it is noteworthy that the black and white lines that cross at the center are considered to be static relative to the colored figures that spin around the outside. Also, of the two crosses, the black one is graphically more solid and fixed in comparison to the white cross, which, set on the diagonal, gives a feeling of energy that balances the black "X."

Navajo women are considered to have dynamic natures, at least as compared to Navajo men, and women's art reflects this belief. In contrast to the traditional designs that men faithfully copy in their sandpaintings, the lively minds of women always produce new patterns for their weavings, never replicating a pre-existing work. And just as the energy of the mind can be used effectively only when it is controlled by ritual knowledge, the creativity of the

---

On the other hand, not all contemporary Western artists are product-oriented. During his formative years, Jackson Pollock watched Navajo sandpainters at work. Some of his letters indicate that one inspiration for his technique of "action painting" was the Navajos' emphasis on process, rather than product, to say nothing of the procedural similarity found in Pollock's method of dripping paints, lacquers, and even sand onto a canvas lying on the floor (cf. Witherspoon 1977:174–178).

[6]For some sings, however, the singer composes the prayers that are used (cf. Frisbie 1980).

[7]The following stylistic analysis is based on Witherspoon (1977:163–168).

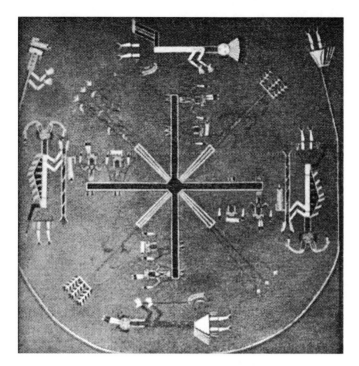

FIGURE 5–5   Navajo sandpainting, *Whirling Logs. (Photo courtesy K.C. Publications.)*

weaver bears fruit only when she successfully controls the diverse elements of the weaving process, from shearing the sheep and spinning the wool, through selecting the proper natural dyes to produce a desired color, to weaving weft threads through the warp to produce a balanced, integrated design (Witherspoon 1981:30).

Ramifications of Navajo Aesthetic Theory

From what has been said thus far about Navajo aesthetics, one could surmise that Navajos make art solely for practical ends such as healing the sick and that, for example, when chants and sandpaintings are used in a Sing to cure a sick person, the participants in the ceremony experience feelings comparable to those of the doctors and nurses in a Western hospital's operating room. Such is not the case. When Navajos discuss art, they emphasize its instrumental value, but sprinkled through the literature one finds comments that, taken together, give some clue to the Navajo affective response to art. For example, based on her research in the 1930s, Gladys Reichard wrote,

The whole fabrication of prayer sticks and [medicine] bundle paraphernalia is an aesthetic occupation, felt as such by the men who pursue it. The materials are handled not only with reverence by the men, but also with pleasure expressed verbally as they work. The same kind of satisfaction is shown in the achievement represented by a sandpainting. (Reichard 1977 [orig 1939]:77)

On a less lofty level, Johnny Blanco told McAllester, "I like the [songs] that have a nice tune. When you hear a nice tune, that makes you happy" (McAllester 1954:83). Navajos' reactions to art rarely include the ecstatic, however. In fact, a person who experiences an odd or dizzy feeling upon hearing Enemy Way music is thought to need the ceremony performed over him- or herself.

Pride in the quality of one's work and a feeling of awe at the master artist's consummate skill are also part of the traditional Navajo aesthetic response.[8] Given the underlying assumptions of their worldview, all Navajos are, in a sense, artists, but some individuals are nevertheless singled out for their exceptional abilities. Kluckhohn and Leighton report,

Experts are richly rewarded in prestige as well as money, and not without reason. Prodigious memory is demanded of the ceremonialist. The Singer who knows one nine-night chant must learn at least as much as a man who sets out to memorize the whole of a Wagnerian opera: orchestral score, every vocal part, all the details of the settings, stage business and each requirement of costume. Some singers know three or more longs chants, as well as various minor rites. (Kluckhohn and Leighton 1946:163, quoted in McAllester 1954:79)

Although Navajo women are eager to find buyers for their weavings and to win prizes in exhibitions of Southwestern Indian arts and crafts, in the noncompetitive atmosphere of traditional Navajo culture, prestige and money were not the primary motives for artistic activity. Even at the present time such considerations seem to be secondary. For example, most weavers today are lucky to receive a payment equivalent to the minimum wage for their long hours at distaff and loom. Given the limited economic resources of many Navajos, it would be sheer romanticism to assume that Navajo artists are indifferent to the income they derive from sales, but besides the profit motive, women also weave for the satisfaction they receive from successfully carrying out the creative synthesis that the craft entails (Witherspoon 1981).

---

[8]Not surprisingly, emphasis was traditionally placed on conceptual skills rather than on perceptual and motor skills, and summoning the mental concentration needed to generate *hózhǫ́* was more important than having the manual or vocal skills necessary for flawless execution. Craftsmanship has, however, risen to paramount importance in arts and crafts made for sale to non-Navajos (cf. Adair 1944:96–101, 199; Leighton and Leighton 1944:51; Bartlett 1950:5–6; Reichard 1936:19; see also the present chapter's Epilogue).

Conclusion

Although most of us usually take our phenomenal world for granted, one sometimes wonders what it would feel like to live inside another person's skin, to look about through his or her eyes, to think with his or her mind while walking through that world. Would the experience be the same as one's own perceptions, thoughts, and feelings, or would these all be different? The accumulation of ethnographic information makes us the first to have systematic, empirical information relevant to these questions, and nowhere is that data more complete than in the case of the Navajos. Those who have studied Navajo culture in depth still disagree about some aspects of Navajo worldview, but their strong consensus is that traditional Navajos do indeed look at the world in a way that is their own. Navajos believe that the world was created in a state of beauty, balance, and harmony that exists in dynamic balance with ugliness, chaos, and evil. These opposing forces persist today, and in the face of the hazards represented by dangerous spirit forces, Navajos seek to maintain and foster *hózhǫ́* by living lives of balanced harmony. By producing the arts needed for Sings, Navajos are confident that, as the conclusion of Shooting Way says, "Conditions of beauty have been restored." Despite their adverse physical and sociopolitical environment, Navajos have not only survived but have actually thrived, in part because of their commitment to *hózhǫ́*.

Epilogue

The resilience of the Navajos in the face of a changing social and political environment is uncommon among world cultures. Despite having adopted many alien practices over the centuries—sedentism, aspects of ceremonialism, and arts such as weaving from the Puebloans who were prior residents of the Southwest; peyotism[9] and silversmithing from Mexican cultures to the south; and everything from gas-powered vehicles to a cash economy from their Anglo neighbors—Navajos remain unique in their lifeways and worldview, and their numbers continue to grow every year. Navajo culture provides a positive model for the ways in which the rising tide of globalization can be taken advantage of for the things such as medical care that would seem to be of value, while avoiding the grave threats of economic exploitation and cultural homogenization.

The transformation of Navajo arts continues apace. The modifications that have occurred in Navajo ceramics over the years offer one example (cf. Hartman 1987). Navajos have long produced pottery, making such items

---

[9]The Native American Church of Navajoland, which uses peyote as part of its religious practice, claims 40,000 members (cf. Bergman 1971).

as ceramic jars, drums, and whistles for ceremonial use, plus tall containers, usually sealed (after firing) with pitch and used for food and water storage. Even before Anglos began directly affecting Navajo arts, however, Navajo pottery was undergoing change: Fearing reprisals after the 1680 Pueblo Revolt, some Puebloans from Jemez, New Mexico, migrated into Navajo land. When the Jemez painted pottery styles merged with traditional Navajo ceramic techniques, the result was Gobernador Polychrome (Figure 5–6).

The unpainted pitch-covered pots remained the dominant Navajo style of pottery, but by the late 1800s this utilitarian ware was increasingly supplanted by pots, pans, and jars of non-Navajo manufacture. Nevertheless, traditional items continued to be made for use in Sings. The conservatism of Navajo ceremonialism had interesting consequences, however. In the early twentieth century, because potters only made items for ritual use, their craft took on an aura of mystery and danger (e.g., "a woman should not allow others to observe her while making pottery" [Hartman 1987:37]). As the restrictions and taboos surrounding pottery increased, they actually may have become a disincentive to learn the craft (cf. especially ibid; see also Tschopik 1938). These restrictions notwithstanding, the fact that Sings such as Enemy Way required ceramic items—and ones free of chips and cracks—kept the Navajo pottery tradition alive. (Also as Hartman notes [1987:40], in the 1930s, some anthropologists began buying Navajo pots for field collections, thereby themselves contributing to the viability of Navajo ceramics.)

FIGURE 5–6 Gobernador polychrome jar. *(Photo courtesy of University of Colorado Museum ca. no. 383.)*

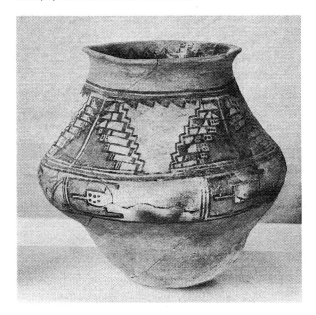

Meanwhile, tourist arts were becoming a major economic force in the Southwestern United States, with expanding markets and eager entrepreneurs encouraging the production of Puebloan pots and Navajo silver. Russell P. Hartman (1987) has recounted the fascinating process whereby the indigenous production of ceramic wares, which many non-Navajos had dismissed as "mud pots," was transformed into a successful commercial venture. With the encouragement and direction of traders as well as a clear economic incentive, by the 1960s individual creativity began to appear in Navajo ceramics, with some potters starting to make nonceremonial items—a significant development in light of the highly constrained nature of the craft during the first half of the twentieth century. By the early 1980s, Navajo pots (Figure 5–7) were receiving major attention in museum exhibitions, and today Navajo potters produce pots in a wide variety of styles. Some ceramists adapt indigenous Navajo styles for commercial sale, others produce pots with traditional Pueblo shapes and decorations, and still others make highly innovative work. For example, a number of Navajo potters (as well as some Puebloan potters) now produce and sell pots with random, fine dark lines on a light background. The irregular patterns are made by placing hair from horses' tails on the pot during firing, a technique that may have had Apache origins. Aided by a 1990–1993 show at the Arizona State Museum in Tucson entitled "Shonto Junction: Where Navajo Potteries Meet," Navajo ceramics are now

FIGURE 5-7 Modern Navajo pot made by Alice Cling. It is traditional in general shape but also in having a lustrous sheen, produced by piñon pitch. *(Alice Cling, Navajo pot, 11.5" high, 8.5" diameter, 6.5" opening. Collection of Jan Musial. Photo courtesy of Jan Musial, Musial's Navajo Arts.)*

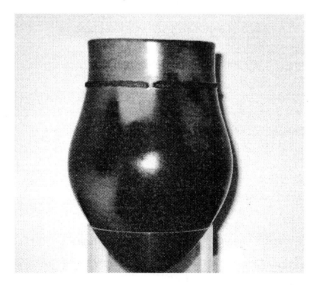

sold in many galleries that specialize in Southwestern art and on the Internet. These developments notwithstanding, some Navajo potters continue to produce items for ceremonial use. (As noted in footnote 6 of this chapter, the Navajo tradition of sandpainting also diverged in the twentieth century into two distinctly separate traditions, one perpetuating the long-established and stylistically conservative designs that are necessary for Sings; the other, created for sale off the reservation and using modified designs. Nancy Parezo [1982, 1983] describes the process whereby this divergence took place, including implications for the division of labor by gender.)

Likewise, Navajo three-dimensional sculpture has evolved from simple figures made of mud and used as toys by Navajo children at least as far back as the 1870s (Rosenak and Rosenak 1994), to a diverse and commercially viable "folk art" tradition. As elsewhere, the developments came about in part by happenstance: An Anglo couple, Chuck and Jan Rosenak, with a long-standing interest in American folk art moved to Santa Fe, New Mexico, in 1983. In the Wheelwright Museum there they saw Navajo toys made from sun-dried clay, and soon they began actively collecting, promoting, and writing about the sculptures they purchased on the Navajo Reservation (Figure 5–8). At the present, the figures are produced for sale in a wide variety of media, including painted and carved wood, glass beads over metal armatures, painted sun-dried clay, as well as hand-woven rugs with depictions of such nontraditional imagery as dinosaurs. Again, although the work is produced for sale off the reservation, it consistently retains enough traditional Navajo

FIGURE 5–8 Navajo folk art: Two people riding in a horse-drawn wagon. Sun-dried clay and paint. *(Courtesy of TwinRocks.com.)*

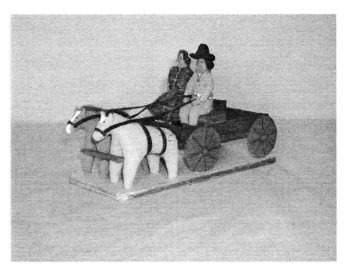

subject matter to remind the buyer—and, of course, its maker—of its place of origin.

The evolution of two-dimensional visual Navajo arts reflects even more diverse factors. In addition to traditional sandpainting, secular figurative pictures were made as far back as the 1700s, either for casual recreation or to inform others of Navajo ways (Brody 1983:30). With increased Anglo presence in the early twentieth century, however, a few individuals began making paintings for sale. An illuminating example is provided by a man, born around 1930, who signed his work Beatien Yazz and whom Anglos knew as Jimmy Toddy.

Showing exceptional artistic ability at an early age, Toddy was encouraged to paint and draw by Anglo trading post owners (Figure 5–9). In his mid-teens Toddy briefly studied at the Studio School, which an Anglo art teacher, Dorothy Dunn, had established as part of the government-run Santa Fe Indian School. He did not, however, immediately adopt the distinctive Studio School technique, characterized by "a flat, decorative style, [with] the patterned movement of figures across the picture plane, and an idealized view of

FIGURE 5–9   Beatien Yazz, *The Road Man* 1977. *(Courtesy of Museum of Northern Arizona Photo Archives.)*

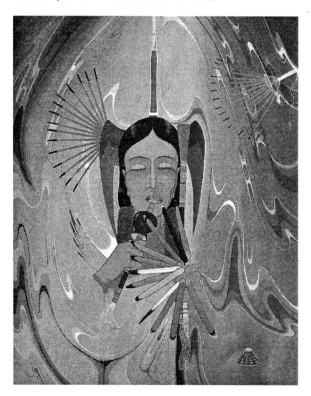

the traditional Indian past" (Berlo and Phillips 1998:216). He did, though, leave the school a confirmed easel painter. In an excellent critical essay on Toddy, J. J. Brody observes, "Before [Toddy] was eighteen, this isolated Navajo artist had seen a great variety of art in . . . such exotic places as Chicago, San Francisco, and Tientsin, China, and these encounters with alien artistic systems helped to shape his work" (1983:29)

The aesthetic hybridization seen in Jimmy Toddy's work is far from unique. In the early 1960s the New Indian Painter movement, whose members came from tribes across the United States and which combined traditional Native American subject matter with fine arts techniques and sensibilities, included the Navajo artists Mary Morez and R. C. Gorman. The nascent movement of Navajo fine art painting continues today with artists such as Emmi Whitehorse (Figure 5–10). Born in 1956 in northern New Mexico, Whitehorse's first language was Navajo, and her grandmother was a traditional weaver. After having received a BA and MFA from the University of New Mexico, Whitehorse's mixed media work reflects various styles. The

FIGURE 5-10 Emmi Whitehorse, *Rushing Water—Green,* oil on paper canvas, 51" x 39.5". 2000. *(Courtesy of Emmi Whitehorse.)*

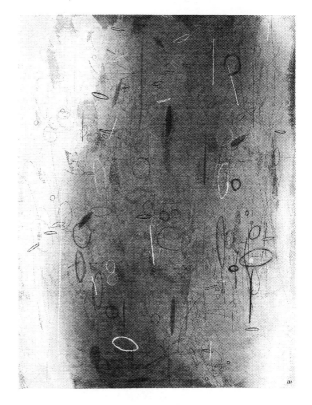

artist says that at one extreme her work was "an exploration of my background: the clan system, the creation stories, the moral stories. The work became very figurative. Birds would float in and out, and a female shape [emerged], Changing Woman, White-shell Woman" (quoted in Regan 1997:2). Later work she describes as being "nonobjective, almost color-field paintings" (ibid.). Nonetheless, Whitehorse's output still belies her Navajo heritage. Like a weaver, she delights in the creative process of art-making; and like a sandpainter, she works not on an easel but with the canvas on the floor or a flat table.

One might naively assume that when traditional cultures are confronted by the cultural and political hegemony of Western nations, their arts would become extinct or reduced to uninventive curios for tourists. The Navajo case shows reality to be far more complex: Some old practices continue to live on relatively unchanged; some very commercial styles have come into existence. However, many creative individuals have forged viable art forms that bring together the old with the new and the indigenous with the alien to produce art of considerable aesthetic and cultural significance.

Further Reading

In the abundant ethnographic literature on the subject, Downs (1972), Iverson (1981), and Locke (1992) stand out as broad overviews of Navajo culture. An important contemporary issue affecting Navajos is the U.S. government's program of resettling residents of the Navajo and Hopi reservations in consolidated lands held by the two groups, a topic ably surveyed by both Benedek (1999) and Brugge (1999). Thorough and nuanced treatments of Navajo intellectual culture appear in Zolbrod (1983/1988), Farella (1984/1991) Witherspoon (1977), and Witherspoon and Peterson 1995, the latter two works giving extended consideration also to Navajo language, art, and aesthetics.

Other treatments of Navajo art focus on specific media. The central role of the performing arts in Navajo ceremony is discussed by Faris (1995) and Frisbie (1993); and Parezo (1982, 1983) provides an extended account of the emergence of commercial sandpainting. Excellent treatments of Navajo textile traditions are provided by Kent (1985) and Hedlund (1988, 1994); the classic study of the early development of Navajo silversmithing is Adair (1944). Of the many works that favor photography over text, two noteworthy books are by Jacka and Jacka (1994, 1995).

Accounts of the transformations that traditional Navajo arts have undergone also tend to be media specific, with Hartman (1987) documenting changing ceramic traditions and Chase (1982) focusing on Navajo painting. Rosenak and Rosenak (1994) describe the work of the new generation of Navajo producers of "folk art."

The life and artistic output of Jimmy Toddy is insightfully analyzed by J. J. Brody (1983), accompanied by two essays, one by Sallie R. Wagner, a trading post owner and lifelong supporter of Toddy, and one by Toddy himself. Berlo and Phillips (1998:217–220) provide a brief overview of the interaction in the Southwest between fine art and traditional art approaches as seen, for example, in the work of Emmi Whitehorse. It should be noted that Berlo and Phillips' important survey text sets a new standard for the study of native North American art, providing sophisticated art historical and critical analysis in a rigorous ethnographic context.

6

YORUBA AESTHETICS

Goodness and Beauty

in West Africa

A man may be very, very handsome
Handsome as a fish within the water,
But if he has no character
He is no more than a wooden doll.

(Yoruba verse, quoted in Thompson 1983:11)

European and American fascination with West African art goes back at least a hundred years to a time when Picasso, Vlaminck, and other Parisian artists became intrigued with the ways that African carvers portrayed the human face and figure. Since then, interest in West African art has spawned a vast literature that describes the colorful and varied arts of the Guinea Coast as a rich and sweeping panorama, while also illuminating many specific topics in minute detail. For example, a doctoral dissertation by Henry Drewal records, among other things, the events that took place in the Yoruba town of Aiyetoro, Nigeria, beginning on the afternoon of March 27, 1971, and continuing for the next twenty-four hours. Most of the present chapter describes Yoruba aesthetics in general and abstract terms, but to evoke the spirit of Yoruba art, I will begin by recounting the happenings on that day, as seen through the eyes of Henry and Margaret Drewal (cf. Drewal 1973; see also Drewal and Drewal 1983 and Lawall 1996).

Anticipation of the activities has been growing in Aiyetoro for days. Various misfortunes have been plaguing the townspeople, and so several weeks ago the town fathers, following custom, consulted the *babalawo*, a priest in the cult of Ifa, the God of Divination (Figure 6–1). The *babalawo's* art was, as always, subtle and complex. From a special, elaborately carved wooden container, he took sixteen palm nuts, enough for a large handful. Again and again he scattered them before himself and then attempted to pick them all up with one sweep of his right hand. After each try, one or two nuts remained behind, but this was as tradition dictated, and each time the *babalawo* made a

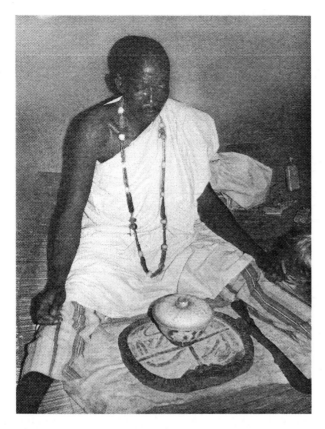

FIGURE 6–1   Yoruba *babalawo* (Ifa diviner) preparing to consult the spirit. Egado, Nigeria, 1978. *(Photo courtesy Henry John Drewal and Margaret Thompson Drewal.)*

mark in the wood dust that he had previously sprinkled on a carved wooden tray to indicate whether it had been one or two nuts that remained. Sixteen attempts yielded a column of sixteen marks in the dust; based on the resultant configuration of marks, the diviner selected one verse from the thousand committed to his memory (Figure 6–2). This verse held a solution to the town's problem: It was imperative that the dual rituals of Ẹfẹ and Gẹlẹdẹ be performed.

Soon after the Ifa diviner prescribed the Ẹfẹ/Gẹlẹdẹ rituals, the men and women who belong to the Ẹfẹ/Gẹlẹdẹ cult gathered in their meeting house and began preparing for the ceremonies, activities that would require an exceptional quantity of art, produced in many different media. First, cult members examined the wooden masks that had been used in past years, giving those in good condition a new coat of paint (Figure 6–3) and commissioning carvers to make replacements for unusable ones (Figure 6–4). Old or

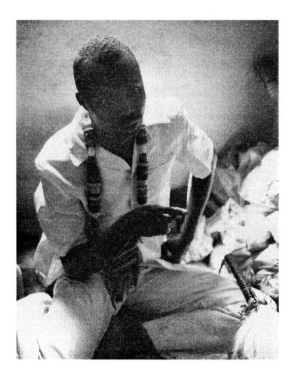

FIGURE 6-2 A *babalawo* consulting during a divination session. Ijebu, Nigeria, 1982. *(Photo courtesy Henry John Drewal and Margaret Thompson Drewal.)*

new, Ẹfẹ/Gẹlẹdẹ masks are complex creations, often incorporating intricate linear elements to produce complex sculptures in the round. But mask makers are not the only residents of Aiyetoro who have been busy with preparations. Other Ẹfẹ/Gẹlẹdẹ members have been making elaborate costumes to be worn with the masks. Although the actual performers are men, they will portray both males and females. Masculinity is conveyed by a bamboo hoop around the torso, over which flow layers of richly embroidered and appliquéd cloth, giving the wearer a massive appearance. Femininity, by contrast, is indicated by a costume that gives the dancer a small waist and artificially enlarged breasts and buttocks.

Still other cult members have been composing the songs that will be a principle attraction of the ceremonies. The Ẹfẹ performance lasts all night, and since new songs are composed each year, the Ẹfẹ/Gẹlẹdẹ song writers clearly face a daunting task before the rituals can be performed.

But now, several weeks later, all such preparations in Aiyetoro have been completed. In the morning, cult leaders went to a sacred grove and offered the resident spirits various gifts of kola nuts, whiskey, a white ram, and finally, a soup of cornmeal and waterleaf. These, along with prayers and songs, were given to ensure good fortune not just for the Ẹfẹ/Gẹlẹdẹ ceremonies but for the entire coming year. In the village itself, the air has become increasingly charged with anticipation; as the excitement grows during the day, so do the

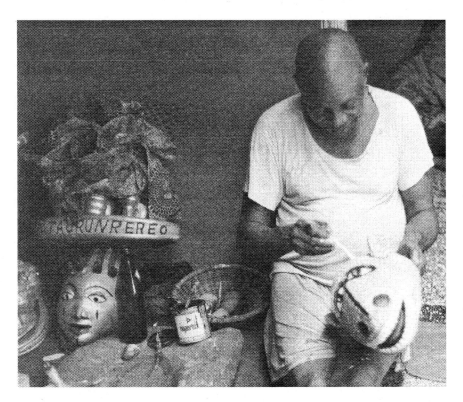

FIGURE 6-3   Elder in the Gẹlẹdẹ society painting a mask in preparation for a festival. Lagos, Nigeria, 1978. *(Photo courtesy Henry John Drewal and Margaret Thompson Drewal.)*

crowds. Although Ẹfẹ/Gẹlẹdẹ members constitute only a small portion of Aiyetoro's total population, many other Yoruba, traditionalists as well as Christians and Muslims, provide an eager audience. Word has spread beyond the boundaries of the village itself, and some of the visitors have traveled as many as 150 miles to witness the events of the next twenty-four hours.

There are variations in Ẹfẹ/Gẹlẹdẹ performances from village to village, but if the ceremonies at Aiyetoro parallel those in Ketu and Idahin (as described by the Drewals), then shortly after nightfall between 1,000 and 1,500 spectators will bring their lamps, food, mats, and chairs to the central market square in anticipation of the performance that will last till dawn. A special enclosure made of palm fronds stands at one side of the square, but the opposite side of the square gives the first clear evidence that the ceremony is about to start. Five drummers begin the insistent, powerful beat that will continue through most of the night. Their playing provides more than just a rhythmic background to the festivities. The largest of the drums, the *iyalu* or "mother drums," are literally "talking." By mimicking the rhythmic and melodic patterns of the Yoruba language (which is tonal in nature), the mother drums

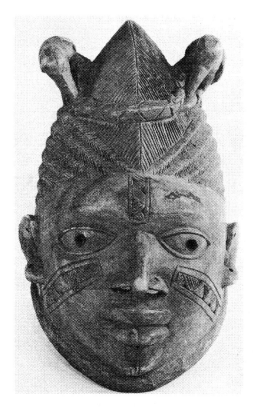

FIGURE 6–4 Yoruba Gęlędę society mask, carved from cottonwood. *(Courtesy, Field Museum of Natural History, Chicago, neg. no. 109311.)*

sing out verbal messages, praising the Yoruba gods, remembering revered ancestors, and honoring illustrious elders—as well as giving voice to many well-known Yoruba proverbs. Against the mother drums, the beat of the smaller drums, tuned to various pitches, adds a complex polyrhythmic counterpart.

At last masked Ẹfẹ/Gẹlẹdẹ members begin to emerge from the enclosure and approach the opening in the center of the crowded square (Figure 6–5). Some of their masks have moving parts that fascinate the younger spectators, who cheer and push to get a closer look. Other, more serious masks, represent specific supernatural figures. One group of cult members forms a chorus that sings a hearty praise as each masked performer emerges from the palm frond enclosure, and they are soon joined by others from the crowd of onlookers. When a figure known as Pa-ni-ina-njako rushes into the square with a pot of fire on his head, the people excitedly sing,

> The burning of the bush comes without warning.
> You farmers with fields near the bush,
> You are warned to take precautions.
> (Quoted in Drewal 1973:73)

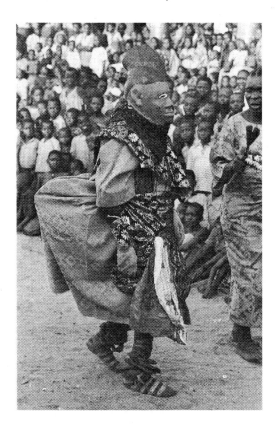

FIGURE 6-5 Masked Gẹlẹdẹ dancer. Lagos, Nigeria, 1978. *(Photo courtesy Henry John Drewal and Margaret Thompson Drewal.)*

Upon Pa-ni-ina-njako's entrance, all lamps are extinguished. The square remains dark, making later events all the more dramatic.

Sometimes the masked performer himself sings; and one, named Tetede, heralds the arrival of the central figure of the Ẹfẹ night ceremony, Oro Ẹfẹ. After much fanfare from his attendants and tentativeness on his own part, the drummers fall silent and Oro Ẹfẹ finally emerges from the enclosure. He is literally larger than life, and the looming Ẹfẹ mask that sits above his head adds to his supernatural stature. Oro Ẹfẹ's iron ankle rattles, six on each leg, sound a slow, steady beat as he enters the square, swaying and stamping. He begins a series of chants honoring Yoruba gods, ancestors, and mothers, and his words are resoundingly seconded by onlookers who fire guns into the air and shout their approval.

After these preliminaries, Oro Ẹfẹ starts a routine that will continue for hours. He begins chanting a song, and soon members of the Ẹfẹ/Gẹlẹdẹ chorus take up the words and move through the crowd teaching it to the onlookers until the thousand-plus voices are singing it in unison. After a while, Oro Ẹfẹ begins another song, and eventually everyone is singing the new one. Finally, as dawn approaches, a masked performer walking on stilts enters the square. As he diverts the crowd's attention, Oro Ẹfẹ makes an unobtrusive exit, and the weary onlookers begin to disperse. So goes Ẹfẹ Night.

The next day is devoted to the Gẹlẹdẹ Dance, staged by the same men who performed Ẹfẹ Night. Late in the afternoon, the crowd begins to gather once more around the market square, and again the cult's drummers take up their position opposite the palm frond enclosure. Their drumming attracts still more onlookers until the expectant spectators are jostling each other for good seats. (A Yoruba proverb says, in translation, "The eyes that have seen Gẹlẹdẹ have seen the ultimate spectacle" [Drewal and Drewal 1987:243].)

Meanwhile, cult members are putting on their costumes; again, masks sit atop their heads and elaborate costumes cover their bodies. The masked dancers are of all ages, and the youngest dancers go first. Boys as young as 5, individually or in groups of two or three, attempt to perform the intricate steps of the Gẹlẹdẹ dance. Happy onlookers reward their efforts with enthusiastic praise—and sometimes with coins. Adolescent and teenage dancers eventually replace the youngsters, and they in turn are followed by adult performers. Finally, the most accomplished of all, the elders, appear. With each successive dancer or group of dancers, the crowd's enthusiasm grows, and the cult members who have been assigned the job of controlling the crowd are barely able to maintain an open space in the middle of the square for the whirling, stamping, explosively energetic dancers. Meanwhile, other attendants vigorously fan those who have already danced so they can redouble their choreographic virtuosity in another effort. After the most experienced dancers have performed to the shouts of encouragement from the crowd—and sometimes accompanied by cult members who cannot resist joining the dance—the Ẹfẹ/Gẹlẹdẹ ceremonies end. The citizens return to their house compounds, happy and confident that the joyous celebration will bring good fortune to the town in the future.

The activities of Ẹfẹ Night and Gẹlẹdẹ Dance constitute a multimedia artistic event, and as such they embody many of the principles at the core of Yoruba aesthetics. Mask making and costumery, song and dance—all are combined in Ẹfẹ/Gẹlẹdẹ to produce a powerful spectacle that is distinctively Yoruba in nature. No witness to Ẹfẹ/Gẹlẹdẹ, whether native or visitor, can fail to appreciate the richness of Yoruba art.

The Drewals' account of Ẹfẹ/Gẹlẹdẹ gives us a vivid sense of a small component of the Yoruba art world. But Ẹfẹ/Gẹlẹdẹ is just one of a large number of equally striking artistic activities in Yoruba life. As we shall see, Yoruba culture is not only rich in art—art plays an important role in the social and moral world of the Yoruba as well.

Yoruba Society

If all the world's societies are placed in some approximate order, ranging from small-scale hunting and gathering groups to large-scale, complex civilizations, the traditional culture of the West African Yoruba (see map, p. xvi) would be closer to the complex end of the spectrum. The Yoruba population, for example, numbers over 25 million people in Nigeria, plus many millions more in neighboring Benin and farther west along the Guinea Coast. Moreover, great number of descendants of Yoruba who had been slaves now live in South America, the Caribbean, and the United States. Cities have existed in this area of West Africa since the distant archaeological past. Modern Yorubaland is the most urbanized ethnic region in sub-Saharan Africa, with half of the Yoruba population living in towns and cities, six of which have more than 100,000 residents (Bascom 1969:3). The largest, Ibadan, has evolved from an agricultural and trade center to a thriving industrial metropolis and the largest inland city in sub-Saharan Africa. But like the much smaller Aiyetoro, whose Ẹfẹ/Gẹlẹdẹ celebration has been described, even Ibadan's population swells when major religious festivals are held (cf. Lloyd, Mabogunje, and Awe 1967).

The Yoruba homeland has seen the rise and fall of powerful political entities for at least a thousand years. Contemporary Yoruba are divided into many kingdoms, each with an elaborate bureaucracy, impressive symbols of state such as beaded crowns and elaborately carved royal stools, and a political hierarchy whose pervasive influence reaches down to the individual house compound (Figure 6–6). Traditional Yoruba culture lacked writing, but formalized court singing and other genres of oral literature communicated a wealth of historical information.

Yoruba society has many other sorts of specialists besides those of political process. On market days, traders (most of whom are women) sell everything from chickens and goats to ingredients for charms and medicines. Most Yoruba do at least some farming, but many people additionally practice semiprofessional vocations. There are guilds of weavers, dyers, iron workers, brass casters, woodcarvers, carvers of calabash gourds, leather workers, and potters, as well as drummers, diviners, and circumcisers, to name only some of the Yoruba specialists.

Two features of Yoruba culture stand in marked contrast to the West: kinship and religion. Both play a more important role in the day-to-day lives of traditional Yoruba than they do for most Westerners. The Yoruba reckon descent patrilineally, which is to say that for most practical purposes, every person belongs only to his or her father's clan. The clan overshadows the nuclear family in importance, and every clan member lives under the authority of the *bale*, the clan's oldest male member.

Religion also plays an important role in the lives of most Yoruba. Although many Yoruba are now Christians or Muslims, traditional religion is also a powerful force—as the Ẹfẹ/Gẹlẹdẹ ceremonies demonstrated. Yoruba religion centers around several types of supernatural beings. First is Olodumare (also called Olorun), a male supreme being who is the source of all life. Although he represents beauty *par excellence*, Olodumare never appears in

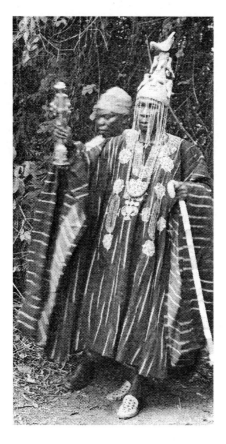

FIGURE 6-6 Yoruba king with beaded crown and staff of authority during annual rites of kingship. Ijebu, Nigeria, 1978. *(Photo courtesy Henry John Drewal and Margaret Thompson Drewal.)*

Yoruba iconography, and, unlike other Yoruba supernaturals, he has no cult of devotees for his propitiation. However, his coeval, Onile, does play an active role in the affairs of living men and women. As owner of the earth, she is attended by a special cult, Ogboni. Onile is the goddess of motherhood, worshipped by all mothers.

Beneath Olodumare and Onile are the *orisha*, a large group of supernatural beings. Many are associated with specific natural phenomena (e.g., Shango, the god of thunder and lightning [Figure 6–7] and human activities (e.g., Ogun, the *orisha* of ironworking). Other *orisha* are the spirits of deified ancestors. The *orisha* directly influence the lives of mortals, so to entice them to act favorably, each *orisha* is served by a cult of mortal worshippers. Cult members may honor and feed the *orisha* by making sacrifices to it; they may wear distinctive clothes or ornaments to glorify it; or (and of particular interest to us) they may use sculpture, music, dance, and oratory to publicly praise their *orisha* and thereby win its favor. As we have seen, Efe/Gelede cult members in western Nigeria spend an entire night in public singing and another

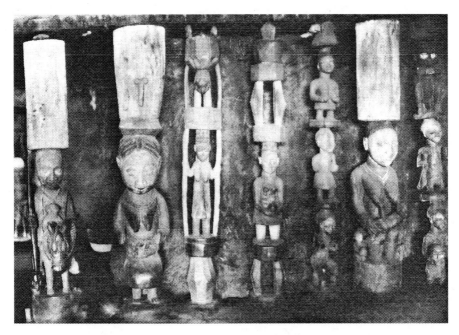

FIGURE 6-7 Interior view of cult house for Shango, Yoruba God of Thunder. Ibadan, Nigeria. *(Photo courtesy Field Museum of Natural History, Chicago, neg. no. 70014)*

day in dancing. They do this in a concerted effort to please their *orisha*—in this case, Ẹ̀fẹ̀, another spirit of motherhood, who embodies powerful procreative, nurturant, and pacifying capabilities. At the same time, cult members hope that their ceremonies will nullify any harm that might come from women who are witches.

Yoruba Art Production

The Guinea Coast, a 200-mile (320-kilometer) strip of land that begins in Sierra Leone in the west and runs 1,500 miles (2,400 kilometers) eastward to include the southern portions of the Ivory Coast, Ghana, Togo, Benin, Nigeria, and Cameroon, is extremely rich in art production. Why it has produced such enormous quantities of art is a matter for speculation (cf. Bascom 1973b:184–187) but whatever the reason, Guinea Coast art has had a magnetic appeal for Western sensibilities. The sensuousness, vitality, and visual inventiveness that Matisse, Picasso, and Brancusi found so striking in Guinea Coast art in the first decade of the twentieth century continue to excite Western collectors and museum goers today. For their part, scholars have been so fascinated by West African art that they have carried out more field studies and published more books and articles on West African art than on art from anywhere else in the world except the West, the Far East, and India.

The diversity of Yoruba art production is reflected in the training of Yoruba artists. Some families specialize in particular crafts, in which case a child's years of artistic training are an integral part of growing up. Alternatively, the child whose interests and talents do not coincide with the family profession may be apprenticed to a master artist in another medium. In any case, the degree of specialization is remarkably high. For example, the guild of male weavers who use a horizontal loom to make narrow bands of material is separate from the guild of women weavers, who use a vertical loom to weave wider fabric (Bascom 1973a:66). As the Ẹfẹ/Gẹlẹdẹ activities showed, Yoruba visual arts often occur in the context of the performing arts—music, dance, drama, and oratory. If anything, these media play an even greater role in West African aesthetic sensibilities than do the visual arts (cf. Borgatti 1982:29).

The Yoruba distinguish between decorative and utilitarian arts, calling, for example, the carver of masks (Figure 6–8), *gbẹnegbẹna*, whereas the carver of mortars and other practical items is *gbẹgibe-gi* (Bascom 1973a:64). But even the carver of masks is not a full-time artist and must rely on farming to supplement the income he receives from commissions and the occasional apprentice.

Although Yoruba art serves several purposes, religion is the most important. Hundreds of different cults exist in Yorubaland, each associated with a specific *orisha,* and most cults' duties require the use of art. Recall again the Ẹfẹ/Gẹlẹdẹ ceremonies. Not only did the dancers and singers use many masks, but also each dancer wore an elaborate costume. Furthermore, complex drumming, dancing, and singing were all incorporated into the performance.

Or consider another cult, that of the *babalawo,* the diviner who asked his own deity, Ifa, whether the time had come for the Ẹfẹ/Gẹlẹdẹ celebration. He probably stored the sixteen palm nuts needed for the divination ceremony in an elaborately carved container; he used a brass bell to attract Ifa's attention; and Figure 6–9 shows the handsome wooden tray upon which one *babalawo* scattered sawdust. Finally, the *babalawo* himself is distinguished by the decoration of his person: Bracelets of alternating green and tan beads (see Figure 6–2) are the emblem of the *babalawo.* The elaborate visual and performing arts associated with the cults of Ẹfẹ/Gẹlẹdẹ and Ifa are matched by many other Yoruba cults, so the quantity of Yoruba religious art is clearly enormous (Figure 6–10).

Still more Yoruba art is produced for secular purposes, primarily as a means of communicating social status. Each ruler of a Yoruba kingdom has his own royal stool, beaded crown, umbrellas, fly whisks, scepters, gowns, slippers, and other regalia of state, and the finest carving graces his palace. Also, the reputation of a noble lineage is made visible to all by the impressive low-

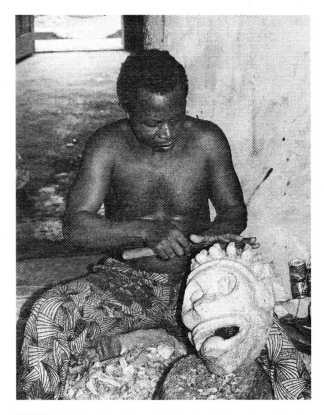

FIGURE 6–8   Yoruba sculptor finishing the knifework on a head-dress for an Egungun masquerade. Awori, Nigeria, 1981. *(Photo courtesy Henry John Drewal and Margaret Thompson Drewal.)*

relief carvings on its compound door. But even this art is not wholly secular in nature. Yoruba religion and politics complement and support each other, and, as we shall see, the Yoruba strongly believe that excellent art, by embodying goodness and rectitude, is a public confirmation of elevated political or religious status.

Yoruba Art Criticism

A thumbnail history of Western understanding of African aesthetics is contained in the following three quotations:

> It is for want of a conscious critical sense and the intellectual power of comparison and classification that the Negro has failed to create one of the great cultures of the world. (Fry, quoted in Thompson 1968:44)

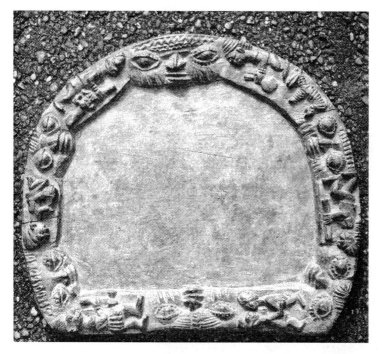

FIGURE 6–9   Ifa divination tray. *(Photograph courtesy Parkersburg [West Virginia] Art Center, from the Marietta College Permanent Collection, Marietta, Ohio.)*

> It is important for us not to deceive ourselves into believing that we can understand the intention of an African sculptor simply by looking at his work. (Willett 1971:161)

> There exists in Sub-Saharan Africa, locked in the minds of kings, priests, and commoners, a reservoir of artistic criticism. Wherever tapped, this source lends clarity to our understanding of the arts of tropical Africa. (Thompson 1973:19)

Taken together, these statements document a steady intellectual evolution, from Roger Fry's naive ethnocentrism of only seventy-odd years ago that tacitly assumed that "primitive peoples" were incapable of critical thought and subtle philosophical speculation through a growing awareness of our ignorance of the aesthetic underpinnings of art from other cultures, as seen in the second quotation from Frank Willett, and finally the conclusions of Robert Farris Thompson, whose sustained research was instrumental in revealing to Westerners several important components of the Yoruba aesthetic.

Many scholars have contributed to our knowledge of Yoruba aesthetics, and several of them combine the art historian's visual sensitivity to style and form with the cultural anthropologist's rigorous fieldwork techniques. One is

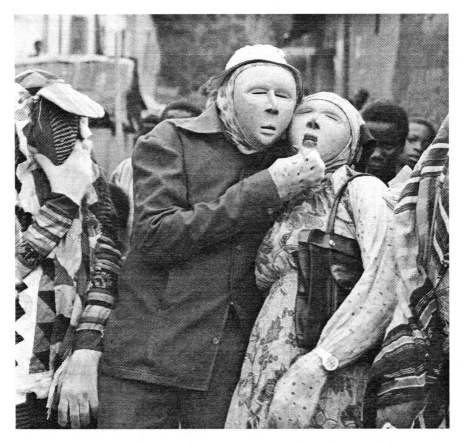

FIGURE 6–10 Humorous Egungun *idan* (miracle) performers masquerading as Europeans. Awori, Nigeria, 1981. *(Photo courtesy Henry John Drewal and Margaret Thompson Drewal.)*

Robert Farris Thompson, who since the 1960s has spent much time in West Africa interviewing Yoruba artists and critics. Although his early fieldwork was done through translators, Thompson was careful to recheck translations (using a native Yoruba speaker), both in the field and again after returning to the United States. Thompson's writing is both lucid and insightful, providing thorough descriptive material as well as thought-provoking analysis.

Thompson has shown beyond doubt that Yoruba culture does possess a living, sophisticated tradition of art criticism. He notes that although no Yoruba individuals make a full-time occupation of being art critics, criticism is a traditionally recognized activity. In fact, a Yoruba dictionary dating from 1858 has two entries that mean "knower of beauty" or "connoisseur" (Thompson 1983:5). A Yoruba art commentator may be king or commoner, male or female, artist or one who commissions art. Of the 200 art critics Thompson interviewed, twenty were farmers, "some of them of very humble economic means, who balanced the simplicity of their material possessions against the riches of their minds" (Thompson 1973:27). Despite their diversity, the critics all spoke articulately and with marked conviction in evaluating Yoruba art works, using a highly developed vocabulary that is called upon only in the context of art criticism.

Thompson describes his technique for collecting information thus:

> Artistic criticism was not requested in any village or town until data about carvers, dating of works, names of woods, and so forth had been collected. The crowd was then asked, while pieces of sculpture brought out for study were still in the sunlight, was someone willing to rank the carvings for a minimal fee and explain why he liked one piece over another? Almost without fail someone would step forward and immediately begin to criticize the sculpture. The rare delays did not stem from lack of verbal skill. Rather some informants were simply afraid that their efforts would not really be compensated. Others wished to study the works with care in the light, turning them around and testing their profile and mass. (Thompson 1973:26)

Using these techniques, Thompson collected a rich body of information from which he extracted the evaluative criteria used by Yoruba art critics. Granted, standards of art criticism exist on a different analytic level from the abstract assumptions that make up the Yoruba philosophy of art, our central concern here. However, the explicit principles of Yoruba art criticism provide the best access into the implicit ideas of Yoruba aesthetics. According to Thompson, the canons of Yoruba statuary criticism are as follows[1]:

- A Yoruba figurative carving should be "not too real and not too abstract, but somewhere in between" (Thompson 1974:26). This value, which Yoruba call *jíjora*, requires that a carved human figure should look like a person but should exhibit none of the idiosyncratic flaws that set that individual apart from others.
- A carved figure should possess *ifarahòn*, or clarity of form and line. It is desirable that the major sculptural masses be clearly demarcated and that the fine lines representing clan scars should be clearly visible. One informant told Thompson, "If you want to marry a person, you have to see the body completely" (Thompson 1973:36), and the elements of a carved figure should similarly be visible for all to see.
- A carving should also have a smooth surface, giving the piece a shining luminosity or *dìdón*. Creating such a high polish is one sign of the

---

[1] Morton (2000:6) has asserted that "The Yoruba's language of aesthetic discourse . . . [applies] across the board, whether they are evaluating the words spoken by priests, priestesses, and the chanters, or the Ifa poetry recited by their poets, or the creative products of carvers, blacksmiths, potters, weavers, or the fluid motions of dancers, and the rhythmic music of musicians."

carver's art: "The adzemarks of the master, where the edges show, shine while the adzemarks of the apprentice lack formal separation and do not shine" (Thompson 1973:37).

- Yoruba art critics are sensitive to several factors of composition. All parts of a figure should be properly positioned relative to each other, and their sizes should be correct—which is to say, neither too big nor too small.

- Surface details of carvings should be finely made, and delicacy is much appreciated.

- Roundness—in buttocks, breasts, and other major body parts—is held in high esteem, but again, only in moderation. "Excessive curved swellings" and "sinister bulges" are appropriate only in the rare portrayals of the grotesque that are made for purposes of satire, moral inquisition, and psychological warfare, situations that require carvers to violate the principles of beauty.

- Proper Yoruba sculpture usually displays a marked bilateral symmetry. The carver seeks to produce a noble, upright posture, giving figures an appearance of calm dignity.

- Yoruba art connoisseurs recognize and appreciate the carver whose work demonstrates exceptional skill. The master carver's talents are often alluded to in his oríkì, or attributive name. For example, an early twentieth-century carver named Taiwo was known far and wide by his praise name, Onípàsónòbe, which means, "possessed of a knife like a whip" (Thompson 1973:56).

- A final Yoruba canon of beauty is ephebism (òdó), or "the depiction of mankind at the optimum of physicality between the extremes of infancy and old age" (Thompson 1971:378). The Yoruba have the highest regard for the sagacity of the elders, but when they are portrayed in wood carvings, old people are flattered by being given the robust appearance of a person at the physical prime of life. On inspection, it is clear that several of the preceding principles of Yoruba art criticism derive from ephebism. A statuette should not portray the slack, wrinkled skin of old age, but the *smooth* appearance of *lustrous* skin over firm muscle, with clan scars still clearly *visible*. It should show not the stooped posture or hobbled gait of the elderly but the confidently *erect* and *symmetrical* stance of early maturity, not the withered breasts and buttocks of a grandmother but the sensual *roundness* and swelling fullness characteristic of a woman just starting her reproductive years, and, most of all, not the ungainly frame of youth but the harmoniously *proportioned*, proudly *demarcated* elements of the mature body.

Yoruba arts constitute an integrated stylistic system, so it is not surprising that the criteria of dance and music criticism parallel those for carving.

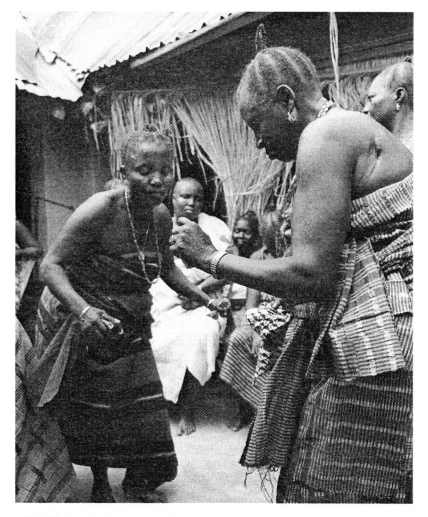

FIGURE 6–11   Odudua devotees dancing during a ceremony. Ijebu, Nigeria, 1982. *(Photo courtesy Henry John Drewal and Margaret Thompson Drewal.)*

For example, the vitality implicit in ephebism is as important in dance as it is in carving. Yoruba dancers display both athletic energy and a sensitivity to rhythmic complexity that only years of practice can give (Figure 6–11). Thus, a dancer's hands and feet may be following the four-four beat of one percussion instrument, the hips a three-four beat of another, and the back and shoulders a five-four beat of still another! But instead of executing this polyrhythmic wizardry with ostentatious bravado, the audience expects the dancer to maintain composure, as reflected in a "cool," unsmiling face (Thompson 1974:45). The principles of Yoruba art criticism, then, are complex, elaborate, and sophisticated. Taken as a whole, they constitute a unique applied aesthetic, one significantly different from Western aesthetics.[2]

Moral and Ethical Bases of Yoruba Criticism

Although these principles of Yoruba art criticism are both broad and subtle, they address only the superficial appearance of an artwork, primarily as it relates to the human form. As such, they seem arbitrary, perhaps only a rationale for sensuality. But if one looks more deeply into Yoruba philosophic assumptions, as manifest in Yoruba myth, religion, and secular belief, there emerges a profound system of reasoning from which these standards of beauty are derived.

Roy Sieber has said that African sculpture is rarely made as art for art's sake; it is, rather, art for life's sake (Sieber 1962:8). This axiom lies at the heart of Yoruba aesthetics. Most Yoruba art serves religious purposes; but the emphasis, we must be clear to say, is not on attaining spiritual enlightenment but on using religious means to attain material well-being for the population at large. Yoruba theology is thoroughly pragmatic, based on the belief that if the gods are praised, they will provide prosperity, fertility, and good health to those who honor them. (Sculptures of Yoruba *orisha* are not considered to be the gods themselves; rather, they are vehicles that link mortals with the spirit world [Lawal 1974:244]).

In artistic contexts this means that if the *orisha* are praised through beautiful art, then they will be compelled to bestow their blessings upon the mortals who present the art.[3] This reasoning accounts for several of the formal criteria of Yoruba art reported by Thompson, such as the criterion of "midpoint mimesis," which requires that a representation of a person should be generalized to the degree that it portrays the finest and best in the human form. Thompson's informants often praised a sculpture with the phrase, *nitori o jo enia*—"the image is beautiful because it resembles mankind" (Thompson 1976: Chapter 3, p. 1).

---

[2]"I would frankly doubt that curators, of whatever sensitivity, could, without careful study of the Yoruba aesthetic, make judgments which would unerringly coincide with those of the Yoruba connoisseurs. The canon of ephebism, for example, might intervene as an overlooked variable and it is not at all certain that eyes conditioned by a visual culture of abstract expressionism, Pop, and later modes are *ipso facto* in tune with the relative symmetries, straightness, and delicacy of the Yoruba round of art" (Thompson 1976: Chapter 3, p.4).

[3]Other African societies have similar beliefs. For example, Vandenhoute found that among the Dan peoples, only masks that are beautiful are thought to bring favors to mortals from their revered ancestors (cf. Gerbrands 1957:91). Similarly, many individuals among the Baule own statuettes that are meant to please a spirit lover. If this spirit lover is made to feel content, it will give both riches and children to the statuette's owner (Vogel 1979, 1980).

To please the inhabitants of the spirit world, a sculpture should possess exemplary beauty not only in physique but also in representing the highest ethical standards. This principle leads us to a still deeper level of Yoruba aesthetics, one that relates criteria of beauty to standards of ethical and moral worth. For example, the Yoruba carver focuses a disproportionately great amount of his attention on his subject's head, which is considered to be the seat of consciousness and moral capacity. The Yoruba, like other West Africans, see more in a face than Westerners commonly do. Not just the eyes, but the entire visage is, apparently, a "mirror of the soul" (cf. Abiodun 1987; Deregowski, Ellis, and Shepherd 1975; Borgatti 1982:34). Thus, heads are depicted as being overly large relative to the rest of the body, a psychological realism that conveys its own kind of truth.

The equation between sensuous beauty and ethical goodness is found again and again in Yoruba life. It has been clear for some time that the (seeming) idiosyncrasies of a language can provide useful clues for cross-cultural understanding, and that the things that appear exotic in another tongue may provide the key to unlocking the speakers' way of seeing things. In this case, the equation of goodness with beauty in sub-Saharan African languages provides a valuable insight into the aesthetics of the Yoruba and other African peoples.[4]

The equivalence between goodness and beauty prompts the question, In African thought, just what *is* goodness? In general, the cultural context of language usage shows that the criteria of goodness-and-beauty are not thought to come from natural laws or from religious revelation; they are firmly grounded in social reality. "Goodness" means ethical goodness, moral goodness; exemplary conduct is the foundation of all beauty. Consider, for example, these remarks by John Miller Chernoff, based on his many years' experience of learning the art of traditional drumming in Ghana: "My education in African music was an education in my awareness of spiritual and ethical principles, the prerequisites of the clear mind and experienced judgment I would need to play really well" (Chernoff 1979:140).

---

[4]Scholars have learned that in many African languages, the same word means both "good" and "beautiful." For example, Daniel Crowley, whose extensive fieldwork in central Africa focused on the arts of the Chokwe, has reported that although the Chokwe language has an extensive vocabulary for differentiating such things as degrees of kinship and types of musical instruments, it lacks a lexical distinction between "good" and "beautiful," both of which are termed *chimba* (Crowley 1971:322). Similarly, Harold Schneider found that in the language of the Turu of Tanzania, the word *majigha* means "beauty, a lovely thing," but "more precisely, it is a voluntary action which makes people happy" (Schneider 1966:158). In a review of the literature on this subject, Leiris and Delange note additional African languages in which "good" and "beautiful" are expressed by the same, or closely related, terms. In some cases, however, the situation appears to be more complex. For example, the Bulu, in Southern Cameroon, are said to "use the word *abeñ* (beauty) when speaking of a woman, a house or the weather, while other words are used indiscriminately to describe 'good' or 'fine' " (Leiris and Delange 1968:42).

Returning to Yoruba we find that here too language illuminates the relationship between goodness and beauty. The Nigerian art historian, Babatunde Lawal, himself a Yoruba, has reported that the word *ewá* refers to manifest beauty, but that it has two distinctly different levels of meaning. *Ewá ode,* or "facial beauty," refers to the outer beauty of a thing—the attractive appearance of an object or the sensuous good looks of a person. But *ewá inu,* "inner beauty," refers to the genuine, intrinsic worth of a thing. In an inanimate object, this utilitarian value is paramount, far exceeding the importance of outer beauty. Thus, "a good-looking but fragile cutlass is useless and is dismissed as . . . superficial beauty" (Lawal 1974).

In man or woman, the inner beauty of *ewá inu* is determined by the person's *iwà,* or character. The concept of *iwà* leads us to a still deeper level of Yoruba aesthetic theory. Lawal says,

> *Iwà* is the very stuff which makes life a joy because not only does it please *Olorun* (the High-God), it also endears one to the hearts of all men. . . . The person who is outwardly beautiful but inwardly ugly or lacks character is called *awobowà* (literally skin covers character). . . . The physical beauty of such a person may be at first admired, but as soon as his inner ugliness surfaces he becomes repulsive. His beauty is immediately beclouded by the flames of his character: for the Yoruba see character as manifesting itself like a flame. (Lawal 1974:240–241)

A Yoruba verse quoted by Thompson (1983:11) shows the importance attached to personal character:

> A man may be very, very handsome
> Handsome as a fish within the water
> But if he has no character
> He is no more than a wooden doll.

Iwà: Good Character

The Nigerian art historian Rowland Abiodun has written that *iwà* "pertains not so much to the superficial physical appearance of things as to their deep essence in Yorùbá culture and metaphysics" (1990:66), going on to note that it "can mean either 'character' or 'existence'" (ibid.:67).[5] What are the essential traits of *iwà*? They are perhaps best summed up by the words *harmonious energy*—a phrase that finally stands at the very foundation of Yoruba aesthetic thought. Thus, we must examine the implications of harmony and energy in the world of Yoruba society and art.

---

[5] Abiodun also says that *iwà* applies directly to artists themselves, calling for such traits of "gentle character," "good hearing,," and "teachableness, obedience, and understanding" (Abiodun 1990:78).

The person of good character maintains *harmony*, as it were, in two different dimensions. From a diachronic perspective, he or she lives in accord with the ancestors and the storehouse of Yoruba tradition that has been handed down from the past and that perpetuates the beliefs and institutions of the forebearers. However, from a synchronic perspective, Yoruba culture encourages harmony with one's contemporary social environment. The Yoruba expect all adults to maintain a cooperative spirit in dealing with others and to be submissive to legitimate authority, be it the political authority of the king or the familial authority of the clan headman, the *bale*.

This goal of harmonious living has many implications for day-to-day Yoruba life. Emotions should always be kept in check, and one should maintain a tranquil countenance, whether engaging in a heated political debate or participating in a vigorous dance. Lawal states, "*Iwà* fosters social harmony among men, thereby generating law and order in society" (Lawal 1974:247). Of course, the high value placed on harmonious living makes good sense in Yoruba culture, with its traditionally high level of urbanism and also with all the psychosocial challenges of living together in large house compounds, where many extended family members are in continual, face-to-face contact with each other. The Yoruba recognize the importance of people getting along with each other. As a consequence, harmony stands as a pillar of the Yoruba value system.

The quest for harmonious living is reflected in Yoruba art and aesthetics in several ways, such as the recurrent concern with *moderation*. Recall, for example, that carved statuettes ought to be neither too realistic nor too idealized; body parts should be clearly delineated but not exaggerated; surfaces have to be curved but "sinister bulges" must be avoided; and sculpture should be compositionally balanced, with a high level of bilateral symmetry.[6]

The performing arts of the Yoruba also reflect a respect for social harmony. No matter how energetic the choreography or how demanding the polyrhythmic beat of the drums, a Yoruba dancer should not spin about the dance area with abandon but must maintain control, staying "inside" the tempo, keeping a "cool" look on his face (cf. Thompson 1971). The content of Yoruba art reflects a similar concern with maintaining social equilibrium. For example, the songs composed for Ẹfẹ Night often ridicule individuals who have been antisocial during the preceding year (cf. Drewal 1973:92).

The striving for *harmony* in Yoruba art and culture is not the whole story, however. A life of total accord, devoid of creative novelty and social friction, is

---

[6]Lawal notes that this striving for harmonious moderation leads to an interesting dilemma in Yoruba ideas about human beauty. For example, although tall, good-looking, well-complexioned men are, in theory, the most handsome, "beauty is also seen in the mean (*iwontún wonsi*), i.e., average height, complexion and looks. In fact most Yoruba would prefer the mean because while the extremely ugly is often despised, the extremely beautiful is often held suspect" (Lawal 1974:239).

as stultifying in theory as it is impossible in practice; and the ideal of "harmonious *energy*" brings distinctly different values into play. Energy is conveyed by the Yoruba term *àṣẹ*, an important word that denotes "authority" and carries connotations of "spiritual command, the power-to-make-things-happen, God's own enabling light rendered accessible to men and women" (Thompson 1983:5). Power, growth, and individual uniqueness are basic character attributes, and little thought is needed to see that these too are not arbitrary values but spring from vital concerns of life. To ensure protection from dangers such as drought, disease, and foreign invaders, one must be physically strong; and to provide for the welfare of one's family, one must lead a vigorous, active life. Moreover, although Yoruba culture is hierarchical and has distinctly conservative tendencies, Yoruba social life also includes a measure of competitiveness. In the political arena, for example, the self-made man can rise to a position of some power (Barbar 1981:724). All these needs and wishes require an outlay of energy.

A striving for energy, power, and prosperity is, if anything, even more apparent in Yoruba art than is the quest for harmony. The pre-eminent value of ephebism, of portraying individuals at their peak of physical dynamism, springs from *àṣẹ*, but so do such stylistic details as the flexed legs so often seen in carved figures. The feeling of equipoise conveyed by a carving's bilateral symmetry contrasts with its powerful lower body that, from the tense angle at the hip and knee, seem ready to send the subject leaping into the air.

As with harmony, the Yoruba striving for energy has both synchronic and diachronic aspects. An individual should have power in the present, but one's influence and renown should also continue into the future. Thus, since tomorrow is in the hands of the next generation, considerations of reproduction and sexuality play a role in Yoruba moral and aesthetic thought. The Yoruba place a high value on having many healthy children, and this too influences the plastic and performing arts. Women's breasts nourish suckling infants, so Yoruba art critics praise statuettes of women with breasts that are thought to show promise of feeding many children.[7]

Perhaps because there are few visible indications of an individual's fertility, the reproductive emphasis in Yoruba arts often extends to secondary sexual characteristics. In practical terms, men's muscular arms, legs, and torsos provide food and protection for their families, but when found in Yoruba sculpture and dance, these traits are handsome in themselves. Similarly, smooth, lustrous skin combines practical and sensual considerations. Such skin is an indication of good health and personal hygiene, but again it is considered to be intrinsically—and erotically—beautiful. Sizable buttocks may reflect the luxuries of the ample diet available to a prosperous family, and (as

---

[7]Interestingly, the Anang, the Yoruba's not-too-distant neighbors, prefer carvings of women with pendulous breasts, evidence that they have already fed many children.

has been hypothesized by Tobias [1961] concerning steatopygous San women) they may provide nutritional insurance for a nursing mother during periods of food shortage. But these practical factors merge with a sensual and aesthetic appeal. They reflect present wealth and prosperity, and at the same time they contribute to the well-being of the next generation.

The core Yoruba value of *àṣẹ*, or dynamic power and growth, informs art on several different levels. In sculpture *àṣẹ* justifies sensuous ephebism and vitality; it provides a rationale for the pulsing energy of music and dance; and it engenders a creative force in the arts as a whole. Drewal and Drewal (1983) believe that the wide diversity they found in Gẹlẹdẹ dance is a direct consequence of the inventiveness and spirit of growth that permeates Yoruba culture and art.

In Yoruba thought, anything that is beautiful is necessarily *good*, not just aesthetically but also socially, politically, and ethically (Figure 6–12). But the

FIGURE 6-12   Araba, the head Ifa priest of the community, dancing during Ifa festival. Lagos, Nigeria, 1977. *(Photo courtesy Henry John Drewal and Margaret Thompson Drewal.)*

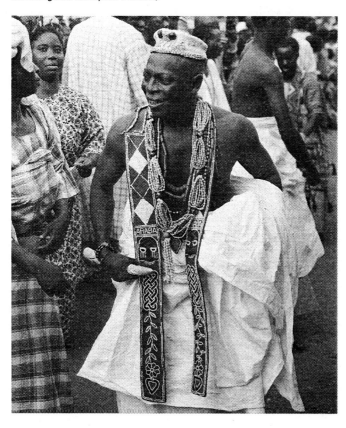

Yoruba philosophy of art is more than an after-the-fact rationalization for the superiority of the Yoruba elite. At its foundation, art makes a crucial contribution to Yoruba culture by conveying the fundamental theme of *harmonious energy*. This concept is important because it embodies a basic existential contradiction. On the one hand, when Yoruba art, through its subject matter and stylistic conventions, admonishes people to lead lives of *harmony*, it is calling for acquiescence to authority, obedience to custom, and ultimately a reliance on the security of hearth and home. *Energy*, by contrast, requires a person to increase his or her own income and autonomy, usually at the expense of others, or else to abandon traditional life ways in order to forge new means of success. At the very least, the energetic life requires one to leave the safe haven of home in search of a spouse with whom to raise a family and to prosper. Thus, the imperatives of harmony and energy inevitably pull in opposite directions, and the wonder of Yoruba art lies in its combining these contradictory motives. Think again of the dancers of the Ẹfẹ/Gẹlẹdẹ cult who opened this chapter. Their choreographic style says, "Live well with others, but develop your own potentialities too." The merits of such a message are clear. In his *Flash of the Spirit*, a study of the aesthetic influences of Black Africa on the arts and cultures of Black Americans in the New World, Robert Farris Thompson has argued that "a civilization like that of the Yoruba, and the Yoruba-Americans, pulsing with ceaseless creativity rightly stabilized by precision and control, will safeguard the passage of its people through the storms of time" (Thompson 1983:97).

Phrased in these terms, Yoruba art addresses a universal human problem, a dilemma faced by every person in all societies—namely, the precarious balance between social cohesion and individual autonomy. Everyone ultimately must ask, How can I conform to the demands of society and still be true to myself? Yoruba art does not dispel or resolve the predicament, but by simultaneously embodying principles of both harmony and energy, it says unequivocally that neither goal should be pursued to the extreme, that each must always be balanced and held in check by the other.

Conclusion: The Metaphysical Basis of Yoruba Art

The literature on Yoruba art is quite rich, but most of it is focused on its capacity to convey important—indeed profound—social and ethical messages. But there is evidence of yet another, more conceptual, level of Yoruba aesthetics. In fact, the existence of such a metaphysical foundation for Yoruba art should have been expected. After all, how could a culture invest art with such vital information unless it attributes to art a communicative efficacy of considerable power?

Margaret and Henry Drewal have suggested one source of art's power in Yoruba thought. Based on extensive fieldwork, they have reexamined the

Yoruba concept of *àṣẹ*, that is, "energy" or "authority." As noted earlier, *àṣẹ* applies to personal behavior, as exemplified by the vitality of a master drummer or the stamina of a consummate dancer, but the Drewals have learned that *àṣẹ* also has a more abstract meaning as a "sheer activating [or] generative force" (Drewal and Drewal 1987:225). In Yoruba intellectual thought, *àṣẹ* is conceptualized as wind; inasmuch as speech is impelled by wind from the speaker's lungs, words are believed to have a power all their own. Words that are uttered in ritual contexts (in the form of proverbs, songs, and incantations) can actually make things happen; and when many voices speak as one, as in the songs sung by the hundreds of participants and observers in Ẹfẹ ceremonies, the words have an irresistible force (Drewal and Drewal 1987:226).

The Yoruba scholar, Rowland Abiodun, claims that the power of *àṣẹ* is dependent upon yet another Yoruba concept, *Ọrọ̀*. A passage from the Yoruba creation story provides a valuable clue regarding *Ọrọ̀* and the metaphysical foundation of art. According to the oral literature associated with Ifa divination, at some time in the mythic past the high god, Olodumare, "realized that he needed an intermediary force, since he was too charged with energy to come into contact with any living thing and have it survive" (Abiodun 1987:254). Therefore, he produced the three seminal elements of creation: *ogbón* (wisdom), *ìmọ̀* (knowledge), and *òye* (understanding), known collectively as *Ọrọ̀*. Holding them in the palm of his hand, Olodumare told Wisdom, Knowledge, and Understanding to fly away and look for a place of their own to live. None was successful, however, and one by one they flew back to him, causing an annoying, bee-like din. Olodumare then swallowed them. This situation prevailed for a long, long time, but eventually Olodumare lost patience with the incessant humming of the three energized entities in his stomach. To get some peace for himself, he expelled them and ordered them to go down to earth, an event that Abiodun describes in dramatic terms: "Since they were heavily charged lifeforces from heaven, their descent was accompanied by lightning and thunder. All solid matter melted and became jell-like. For a while, *Ọrọ̀* was suspended in mid-air like an egg and did not melt, but then it dropped to earth and split" (Abiodun 1987:255).

On earth, Abiodun says, *Ọrọ̀* is associated with several things: On a literal level it is identified with Ifa, the *orisha* of divination, and in particular with the proverbs *(Òwe)* that the *babalawos* use to divine the future; but of central interest to us is the fact that by extension *Òwe* "can metaphorically apply to the communicative properties of sculpture, dance, drama, song, chant, poetry, [and] incantations" (Abiodun 1987:255). Thus, the Yoruba conceptualize the verbal and visual ritual arts as *earthly incarnations of divine Wisdom, Knowledge, and Understanding.*

There is another way to portray this situation: In Yoruba thought there are two kinds of beings, the "people here on earth" *(Ará Ayé)* and the "beings in heaven" *(Ará Òrun)* (Abiodun 1987:256), and each category has a profound need for the other. For their part, divine Wisdom, Knowledge, and Understanding are too energetic and restless to remain in heaven: They require earth as their dwelling. At the same time, mortals must have the help of the deities on high in solving their own mundane problems. Significantly, art provides both parties with a means to meet their needs. *Òrò* descends to earth via the oral literature of Ifa divination, and, reciprocally, the performing and visual arts provide a channel or conduit whereby the individual can communicate with *Orí-isese*, the "primal head" in heaven.

These are by no means simple ideas, and much detail has been omitted (Figure 6–13). Further, the situation is likely to become more complex as scholars pursue additional research along these lines. For example, a rough congruity is emerging between accounts of Yoruba aesthetics based on Yoruba art criticism (by Robert Farris Thompson), *Ifa* divination (by Rowland Abiodun), Yoruba everyday language (by Babatunde Lawal), and the moral philosophy expounded by Yoruba traditional herbal healers (as reported in Hallen 2000). But already it is clear that the visual and performative sophistication of Yoruba art is matched by an equally complex body of abstract, philosophical thought that attributes to art a central role in both Yoruba society and Yoruba intellectual culture.

Epilogue

Robert Farris Thompson has observed that at one time, "Yoruba traditional culture and religious art had seemed destined for total obliteration in the

FIGURE 6–13   Gęlędę masks dancing in Ijio, Nigeria. *(Photo by Doig Simmonds, Courtesy of Babatunde Lawal, Virginia Commonwealth University.)*

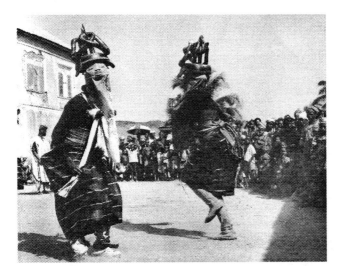

wake of the slave trade, civil wars, and modernization" (1983:16). But as he goes on to demonstrate, the Yoruba people and their system of aesthetic thought had more than sufficient vitality—the "flash of the spirit," to use his phrase—to overcome these threats and to thrive in modern times. Not only are Yoruba arts still found in traditional communities in southwestern Nigeria, but in other settings they have evolved in several surprising ways.

For one thing, when Yoruba were brought as slaves to North and South America and the Caribbean, much of their culture came with them. But soon, a transformation began whereby elements of Yoruba belief combined with the ideas of slaves who had come from other parts of West and Central Africa, plus an admixture of elements from Western Europe. For example, a wide-ranging syncretism occurred between Roman Catholicism and traditional Yoruba *orisha*-based religion. "Thus," Thompson says, "the Virgin Mary was sometimes equated with the sweet and gentle aspect of the multifaceted goddess of the river, Oshun. Thus Shàngó, the Yoruba thunder god, in Cuba was frequently equated with Saint Barbara, whose killers were struck dead by God with lightning" (Thompson 1984:17–18). Thompson goes on (1983:18–99) to give a detailed account of the process whereby several other *orishas* were transformed in the New World. In a later work, he gives a richly nuanced description of numerous altars constructed for Esu, Ogun, and other *orishas*, not only in West Africa but also in the Americas, from New York City to Buenos Aires, noting Yoruba elements in the performances of such icons of popular culture as Desi Arnaz and Carmen Miranda (1994:228). As an example of the complex cultural roots of some religious altars created by African Americans in the New World, Thompson describes one in southern Brazil, made by a woman who followed a syncretic religion called Umbanda (Figure 6–14). "Umbanda," Thompson says, "blends Kardecist spiritualism from France with Roman Catholic elements, plus the names and concepts of the *òrìsà*, plus some of the principal animate medicines of God from Kongo, plus romanticized Native American images from the forests of the interior of Brazil. The mix is rich" (ibid.: 233).

But the river of culture change seldom runs predictably, and a countercurrent to such syncretism emerged in the United States in response to the Black Power movement. Of particular relevance is the creation in 1970, near Sheldon, South Carolina, of Oyotunji, a village based on traditional Yoruba cultural principles. According to John Mason, "Oyotunji served as the focal point in the United States for the renaissance of traditional Yoruba art from earlier times. There was a conscious, all-out effort to remove Catholic/slave vestiges from Yoruba worship and to reclaim the best parts of an ancient and valued past in order to build a free and enlightened future" (1994:244). Significantly, the founder of Oyojunji, an African American named Oseijeman, and another leader, Babalosa Orisamola Awolowo, were both trained as artists. According to Mason, they "spearheaded [a Yoruba] art revival and . . .

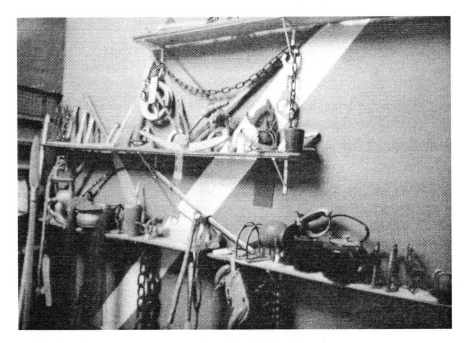

FIGURE 6–14   Umbanda Ogun shrine. Rio Grande, Brazil. *(Courtesy of Robert Farris Thompson.)*

served as inspirational models for a host of young artists who visited, studied, or lived at Oyotunji" (ibid.:244). Thirty years after its creation, although small, Oyotunji residents (and their frequent visitors) still follow traditional Yoruba religion and culture and carry out an annual round of ritual celebrations.

Meanwhile, the Yoruba artistic impulse has also been in flux in Nigeria. Several individuals such as Yemi Bisiri and Romuald Hazoume have endeavored to merge the theory and motifs of Yoruba art with Western fine arts traditions. Perhaps the best known of this group is a man born as Taiwo Olaniui Salau but who works under the name Twins Seven-Seven (a reference to his being the only survivor of seven sets of twins in his family). Twins Seven-Seven, whose creative efforts were initially channeled into music and dance, began by working on paper but then changed to drawing on plywood (Figure 6–15). About his work, André Magnin says, "With the exception of a few paintings which represent 'profane' themes (for example, a satirical painting that portrays politicians as animals), the universe of Twins Seven-Seven is thoroughly rooted in Yoruba visionary imagery, both religious and folkloric. In this regard, the very rich pantheon of the Yoruba religion constitutes a powerful stimulus to creation, verbal as much as pictorial or sculptural" (1996:61).

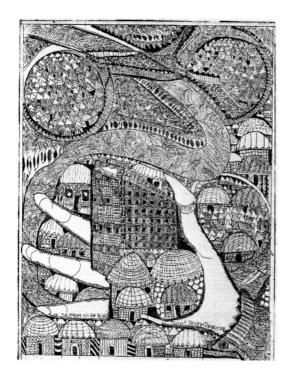

FIGURE 6-15 Twins Seven-Seven, of Oshogbo, Nigeria, *Lagos in the Palm of an Architect*, etching, 12 x 9. *(Photo courtesy Indigo Arts Gallery.)*

Twins Seven-Seven's first foray into the visual arts came about as a result of a chance meeting with some members of the Mbari Mbayo Club, a group of artists in the town of Oshogbo, and the Oshogbo School represents one more permutation in Yoruba art and aesthetics (cf. Kennedy 1992:58–86). Although traditional arts had disappeared from the bustling trading center of Oshogbo, several elaborate "Brazilian" or "San Salvador" houses were built there, reflecting a style brought back to Nigeria by returning slaves in the nineteenth century. Moreover, the town was the site of a large annual festival celebrating the local king's legendary first meeting with the goddess Oshun. In 1950, Suzanne Wenger, an Austrian painter who had been working in Paris, moved to Oshogbo. She was fascinated by Yoruba culture and undertook formal study of Yoruba poetry and philosophy under a widely respected cult leader named Ajagemo. Eventually, Wenger changed her name to Iwin Funmike Adunni and was made a "priestess" by traditional religionists in Oshogbo (Kennedy 1992:61). Before his death, Ajagemo asked Wenger to start rebuilding cult houses for local *orishas*. Working with local people, the shrines Wenger built represent a striking synthesis of styles. Wenger has said that she was "using the language of the local flora and fauna as well as the local religion and philosophy" (quoted in Kennedy 1962:61).

In 1950, German-born Ulli Beier also left Paris for Africa. Beier took a position teaching English at the University of Ibadan (Nigeria), but soon the widely traveled professor and author took up residence in Oshogbo, living in the compound of Duro Ladipo. Besides being a school teacher, Ladipo himself was a musician. After a musical success at a cultural center in Ibadan called the Mbari Club, he returned to Oshogbo to set up the Mbari Mbayo Club. The club became a hotbed of all sorts of artistic activity, ranging from music and theater to the visual arts. Also instrumental in supporting the movement was Georgina Beier, a London-born artist and the wife of Ulli Beier, who came to Nigeria in 1959.

Suzanne Wenger, Ulli Beier, and Georgina Beier, each in his or her own way, encouraged and promoted a generation of African artists, individuals who came from all over the continent and whose work was recognized throughout the world. The Yoruba artist Twins Seven-Seven, mentioned above, is a case in point: In the summer of 1964 Georgina Beier organized a week-long printmaking workshop in Oshogbo. The event "was attended by actors from Duro Ladipo's theater troupe who participated as much out of curiosity as any notion of future careers. They were joined by passers-by and the result was a kind of festival of activity. During this workshop, the talents of four more artists—Adebisi Fabunmi, Muraina Oyelami, Jimoh Buraimoh, and *Twins Seven-Seven*—emerged" (Kennedy 1992:70, emphasis added).

Thus, as elsewhere in the world, recent decades have not witnessed the extinction of Yoruba arts. Rather, they have been transformed in ways that could not have been predicted but that reflect the complex interplay between cultures that has taken place. Some traditional arts are still practiced, but to them have been added works that are breathtaking in their vitality and uniqueness.

Further Reading

The corpus of published literature on Yoruba art and culture is daunting in size. Bascom (1969) provides a succinct overview of traditional Yoruba social institutions. Detailed descriptions of the elaborate ceremonies of the Efẹ/Gẹlẹdẹ cult appear in Drewal 1973, Drewal and Drewal 1983, and Lawall 1996.

Yoruba art in itself has prompted a significant body of writing in English. A concise statement of Thompson's findings on Yoruba art connoisseurship appeared in *Art News* (1968); a later book (1974), broadened his analysis to include Yoruba music and dance. The artist in Yoruba society—primarily, the visual artist—is the focus of Bascom (1973a) as is a later volume edited by Abiodun, Drewal, and Pemberton (1994).

Substantial commentaries on Yoruba religion, philosophy, and aesthetics are Bascom (1991/1969), Lawal (1974), Abiodun (1987, 1990), and Hallen (2000).

Oyotunji Village is the subject of Hunt (1979) and Mason (1994). The arts of the African Diaspora are the subject of Thompson (1983, 1994). Both Magnin (1996) and Kennedy (1992) provide excellent surveys of contemporary fine art developments in Africa, including Yoruba art generally and the events at Oshogbo in particular.

7

AZTEC AESTHETICS

Flower and Song

Jade shatters,
the quetzal feather tears apart.
Oh God, you mock us.
Perhaps we really do not exist.

(León-Portilla 1971:448)

The aesthetics of the pre-Hispanic Aztecs deserve our attention for several reasons. For one thing, the Aztecs, along with the Olmecs, Mayas, and other Mesoamerican societies, made a prodigious quantity of artwork, most of it reflecting superlative standards of craftsmanship. Also, these states, like the handful of other complex civilizations that emerged during the long course of human history, possessed a high level of economic specialization, with some people farming, some trading, some producing artworks—and some creating an intricate aesthetic system, one that was discussed extensively and, at times, hotly debated.

Another compelling reason to examine Aztec aesthetics is that the New World civilizations are usually thought to have developed independently of Old World traditions. Therefore, if parallels exist between New and Old World aesthetics, they are unlikely to have resulted from diffusion but probably represent independent, convergent development. And this in turn has an important bearing on the question, To what extent do aesthetic systems reflect fundamental, pan-human predispositions toward art?

The Aztecs in Mesoamerican History

When the Spanish Conquistadors arrived in the early sixteenth century, they found a land dominated from the Gulf Coast to the Pacific, from the deserts of north-central Mexico to the forests of Guatemala, by the mighty military state of the Aztecs. A few small groups existed as autonomous enclaves, but the Aztecs, ruling from their capital of Tenochtitlán,[1] were the lords of the land.

Tenochtitlán itself was a wonder to the Spaniards. Built on an island in Lake Texcoco (which is now dry land, the site of modern Mexico City), Tenochtitlán had a population of perhaps 200,000 (see Figures 7–1 and 7–2). In all the world, only Paris and Istanbul were larger at that time. The biggest city the conquistadors were likely to have seen, Seville, Spain, was less than one-third the size of Tenochtitlán. The city's massive stone architecture, including impressively decorated temples, had few European parallels and the fine arts flourished there in a way envied by many Europeans of the day. For example, Albrecht Dürer, after viewing some of the spoils of conquest, wrote, "All the days of my life I have seen nothing that rejoiced my heart such as these things, for I saw amongst them wonderful works of art and I marveled at the subtle ingenuity of men in foreign lands" (quoted in Fraser 1971:25).

The impressive Aztec state of 1520 represented the culmination of several thousands of years of economic, political, and cultural change in Mesoamerica. Before about 10,000 years ago, two different groups existed in the area. Now called the Big Game Hunters and the Seed Gatherers, their names accurately reflect a significant difference in subsistence specialization. A decline in the availability of large game animals, such as mammoth, llama, and bison, gradually tipped the balance in favor of the better adapted Seed Gatherers. Around 8,000 years ago, these peoples took a step that was unprecedented in the New World and that eventually had enormous consequences: They started encouraging some plants to grow when and where they met human requirements, rather than tailoring human needs to the plants' natural life cycles. In doing this, these early Native Americans started down the path that led to agriculture. Eventually, maize (corn), beans, squash, and many other plants were domesticated, and by 4,000 years ago, some groups in central and southern Mesoamerica had become full-time farmers.

As in the other areas of the world that witnessed the "Neolithic Revolution," Mesoamerican farmers eventually developed the whole constellation of traits associated with civilization. As farming became more intensive, the formerly nomadic hunter-gatherers found they could support not only permanent villages but also larger and larger urban centers, culminating in ceremonial centers inhabited by priests and graced with monumental architecture. The division of labor became far more complex, and calendars and record-keeping systems came into use. Development was not an even, gradual

---

[1]Regarding the pronunciation of Aztec words, all letters have the same sound as in Spanish except that *h*s are aspirated as in the English *hog; x* is pronounced as in the English *sh;* and the sound indicated by *tl* is pronounced as a single consonant, not as two distinct consonants, the same being true for *tz.* Stress is usually on the next to the last syllable, with exceptions, such as Tenochtitlán, indicated by an accent mark.

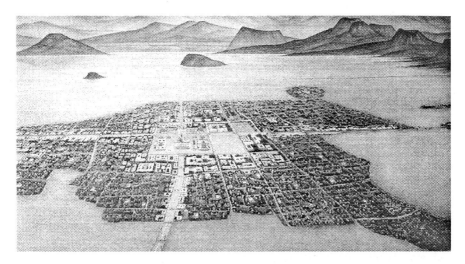

FIGURE 7-1   The city of Tenochtitlán, as conceived by Luis Covarrubias, Mural in the National Museum of Anthropology, Mexico City. *(Courtesy National Museum of Anthropology.)*

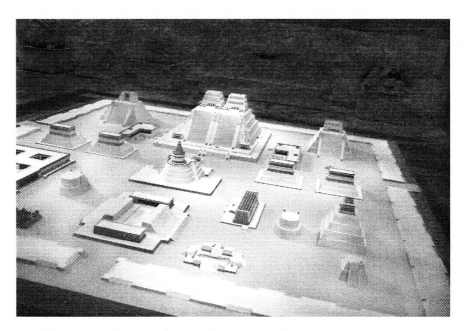

FIGURE 7-2   Model of the city of Tenochtitlán, as conceived by Luis Covarrubias as it may have looked before the Spanish arrived. National Museum of Anthropology, Mexico City. *(Courtesy National Museum of Anthropology.)*

process, but instead there was a succession of different peoples and places at the forefront of change. Olmec culture, near the Atlantic coast of southern Mexico, flourished from about 1500 B.C.E. to 400 B.C.E. During the later so-called "Classic" Period from 300 A.D. to 900 A.D., the distinctive Mayan civilization emerged in what is now southern Mexico, northern Guatemala, and neighboring regions. At about the same time, Zapotec culture flourished to the west in Oaxaca, and in central Mexico the city of Teotihuacán was the center of a third vigorous culture.

Toward the end of the Classic Period, all three of these kingdoms fell into disarray, due at least in part to incoming Chichimec ("barbarian") groups from the north. Arriving with the simpler hunter-gatherer technology of the ancient Seed Gatherers, these nomads quickly adopted the sedentary, horticultural lifestyle of the people they had invaded. One such group was the Toltecs, who were to build a spectacular city at Tula, not far from the fallen Teotihuacán, and who established their own political hegemony in the Valley of Mexico until, in the twelfth century, they too fell to later waves of newcomers. The Toltecs are particularly relevant here because they spoke a Nahuatl language and were eventually adopted as the putative forebears of another Nahuatl-speaking group of hunter-gatherer-fighters that arrived from the north in the thirteenth century, the Aztecs.

The Aztecs' legendary histories claimed that around 1300 they began their travels at Aztlán (hence their current name, Aztec). Along the way, their own principal deity, Huitzilopochtli ("Hummingbird-on-the-left"), a god of sun and war, told them that they were destined to rule the world and that they should change their name to "Mexica," after the place he told them to go, the Valley of Mexico. Spurned there by the earlier residents, the Aztecs eventually settled on an inhospitable island in Lake Texcoco, founding their city of Tenochtitlán in 1337. Within a hundred years, they were rapidly expanding their influence by warfare and alliance to become the most powerful single state in Mexico. By 1502, their capital of Tenochtitlán had grown to 200,000, and their empire extended over most of Mesoamerica. It was this realm that Hernán Cortés encountered upon his arrival in the New World in 1519.

The Aztec hegemony lasted only from about 1480 to 1520. By 1521, the Spanish had conquered Tenochtitlán and the Aztec empire was in ruins. Several factors led to the rapid defeat of the Aztecs, not the least of which was the willingness of many of the peoples whom the Aztecs had conquered to side with the Spanish against the Aztecs.[2]

---

[2]The surveys of Aztec culture by Carrasco (1998) and M. Smith (1996) both discuss the numerous factors that lead to the Spanish conquest of the Aztecs. It is not certain, however, that the Aztecs initially welcomed the Spanish because they thought that Cortés was their god Quetzalcoatl, returned from the East, and that his arrival fulfilled an ancient Aztec myth and more recent omens and signs. Gillespie (1989:173-201) believes this thesis to be a post-contact

Our Knowledge of Aztec Thought

Excavations in Mesoamerica began in 1839, and since that time a wealth of artifacts and information has been uncovered by the archaeologist's shovel and trowel. Scholars usually face the task of reconstructing the past by studying the mute bones and stones of a forgotten era, but evidence of the late Mesoamerican civilizations exists in another valuable form—the written word. Since the 1950s, there has been a steady growth in the field known as ethnohistory, a discipline that gleans information about no-longer extant cultures by examining written documents dating from the era when the society still existed. For the Aztecs, such resources are comparatively rich. Like the other areas of the world where the Neolithic Revolution ran its course, Mesoamerica developed notation systems for record-keeping—at first for dates and the individual names, but later for more complex information. The Spanish conquerors found native Aztec libraries of codices (singular, codex) that dealt at length with such topics as history, astronomy, and astrology by use of pictographs and ideographs (see Figure 7–3).

Although the European invaders destroyed much of this native literature, they themselves created an extensive body of what amounts to Aztec ethnography. Eight years after the collapse of the Aztec Empire, a Franciscan missionary, Fra Bernadino de Sahagun, arrived in "New Spain" and began (along with several other early Spanish chroniclers) two decades of systematically recording the beliefs and customs of the Aztecs. Sahagun and his Aztec "research assistants"—young men of the nobility who would have become priests had the Spanish not arrived—collected information on a wide range of subjects. Between the deductions from the archaeological record and the commentary in such ethnohistorical sources as these, we have a surprisingly complete picture of life in a complex, thoroughly non-Western culture as it existed nearly 500 years ago.

Aztec Culture

The Aztec Empire was far too complex a social system to be analyzed here in detail, but a few of its features require brief mention. With regard to its economy, remarkably fertile "floating gardens" *(chinampas)* in Lake Texcoco produced as many as seven harvests per year. In addition, conquered territories had to pay large amounts of food to Tenochtitlán as tribute. Aztec documents reveal that every year the capital received tens of millions of pounds of corn, beans, and other foodstuffs, as well as many cotton cloaks, shields, feathers, precious stones, and other items.

---

construction, created by the Aztec nobility in an effort to understand and rationalize their defeat.

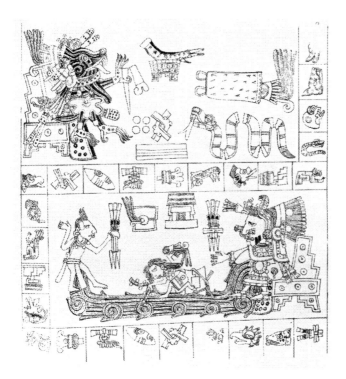

FIGURE 7–3   A page from the Codex Borgiano, probably of Aztec origin. *(Courtesy, Field Museum of Natural History, Chicago, neg. no. 2561.)*

Aztec society was composed of twenty ranked clans, each with many lineages that were also ranked, ranging from the highest aristocratic families from which members of the priesthood were drawn, to the larger, lower clans of land-holding farmers. The vast infrastructure of the Empire, from priests and bureaucrats to temple schools and the army, was supported through taxes paid by the farming populace. Such a structure provided kinship bonds among the Aztec people and embodied a hierarchical spirit that permeated Aztec society. Above the twenty clans was the family of the emperor and below them was a large population of non-Aztec laborers (including guilds of artists and craftsmen), largely drawn from conquered tribes and chiefdoms. Although they were bound for life to their trade or to the Aztec families they worked for, these individuals were not quite slaves, inasmuch as they could own property, maintain families, and see their children grow up to become free men and women. *Pochteca,* or traders, made up another growing class in the last years of the Empire. All Aztec men, including priests, periodically bore arms for the state, and an atmosphere of militarism colored Aztec life and thought.

Aztec religious practice lay primarily in the hands of a priesthood that was both influential and numerous—Tenochtitlán alone probably had 5,000 priests. Their chief responsibility was a series of ritual ceremonies that recurred annually and was organized into an elaborate fifty-two-year cycle. Aztec priests and commoners alike thought that their gods had created the world and everything in it through strenuous effort and dramatic sacrifice, thus placing mortals in their great debt. Humans, they believed, were obliged to repay this debt, but there was a pervasive fear that such efforts would ultimately fail and that the four prior creations and destructions of the world would soon be followed by a fifth cataclysm, probably at some crucial juncture of the fifty-two-year ritual cycle. Only through their gifts of sacred energy to Huitzilopochtli, Tlaloc, and the other deities might this apocalypse be forestalled.

Aztec Art

Like people in other complex societies, the Aztecs produced and consumed much art. Part-time artisans, working in their homes, made utilitarian goods in a wide range of media, including items woven from native cotton as well as from the fibers from maguey plant, pottery vessels, and tools made from obsidian and copper. By contrast, the workshops of full-time specialists supplied their elite patrons with luxury goods, such as jewelry and stone sculptures. (Aztec myth had it that their ancestors were first taught stoneworking, as well as weaving, by the plumed serpent deity, Quetzalcoatl.) The most spectacular Aztec art form was architecture. Commoners' houses and secular public buildings were modest in design, but temples were ambitiously large stone structures that included huge, stepped pyramids on whose truncated tops stood small wooden structures. In most cases, large stone figures surrounded the pyramid's base (see Figure 7–4) and brightly painted mural frescoes decorated the pyramid itself. Small items, both religious and decorative in purpose, were also carved in stone. Wood carving also was practiced, but little of it remains today.

As we might expect in such a hierarchically oriented society, elaborate body decoration distinguished members of one social level from another, as well as one individual from another. Aristocratic women, perhaps with the aid of obsidian mirrors, used yellow coloring, derived from insects and cooking oil, to color their skins. They also scented their bodies with perfumes, and they chewed gum to freshen their breath. Bray (1968) gives this account of Aztec clothes and ornamentation:

> The Mexicans loved display and were uninhibited in their use of jewelry and such accessories as fans, fly-whisks, and head-dresses made of green or red feathers. Beads were made of rare stones or of gold cast into the form of crabs, scorpions, birds, or sea shells, and necklaces were hung with bells which tinkled

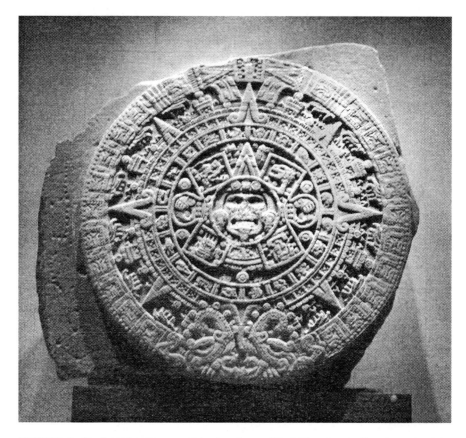

FIGURE 7–4 The Aztec Sun Stone, a olivine basalt monolith, 3.57 meters in diameter and weighing 24.5 tons. Originally part of the High Temple, it is now on display in the National Museum of Anthropology, Mexico City. *(Courtesy The Field Museum.)*

> when the wearer moved. The same materials were used for pendants and chest ornaments and the limbs of rich young men were adorned with leather or gold bands set with jade and turquoise mosaic. Poorer folk wore ornaments of a similar kind, but substituted shells or less expensive stones for the precious materials used by the aristocracy. (Bray 1968:28, quoted in Carrasco 1998:121)

The emperor wore the most elaborate costume of all. According to the *Florentine Codex,* for public performances his hair was decorated with quetzal feathers "set off with gold," and he wore a "finely wrought headdress of red spoonbill features, with flaring quetzal feathers, and with it a drum [covered] with gold." In addition, he wore gold earrings, a lip plug made of greenstone set in gold, and any of a wide number of gold lip pendants in forms ranging from pelicans and eagles to fire serpents and boating poles (Carrasco 1998:128).

Aztec painting merged with calligraphy to produce the illustrations of the Aztec codices. A black-on-orange decorated pottery was made in a style that had its origins many centuries earlier in Teotihuacán culture. Fiber artists wove fine textiles, including velvets and brocades, and these were further embroidered, tie-dyed, or served as the ground for feather mosaic. Mosaics were also made of shells, turquoise, and other semiprecious stones. When the Spanish arrived in Tenochtitlán, they found great quantities of gold and silver that Aztec craftsmen had worked using lost wax casting and other complex techniques. Religion provided the subject matter for most Aztec art; however, it should be borne in mind that the goals of Aztec religion and politics were indistinguishable and that both were focused on repaying the Aztecs' debt to their deities, thereby forestalling the apocalypse and realizing the Aztecs' promised destiny as rulers of the world.

Perhaps the religious basis of Aztec art is the reason why an aesthetic sensibility pervades so much of Aztec culture. Citing a native account of a young girl's education, David Carrasco says,

> "Seize the broom, be diligent with the sweeping." Here began the "art" of the woman's life, which was care of the home. "The art of good drink, the art of good food, which is called one's birthright" meant to get to work sewing, grinding cornmeal, and cooking; but, as with everything else, do it in Aztec style. This style included a pronounced emphasis on artistic sensitivity. Young women were encouraged to observe and take in the arts of feather working, embroidering, and "color-working"—the creation of art. (Carrasco 1998:107)

Covarrubias (1957:321–326), himself a Mexican painter and art historian, has asserted that Aztec artistic style had three components—a generalized geometric propensity that is indigenously Aztec; a graphic, pictorial style borrowed from the Mixteca-Puebla tradition; and many architectural conventions copied directly from the pyramids of the Toltecs. Like the European art patrons of the Renaissance who glorified classical Greek and Roman culture, the Aztecs looked back upon the Toltec and early Mixtec civilizations as their cultural and intellectual forebears. As the Aztecs expanded their empire, they brought master Toltec and Mixtec artisans to Tenochtitlán to produce the art they desired.

Aztec style was an amalgam of both naturalism and conventionalized representation. Mortal humans and animals were rendered with extreme subtlety, and the Aztecs visualized their gods as fierce, anthropomorphic beings with faces resembling native Mesoamericans, albeit clothed and decorated with the elaborate regalia appropriate to deities. The iconographic traits that identified a given god included the color of his face (Huitzilopochtli's was blue with a horizontal yellow stripe) and the shape and color of his nose and ear ornaments, headdresses, items worn in his hair or on his head and neck, plus objects—frequently shields—held in his hands (cf. Nicholson 1976).

Dance was another important component of the Aztec arts. From the codex texts we know that both sacred and secular dances were performed, and from their illustrations and from Aztec ceramic figurines, we even have some idea of the patterns of movement that characterized Aztec dance (cf. Marti and Kurath 1964).

In sum, Aztec society produced a tremendous quantity of art with a high degree of craftsmanship and technical sophistication, reflecting its being made by full-time, as well as part-time, specialists.

Aztec Aesthetics

Evidence bearing on the nature of Aztec aesthetics was long thought to have disappeared. Vaillant, in his classic *The Aztecs of Mexico,* stated flatly, "We have no way, except by analogy with living groups, to ascertain the Aztec attitude toward their art" (Vaillant 1944:156). Two decades later Westheim, surveying Aztec art and aesthetics in the thoroughgoing tradition of German art history, stated, "There does not seem to have been a Mesoamerican Aristotle. At least, no maxims [about aesthetics] such as his have been preserved. We must derive the esthetics expressed in that art from the works of art that have been saved" (Westheim 1965/1950:54–55).

Despite these statements, both common sense and ethnographic parallels lead us to expect that Aztec art was indeed grounded in a canon of aesthetic theory, and a few remarks by the early Spanish invaders support this assumption. For example, the Spanish chronicler Díaz, in a description of a battle that occurred just before the fall of Tenochtitlán, said that many Spanish soldiers drowned because they overloaded their boats with loot of gold and silver, whereas he himself survived because he took only jade beads, jade being more valuable to the Aztecs than either silver or gold (cited in Covarrubias 1957:319).

Since the mid-1950s, through the efforts of ethnohistorians such as Angel Maria Garabay K. and Miguel León-Portilla, the major themes of Aztec philosophy have come to light. Contrary to Westheim's remark, Mesoamerica *did* have its Aristotles—a category of priests called *tlamatinime* (singular, *tlamatini),* or knowers-of-things, who were respected for their wisdom, whose chief interest lay in speculative thought, and who, like many Western philosophers, sought to illuminate major metaphysical questions by examining traditional beliefs, correcting and extending them when possible. One codex described the *tlamatini* in the following terms:

> He is the way, the true guide of others . . .
> teacher of the truth, he never stops reproving . . .
> He holds a mirror before others,
> he makes them mindful and judicious . . .

He shines his light on the world,
he inquires into the region of the gods above,
and into the region of the dead below . . .

> (*Codice Matritense* fol. 118rx, cited in León-Portilla 1971:448)

As noted previously, one of the Aztecs' central concerns was the belief that a fifth and final destruction of the world was imminent. The *tlamatinime* translated this popular fear of an impending apocalypse into questions of a more philosophical nature, the foremost of which concerned the tentative-ness of the material world in general and of human mortality in particular. For example, a late Aztec philosopher wrote the following lines of lament about the fifteenth-century king, Itzcóatl, who had glorified the Aztecs as the People of the Sun:

You were celebrated, Oh Itzcóatl,
exquisite were the words you spoke,
but you are dead. . . .

> (*Cantares Mexicanos,* 1904, fol. 29v, cited in León-Portilla 1971:448)

The Aztec wise men realized that *all* earthly things are transient and doomed for destruction:

Hence, I weep,
for you are weary,
oh God.
Jade shatters,
the quetzal feather tears apart.
Oh God, you mock us.
Perhaps we really do not exist.
Perchance we are nothing to you?

> (*Cantares Mexicanos,* 1904, fol. 12v, cited in León-Portilla 1971:448)

The logical consequence of the *tlamatinime's* concern about the imper-manence of all things is summed up in the penultimate line of the preceding excerpt: *Perhaps we really do not exist;* perhaps life

. . . is just a dream . . .
And here no one speaks the truth. . . .

> (*Cantares Mexicanos,* 1904, fol. 13r, cited in León-Portilla 1971:450)

If life is transitory or only a dream, the *tlamatinime* asked, how should one live out one's days? A codex records one proffered answer—to experi-ence life to the fullest during the brief time that remains:

Here man lives on earth!
Here there are lords, there is power, there is nobility. . . .
There is ardor, there is life, there is struggle,
the search for a woman, the search for a man.

> (*Florentine Codex*, bk. 6, fol. 44r, cited in León-Portilla 1971:449)

This *carpe diem* doctrine appears to have been only a minority opinion, however. Other *tlamatinime* held different views about *neltiliztli*, or truth that is solidly established and "rooted" in the fundamental nature of things. The most relevant for our purposes is a theory that had a wide currency but that found its most complete elaboration in the works of a sage named Tecaye-huatzin and his associates. According to this school of thought, the only things in life that are real, the only things that are rooted, are "flower and song."

The phrase "flower and song" appears often in the writings of the *tlamatinime;* it is an example of "difrasismo," whereby two words are conjoined to convey one important idea.[3] The concept conveyed by "flower and song" is *art* in the broadest sense of the word, including poetry, symbol, metaphor, and all that has meaningful beauty (see Figure 7–5).

Using "flower and song," a *tlamatini* named Nezahualocóyotl explained one way out of the dilemma of transience and death:

Finally, my heart understands it:
I hear a song,
I see a flower,
Behold, they will not wither!

> (Ms. *Romances de Los señores de la Nueva España*, fol. 19v,
> cited in León-Portilla 1966:35)

Elsewhere Nezahualocóyotl said,

They will not end, my flowers,
they will not cease, my songs. . . .
Even when the flowers
wither and grow yellow,
they will be carried thither,
to the interior of the house
of the bird with the golden plumes.

> (*Cantares Mexecanos*, fol. 13v, cited in León-Portilla 1966:36–37)

---

[3]In a similar way, English speakers sometimes use the phrase "bread and butter" to refer to subsistence generally.

Flowers apparently had more than just a metaphorical significance for the Aztecs. Covarrubias (1957:321) relates that at the time of conquest, "The Spaniards were much impressed with the haughty manner of the Aztec nobility toward them, and wrote with candor of the nobles' extreme cleanliness: They bathed often and held bouquets of flowers to their noses whenever they had to approach a Spaniard."

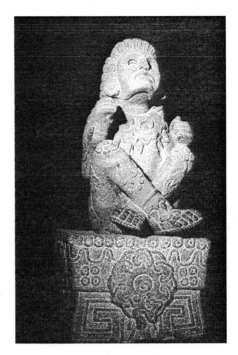

FIGURE 7-5 Stone sculpture of Xochipilli, Aztec god of song, poetry, theater, love, dance, vegetation, and springtime. Some of the decorations on his throne represent flowers. Height, including throne, 1.15 meters. *(Photo courtesy Garcia Valades Editores, S. A.)*

That is, art is everlasting, and even if the tangible embodiment of art should fade, its essence will, like the Gods to whom it is dedicated, last forever.[4]

Discovering the origin and true nature of "flower and song" was so important an issue that the Nahuatl manuscript *Cantares Mexicanos* describes a meeting convened by Tecayehuatzin and attended by various *tlamatinime* at which the metaphysical efficacy of "flower and song" was debated at length. The host of the gathering began by asking whether "flower and song" are perhaps the only things that are genuinely real and lasting. The first response came from Ayocuin Cuitzpaltzin who asserted that art is simply the gift of the gods through which we humans, in our clumsy way, may find immortality:

> From the interior of heaven come
> the beautiful flowers, the beautiful songs.
> Our desire deforms them,
> our inventiveness mars them. . . .
> Must I depart like the flowers that perish?

---

[4]Jane H. Hill (1987) has demonstrated the pervasiveness of the metaphoric association between "flower" and poetry throughout the Uto-Aztecan language family, extending well north of the Rio Grande.

> Will nothing of my fame remain here on the earth?
> At least my flowers, at least my songs.
>
> (*Cantares Mexicanos,* fol. 10r, cited in León-Portilla 1966:51–52)

The poet's reasoning here may have been that inasmuch as genuine art comes from the gods, it will (like the gods) last forever. That is, even after the inevitable disintegration with the passage of time of the material artwork, the *essence* that it once embodied is true and eternal. This, at least, seems to have been in the mind of a second speaker, Azuiauhtzin, who suggested that "flower and song" "are the form of invoking the supreme giver of life. The giver of life may perhaps become present by way of the world of symbol" (León-Portilla 1966:52). Just as one might take a gift of flowers when visiting a friend, the gift of sacred art may warm the gods' reception of mortals and thus give the makers of the art some prospect of immortality.[5]

Then another participant, Cuauhtencoztli, questioned whether "flower and song" have any worth at all, to which the host, Tecayehuatzin, replied that at least they have value in that they can alleviate sorrow and bring joy to one's life. After all, the person who is genuinely engaged by art is oblivious both to the passage of time and to the troubles of the mundane world, a condition not unlike immortality itself, forestalling at least for the moment the approaching cataclysm. In this, the Aztecs give us an important observation about the power of art: So long as art profoundly engages the mind and spirit, it gives release from the worries and cares that are part of mortal life.

But a final speaker, Xayacámach, says that this line of reasoning is shallow, questioning whether "flower and song" are merely

> like hallucinating drugs, the best means of intoxicating the heart and making oneself forgetful of sadness here. When in the sacred gatherings the drugs are consumed, one sees marvelous visions, evanescent forms of different colors, all more real than reality itself. However, afterward this fantastic world vanishes like a dream, leaves the man weary, and no longer exists.[6] (León-Portilla 1966:53)

The meeting eventually closes on an ambiguous note. The host admits that the matter has not been resolved and that "his heart continues to be open to doubt," but all present will agree that, "if nothing else, 'flower and song' at least make possible our friendship" (León-Portilla 1966:53), presumably by providing a topic for stimulating discussions such as the one in which they have just participated.

---

[5]The practice of giving art objects to the gods in return for favors had parallels in the earthly realm of Aztec society in that it was fairly common for Aztecs to give craft items to those whom they asked for favors. (See Brumfiel 1987.)

[6]This note of skepticism may reflect the speaker's belief that the philosophy of "flower and song" is less effective than a competing idea that saw military victory and blood sacrifice as the only means of propitiating the gods (cf. León-Portilla 1983).

Two themes may be discerned in this debate regarding "flower and song." First, some of art's secular functions are noted. Art can serve as a source of pleasure and provide a basis for friendship. But the second and more serious use of art relates to the human soul. Art invokes the gods and insures the maker's immortality, no small accomplishment in a world whose imminent destruction was taken for granted both in Aztec popular thought and in the more rarified philosophies of the *tlamatinime*. Aztec aesthetics is founded on a belief that true art comes from the gods and is manifest in the artist's mystical revelation of sacred truth. Through such knowledge the artist transcends mortality and the transient world of the senses and partakes of the eternal. The Aztec sages believed that art is the only thing that is actually real, and as such it can protect humans from the inevitable destruction of the fragile and temporary world.[7]

The application of this theory to actual Aztec art production is interesting. The *tlamatinime* presumably considered themselves to be spiritually enlightened, and they believed that their poems embodied "flower and song." But as previously noted, the visual arts were created not by Aztec nobles, or even by Aztec commoners. Instead, most visual arts were created by craftsmen brought to Tenochtitlán from subjugated peoples. A few artists were Mixtecs, but most were Toltecs. Indeed, the Nahuatl word *toltécatl* actually meant "artist," and the highest form of artistry was identified with Toltec production.

This seeming paradox—that although art was viewed as the gods' blessing upon the Aztecs, in practice most visual art was produced by non-Aztecs—is perhaps resolved by recalling the high regard in which the Aztecs held Toltec culture. A memory of the elegance and sophistication of the long-fallen Toltec kingdom haunted the parvenu Aztecs. Therefore, they were willing to accept art being made by the illustrious Toltecs—especially since the Aztecs saw themselves as the spiritual heirs of the Toltec civilization and were, in any case, the undisputed masters of Toltec artists.

These views become even more credible in light of Aztec beliefs about artistic talent, which was thought to depend on two factors. First, one must have been born on a propitious date (the day One Flower was good) and second, one must possess the proper temperament to seek, through meditation, the spiritual enlightenment of a "deified heart." One codex described the characteristic qualities of artists in the following lines:

The artist: disciple, abundant, multiple, restless.
The true artist, capable, practicing, skillful,
maintains dialogue with his heart, meets things with his mind.

---

[7]It is an uncanny fact that the Aztec's world *was* soon destroyed, not by fate and fierce Aztec gods but by the conquering Spanish. This irony is heightened when one realizes that the essence of Aztec culture *did* survive this cataclysm largely through art works such as architecture, the illustrated codices, stone sculpture, and so on.

The true artist draws out all from his heart;
works with delight; makes things with calm, with sagacity;
works like a true Toltec; composes his objects; works dexterously; invents;
arranges materials; adorns them; makes them adjust.

The carrion artist works at random; sneers at the people;
makes things opaque; brushes across the surface of the face of things;
works without care; defrauds people; is a thief.

> (*Códice Matritense de La Real Academia* VII, fols. 115, v and 116, r,
> cited in León-Portilla 1963:168)

The same manuscript goes on to specify the traits of the practitioners of various crafts. For example,

The good painter is a Toltec, an artist;
he creates with red and black ink,
with black water. . . .

The good painter is wise,
God is in his heart.
He puts divinity into things;
he converses with his own heart.

He knows the colors, he applies them and shades them;
he draws feet and faces,
he puts in the shadows, he achieves perfection.
He paints the colors of all the flowers,
as if he were a Toltec.

> (*Códice Matritense de La Real Academia,* fol. 117,v,
> cited in León-Portilla 1963:172–173)

Carrasco has paraphrased this passage thus:

To be a true painter, a person had to develop an inward sense of feeling and understanding about the nature and intention of the god. This was called "conversing with one's heart," which resulted in the painter becoming a *yolteotl,* or "a heart rooted in god." A person who had taken a god into his or her heart could then transfer the images and purpose of the divine reality into the painting, codices, and murals that were so important to the Aztecs. (Carrasco 1998:163)

In sum, the Aztecs maintained what León-Portilla calls an "aesthetic conception of the universe and life [because] 'art made things divine,' and only the divine was true" (León-Portilla 1963:182).

Conclusion

The sophistication of Aztec aesthetics should not be seen in an ethnographic vacuum, and the forgoing account of the Aztec philosophical system requires as a postscript some mention of the dark side of Aztec culture. Not only was their empire created by bloody wars and political maneuvering, but after its boundaries were extended to the limit, the Aztecs continued their policy of extreme militarism. The Aztecs glorified war *per se:* "There is nothing like death in war, nothing like the flowery death so precious to Him who gives life: Far off I see it: my heart yearns for it" (cited in Coe 1962:168). As this passage suggests, the term "flower" referred symbolically not only to art but also to warriors.

The "flowery wars" of the late Aztec Empire provided another means—in addition to the "flower and song" of art—by which the Aztecs hoped to give gifts to their deities and postpone the final destruction of the earth, namely through providing captives for human sacrifice. Ritual execution, as well as self-mutilation, had been practiced by earlier Mesoamerican civilizations, such as that of the Maya. Mortals' debt to the gods, it was thought, could be repaid in the currency of human blood.[8] With respect to human sacrifice, however, the Aztecs seem to have significantly outstripped their predecessors (cf. León-Portilla 1983:10–23). Cortés's chronicler, Díaz, reported what he saw in one city: "I remember that in the plaza . . . there were piles of human skulls so regularly arranged that one could count them, and I estimated them at more than a hundred thousand (Figure 7–6). I repeat again that there were more than a hundred thousand of them" (quoted in Farb 1978:190). Today we cannot know the actual frequency of Aztec human sacrifice because the Spanish chroniclers sometimes recorded inflated numbers to justify their own colonizing practices. Estimates range widely, from thousands of victims per year to hundreds of thousands. Moreover, as David Carrasco (1998:206) has observed, even the highest numbers pale by comparison to the 24 million Mesoamerican lives lost between 1500 and 1600 as a result of diseases introduced by the Europeans, warfare, massacres, and the inhumane working conditions that prevailed in mines and other Spanish enterprises. Nonetheless, there can be no doubt that Aztec society, for all its high-minded metaphysics and elegant aesthetic theories, also had a horrific side that gloried in blood and death (see Figure 7–7).

Epilogue

The fatalistic prediction of the Aztec codexes—"jade shatters, the quetzal feather tears apart"—turned out to be true. With the arrival of the Spanish, Mesoamerica was forever altered. Despite their political defeat and decimated numbers, however, fifty years after the Empire's fall, native Mesoamericans were still engaged in a wide range of crafts, although they were principally of Spanish origin, such as glove-making, saddle-making, and glass

---

[8]In addition to the religious rationale for human sacrifice, Mesoamericans were not unaware of its use as a means of intimidating enemies and subject populations.

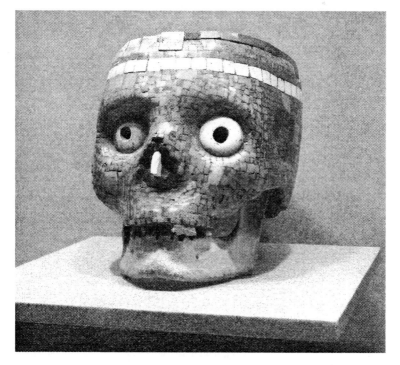

FIGURE 7-6 Human skull with turquoise overlay. *(Courtesy of National Museum of Anthropology, Mexico City.)*

working (Gibson 1964:397–398). Artisans were still were mostly Toltecs, who proved to be adept at learning the new trades, perhaps due both to their comparatively good wages and also to their history of making goods in accord with their masters' wishes.

Aztec art and culture were not altogether extinguished, however. In fact, there are still more than a million Nahuatl speakers living in Mexico today, and in their language and their day-to-day lives, many of them carry on traditions whose roots go back to pre-Hispanic times. Many elements of Aztec culture can be found that are not only alive and intact but are positively thriving in the world today. For example, the Mexican flag dramatically displays an eagle, perched on a cactus and gripping a snake in its mouth, a device that comes from the Aztec's traditional tale of the founding of Tenochtitlán: During their migration from Aztlán, their god, Huitzilopochtli, had told them to journey southward until they saw such an eagle and when they did, to settle there and begin building an empire. The Aztec calendar stone (Figure 7–4), which appears in so much public imagery in contemporary Mexico, similarly links the present to the past. As Michael E. Smith (1996:299) has observed, in

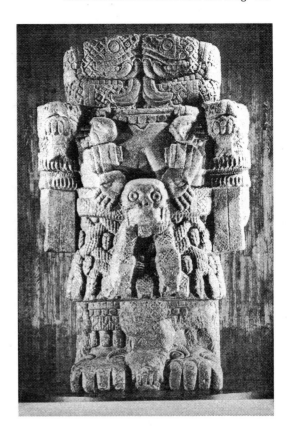

FIGURE 7-7 Stone sculpture of Coatlicue, Aztec goddess of the earth and death. She wears a necklace of human hearts and hands, and her skirt is made of serpents. 2.57 meters high. *(Photo courtesy García Valades Editores, S. A.)*

the same way that the Aztecs brought legitimacy to their civilization by adopting the Toltecs as their putative ancestors, modern Mexico—both in its national government and among many of its peoples—looks back to the Aztecs as a source of pride and authenticity.

Other artistic accoutrements of pre-Hispanic culture also remain current in Mexico—and beyond Mexico. The tortilla and the tamale, as well as mole and chili sauces, were as characteristic of traditional Aztec cuisine as they are of Mexican food today, whether served in Mexico itself or in the United States, Europe, or Asia.[9] Also, Zantwijk (1957:108–114) has claimed that traces of the Aztec worldview still linger in some contemporary Nahuatl poetry.

In the visual arts, the Aztec spirit is also alive and well. The back strap loom, used by Mesoamerican weavers before the arrival of the Spanish, may

---

[9]In 1999, Grupo Maseca, Mexico's biggest tortilla producer, opened a large tortilla factory in Coventry, England—the first in Europe; and a web page—http://www.bento.com/r-mex.asp—lists thirty Mexican and Tex-Mex restaurants in Tokyo, Japan.

still be found, although wool and imported cotton have largely supplanted indigenous varieties of cotton and maguey fibers. The woven products find a variety of uses, from utilitarian clothing in Mexico's rural areas, to decoration
for the homes of middle class Mexicans and foreign visitors to Mexico. Also,
Tony Cohan (1998) has observed that the intense, saturated colors that give
such a distinctive appearance to many contemporary Mexican house facades,
textiles, ceramics, and the displays of market vendors, has a pre-Hispanic
precedent with some structures painted "cerulean blue, yellow, red, orange,
ocher, black" (1998:9).

But it is in the art of large-scale wall murals that Aztec iconography has
had perhaps its most prolific and politically significant reincarnation in modern Mexico. In 1921 the Mexican minister of education, José Vasconcelos,
began commissioning several artists (among them Diego Rivera, José
Clemente Orozco, and David Alfaro Siqueiros) to create large paintings on
the walls of public buildings. The goal was to raise citizen literacy and awareness of Mexico's proud past, and the resultant murals often contained characters and events from Aztec history. For example, true to his populist
sympathies, Rivera's *The Great City of Tenochtitlán,* created in the National
Palace, Mexico City, includes a small background vignette of the pyramids and
central district of the Aztec capital city, while the foreground is filled with la-
boring masses of Aztec workers, such as the sellers of reed mats (Figure 7–8).

Rivera, Orozco, and Siqueiros continued to create murals in Mexico,
the United States, and elsewhere throughout their lives; but after their careers had come to an end, the social movements of the 1960's breathed new
life into the muralist movement. Today in Mexico (and in other countries

FIGURE 7–8   Diego Rivera (1866–1957), *The Great City of Tenochtitlan,* 1945, detail of mural,
4.92 x 9.71 m. Patio Corridor, National Palace, Mexico City, D.F. Mexico. © 2003 Banco de Mexico
Diego Rivera & Frida Kahlo Museums Trust.Av. Cinco de Mayo No. 2, Col. Centro, Del. Cuauhtemoc
06059, Mexico, D.F. Reproduction authorized by the Instituto Nacional de Bellas Artes y Literatura.
(Photo credit: Schalkwijk / Art Resource, NY)

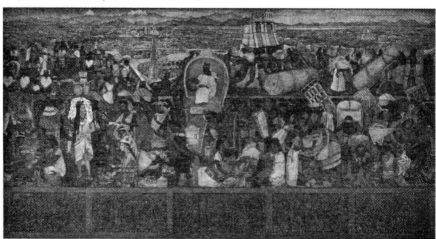

with large Hispanic populations, such as the United States, one often sees large-scale arts on public walls that incorporate Aztec thematic material. Carrasco (1998:248–253) briefly surveys work by three noteworthy muralists—Ray Patlan's work at the Casa Aztlán, a community center in Chicago's Pilsen neighborhood, a mural by José Antonio Burciaga at Stanford University, and works in Los Angeles by painter George Yepes. But with only a little effort, many people can find very impressive Mexican-influenced wall art in their own city or town (Figure 7–9 and 7–10).

Although elements of Aztec art are still to be found, the *tlamatinime's* rarefied theories about "flower and song" seem to be gone. In the early 1960s, Peggy Golde (cf. Golde 1963; Golde and Kraemer 1973) carried out an interesting study of aesthetic values among contemporary descendants of the Aztecs in an isolated Mexican village. She found that although the aesthetic preferences of the people she interviewed varied somewhat, two-thirds shared several aesthetic norms. When shown photographs of pottery, most preferred pieces that (in descending order of importance) reflected intensive work by the potter, whose surface had "clarity" (as judged by the fineness of surface, care of decoration, and meaningfulness of subject matter), and that depicted people of robust good health and endurance. Valid though they may be, these criteria are far removed from the aesthetic beliefs of the Aztec *tlamatinime*, who 500 years ago believed that art was divine in origin, that it was the only lasting true reality, and that art (along with the blood of human sacrifice) provided the only means of saving an otherwise doomed world.

FIGURE 7–9 Juan Moya, street mural, from the West Side neighborhood of Kansas City, Missouri, that combines Aztec imagery—the eagle and snake—with Christian iconography—the head of Christ and a verse from the *New Testament*—plus a reference to the West Side. *(Designed and painted by Juan Moya.)*

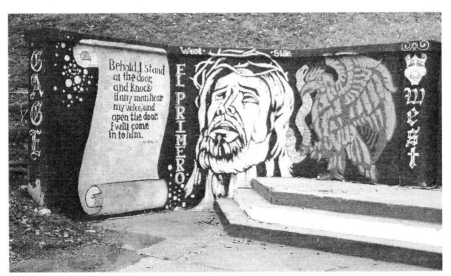

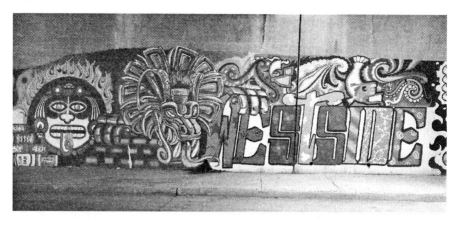

FIGURE 7-10 Carlos Gonzalez, a mural from Kansas City's West Side that directly links the neighborhood to pre-Hispanic images. *(Designed and painted by Carlos Gonzalez.)*

Further Reading

Two authors, Carrasco (1998) and M. Smith (1996) do an excellent job of combining archaeological, ethnohistorical, and ethnographic information to provide broad descriptions of Aztec culture, including Aztec art, as well as such topics as the Aztecs' confrontation with the Spanish invaders. Aztec visual arts receive thorough art historical treatment in Pasztory (1983). The writings of Léon-Portilla (1963, 1966, 1971, 1983) provide an excellent and in-depth account of Aztec philosophy, including the Aztec philosophy of art, and a recent anthology edited by Léon-Portilla and Shorris (2001) gives students direct access to Aztec documents. Friedlander (1975) presents an ethnographic picture of a modern Nahua village, including its weavers, and Nutini (1988) describes Day of the Dead activities in a Tlaxcala village in the Valley of Mexico, including a symbolic analysis of their pre-Hispanic roots.

8

AESTHETICS IN EARLY INDIA

Rasa and the Theory

of Transcendental Enjoyment

Two birds, deepest of friends,
live on the same tree.
One eats the sweet fruit.
The other, without eating, watches.

(Abhinavagupta, 10th century A.D.)]

The Indus River valley occupies a special place in Western thought. It was one of the few locations where our distant human ancestors discovered agriculture, an innovation that eventually had sweeping consequences in that people exchanged their earlier transient existence for sedentary village life based on farming. Populations grew dramatically in size, and in south Asia, the Indus River valley saw the rise of a civilization whose size and complexity were unprecedented in the Indian subcontinent. By 2000 B.C., there were cities with such luxuries as wide, well-drained streets and lined spacious, two-storied houses. From grand palaces, the emperors of the Indus Valley civilization ruled an extensive and sophisticated state.

But there is another reason for the perennial Western fascination with Indian civilization. India probably had trade links with the civilizations of Mesopotamia, and thus it may be thought of as a "first cousin" to Western culture. Not only are the populations of India and Europe closely related genetically, but several important languages of the Indian subcontinent such as Sanskrit and Hindi are members of the far-flung Indo-European language family, which also includes most European languages.

For all their kinship, however, India and the West remain alien to each other in many respects. The Westerner may be astounded at the aesthetic sophistication of Indian sculpture, such as the bronze Shiva shown in Figure 8–1, a masterpiece of craftsmanship and elegant grace. But although the beauty of such metalwork dazzles the eye, traditional India did not consider sculpture (or, for that matter, painting) to be a major "art." Dramatic poetry,

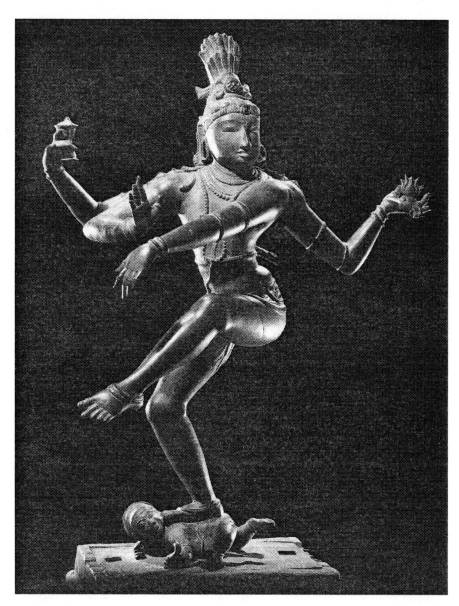

FIGURE 8–1   Shiva Nataraja, the Dancing Lord. 1200–1300 A.D., bronze sculpture, 34 1/4" x 27 1/2" x 13" (87.0 x 69.9 x 33.0 cm). *(The Nelson-Atkins Museum of Art, Kansas City, Missouri [Purchase: Nelson Fund] 34–7.)*

architecture, and music—those were the true arts in the minds of early Indian theorists. Or, to note another seeming incongruity, the Westerner quickly learns that almost all Indian art has religious subject matter—only to be confronted by examples of Indian sculpture and literature that are blatantly erotic in subject matter (Figure 14–4).

How can these apparent anomalies be explained? Certainly not by relegating them to the status of "errors" and assuming that Indian artists were unaware of what they were doing. To the contrary, few of the world's artistic traditions have been as carefully scrutinized by native aestheticians as those of India. When Indian art surprises us, it is due to our ignorance of the aesthetic system that has informed Indian art for nearly 2,000 years.

Some familiarity with this system of thought helps resolve such seeming contradictions. The belief that sculpture and painting are, at best, secondary in importance, makes sense when one accepts the Indian assumption that art should have a dimension of time. A painting or sculpture freezes the action of its subject in a single instant, whereas drama unfolds an elaborate narrative. Indian aestheticians believed that this time dimension makes drama intrinsically superior to painting and sculpture.

An explanation of the presence of erotic subjects in otherwise sacred art works is more complicated. To understand its rationale, we must recreate the historic, artistic, and philosophical context that produced the theory of *rasa,* a concept that distinguishes Indian aesthetic theory from all other philosophies of art.

Background: Indian History, Art, and Aesthetic Writing

The empires of the early Indus Valley civilization fell into disarray by about 1500 B.C., and although successive events in Indian history are complicated, they generally follow a pulsating pattern whereby periods of unification alternated with intervals of political breakdown, often coinciding with invasions from the west or north. Our interest lies in the classical and medieval periods of Indian history, which spanned the third to thirteenth centuries and which saw the maturation of a distinctively Indian aesthetic system, with the most exciting developments taking place between the ninth and eleventh centuries.

The dominant religion of India during that period was Hinduism, although Buddhism and several other religious traditions also had some influence on the aesthetic thought. The foundation of Hinduism lies in the four Vedas, or collections of ancient Sanskrit sacred writing that record prayers, hymns, and rituals. The last section, called the Upanishads, contains the mystical and speculative core of Hinduism. The Upanishads claim that ultimate reality takes the form of Brahman, which is sometimes personified as a god but which more accurately is the abstract Absolute—pure consciousness and pure bliss, permanent and immutable. The world of the senses, being neither perfect nor immutable, is deemed unreal, so the proper goal of life should be transcendence by means of ritual, self-control, and meditation. The striving to attain such an end began in each person's past life and will continue in future incarnations until an ultimate merging with Brahman occurs.

Speculative thought in India was the domain of a small caste of priests, called brahmins (see Figure 8–2). Similarly, art production was confined to professional, technically adept members of specific subcastes. Religion provided the subject matter for most Indian art, much of which was narrative in nature.

FIGURE 8–2   Brahmin at worship, Madras, India. *(Courtesy, Field Museum of Natural History, Chicago, neg. no. 86507.)*

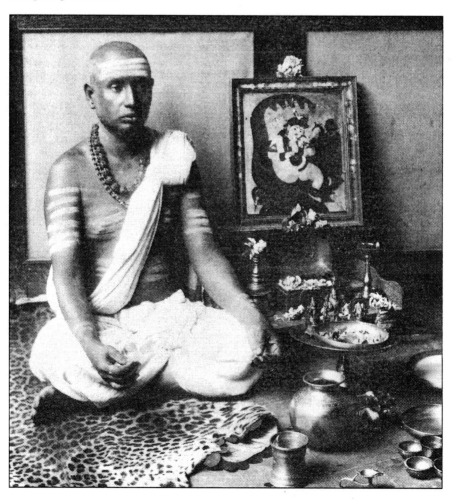

During the classical and medieval periods, numerous intellectuals of the brahmin caste focused their attention on art. They asked, Is art a part of the Absolute or is it a component of the mundane, illusory world of the senses? And in either case, What are the varieties of art, and how can art have such a strong affect on human consciousness? The brahmins often wrote down their speculations, and although most of the original documents are lost and others remain in only fragmentary form, scholars have reconstructed many early theories, sometimes by using the commentaries of later brahmin writers.

Of the dozen or so sources of early Indian aesthetics, two writers deserve particular mention. The oldest document in the Indian aesthetic tradition is the *Nāṭyaśāstra*, which dates from about the third century in the current era and is ascribed to "Bharata," a name that, like the ancient Greek "Homer," probably stands for several anonymous authors. Bharata was chiefly concerned with the practical problems of drama, such as instructing writers, stage managers, and actors on the proper constituents of plays, but he also addressed several theoretical points. In one important passage, he says, "Without *rasa* no dramatic device is of any importance" (quoted in Masson and Patwardhan 1970:1), a remark that, as we shall see, opened a line of inquiry that engaged Indian aestheticians for a thousand years.

If Bharata represents the beginning of Indian aesthetic writing, the tenth-century work of Abhinavagupta was the high point of the tradition. Like many later Indian aestheticians, Abhinnava was born in Kashmir and was influenced by Tantricism. Although he absorbed and synthesized earlier aesthetic writings, he gave more attention to the philosophical and religious dimension of art than did other Indian writers. His two surviving works are *Abhinava bhāratī*, a commentary on the ideas found in Bharata's classic text, and *Dhvanyālokalocana* (or simply, the *Locana*), a commentary on a work by Anandavardhana, which is itself another commentary on Bharata's writings. Both treatises are difficult, so complex in reasoning, so elliptical in style, and so fragmentary in their current state of preservation that competent Sanskrit scholars often disagree significantly on the meaning of crucial passages.

There were additions to the Indian philosophy of art after Abhinavagupta's time, but the ancient writings are still studied in India. This may be a testament to the richness of the writers' speculations, for there is no doubt that Bharata, Abhinavagupta, and others produced an aesthetic theory as profound and complex as can be found in any human culture.

Art as the "Fifth Veda"

In the first pages of the ancient *Nāṭyaśāstra*, Bharata recounts the story of the origin of art. In this tale, Brahman is anthropomorphized as the leader of many lesser gods who come asking him for something to amuse themselves with besides the purely religious writings found in the four Vedas. Brahman says,

> Since these [original] Vedas cannot be heard by women, by Sudras and other classes, I will create a fifth Veda, different from these, that will be for *all* people. I will create a fifth Veda called "drama" out of past stories, that will lead to righteousness, to material gain, to fame, with good advice and full of wise sayings. It will display the deeds of all people in the world to come. (Masson and Patwardhan 1970, vol. 1:18–19)

In this passage, the speaker was, of course, referring to art, identifying two distinct reasons for art's existence. Art gives pleasure to mortals, and at the same time it shows them how to better themselves. In saying this, Bharata gave voice to an enduring belief in Hindu thought inasmuch as the aesthetic principles of pleasure and edification were still accepted by brahmin writers who lived a thousand years after Bharata. Although most believed that the more important of the two functions is art's capacity to engage a person's emotions, it is easier to explain Indian aesthetics by starting with the other rationale for art—namely, that it provides an excellent means of instruction.

Art as Instruction

As noted previously, the Vedas portray humans as existing in greater or lesser states of imperfection. We mortals are inherently ignorant and often waste our lives on sensuality and lust. The arts, however, can liberate us from this sorry condition and put our passions to good use. Just as the Vedas instruct devotees regarding the path to unification with the Absolute, *the arts lead to the moral betterment of those who experience them.* This is the first axiom of classical Indian aesthetics. We must be clear, however, about what the Vedas consider to be "moral betterment." The phrase may suggest a purely spiritual development to Westerners, but from a Hindu perspective, moral betterment implies the successful pursuit of the *puruṣārthas*, the four proper goals of life, which include not only righteousness and spiritual emancipation but also the acquisition of material prosperity and the enjoyment of refined, worldly pleasures. So when Indian writers say that art exists to help a person progress along the path to Brahman, they are thinking of improvement in what Westerners would consider both the sacred *and* the secular dimensions of life.

Many centuries after Bharata told the story of Brahman creating the arts for (among other things) the edification of lesser gods and mortals, Abhinavagupta was still convinced that an important value of art lies in its capacity to instruct "in the ways of the world and in the means leading to the [four] goals of life" (quoted in Masson and Patwardhan 1969:55). But again, "instruction" must be understood in its Vedic context. Abhinavagupta did not condone didactic art that preached an obvious sermon or told a narrow, cautionary tale. Immediately after his claim that art should teach people how to attain the four goals of life, Abhinavagupta asked, "Question: does the drama instruct the way a teacher (or an elderly person) does? (Answer:). No. Rather it causes one's wisdom to grow" (ibid.).[1]

A later writer, Mammat, elaborated on art's ability to teach. Art instructs, he said, "in the delicate, subtle manner of a beloved wife, not in the high hortatory tone of a master nor in the indifferent 'take it or leave it' manner of an acquaintance" (paraphrased in Dhayagude 1981:167). Instruction via art is more subtle than other forms of learning, but also the recipient of instruction is no ordinary student. Abhinavagupta says, "Even a stupid man can learn [philosophy] from the teachings of his professor. But poetry is only given to the person who has the imaginative genius—and that only once in a while" (Masson and Patwardhan 1969:19).

Art's special instructional efficacy becomes more understandable in light of Vedic metaphysics. If Brahman is the only reality, then the individual self, still striving to attain Brahman, obviously is less than real. On the other hand, the creators of Hindu philosophy realized that it is counterintuitive to believe that the phenomenal world and human consciousness are totally unreal. One does, after all, *experience* the world and one's self. The solution lies in the concept of *māyā*, which asserts that the world of the senses is neither real nor unreal, but that it *is* empirically true.[2]

Art, too, is *māyā,* at least for the more theoretical Indian writers. The world portrayed in art does not have the same reality as the subject matter it portrays, but even the most empirically oriented observer must admit that it does have some sort of substantiality because art can prompt a powerful emotional response in the percipient. Because of this, art can instruct in a way that is different from, and superior to, the education that one might receive through formal channels. As Masson and Patwardhan (1969:5) put it, "Preachers inform us; only poets invite us to experience."

The Transcendental Pleasure of Art

Abhinavagupta's writings stand at the pinnacle of Indian aesthetic thought. The breadth of his learning and the depth of his analysis could suggest a man

---

[1]It is common practice for modern translators of Sanskrit to add words, enclosed in parentheses, that they believe to be likely replacements for those now missing from the original documents. I have followed the same convention in this chapter, although I have omitted the Sanskrit words that typically are left in texts (in parenthesis) by some translators. By contrast, I have used brackets to add my own clarifying word or two in direct quotations that otherwise would not make sense outside their original context.

[2]To explain the apparent contradiction between the sensible world seeming to be simultaneously real and unreal, "Sankara, the great teacher of Advaita Vedanta, uses the analogy of a rope which appears to be a snake because of darkness or defective sight. Here the snake is pure illusion since it has no correspondence with the reality of the rope. Still the apprehension of the snake is real enough for it produces fear which is an undeniable empirical fact" (Dhayagude 1981:11).

who possessed the combined talents of Plato and Aristotle. But before we form an image of him as a dry intellectual, engrossed in purely cerebral activities, we should consider the following description of Abhinavagupta. It is the only extant account of him and apparently was written by a person who actually saw Abhinava at work.

> He sits in the middle of a garden of grapes, inside a pavilion made of crystal and filled with beautiful paintings. The room smells wonderful because of flower garlands, incense-sticks and (oil-) lamps. Its walls are smeared with sandal-paste and other such things. The room is constantly resounding with musical instruments, with songs and with dancing. There are crowds of women Yogins and realized beings with magic powers. It is equipped with a golden seat from which pearls are hanging. It has a soft awning stretched over it (as a canopy). Abhinava is attended by all his numerous students, with Kssemaraja at their head, who are writing down everything he says. To his side stand two women, partners in Tantric rites, who hold in one hand a jug of wine and a box full of betel rolls, and in the other hand a lotus and a citron. Abhinava has his eyes trembling in ecstasy. (Masson and Patwardhan 1969:38–39)

The account goes on to describe a mark of ashes on Abhinavagupta's forehead, a bead dangling from one ear, and flower garlands hanging about his neck. Then, "One hand is held on his knee holding a rosary with his fingers clearly making the sign that signifies his knowledge of the highest Siva. He plays on his resonating lute with the tips of the quivering fingers of his lotus-like left hand" (Masson and Patwardhan 1969:39).

So much for the picture of Abhinavagupta as a dusty old pedant who thought art should be used principally for instruction. It has been said that if one side of Hinduism is ascetic and world-denying, its other side is sensual and resolutely life-affirming (cf. Organ 1975). The latter impulse is especially evident in the sect known as Tantricism. Tantricism emphasized identification with the Absolute through meditation and also through rituals that included the religiously sanctioned eating of (otherwise forbidden) meat, the drinking of wine, and engaging in ritualized sexual intercourse. Clearly, the above description portrays Abhinavagupta as a central participant in a Tantric ritual.

Although the major Indian writers recognized that art can teach a person how to attain the four goals of life, they consistently placed greater stress on the second axiom of Indian aesthetics, the idea that *art can give pleasure that verges upon transcendental ecstasy.*

Rasa Theory

In Sanskrit, *rasa* refers to (among other things) the emotional satisfaction that one experiences in reaction to art, and the history of Indian aesthetics is

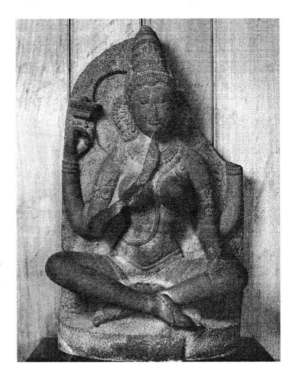

FIGURE 8-3   The Mother Goddess as a Yogini. Indian sculpture, Pallava-Chola transition, late 9th to early 10th century, greenstone (chlorite-actinolate), H: 52 1/2" (133.4 cm). *(The Nelson-Atkins Museum of Art, Kansas City, Missouri [Purchase: Nelson Trust] 44-27.)*

largely a chronicle of speculation about the multifarious nature of *rasa*. From the beginning of Indian aesthetics (recall Bharata's claim that "without *rasa* no dramatic device is of any importance") through Abhinavagupta (whose *Locana* says, "*rasa* alone is the soul of poetry" [Masson and Patwardhan 1969:81]), Indian aestheticians were unanimous in placing *rasa* at the center of their theories.

Rasa has more than one meaning, however. Most literally, the word may be translated as "taste," "flavor," or "relish," prompting Bharata to use an analogy with food to convey his conception of *rasa*:

> Relish is produced from the combination of various spices, herbs and other materials. . . . Just as people enjoy relish while partaking of food made relishable by various ingredients, and experience happiness, etc., even so enlightened spectators relish the permanent feelings made relishable by the operation of the various elements accompanied with verbal, physical and emotional gesticulation, and experience happiness. (Dhayagude 1981:179)

Indian writers select their metaphors with care, and Bharata's likening of *rasa* to the delight that savory food can produce is no exception. For example, a distinctly piquant flavor is characteristic of the spice that in English is called "curry powder"; the taste is the *essence* both of the spice and of the dish the spice is used in. The subjective experience of the curry powder, however, is qualitatively different from the cumin, turmeric, ginger, and so on, that blend together to make it up. Although curry is a substance, its significance, in a sense its reality, lies in its distinctive taste.

The situation with art is similar. Art does have an existence in the world of the senses. For example, on one level a play is made up of living actors on actual stages who make audible utterances, just as curry has its own specific component spices. These are only a secondary feature of drama, however. Art's fundamental and essential existence is found not on this empirical level but in the distinctive aesthetic reaction that the play prompts in the properly attuned audience member. So a deeper and more important meaning of *rasa* is the state a person is in when totally engaged by a work of art.

The analogy of *rasa* with food has additional dimensions. Just as curry powder is a blend of several individual spices, the total emotional response of a person who perceives art may be—indeed, should be—a combination of several elemental emotions. *Rasa* theorists specified that of the eight (or, for some writers, nine) recognized emotions (see p. 202), a successful poem should be dominated by only one, the others being relegated to secondary roles that complement the pervading mood of the poem.

Finally, like a food's flavor, *rasa* is characterized by a feeling of indivisible immediacy, an instantaneous experience of oneness between the audience and the artwork. The person engrossed in art cannot draw a boundary between where the self ends and where the aesthetic response begins any more than the eater can distinguish between the tongue and the taste upon it. Thus, *rasa* means not only *taste* but also the sensuous pleasure that the aesthetically attuned individual may experience as a result of art—the thrill of excitement or the soothing of grief that can come about when one is immersed in an artwork.

Other Indian theorists go beyond the sensuous level of *rasa*, reminding us that art may be gratifying not just to the senses but to the spirit as well. This line of reasoning brings us back to the previously mentioned belief that art may serve as a means of instruction and spiritual liberation. To quote Abhinavagupta, "Delight (can be said to be) the cause of moral instruction. Imaginative experience consists in delight; delight is (the essential part of) drama, and drama is the only Veda" (Masson and Patwardhan 1970, vol. 2:22). Thus, he concludes, "Delight is the final and major result [of art]" (Masson and Patwardhan 1969:55).

The early Indian view was that anything that is morally uplifting or that leads to a more prosperous life must necessarily give pleasure; conversely, nothing could be enjoyable if it despoils one's character. Goodness and happiness are inseparably linked in Vedic thought. Moral betterment is not just a means to a higher plane of consciousness in some future incarnation. Since spiritual improvement brings a person closer to the pure bliss of Brahman, the experience itself is deeply satisfying. Abhinava also wrote, "What we call bliss is nothing but a full illumination of one's own being, accompanied by a form of cogitation which pervades all one's own nature, one's own Self" (Gnoli 1968:xlii). Although art is not the only path to enlightenment (meditation and ritual are alternative means), it plays an extremely important role in Indian thought because it brings one closer to Brahman, the Great Enjoyer, and his *Ras Lila*, the Play of the Universe (cf. Raffé 1952:105fn).

The Source of Art's Power

How does art accomplish this feat? *Rasa* theorists debated this question for centuries, but all concur that *conscious* use of art to obtain pleasure and moral betterment should not be necessary; poetry should be intuitively enjoyed, not laboriously studied (Masson and Patwardhan 1970, vol. 1:20). Nor should art explicitly exhort audience members to elevate their minds or spirits.[3]

One source of art's efficacy is its subject matter. Classical and medieval Indian drama was concerned with the actions of heroic supernaturals, and one theory of *rasa* held that in watching divine characters play out their roles, the sympathetic viewer would identify with the enlightened actions of the gods and thereby would be raised to a higher level of spiritual development. Again, however, the relationship between an artwork and its moral lesson should not be explicit; one should not come away from a dramatic performance with a resolution to emulate the holiness of the characters in the play. Instead, *rasa* should arise "from the apprehension of the Absolute, characterized by complete identity between the subject [i.e., the viewer] and the [*rasa*-inspiring] object. In it the mind contemplates itself in its freedom and as such is infinite and attaining the stage of the Absolute" (Pandy 1952:485). Moved by art, the properly attuned audience member forgets the personal, idiosyncratic self and merges with the cosmic Self that is Brahman.[4]

Other Indian writers attributed art's power to its stylistic conventions rather than its subject matter. Poetry, for example, was characterized by its hypereloquent language, dramatic figures of speech, and various other embellishments. Certainly, they argued, art does not gain power through its

---

[3]Dhayagude observes that although there might seem to be a contradiction between art's affective function, as manifest in the doctrine of *rasa*, and art's instructional function, the conflict "disappears if we bear in mind that the instruction which poetry gives is inseparable from the delightful experience which it occasions. If there is no *rasa* there is no poetry; if there is *rasa* but no instruction, one need not complain; if there is *rasa* and instruction, one need not quarrel. But in poetry instruction must not be superadded; it must accrue as part of aesthetic experience; it must be inseparable from the enjoyment of *rasa*" (Dhayagude 1981:169).

[4]Indian aestheticians believed that the audience member's being engrossed in an artwork is qualitatively equivalent to the total immersion of the artist in his or her work. The *Brahma Sutra* says, "The arrow-maker perceives nothing beyond his work when he is buried in it; but he has nevertheless consciousness and control over his body" (cited in Coomaraswamy 1924:21).

imperfect imitation of specific individuals and actions. Instead, the truths found in art are generalized and relevant to all times and places. By its nature, poetry does not portray its subject in particularities; instead, its stylistic conventions allow it to convey universal principles. The superficial details of the dramatic action should not distract the "percipient" (the person who perceives the artwork). Not *this* actor with *these* mortal idiosyncrasies, but rather the eternal, omnipresent god that the actor represents.

As with many other issues, Abhinavagupta went further than others in analyzing the source of *rasa's* power. Because every mortal has lived a multitude of previous lives since Brahman first set the universe in motion, and since we have experienced all possible emotions during our past existences, Abhinava suggested that we all come into our present lives with an instinctive capacity to feel all eight of the possible emotions—happiness, pride, zest (or laughter), sorrow, anger, disgust, fear and wonder (cf. Dhayagude 1981:182). Thus, when a person clears the mind of all distractions and becomes totally immersed in an artwork, these eight inborn emotions are transformed into the higher affective responses that we associate with art. For example, one's innate capacity to feel delight is the basis of erotic art, laughter is elevated to comedy by art, sorrow is transmuted into pathos, and anger is transformed into furious art.

There is a pervasive tendency in Indian philosophy to typologize, enumerate, and systematize. Writers long before Abhinava's time had equated the eight emotions with eight *rasas,* but Abhinava added a ninth, *śānta,* the artistic manifestation of tranquility. Furthermore, although all nine types of *rasa* are highly desirable, he considered some to be more elevated, deindividualized, and universal than others. For example, *kama,* the *rasa* of the erotic, was considered somewhat lower than *śānta*—not as a result of prudishness but because the transcendence that occurs via sensuality is highly dependent upon the senses, whereas the meditative experience of tranquility found in *śānta* has no such ties to the material world and can bring one directly to Brahman (cf. Munro 1965:76).

Whether art's power comes from its portrayal of divine subject matter, from its ability to use stylistic devices to transcend the particular to attain the universal, or from its capacity to transform the emotional history of past lives into the higher spiritual responses that pave the way to the pure bliss of the Absolute, the aesthetic writers of classical and medieval India clearly respected art's significance in human life. Like the other four Vedas, the "fifth Veda" of art provides a means of escaping the limitations of our mortality and of ascending to a higher plane of existence.

Implications of *Rasa* Theory

Having examined the core of the theory, we can complete our discussion of *rasa* by looking at it in the broader context of medieval Indian thought and

FIGURE 8-4 Shiva Vishapaharana. Bronze with green patina, dating from the ninth or tenth century. Eastern Chalukya period (615–1070), India, bronze with green patina, 18 1/2" x 8" (47.0 x 20.3 cm) *(The Nelson-Atkins Museum of Art, Kansas City, Missouri [Nelson Trust] 50-17.)*

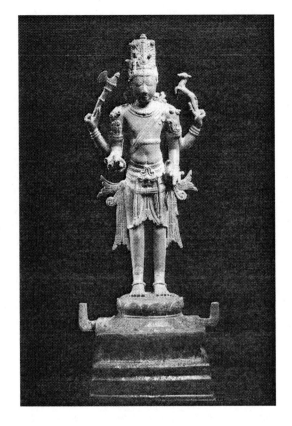

art. First, although being in a state of *rasa* resembles religious meditation, Indian aestheticians clearly separated the two. The rare mortal who attains complete spiritual emancipation is completely removed from the phenomenal world (Dhayagude 1981:23). By contrast, although *rasa* can free the *rasika* (susceptible person) from the passions and petty distractions that life holds, the artwork itself continues to link the *rasika* to the world of the senses. Even *śānta* must be prompted by an actual work of art. As Pandy puts it, *rasa* "is different from the mystic experience of the brahmin because it is a limited experience, though without the consciousness of limitation at the time it takes place" (Pandy 1952:478). On the other hand, the bliss of the lover differs from the bliss of the *rasika* in that its fulfillment requires reciprocal feelings from the loved one.

On a less ethereal level, we do not know the extent to which the theory of *rasa* influenced those individuals who actually produced art in early India (cf. Vatsyayan 1968:103; Organ 1975:12; Saraswati 1969:89). *Rasa*-theorists agreed, however, that artists—especially poets—have great potential power. After all, their creations can alter the course of a person's material and spiritual life. In the *Dhvanyāloka*, another major record of Indian aesthetics, Anandavardhana says, "In the shoreless world of poetry, the poet is the unique creator. Everything becomes transformed into the way he envisions it" (Masson and Patwardhan 1969:12).

However, it is not a personal, subjective vision that makes the artist a serious force in the world, nor is the percipient's private and distinctive reaction to art particularly significant. Indian aestheticians relegate an individual's idiosyncratic, subjective response to art to a position of minimal importance. Artist and audience member alike tap the powerful energy of art only insofar as they engage the various emotions that are part of *rasa* theory.

The literary arts—poetry and drama—provide most of the examples used by *rasa*-theorists, although some writers occasionally refer to other media, including the other Indian "fine" arts, music and architecture. In Pandy's words, for example, "Music idealizes the sensible. It represents in tone, not the material extension, but only the movement and quivering of the inner parts of the material body. . . . Music is beautiful because in it the Absolute shines through the pleasant sound" (Pandy 1952:484–485). Likewise, architecture "represents heaven on earth and therefore arouses wonder . . . , and leads to the aesthetic experience" (ibid.:486). Music and architecture, like drama, provide an avenue whereby one's self is transcended; and in medieval Indian thought, such transcendence is the definitive and invaluable purpose of art.

Conclusion

We cannot hope to totally reconstruct an aesthetic system of nearly a thousand years ago, so several interesting questions remain unanswered. Written records and oral traditions combine to reveal an extensive aesthetic of drama and, to a lesser extent, music and architecture; but what assumptions, explicit or covert, provided a foundation for painting and sculpture, body decoration and dancing? And although we must be grateful for our knowledge of the aesthetic speculations of brahmin intellectuals, one wonders to what extent the people at large knew about—much less agreed with—these rarified ideas.

Despite such gaps in our knowledge, however, the aesthetic system that does remain from classical and medieval India is remarkable for its internal consistency, complexity, and depth. *Rasa* theory begins with an important psychological fact, one that all of us have probably experienced at some time: Art can sweep us away, freeing our spirits of the tedious cares that besiege our daily lives. Momentarily unconcerned about our petty, unfulfilled desires, we cease wondering who we are, what we want, and how we can get it. In the aesthetic moment of suspended self, we experience a focused intensity, a merging with not just the artwork but with the harmony of all creation. The Indian writers knew that although the art experience begins with the senses, it provides a means whereby we can move beyond the sensory world around us and

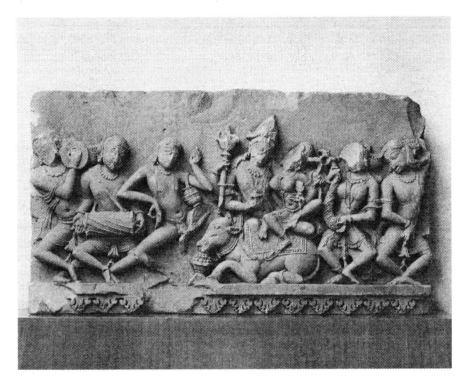

FIGURE 8-5 Shiva and Parvati on the Bull Nandi, attended by musicians and dancers. Buff sandstone (quartz arenite), 18" x 33 3/4" x 5 3/4" (45.7 x 85.7 x 14.6 cm) *(The Nelson-Atkins Museum of Art, Kansas City, Missouri [Nelson Trust] 35–304.)*

escape to a state of superior pleasure, practical betterment, and, ultimately, spiritual bliss.

Further Reading

The aesthetics of early India is not easy to study inasmuch as many of the English language source materials published in India are not commonly available in libraries in the United States. Munro (1965) and Organ (1975) are not difficult to find, but one generally needs time and persistence (and help from the interlibrary loan department) to get many useful studies, including Masson and Patwardhan (1969, 1970), Dhayagude (1981), Gnoli (1968), Krishnamoorthy (1979) and Pandy (1952).

Also to be recommended is *The "Dhavanyāloka" of Ānandavardhana with the "Locana" of Abhinavagupta* (Ingalls 1990). It holds a wealth of information, not only in its text but also in footnotes to the text, Ingalls' introduction (pp. 1–39), and its exhaustive bibliography (pp. 731–748).

9

JAPANESE AESTHETICS

An Exultation

of Beauty and Bliss

Art is an inspiration; life a fact.

(Anesaki 1933)

Contemporary Japan may bring to the Western mind a country of urban bustle and high-tech growth, but a moment's reflection reminds one of another Japan, a land where beauty is cultivated and art thrives. This seeming contradiction cannot be attributed to historical succession, with the delicate aesthetic sensibilities of the past being bowled over by a twentieth-century ethos of materialism. As the following poem shows, a thousand years ago Fujiwara no Kintō juxtaposed a crass vessel of trade, a sailing ship, with the natural beauty of morning mist in a scenic bay to convey a poignant feeling of melancholic loss.

> Dimly, dimly
> The day breaks at Akashi Bay;
> And in the morning mist
> My heart follows a vanishing ship
> As it goes behind an island.
>   (Fujiwara no Kintō, 966–1041)

As the poem suggests, Japan has a long history of simultaneously cultivating art and commerce. Indeed, few societies have been as successful as Japan in maintaining a fundamentally aesthetic sensibility throughout a long history of political, social, and religious upheaval and change. Fortunately for us, Japan also has a tradition of literacy, scholarship, and aesthetic self-awareness that allows us to uncover the primary philosophical and religious principles that have produced a society so pervaded by art that in the considered opinion of one Western scholar, aesthetics constitutes "the very essence of Japanese life."[1]

---

[1]"So important is the aesthetic in Japanese culture that it has been accepted by many students of Japan as the outstanding positive characteristic of Japanese culture as a whole. . . . In comparison with other cultures, the aesthetic has been considered to be the essentially unique

Background: Japanese History and Art

The wealth of available information about Japanese aesthetics and the technical sophistication of Japanese art make Japan a particularly interesting subject of study, but this same richness can overwhelm the nonspecialist. In the following paragraphs, I give only enough information about Japanese history and art to provide a context for our main concern, Japanese aesthetics.

For thousands of years, the residents of the Japanese archipelago lived as nomadic hunter-gatherers. A tribal stage followed, during which the Japanese acquired from the Asian mainland the skills of wet rice cultivation, pottery, metallurgy, and, in the sixth century C.E., writing. Finally, there emerged a society dominated by a few large clans and small kingdoms, each led by a powerful priest-chief. Political unity was established in Japan in the seventh century, and the stability of the resultant Imperial Era lasted nearly until the thirteenth century. This was followed by nearly four hundred years (1192–1568) of the Medieval Period, when provincial lords and their *samurai* retainers engaged in constant civil war. The strict rulers of the Tokugawa Period (1568–1867) reestablished law and order, but in 1867, the repressive and xenophobic policies of the Tokugawa shoguns gave way to the influence of Western powers and the era of modern Japan began. The following account focuses on the art and aesthetics of the Imperial, Medieval, and Tokugawa periods because, except for the oral tradition of Shintoism, scholars know little of Japanese culture before 600, and the principal aesthetic developments since 1867 have resulted largely from Western-style industrialism and trade.[2]

Japanese visual artists have worked in painting, watercolor, printmaking, sculpture, pottery, textiles, and architecture, exploiting all the media used by Western artists. In addition, the Japanese have also used other visual media, such as calligraphy and flower arrangement, that have been only occasionally utilized in the West. Still other activities in Japan, such as sword-making and the tea ceremony, have a distinctly aesthetic dimension that has no counterpart in the West.

As in the visual arts, the history of Japanese literature reveals a complex interplay between mainland and indigenous forces, producing arts of a distinctively Japanese character. For example, although writing came initially from China, by the tenth century the calligraphic characters used in Japanese writing had evolved into forms that were distinctly different from those found in China. Chinese remained the language for state documents during the Imperial Era; consequently, Japanese women, who were considered to be inferior by the standards of traditional Confucian dogma, were not taught

---

expression of spirituality in Japan, as is ethics in China, religion in India, and, possibly, reason in the West" (Moore 1967:196).

[2]Ueda (1967:viii) remarks, for example, that "the history of traditional Japanese aesthetics ends in the mid-nineteenth century."

Chinese, although they did commonly learn to write Japanese. It was predictable, therefore, that when some women began writing stories of their own imaginative creation, they set them down in Japanese, and, free of the strict conventions that applied to writing in Chinese, they invented a unique tradition of Japanese fiction writing. Indeed, because of these women writers' concern with their characters' private lives and psychological states, books such as *The Tale of Genji* and *The Pillow Book* may reasonably be regarded as the world's first true novels. Similarly, Japanese poetry and drama, though influenced by mainland cultures, exhibit characteristically Japanese qualities.

All cultures have their speculative thinkers and their systems of abstract philosophy. Some Westerners assume that religion is the primary vehicle of such thought in small-scale societies, whereas secular philosophy is believed to largely supplant religion in complex societies. Japan, however, does not follow this pattern. As we shall see, although Japan is rich in religious belief,[3] formal philosophy has never been well developed in Japan, as Japanese writers themselves have recognized.[4] Thus, Japanese speculative thought, like Japanese art, often substitutes insinuation and suggestion for explicit, concrete propositions. But this inexplicitness should not be confused with indifference. As we shall see, Japanese religions contain profound concepts that are applicable to many domains of culture—including art.

Shintoism's Seminal Influences on Japan

Of the three principal belief systems of Japan—Shintoism, Buddhism, and Confucianism—only Shintoism is indigenously Japanese, the other two having been imported from the Asian mainland. We have an incomplete understanding of early Shintoism because Japan had no system of writing before the sixth century, and subsequent written accounts of Shintoism may reflect Buddhist and Confucianist influences. However, by combining early historic

---

[3]Religion remains a potent force in modern Japan. A survey of religious affiliation (Hori et al. 1972) identified 165 different Shinto sects and subsects (with about 70 million adherents), 162 Buddhist sects (81 million adherents), and about three-quarters of a million Christians. That the total number of adherents is more than 50 percent higher than the population of Japan reveals that many individuals actively subscribe to more than one doctrine. Furthermore, these figures fail to note that many Japanese also accept the ethical and political principles of Confucianism.

[4]For example, Ienaga (1979:90) says, "there is no denying the poverty of Japanese output in the field of theoretical speculation as compared with the excellence of Japanese achievements in the fields of literature and art." Similarly, Nakamura has observed that although the Japanese language has always had "a rich vocabulary of words denoting aesthetic and emotional states of mind, words denoting intellectual, inferential processes of active thought are notably lacking. . . . It is extremely difficult to express abstract concepts solely in words of the original Japanese" (1967:182; see also Izutsu and Izutsu 1981).

writings with the oral traditions passed down to contemporary Shinto priests, scholars now have a good idea of traditional Shinto belief.

Shintoism is concerned primarily with Kami, or spirits, that are "invisible to the human eye in our normal state of consciousness [but that are] capable of exerting an influence on our visible universe" (Herbert 1967:25). The Kami can have good, bad, or ambiguous natures, and although some Kami are more powerful than others, none are omnipotent or omniscient. Shintoists recognize many Kami, with new ones sometimes being added to the pantheon as others fade into obscurity. Shintoism has little to say about human ethics, nor does it make many pronouncements about morality or an afterlife. Instead, it focuses on rites at shrines, where the more important Kami reside and are offered worship.

Although such a religion might seem just a fabric of what Ienaga (1979:18) calls "magical ceremonies," devoid of philosophical insight, Herbert's interviews (1967) with members of the upper echelons of the Shinto priesthood reveal that a metaphysical dimension of Shinto does exist and that it provides much of the philosophical foundation for Japanese aesthetics. *Change* and *purity* are fundamental concepts in Shintoism. To understand Shintoism's contributions to aesthetics, we must examine each of these in detail.

The Japanese word *masubi* expresses the abstract idea of change. Shinto priests told Herbert that this is the single most enlightening word in their religion. The term, Herbert says, may be translated as "the spirit of birth and becoming, also birth, accomplishment, combination; the creating and harmonizing powers. It embraces everything, including the Deities. Even Magatsuhi, the cause of every evil, is understood as a deviation of *musubi*" (Herbert 1967:67). *Musubi*—change—is personified by the rising sun, a symbol of both Japanese identity and the pre-eminent Shinto goddess, Amaterasu-ô-mi-kami. Moreover, *musubi's* "intangible meaning is a dynamic power uniting a pair of correlative opposites such as man and woman, day and night, and subject and object" (Herbert 1967:67). Such polarities generate change that is neither unilineal nor predictable. Instead, change is spontaneous and triune, with the potentialities of expansion, contraction, and evolution all aptly symbolized by Shinto's emblem, three comma-shaped figures whirling together to form a circle.

Inasmuch as Kami reside in specific locations in nature, if art is to portray the truly significant then it must be a faithful representation of nature (cf. Ueda 1967:214). This principle partially explains the frequent depiction in Japanese visual art of such subjects as landscapes, still lifes, and animals (see Figure 9–1)—a preoccupation whose uniqueness can be appreciated be recalling that humans (or deities that are either anthropomorphic or human/animal hybrids) provide almost all the subject matter for representational art in most of the rest of the world. Admittedly, not all Japanese paintings of nature are meant to represent Shinto Kami. Zen Buddhism, for

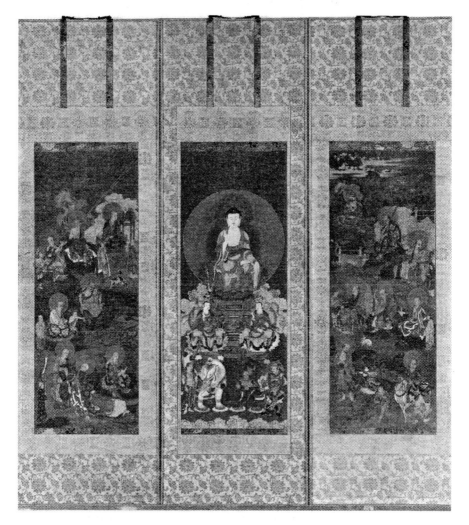

FIGURE 9-1 *Sakyamuni Triad with Sixteen Rakans.* 1400–1449, Early Muromachi (1392–1568). Three hanging scrolls mounted on panels, ink and color with gold pigment on silk. H: 175.2; W (total): 162.0, (each panel) 54.0 cm. Total size — 69" x 63 3/4" (175.3 x 161.9 cm). *(The Nelson-Atkins Museum of Art, Kansas City, Missouri [acquired through the Edith Ehrman Memorial Fund and the generosity of Mr. John W. Gruber]* F86–27 A–C.)

example, has its own tradition of landscape painting. But the naturalistic bent of Japanese art surely reflects to some degree "the most characteristic feature of Shinto [which] is a basic conviction that Gods (Kami), men and the whole of Nature were actually born of the same parents" (Herbert 1967:21).

Like change, the Shinto concept of ritual *purity* has deep roots in Japan, going back to a prehistoric period when people may have feared coming in contact with any contaminating substance such as blood. Not only do Shinto devotees maintain high levels of bodily cleanliness, but paths to Shinto

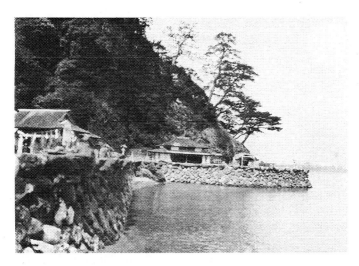

FIGURE 9-2   Photo of a Shinto Shrine at Futami ga ura, Japan. *(Courtesy, Field Museum of Natural History, Chicago, neg. no. 50240.)*

devotees maintain high levels of bodily cleanliness, but paths to Shinto shrines are typically located close to a small fountain or body of water where one is expected to rinse the mouth and otherwise purify the body (see Figure 9–2). At some shrines, the same end is accomplished by routing the path to the shrine over a small natural stream.

The Shintoist equation of beauty with cleanliness and goodness has informed Japanese thought throughout history.[5] Kōsaka (1967:257) observes, "morality in ancient times was aesthetic"; and a distinguished, contemporary Shintoist told Herbert (1967:90), "anything that impairs the aesthetic order is thereby 'impure.'"

The Shinto creation myth sheds much light on Japanese aesthetics. The long and complex story cycle centers around the Sun Goddess, Amaterasu-ô-mi-kami, and the creation of all material things. In a pivotal episode, Amaterasu-ô-mi-kami's brother has frightened the goddess into the Rock Cave of Heaven. Since she is the source of all sunlight, and hence is necessary for the growth and nourishment of all living things, the other Kami desperately need to lure her out of the cave. To this end, they create many things that later mortals value highly, including all plant and animal life. Still frightened, however, Amaterasu-ô-mi-kami continues to cower behind the cave's heavy door, seemingly unmoved by such practical wonders as the plant and animal kingdoms.

---

[5]In modern Japanese the same word—*kirei*—means both "beautiful" and "clean" (Sacchi Tahara, personal communication).

Then, the story goes, a Kami named Ane-no-uzume approaches the door of the cave and begins to play music and dance. As she does so, she exposes her pudenda and nipples, simultaneously suggesting sensuality and revealing the parts of the body most directly related to child-bearing and nursing, thereby reminding the Sun Goddess of her responsibility of bearing and nurturing the entire line of Japanese Emperors. Ane-no-uzume's music and dance pique the curiosity of the timid Sun Goddess, who opens the door just enough to look out of the cave. Having gotten her attention, the Kami hand to Amaterasu-ô-mi-kami a perfect mirror; and this, finally, induces the goddess to emerge from the cave, restoring her life-giving sunlight to the world (see Figure 13–1).

Japanese art and aesthetics reflect several components of this episode in the Shinto creation story. For example, Ane-no-uzume's music came from a bamboo flute and a zither-like instrument, the koto; in fact, the flute and koto are still used in Shinto temples as well as in secular settings. More important are the clues the story gives regarding an underlying Shinto philosophy of art. What is it about the arts that made them so appealing to the Sun Goddess? An old version of the story says that what caught the Sun Goddess's attention was the general merriment taking place outside the Rock Cave, and in one rendition the praise expressed by Ane-no-uzume's song was also an important enticement for the Sun Goddess, who said, "Though of late many prayers have been addressed to me, of none has the language been so beautiful as this" (quoted in Herbert 1967:308).

Thus, the Shinto creation story reflects a belief that making art pleases the all-important spirit world, thereby significantly enhancing human existence. This principle goes a long way toward accounting for the sweeping importance of art in Japanese culture. Mason has observed, "Practicality and beauty are commonly associated in Japan, for the Shinto conception of creative action sees an increase of value when the aesthetic and the practical are united. Art and utilitarianism are more naturally co-ordinated in Japan than in any other country" (Mason 1935:195).

A second important aesthetic principle can be seen in the Shinto creation story. Diverting music and dance may have persuaded Amaterasu-ô-mi-kami to peep out of the Rock Cave of Heaven, but it was the perfect mirror that finally brought the sun's light back into the world. In memory of this, many Shinto shrines still preserve mirrors as sacred relics. Beyond that, however, the mirror of the myth may be thought to symbolically convey an important feature of Japanese visual art. Like a mirror, art should depict a palpable reality; it should portray a subject matter as it objectively is, not the subjective fancies or fantasies of the artist. This is true no matter how spare or abstract the art may seem. Some works, such as Zen ink paintings, may seem cryptic, but their intent is realism nevertheless. The Shinto story of Amaterasu-ô-mi-kami and the Rock Cave of Heaven suggests that life as we know it, including the regenerative powers of the rising and setting sun, was made possible by art, as symbolized by Ane-no-uzume's music and dance and by the perfect mirror itself.

Over 100,000 Shinto shrines, each with one or more simple but elegant architectural structures, dot the countryside of contemporary Japan, and there are many more shrines that have little or no material accoutrements. Moreover, the Shinto creation myth leaves little doubt that art has played a central role in Japanese culture. Quite literally, Shintoists have the arts to thank for the very rising and setting of the sun each day.

Esoteric Buddhism and Japanese Aesthetics

Buddhism began in northern India, but it spread rapidly to the east. By the sixth century C.E., it arrived in Japan, championed by the then-dominant Soga clan. In contrast to the polytheistic beliefs of Shintoism, Buddha's teachings emphasized a unified reality underlying the multifarious gods, and it promised salvation to those who became one with that reality. Buddhists eschew the rituals of Shintoism, attempting instead to gain enlightenment through the powers of the mind. Attachment to personal possessions inevitably causes suffering, they believe, so enlightenment comes only to those who disengage themselves from material things, which in any case are so changeable that they can only deceive the unwary.

Hundreds of years passed before Buddhism became popular with the common people of Japan, and even among the courtly aristocrats, early Buddhism complemented, rather than supplanted, Shintoism. Furthermore, Japanese Buddhism was not initially so much a means of enlightenment as a symbol of the elevated status of the elite, prompting the construction of spectacular Buddhist monasteries and temples.

This situation began to change in 794 when the Japanese capital was moved from Nara to Kyoto, where it would stay during the 400-year Heian period of relative peace and prosperity. Contacts with the Asian mainland continued to bring new concepts to the imperial court, and of particular importance were the preachings of two Buddhist monks who had studied in China, Kūkai (also known as Kōbō Daishi, see Figure 9–3) and Saichō. Kūkai established a sect known as Shingon Buddhism, and Saichō founded Tendai Buddhism; both groups undertook a sweeping reformation of Japanese Buddhism. In contrast to the prior practice of simply saying prayers and performing appropriate rituals in the hope of ensuring the safety of the Japanese state, Kūkai and Saichō emphasized personal faith and spiritual development.

Kūkai was more influential than Saichō during the ninth century because he convinced the Japanese emperor that his Shingon teachings were based on the best form of Buddhism to be found in China. His practice, he said, came from the greatest of Chinese Buddhist monks, who passed on to

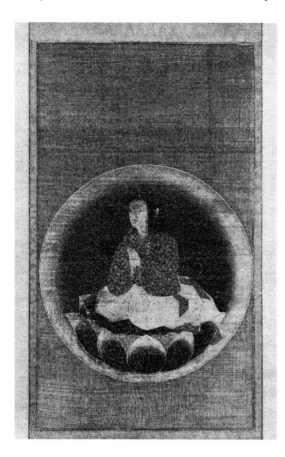

FIGURE 9-3 Chigo Daishi (The Great Master Kukai as a Child)", 15th century, Muromachi Period (1392–1568); Three hanging scrolls mounted on panels, ink, colors and gold on silk. H: 137.2; W: 521 cm (54" x 20 1/2"). H: 66.0 W: 31.8 cm (26" x 15") painting only. Total 69 x 63 3/4" (175.3 x 161.9 cm). *(The Nelson-Atkins Museum of Art, Kansas City, Missouri [Gift of Mrs. George H. Bunting, Jr.] 70–34/1)*

him a doctrine that had come down orally and in a direct line of succession from the Buddha himself, offering "the easiest and quickest means of obtaining Buddhahood" (Ryusaku, deBary, and Keene 1958:146).

The definitive trait of Kūkai's teaching is contained in his assertion that the essence of Buddhism "is called the esoteric treasury; the words are secret and of absolute truth" (Ryusaku, deBary, and Keene 1958:148). It is not unusual for a religion to claim a monopoly on truth, but whereas most religions hold out the promise of salvation to all people, Kūkai asserted that only those few who learned his secrets had any hope of achieving complete enlightenment.

By contrast, Saichō claimed that although his doctrines were quite similar to those of Kūkai, *he* was the one who had received the true, secret word of Buddha. Although Saichō's sect of Tendai Buddhism remained distinct from Kūkai's Shingon, the two faiths are often referred to collectively as "Esoteric Buddhism," reflecting their secret nature, in contrast to "exoteric" Buddhist doctrines, which were accessible to all. Kūkai said, "By these teachings the dust and stains of the world are cleansed away, revealing the splendor and solemnity of the *world of the mandalas*" (Ryusaku, deBary, and Keene 1958:153, emphasis added).

It is mandalas—that is, square or round paintings, decorated with geometric designs or arrays of figures[6]—that link Esoteric Buddhism with Japanese art and aesthetics. In describing his training in China, Kūkai wrote,

> The abbot informed me that the esoteric scriptures are so abstruse that *their meaning cannot be conveyed except through art*. For this reason he ordered the court artist Li Chen and about a dozen other painters to execute ten scrolls of the Womb and Diamond Mandalas, and assembled more than twenty scribes to make copies of the Diamond and other important Esoteric scriptures. He also ordered the bronzesmith Chao We to cast fifteen ritual implements. (Ryusaku, deBary, and Keene 1958:145, emphasis added)

The Womb and Diamond Mandalas that played such important roles in Shingon belief depicted various Buddhas, lesser deities, saints, and other supernaturals and are said to symbolize "the two aspects of cosmic life, its being and vitality. . . . The point emphasized was the harmony between unity and diversity" (Anesaki 1963:126). Followers of Esoteric Buddhism use mandalas as didactic devices, not only to instruct newcomers but also to remind the initiated of the many forms of absolute truth that are manifest in the Buddha and that are potentially present in every devotee. A millennium ago Esoteric Buddhism engendered a powerful aesthetic system, one that justified art's existence in the most convincing of ways: Only through art can one find salvation. And, practicing what he preached, Kūkai himself became a painter and effectively used the visual arts, music, and dance to aid his proselytizing for Shingon Buddhism.

Shingon art was highly formalized (a wrongly colored lotus petal could subvert an entire mandala), but the 400 years of the Heian period saw an impressive quantity of art production, with courtly life filled with ceremonial music, dance, and appreciation of the visual arts. The art-nurturing atmosphere of Esoteric Buddhism prompted the production of secular arts as well. Scroll painting flourished, and books such as the *The Tale of Genji* testify to the richness of the period's literature.

Even after the tumultuous Medieval Period supplanted the Imperial era, the principles espoused by the founders of Esoteric Buddhism continued to influence Japanese religion and art. A thirteenth-century monk named Nichiren called for a renewed commitment to spiritual purity and, like Saichō before him, he claimed to find the only true means to this end in a Buddhist text, the Lotus Sutra. Still later, Hon-ami, the leader of the influential

---

[6]A Tibetan mandala is shown in Figure 13–3.

Kano school of painting, perpetuated the impact of Esoteric Buddhism in Japanese art.

The Aesthetics of Amida Buddhism

Although Esoteric Buddhism continued to exist, the chaos and confusion of medieval Japan spawned additional religious movements. An important reaction to the rarified practices of the aristocracy's Tendai and Shingon Buddhism appeared in the form of Amida, or Pure Land, Buddhism. The Amida sect exchanged arid intellectualism for personal fervor, and by the twelfth century, Amida Buddhism had become a genuine mass movement.

Whereas Esoteric Buddhists attained enlightenment through knowledge of an array of Buddhas, Bodhisattvas (Buddhas-to-be), and so on, devotees of the new doctrine gained salvation solely by seeking Amida, the Buddha of Boundless Light. They justified this by citing passages in the sutras in which Buddha made an "Original Vow" that promised anyone who called out his name in perfect trust would spend an eternity of bliss in the "Pure Land" that Amida had prepared for his followers (see Figure 9–4).

The appeal of such a doctrine is obvious. Whereas Esoteric Buddhism had given devotees only dispassionate enlightenment, Amida Buddhism offered a life of bliss—a reward that must have seemed especially attractive during the turbulent Medieval Period. Further, whereas success in Esoteric Buddhism required extensive secret knowledge, passed down orally from teacher to a select group of initiates, the new sect promised deliverance to anyone who would call out the name of Amida.

Amida Buddhism had sweeping consequences for Japan. Many monks, giving up their scholarly endeavors, moved out of monasteries and either adopted secular lives or traveled through the land seeking converts to the new faith. Ippen, a thirteenth-century evangelist, reputedly had over two million names on his roster of converts. The popularity of the movement was matched by its members' fervent conviction. A monk named Yokan is said to have repeated the name of Amida 10,000 times a day in his youth and 60,000 times a day during the prime of his life (Hori 1968:119–120).

What was the role of art in Amida Buddhist belief? The contrasts between Esoterism and Amidism are illuminating. Whereas the mysteries of Esoterism were so profound that they could only be conveyed through the highly formalized art of mandalas, the goals and methods of Amida Buddhism were so accessible that proselytizers used popular art to spread the doctrine of Amidism throughout the land. Consider, for example, the techniques of an early advocate of Amida Buddhism named Kūya (903–972): Dancing through the city streets with a tinkling bell hanging from around his neck, Kūya called out the name of Amida and sang simple ditties of his own composition such as,

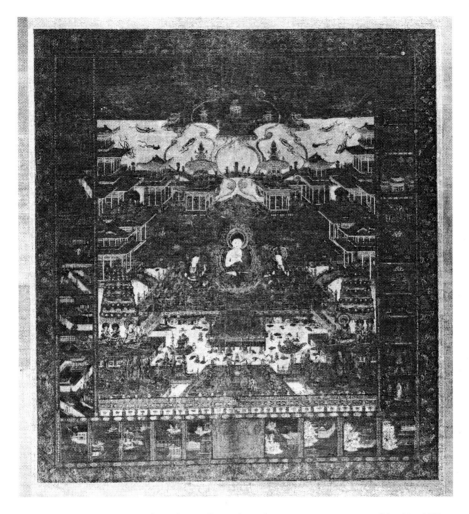

FIGURE 9–4 *The Paradise of Amida Buddha,* early 14th century, Kamajura Period (1185–1392); Hanging scroll, colors and gold on silk; 121.3 x 109.2 cm. (47 3/4" x 43") Painting only. 204.5 cm x 127.0 x 121.3 cm. (80 1/2" x 50") including mounting. *(The Nelson-Atkins Museum of Art, Kansas City, Missouri [Nelson Trust]* 63–12.)

Hito tabi mo	He never fails
Namu Amida bu to	To reach the Lotus Land of
Yu hito no	Bliss who calls,
Hasu utena ni	If only once,
Noboranu wa nashi.	The name of Amida.

In the market places, all kinds of people joined Kūya in his dance, singing out the invocation to Amida, "Namu Amida Butsu" (Ryusaku, deBary, and Keene 1958:193).

In contrast to Kūya, the monk Genshin (942–1017) never left his monastery at Mt. Hiei, but his careful study of the sutras convinced him of the spiritual efficacy of Amida and of the need to spread the message to as many people as possible. To this end, Genshin wrote a book that described the horrors of Hell and the delights of Paradise with such literary power that it became something of a best-seller in tenth-century Japan. Because tradition dictated that Genshin write his masterpiece in a modified form of Chinese that many could not read, however, the writer/poet also created paintings and sculptures in an effort to make his message more widely heard. The result was a dramatically new style of religious art. Forsaking the stiff, formal iconography of Esoterism, Genshin made paintings of Hell and Paradise whose realism was so affecting that they were said to cause nightmares among the ladies-in-waiting at the palace court (Ryusaku, deBary, and Keene 1958:196).[7]

Although Genshin modified the style of Japanese religious art, in certain respects the basic assumptions of Amida Buddhism reflect the Shinto roots of Japanese aesthetics. Art's primary purpose was still to bring about an identification between mortals and the forces of the supernatural world, and this goal was to be attained by realistically portraying the places where the spirits reside. The only difference was that whereas Shinto artists deal with Kami who live in mountains and streams, Amida Buddhist artists depict the paradisal home of the blessed and the hellish land of the damned.

Zen Aesthetics

The twelfth century saw a final major development in Japanese Buddhism, the importation from China of Zen beliefs and practices. Previously, Esoteric Buddhists had placed their faith in a body of secret and exclusive learning as a means of gaining spiritual enlightenment, and adherents to Amida Buddhism sought a paradise of bliss by faithfully repeating the name of Amida. Zenists combined elements of both these sects. Like Esoteric Buddhists, their goal was enlightenment rather than ecstasy, but, like Amida Buddhists, they proposed to attain this end through a technique that was, at least in theory, available to all—namely, silent meditation.

According to tradition, Buddha himself set the precedent for Zen Buddhism. To pass the core of his belief on to his chief disciple, Mahā-kāśyapa, Buddha simply held up a flower, and the student, in silence, smiled. The significance of the event lies in its being a face-to-face encounter between master and student, and in the student's response being intuitive, immediate,

---

[7]Anesaki, who is not prone to overstatement, asserts regarding Genshin, that "as a writer on the vices and miseries of life, on the varieties of existence and on the states of perdition or spiritual beatitude, he may be compared to Dante; while as a painter of paradise and saints he may be called the Fra Angelico of Japanese Buddhism" (Anesaki 1963:151).

and personal, rather than resulting from rational thought and the didactic learning of explicit doctrines. Anesaki says, "Every Zenist should receive his spiritual illumination through the medium of his own soul, directly from the vast sources of the cosmos. All instruction is but as a finger pointing to the moon; and he whose gaze is fixed on the pointer will never see beyond" (Anesaki 1915:49).

Early Zen leaders were divided on many issues—on whether written teachings had any value, on the validity of the Esoteric teachings, on the worth of *koans* (seemingly insoluble riddles given by master to student as a topic of meditation), and on whether meditation was a means or an end in itself. But all Zen sects believed, first, that the material world should be understood for what it is—namely, a place where disorder and flux are inevitable—and, second, that a person can transcend such a world only by replacing passions and consciousness with an intuitive and spontaneous acceptance of the unity of the universe.

Zen Buddhism never gained the wide popularity of Amida Buddhism, but it did find many converts in influential sectors of Japanese society. Besides intellectuals, Zen appealed to Samurai warriors because its doctrines accepted and transcended the rough world in which they lived. Bureaucrats and traders were interested for the same reason, and they also sought the advice of Zen monks on questions of foreign affairs because the holy men had recent and firsthand knowledge of China. For our purposes, however, Zen Buddhism is interesting because it led to a philosophy of art. The twin foundations of Zen aesthetics are *transcendental naturalism* and *spontaneous intuition* (cf. Anesaki 1915:53), each of which warrants our attention.

The transcendentalism of Zen lies in its assertion that all seeming boundaries, as between subject and object or between observer and observed, are illusory. Enlightenment cannot be found in consciously and rationally identifying with nature, but in experiencing a unification with the Oneness or reality. ("The real flower is enjoyed only when the poet-artist lives with it, in it; and when even a sense of identity is no longer here," says Suzuki [1983:184].) Since transcendental reality manifests perfect beauty, as symbolized by the flower that Buddha held up before Mahā-kāśyapa, religious practice becomes, in a sense, an aesthetic endeavor.

Unlike Esoteric and Amida Buddhism, Zen did not use art to explicitly disseminate its message or to gain converts. After all, Mahā-kāśyapa grasped Buddha's meaning in a flash of insight, not as a result of laborious, scholarly study. Nevertheless, the technique of much Japanese art since the thirteenth century, in whatever medium, reflects Zen beliefs. Japanese artists have long thought that "only when the artist's mind is as calm as the surface of a mirror can the real nature of the outside object be grasped" (Kishimoto 1967:117). In this remark, the art-as-mirror metaphor, an image that reaches back to prehistoric, Shintoist Japan, appears once again, but here the emphasis is on the transparency of the artist's sensibility. Far from "interpreting" nature, the Zen artist, in bold and unstudied brushstrokes, removes the apparent divisions between himself and nature.

One product of the Zen approach to art was paintings in which the viewer's own intuitions supply color to an otherwise monochrome drawing (see Figure 9–5). Such emotional reserve and economy of style produced a visual art that differed strikingly from the complex mandalas of Esoteric Buddhism and the dramatic depictions of heaven and hell of Amida Buddhism.

In literature, the sparseness and suggestiveness of Zen aesthetics influenced Nō drama, with its inexpressive masks and minimal plot, as well as the poetic forms known as *tanka* and *haiku,* composed of thirty-one and seventeen syllables respectively. The idea of the artist intuitively merging with nature also encouraged the arts of flower arrangement (see Figure 9–6) and landscaping. The acceptance of Zen Buddhism by members of the Samurai class led to such "martial arts" as sword-making, horsemanship, swimming, and archery. In the latter, for example, the archer's goal is not simply to hit a target. A cleverly designed machine could probably shoot arrows more accurately than the best human archer. From the perspective of Zen, the challenge of archery is essentially spiritual: The bowman attempts to maintain his limbs in a relationship of mutual harmony, to calm his soul, and to concentrate his mind. If he successfully accomplishes this, his arrow will inevitably be unified with the target (cf. Anesaki 1933:121–122).

Zen was the last major innovation in Japanese Buddhism, and it may not be coincidental that Japanese art also changed little after the fifteenth century. During Buddhism's first thousand years in Japan, however, the permutations that occurred in art were as rich and varied as those in religion. New art styles and media accompanied the earliest phase of Buddhism when it was still the private domain of a small, status-conscious aristocracy. With Esoteric Buddhism came the belief that only the art of the mandala could convey the profound teachings that pointed the path to enlightenment. Then Amida Buddhists used music and dance to attract converts, and paintings of heaven and hell strengthened believers' convictions. Finally, Zen beliefs provided a metaphysical theory of art production: Total focusing of concentration, nurturance of inspired insight, and a rigorous mental discipline that could demolish the apparent boundaries between self and a universe of perfect beauty—all for the purpose of unifying art and reality.

Japanese Confucianism

Confucianism also affected traditional Japanese art, albeit in a more subtle way than Shintoism and Buddhism. Like Buddhism, Confucian doctrine entered Japan from the Asian mainland in the sixth century; but whereas Buddhism strongly influenced Japanese religious and philosophical thought, Confucianism was primarily applied to secular matters, especially ethics and

FIGURE 9-5 *Priest Sewing Under Morning Sun,* painted by Shokado Shojo, 1584–1639, inscribed by Ryutan Shuken. Ink on paper, 43 1/2" high. Purchased with fundsfrom the Pan-Asian Trust Account administered by the Guaranty Bank, 1982.58. © *(Courtesy Denver Art Museum. All rights reserved.)*

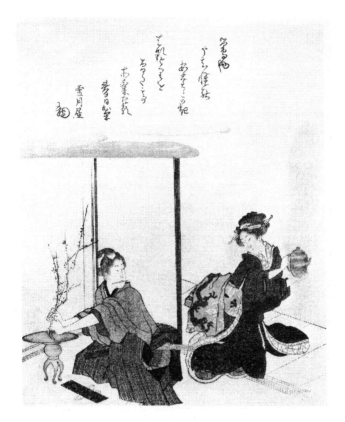

FIGURE 9–6   *Young Man Arranging Flowers. (Courtesy, Field Museum of Natural History, Chicago, neg. no. 49367.)*

government. It emphasized such abstract and general human qualities as virtue, magnanimity, and humanheartedness, as well as social values such as loyalty, courage, and politeness. Whereas Buddhism encouraged its adherents to turn away from the material world because of its changeable nature, Confucianism attempted to negate change by encouraging cultural stability. By codifying both the leader's responsibilities as well as the follower's duties, Confucianism generally appealed to those who held (and hoped to maintain) privileged positions. Also, Confucian ethics forbids movement from one social class to another, so for a long time the only effect of Confucianism on Japanese art was to increase the tendency for individual families to specialize in certain crafts, generation after generation.

Confucianism became more influential after 1568, when the Tokugawa shogunate restored political unity to Japan after the long period of medieval discord. In the arts, Confucianism primarily meant constructing elaborate temples. In the Shogun's court, it prompted such conservative and "edifying" arts as studying the classics of literature and painting, composing poems in the Chinese style, and writing official histories of Japan's past grandeur (cf. Hall 1959:285).

The motive for these activities was as much political as aesthetic. Whether it was a spectacular neo-Confucianist temple or an account of Japanese history written out in artistic calligraphy and illustrated by refined paintings, Confucian art depicted the glories of the Japanese state at the same time that it displayed and validated the pre-eminence of its current rulers.

Japanese Aesthetic Preferences

"Aesthetics" has to do with abstract ideas about art's fundamental nature and reason for being. "Art," by contrast, refers to paintings, poems, and dances. The richness of information about Japanese culture affords us the rare chance to pursue an interesting question: How are a society's theories of art reflected in its production of art? Obviously, aesthetic assumptions influence the subject matter of art. Esoteric Buddhism, for example, conceived art to be the sole means to spiritual enlightenment, so it is not surprising that the art of Esoteric Buddhism primarily depicts Buddhas, Bodhisattvas, and other deified beings.

Aesthetics may also influence the artistic *style* adopted by a culture. Donald Keene has convincingly argued (1971, 1995) that four stylistic traits—suggestion, perishability, irregularity, and simplicity—characterize most Japanese art. Have these qualities emerged autonomously or did they grow out of the Shinto, Buddhist, and, to a lesser extent, Confucian foundations of Japanese art? An examination of them, one by one, reveals that they *are* related to Japanese aesthetic values, but that their relationship to those values are complex, sometimes inverted, and always subtle.

For Westerners, perhaps the most alien feature of Japanese art is its avoidance of the straightforward and the explicit and its preference for the implied and the *suggested*. Consider again the poem on page 206, near the beginning of this chapter.

> Dimly, dimly
> The day breaks at Akashi Bay;
> And in the morning mist
> My heart follows a vanishing ship
> As it goes behind an island.

Fujiwara no Kintō wrote this *tanka* about a thousand years ago to illustrate standards of excellence in poetry, especially the criterion of suggestiveness. The poem is vague about the scene's placement in time: It is after daybreak, but the "morning mist," far from conveying a specific hour, reminds us of a hazy morning when, lacking an unequivocal sunrise, we feel suspended in a timeless state. The poem is also suggestive in being about a virtual non-event. A sailing ship is involved, but all we know is that it has just disappeared! Its size, appearance, and destination are all left to the reader's imagination. (Similarly, the title of the Zen painting in Figure 9–5 is *Priest Sewing under Morning Sun,* but we view the priest from behind and can only guess at the work that presumably lies on his lap.) The emotional core of Fujiwara no Kintō's poem is the statement that his "heart follows" the ship, but again we are left to speculate on the reasons for these feelings. Was a loved one on the boat? Did the poet long to leave on the boat for another land? Fujiwara no Kintō believed that his *tanka* benefited by suggesting many possibilities rather than explicitly stating a set of factual events. A similar taste for suggestiveness pervades most Japanese literature and art—the *haiku,* with its spare seventeen syllables, the cursory treatment of subject matter in a Zen ink painting, or the Nō theater.[8]

Japanese artists' awareness of the importance of suggestiveness is seen in their many discussions of *yūgen.* In the fifteenth century, Shotetsu Monogatari said that *yūgen* is "suggested by the sight of a thin cloud veiling the moon or by autumn mist swathing the scarlet leaves on a mountainside" (Ryusaku, deBary, and Keene 1958:285). The theory of *yūgen* focuses on an individual's emotional reaction to an aesthetic situation. Mumyo Hisho wrote that *yūgen* is experienced "when we look at the sky of an autumn dusk. It has no sound or color, and yet, though we do not understand why, we somehow find ourselves moved to tears" (Ryusaku, deBary, and Keene 1958:285).

The most obvious place to seek the roots of *yūgen* is in Zen Buddhism. Zenists, after all, forsake the conscious study of explicit dogmas and seek instead the spontaneous, intuitive insights of meditation. The parallels between this technique and the artistic sensibility associated with suggestion lie in their shared emphasis on the personal, unconscious response, attained by the use of a suggestive stimulus—the Zenist's *koan* or the artist's subject matter.

However, inasmuch as *yūgen* theory seems to have existed in Japan several centuries before the arrival of Zen Buddhism, the former could not have sprung from the latter. At most, Zen nurtured a stylistic preference that already existed. Buddhists had long displayed a preoccupation with the obscure and with the belief that the palpable, sensory world is only a reflection (or suggestion) of the invisible world of true Buddhahood. After all, the sutras record the tale of Mahā-kāśyapa's spontaneous smile when Buddha held up a rose.

---

[8]Keene says of Nō: "The undecorated stage, the absence of props other than bare outlines, the disregard for all considerations of time and space in the drama, the use of language that is usually obscure and of abstract gestures that are scarcely related to the words, all make it evident that this theater . . . was meant to be the outward, beautiful form suggestive of remoter truths or experiences, the nature of which will differ from person to person" (Keene 1971:16).

Zeami Motokiyo (1363–1443), the pre-eminent theorist of Nō drama, has suggested another possible source of suggestiveness of Japanese art. He believes that *yūgen* should not be sought as an end in itself, but as a means of gaining deeper truths: "Yūgen, then, is the beauty not merely of appearance but of the spirit; it is inner beauty manifesting itself outwards" (Ueda 1967:61). This Shintoist concern for things' inner spirits prompted the sixteenth-century aesthetician Tosa Mitsuoki to remark, "All good works of art are lifelike, not so much in the sense that they copy all the outward details of real life, as in the sense that they observe all the inward laws of nature" (Ueda 1967:131). Moreover, Shintoism, like Buddhism, encouraged artists in Japan to focus on the inner spirit of an art work and to recognize that the work's tangible manifestation could never be more than a "suggestion" of this essence.

Perishability is another stylistic trait found in much Japanese art. Keene says,

> Whatever the subject matter of the old poems, the underlying meaning was often an expression of grief over the fragility of beauty and love. Yet the Japanese were keenly aware that without this mortality there could be no beauty. Kenko wrote, "If man were never to fade away like the dews of Adashino, never to vanish like the smoke over Toribeyama, but lingered on forever in the world, how things would lose their power to move us! The most precious thing in life is its uncertainty."[9] (Keene 1971:24)

An infatuation with perishability sheds light on the Japanese love of cherry blossoms. Although their appearance and scent are not unlike those of plum blossoms, cherry blossoms are short-lived and, like the ideal *samurai* warrior, they fall at the peak of their beauty (Keene 1971:12–13). Both common experience and contemporary psychology support the Japanese belief that the gratitude we feel for something increases when we understand its impermanence. Nonetheless, artists in most cultures, especially those in complex societies, strive for permanence. Where does the Japanese preference for perishability come from?

If a Japanese love of suggestion derives from the concept of *yūgen*, artistic perishability is related to *aware* (or *mono no aware*). When it first appeared in Japanese writing, *aware* meant "an exclamation of surprise and delight," or one's reaction to "the 'ahness' of things" (Ryusaku, deBary, and Keene 1958:176). The concept evolved with the passage of time, however, so that by the eleventh century, it meant "pity and sympathy" (Anesaki 1963:156), often in relation to unrequited love.

Like *yūgen, aware* has a curious relationship to Buddhism. Granted, the ephemerality of the sensory world is, for Buddhists, the strongest evidence of

---

[9]Adashino was a graveyard, and Toribeyama the site of a crematorium.

its being inferior to the realm of the spirit, or true Buddhahood. But this line of reasoning leads most Buddhists to renounce the material world rather than to glory in its supposedly greatest flaw, its impermanence. So perhaps the high value that has been placed on perishability came about in part as a reaction against the world-denying aspect of Buddhism or else against the restrictive, impersonal, and unemotional code of conduct prescribed by Confucianism (cf. Anesaki 1963:159).

Motoori Norinaga, a contributor to the eighteenth-century Shinto revival, gives a clue to a possible Shinto origin of *aware*. Norinaga was highly critical of rationalism and placed his faith in the prescient, creative, and seemingly irrational Shinto deities (Ueda 1967:196). The alternative to unproductive rationalism, Norinaga said, was *mono no aware*; by means of feelings, one touches true meaning. Thus, "through literature man can return to his innermost self—the self that is energetic and creative as bestowed by the God of Creation. Literature helps one approach Shinto gods, who are more truly human than modern men" (Ueda 1967:212).

Admittedly, Norinaga was writing long after *aware* had become an influential concept in Japanese art style, and he does not explicitly emphasize the implications of *aware* for the Japanese concern with perishability. But he does point the way to a possible link between *aware* and perishability. The Shinto deities, as spirits of nature, are unmoved by human reason, but, as we are reminded by the dance of Ane-no-uzume that enticed the Sun Goddess to peep out of the Rock Cave of Heaven, the Kami do respond to more elemental forces such as delight, fear, and simple aesthetic pleasure. Herbert, speaking not of artists but of Shintoists, says that "one of their key phrases is *mono-no-aware*, sympathy with all creatures" (Herbert 1967:21).

So the philosophical basis of the Japanese fascination with perishability in Japanese aesthetics may be this: Buddhism and Shintoism both emphasize the sad fact that all material things have only a brief existence. Humans, too, are not long for this world. In the transience of art works, one sees one's own fate, a vision that prompts the strongest of emotional reactions.

Keene (1971:18–23) cites many examples to illustrate the Japanese penchant for stylistic *irregularity* and *simplicity*. Prime numbers, for example, play an important role in the poetic form of the *tanka*, whose thirty-one syllables are broken into five lines of five, seven, five, seven, and seven syllables each. Also, although Japanese Buddhist monasteries were originally patterned after Chinese structures that had symmetrical floor plans, Japanese architects soon began using asymmetric plans for their own buildings. Japanese ceramic works are often irregular, both in shape and in glaze, and the famous rock gardens of Japan stand in striking contrast to the precisely geometrical layout of formal gardens in the West.

The traditional Japanese tea ceremony may be the best example of irregularity and simplicity, however. An early form of tea had inspired a small tea cult as long ago as the eighth century, but green tea did not appear in Japan until it was brought from China by Eisai (1141–1215), the Buddhist monk who also introduced Zen Buddhism. Although monks initially used tea to avoid falling asleep when they meditated, tea soon became popular beyond the walls of the monastery (Hayashiya, Nakamura, and Hayashiya 1974).

The traditional tea ceremony takes place in a small structure that is notable for its simplicity. Only muted colors and a minimum of adornments are found within. This, complemented by the faint scent of astringent incense, creates a pervasive feeling of tranquility. The tea itself is prepared and served by the use of implements that, though costly, are unostentatious. When the tea has been poured, "it is placed before the visitor, who must lift the cup in both hands, feeling its texture and warmth. He drinks the tea, not in one gulp but three sips, savoring the liquid as refreshing as some precious elixir though made of a most common, ordinary leaf" (Ryusaku, deBary, and Keene 1958:266). In the past, masters of the tea ceremony have explicitly called for simplicity, or *wabi*, in the preparation and drinking of tea (Tanaka 1998:73–77).

The tea ceremony's symbolism, which is too elaborate to describe here in detail, reflects Zen beliefs.[10] For example, although the privy that typically stands outside the tea house may seem anomalous to the Westerner, it suggests to tea ceremonialists "the incessant changes through which the human body passes" (Ryusaku, deBary, and Keene 1958:264). Also, just as Zen meditation should lead to spiritual enlightenment, the tranquil setting of the teahouse should promote *furyu*—a combination of elegant refinement and simple amusement (Hayashiya, Nakamura, and Hayashiya 1974). Similarly, the irregularity and asymmetry found in the tea house's design, its decorations, and the ceremony itself reflect an appreciation of the uniqueness of every artwork and the idiosyncratic aesthetic response of every individual, a principle in keeping with Zen beliefs.

Again, however, the facts of history confound the analysis because the Japanese taste for irregularity and asymmetry predate Zen Buddhism. They might reflect the perennial Buddhist belief that the material world's diversity and imperfection conceal an underlying unity of the cosmos. Shintoism also may be involved—in two ways. First, it seems logical that the Shinto quest for purity would lead to a preference for the clean and simple over the fussy and ornate. Second, Shintoism's emphasis on nature may have contributed to the Japanese avoidance of symmetry. As Anesaki has pointed out, nature itself is rarely symmetrical (Anesaki 1933:18–19).

---

[10]"A lot of the preparations involved are a reflection of Zen thought, so much so that in later days the expression 'Zen and Tea are one and the same' came to be used" (Tanaka 1998:78).

As in most of this analysis of the relationship between Japanese style and aesthetics, this argument seems strained, and we must conclude that although theory usually influences practice, aesthetic philosophy and artistic production are, at most, only loosely linked to one another.

Conclusion

The richness of the literature on Japanese art, religion, and culture allows us to understand Japanese aesthetics in greater depth than is possible in almost any other society. But this same richness is also humbling, making one aware of the incompleteness of even our best efforts. A central assumption of Buddhism is that reality is fundamentally enigmatic; similarly, as Ueda has remarked, "Japanese aesthetic writings tend to be metaphorical rather than analytical, and impressionistic rather than rationalistic" (Ueda 1967:225).

If the essence of Japanese thought is elusive, some of its more superficial aspects are also unclear. For instance, this account has said little about the psychological functions of art. What emotional reaction should art prompt in the audience member? A review of literary theorists has led one scholar to claim that the aesthetic response should be cathartic, that it should liberate one from life's inevitable pettiness and boredom, and that it should evoke the joy of learning (Ueda 1967:23–35), but this important subject has not been sufficiently explored.

Equally uncertain is the way in which Confucianism has influenced Japanese art and aesthetics. The early poet Ki no Tsurayuki (868–946?) claimed that poetry "strengthens men's moral sense and helps create order in this world. Rulers educate their people by means of poetry, and people advise their rulers by means of poetry" (quoted in Ueda 1967:23); and 500 years later, another poet, Yoshimoto, asserted that the Confucian axiom, "That which makes all men follow is good" (Ueda 1967:39), applies to literature. These remarks only whet one's curiosity regarding the general influence of Confucianism on Japanese aesthetics.

Despite such shortcomings, the study of Japanese aesthetics does pay substantial dividends. Japan has been called an "aesthetic culture," and an examination of Japanese history and society indicates this to be true on several levels. First, art plays a crucial role in numerous influential religious traditions. Shintoism accords art a special place in its creation myth, and a striving for harmony, purity, and creativity are fundamental to Shinto thinking. Buddhism also stresses unity and intuitive development, and several Buddhist sects proclaim art's efficacy for spiritual development. Specifically, the message of Esoteric Buddhism is believed to be so subtle as to be communicable only via the art of the mandala; Amida Buddhism uses song, dance, and other popular art forms to gain converts and to ensure their loyalty through graphic depiction of the horrors of hell and the bliss of heaven; and the meditation required of Zen Buddhists promotes an intuitive sensibility and focused concentration that are as valuable in art as in religion.

A second reason for considering Japan to be an aesthetic society is the extent to which artistic factors influence many day-to-day activities. Keene notes that the visitor to modern-day, industrialized Japan is inevitably impressed by "the flowers gracefully bending down from a wall-bracket over the toilet; or the artistically brushed signboard in the railway station which proves to mean 'Left Luggage Room'" (Keene 1971:11).

The rich literature on Japanese art and thought also allows us to get a rare insight into the relationship between, on the one hand, the abstract principles of aesthetics and, on the other, the stylistic traits that give Japan's art its distinctive qualities. The four values that Keene discusses—suggestion, perishability, irregularity, and simplicity—are highly consistent among themselves, but their relationship to Japanese aesthetics seems complex. Certainly, there are resonances between the two systems, but it is equally certain that each possesses a fair amount of autonomy from the other.

Finally, some grasp of the complex history of aesthetic thought in traditional Japan is necessary for an understanding of art in modern Japan. This chapter has looked only at developments through the end of the Tokugawa Period in 1867. However, if Buddhism and Confucianism from China had a powerful influence on Japanese art before that time, Western technology and trade have had a great impact on Japan since then. Conversely, Japan is a major force in an emergent global aesthetic.

Consider, for example, the distinctive form of video animation known as anime. Some of its roots are Japanese, going back to seventeenth century picture stories known as Ukiyo-e Monogatari, or Tales of the Floating World. After World War II, a graphic artist named Osamu Tezuka, influenced by American animated films (he is said to have seen the Disney *Bambi* eighty times) and European cartooning, invented a distinctive type of cartoon book for adults called *manga*. The name came from the early nineteenth century Japanese printmaker, Hokusai, for whom it meant "irresponsible pictures." In the 1960s, an animated version of manga, called *anime*, developed in Japan, where its adult contents and creative visual style made it a major popular art form. By 1980, anime's audience had expanded well beyond the shores of Japan, extending from mainland Asia to the West. In America, anime (with adult themes removed) became a staple of television programming for children, but also (*with* adult themes) it was an important component of a new cyberpunk subculture. Such are the cultural cross-currents that make our world exciting. Japan is especially important in this phenomenon, in part because of the uniqueness of its own traditional aesthetic principles, but also because it continues to meld them with artistic elements from abroad to produce remarkable and vital hybrid forms of art.

Further Reading

The volume of writing in English on Japanese culture, religion, and art is enormous, more than the non-specialist can hope to master. I list here only sources that I have found the most helpful.

The account of Shintoism by Jean Herbert (1967) is valuable for its methodological rigor and objectivity. The work of Masaharu Anesaki (1915, 1933, 1963), though far from recent, is useful on Japanese Buddhism.

Two anthologies that contain a variety of important essays and excerpts from seminal works are those edited by Ryusaku, deBary, and Keene (1958) and by Hume (1995).

Books that go beyond mere description to examine the underlying principles of the Japanese tea ceremony are Hayashiya, Nakamura, and Hayashiya (1974) and Tanaka (1998).

The idea that Japanese art has a distinctive affinity for suggestion, perishability, irregularity, and simplicity comes from the eminent Japanese scholar, Donald Keene (1958), and has been reprinted in various anthologies, such as the volume edited by Hume (1995), mentioned above.

Although not discussed in detail in this chapter, Japanese aesthetics continued to evolve after the mid-1800s. Marra, ed. (2000) and Marra and Marra, eds. (2001) are excellent English-language overviews of these developments.

10

WESTERN AESTHETICS

A Quartet of Traditions

Aesthetics is for the artists as ornithology is for the birds.

(Barnett Newman, quoted in Wolfe 1975:79)

By looking at others, we gain new perspectives on ourselves—on the society that bore us and on the psychological terrain of our own minds. In short, the study of the Other can foster a deeper and more critical understanding of Self. So, armed with some understanding of aesthetics in nine other societies, we now look into the mirror to scrutinize Western thinking about art, subjecting it to the same questions that aided our examination of philosophies of art elsewhere.

We often assume that the hallmark of the West is its science and technology, or else the amazing productivity of its business economy. After all, these were the features that led to the West's partial or total domination of many of the societies we have already discussed. In such a view, the aesthetic dimension of Western culture is of secondary importance.

If we are to avoid semantic confusion, however, we must apply the same definition of "art" to the West that we have been using in previous chapters, taking the word to include not just those things and activities that were created by full-time specialists to fulfill "aesthetic" (in the narrowest sense of the word) needs, but also such things as body decoration, recreational music, oral literature, decorated religious artifacts, and so on.

Applying such a broad definition of art to Western culture reveals just how artistically fertile Euro-American civilization has been and continues to be. For example, consider your own situation at this very moment. You are reading a book that was printed using a *style* of type that was created by an individual trained and experienced in designing type faces that are (among other things) both *expressive* and *pleasing to the eye;* the book's cover and overall *design* received the same attention by others. *Architects* planned the building and room in which you sit, again prompted by considerations of function, cost, and *appearance,* and you (or interior designers) gave similar thought to the room's *decorations.* Your clothes reflect not only your *tastes* but also the *fashions* of our era. If not just now, then probably sometime today you will hear *music* of one *genre* or another, and this evening, the *dramas* or *light come-dies* of television will be available for relaxation unless you choose to end your day by seeking more active activities such as *live music, theater, film,* or *dance.* Then again, you might indulge your taste for *literature* by settling down with a good—or, at least, engrossing—book. Viewed in this light, art is all around, for every waking moment of your life!

Or consider the role of art in weddings. Surveys indicate that the average American couple spends about $20,000 (roughly 40 percent of their yearly income) on their wedding, honeymoon included (Anonymous 1990, 1991),[1] almost all of it for things that are art or art-related. Much of it falls in the category of what, in a small-scale society, would be termed "body decoration": special clothes for the bride, groom, bridal attendants, bride's mother, best man, and ushers; engagement and wedding rings; trousseau and honeymoon clothes. Also, most couples go to some trouble to make the wedding into something of a theater event, paying for a special person (clergy) to direct the ceremony, using an aesthetically special place (church, synagogue, or perhaps even the rose garden of a public park) in which the event is staged—all preceded by a rehearsal (and rehearsal dinner) and followed by a reception, both of which feature music, dance, and special food including the all-important, and often spectacular, wedding cake. Flower arrangements are almost always included, and the wedding invitations and announcements are usually printed on special cards, complete with formal calligraphy. Then there is the limousine (not a jalopy, but a specially designed, perfectly maintained vehicle), as well as photographs (again, not just snapshots, but large photos made by a professional photographer). Obviously, none of this is necessary for a legal wedding; but it is equally clear that most couples feel a profound need to include a great deal of art in the ritual.[2]

Some of the activities that fill our day-to-day lives cannot be considered to be "art," much less "great art," but when one considers the pervasive concern with objects and activities that are "expressive" and "pleasing to the eye," that reflect "taste," "fashion," and "style," or that are popular manifestations of traditional art media—music, drama, dance, and so on—then one realizes just how much art surrounds us at every moment. The affluence of Western society is well known, and it allows us not only to meet our primary needs of

---

[1]Data such as this from bridal magazines is clearly unrepresentative of Americans as a whole in that the publications seek a middle- and upper-class readership, and magazine publishers seek statistics to convince advertisers of the lucrative market to which they provide access. The figures in these surveys do, however, receive some corroboration from reports of annual revenues from the sale of wedding accouterments such as wedding gowns and rings. Surveys in 1999 continue to give average wedding costs as about $20,000.

[2]In *American Muse: Anthropological Excursions into Art and Aesthetics,* I explore more fully the popular arts that accompany contemporary American rituals and holidays (Anderson 2000:41–58). I also discuss at greater length the premise that there is more art in our everyday surroundings than one might at first suppose [ibid.: 17–40].

food, shelter, and reproduction, but also to profusely decorate and sensuously enhance virtually everything we make and do, to say nothing of creating art for its own sake. An evaluation of the relative merits of fine art versus popular and folk art is not the issue here (cf. Gans 1974). What *is* relevant is the simple conclusion that the West has produced, and continues to produce, vast quantities of art.

Likewise, the West has a considerable storehouse of speculative thought related to the art it has produced. We are all "natives," and although we may disagree about the "gray" areas between what is and is not art, between good and mediocre art, and between valid and spurious reasons for art's existence, few of us would be unable to give examples that fall unequivocally in "black" and "white" areas on each of these questions. Thus, Da Vinci's *Mona Lisa* is an instance of fine art, a police "mugshot" is not; the Rolling Stone's "Satisfaction" is an example of popular art, and the "rat-tat-tat" from a jackhammer outside the window is not.[3]

Overview: A "Quartet" of Aesthetic Systems

During the course of Western history, countless views have been aired concerning many of the same questions addressed in the nine previously discussed societies. Although diverse writers claim that theirs is the one and only embodiment of truth, in fact distinct patterns of aesthetic thought are evident. Close inspection reveals that nearly all Western philosophies of art fit into one of four categories. Indeed, although the historians of philosophy who have attempted to systematize Western aesthetic theories have sometimes used different labels in their taxonomies, there is a surprising degree of agreement that there has been a "quartet" of aesthetic traditions in the West, with each voice in the ensemble representing a tradition that can be traced back to ancient Greece and that is still heard today (cf., e.g., Abrams 1953, Stolnitz 1960; Pepper 1945).[4]

Examinations of the four major theories of Western aesthetics will form the main part of the present chapter, but before looking more closely into

---

[3]Of course, it is possible that either of these—a mugshot or a jackhammer's sound—might be transformed (through selection and method of presentation) into art by a conceptual artist.

[4]Three provisos must be made at this point. First, although specific Western aesthetic *theories* tend to fall into one of four categories, actual *people* and *artworks* cannot be so straightforwardly classified. A person inevitably uses different aesthetic criteria to evaluate varied artworks, and a particular work may be responded to from more than one aesthetic perspective. Second, although the four traditions are usually distinct from each other, at times they overlap or are complementary in their concerns. Third, Western theories of art *criticism* are more numerous and varied than Western art *philosophies*, which deal with the ultimate nature or purpose of art.

the first of these, a very brief overview of all four of the theories is in order to provide a comparative perspective for each theory.

- *Mimetic theories* focus on the relationship between the work of art and some material object in the sensible world that the artwork "imitates," either literally or else by capturing it in an idealized form.

- *Instrumental theories* emphasize the functional capacity of art, requiring art to make some sort of positive contribution to the well-being of individuals or society. Religious art, with its goal of enhancing the spiritual condition of the art audience, constitutes the most common type of instrumental art, but political art is also instrumental.

- *Emotionalist theories* center on neither the material nor the social world but on the psychological realm of inner experience and feelings of the individual. Again, the specific locus of interest varies. Emphasis may be on the artist's expression of emotion, on cathartic purging of audience members' feelings, or on the creative act.

- *Formalist theories* do not deal with material, social, or psychological issues, but rather with the aesthetic or technical challenges of the art work itself. Under the paradigm of formalism, art is thought to be a unique manifestation of "significant form," a manipulation of an artistic medium that is capable of producing a unique and arresting response in the aesthetically attuned audience member.

In every era, one of the theories has generally prevailed over the others, so in the following pages we shall begin with the mimetic tradition, which dominated aesthetics in the classical civilizations of ancient Greece and Rome, then move on through instrumental and emotionalist theories, and conclude with formalism.[5]

Besides chronology, the following remarks will also be given structure by distinguishing between "fine" and "popular" arts. To judge from the writings of philosophers, the four major traditions have to do with the stylistically sophisticated fine arts that thrived in the West under the perennial patronage of a political and economic elite. But the West has a long and fertile tradition of producing popular art as well, and I believe these arts also rest on the same four aesthetic traditions mentioned above. Therefore, of the sections that follow, each aesthetic theory will be described in relation to the fine arts and then examined for its applicability to the popular arts. The final picture that emerges is of a culture that has not only created prodigious quantities of fine and popular art but that also has produced a rich and complex body of speculative thought concerning art's meaning and role in human affairs.

---

[5]Postmodern theories have generally reincorporated instrumental—and to a lesser extent, mimetic and emotionalist—concerns into the previously reigning paradigm of formalism.

Mimetic Theories

If the four Western aesthetic theories are thought of as constituting a vocal quartet, with one paradigm singing the melody while the others provide backup harmonies, then mimetic theories were the first to carry the tune. A Greek-derived term related to such English words as "mime" and "imitate," the word *mimetic* refers to art that is made to represent some concrete, specific, extra-artistic subject matter. Myron's sculpture portraying the quintessentially athletic *Discus Thrower* (or the Roman *Male Torso* seen in Figure 10–1); Leonardo da Vinci's portrait of a burgher's smiling young wife, *Mona Lisa;* and the battle for Leningrad during the Russian Revolution, as depicted in Sergei Eisenstein's film, *Potemkin*—each is an example of a classic work of art that was created in an effort to portray some specific subject.

No matter what divergent courses art theorists have followed, Western artists have always attached great importance to art's capacity to imitate the world around them. For example, in his *Treatise on Painting,* Leonardo asserted that among various paintings, "That painting is most praiseworthy which conforms most to the object portrayed" (quoted in McMahon 1956, frag. 433). Many developments in the visual arts, from the Renaissance down to the present day, have been prompted by artists' efforts at simple, mimetic art, be it fourteenth-century Italian painters' discovery of ways to depict geometric perspective or nineteenth-century French impressionists' attempts to render the dazzling play of sunlight on natural subjects. And, equally obviously, an impulse toward realism remains a very important force in contemporary popular art forms, such as television drama and charcoal portraits made by sidewalk artists.

Straightforward, literal imitation has found only limited support among Western speculative thinkers on art, however. Of the major philosophers, only Plato conceived art to be no more than an imitation of sensible reality, and for this reason he belittled art's value. After all, if ultimate reality resides in abstract Platonic Ideas, and material objects are mere shadows of such Ideas, then an artwork that portrays material objects could be no more than "shadows of shadows," twice removed from reality! Artists, too, often admit that there may be more to art than simple imitation. For example, even the most realistic of artists (such as the nineteenth-century artist, William Harnett, who was arrested by Treasury Department agents for his *trompe l'oeil* paintings of U.S. currency) have not been able to resist the temptation to heighten the color and texture of their subjects (Stolnitz 1960:115–116).

Plato's student, Aristotle, sounded a note that has been repeatedly heard in the mimetic tradition. In *The Poetics,* he argued that art can accomplish far more than literal imitation—it can convey the *essence* of the subject matter at hand. Aristotle asked, for example, What makes poetry different from other kinds of serious writing, such as history? His answer was that whereas history merely replicates nature, poetry "is a more philosophical and

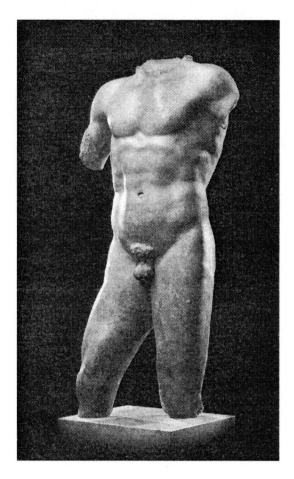

FIGURE 10-1 *Male Torso,* second century B.C., Greek. Marble, 36 1/2" x 20" x9 1/2" (92.7 x 50.8 x 24.1 cm). *(The Nelson-Atkins Museum of Art, Kansas City, Missouri [Nelson Trust]* 41-48.)

a higher thing than history: for poetry tends to express the universal, history the particular" *(Poetics,* 1451a 36).

This idea provided a goal for a different sort of mimetic aesthetic. Art was still conceived as being an imitation of some specific subject matter, but although the artist might begin with a particular, concrete subject, the artwork ultimately transcends this literal subject to convey abstract, ideal concepts. Aristotle himself argued that the definitive trait of tragedy lies in its portrayal of characters who embody pan-human weaknesses and struggles. Thus, the visual arts should depict ideal and perfect beauty (see Figure 10–2), not the unique imperfections and idiosyncrasies that distinguish one person from another. (An often-repeated story recounts that the Roman painter Zeuxis, in an attempt to sculpt the divine beauty of Juno, "had the young maidens of the place stripped for examination, and selected five of them, in order to adapt in his picture the most commendable points in the form of each" [cited in Abrams 1953:37].)

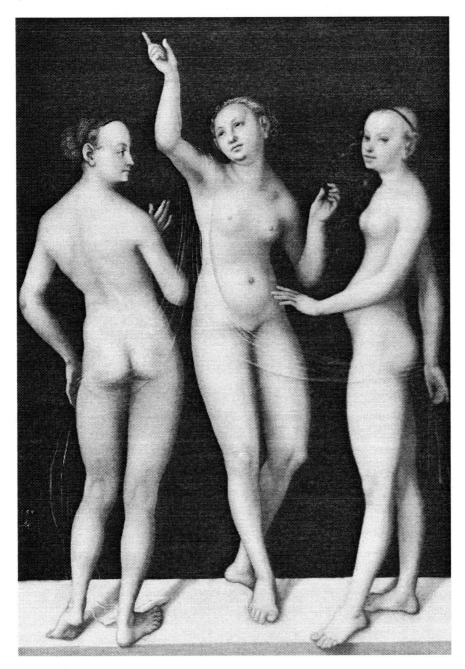

FIGURE 10-2   Lucas Cranach the Elder, *The Three Graces*. Oil on panel, 1535; 19 7/8" x 14 1/6" (50.5 x 35.7 cm). *(The Nelson-Atkins Museum of Art, Kansas City, Missouri [Nelson Fund]. 31-90.)*

During the Middle Ages, artists and writers continued to assume that art was basically mimetic, but they emphasized the religious functions of mimesis, a theme that will be discussed later along with other instrumental theories. But the Renaissance brought a renewed interest in mimesis for its own sake, and the result was the invention of perspective drawing and the sophisticated figurative painting techniques that typify the era (Figure 10–3).

With the neo-classical period, 1550–1750, the mimetic impulse merged with idealism, leading the visual and literary arts to depict not only classic beauty but also ideal principles of ethical and moral perfection. The old Aristotelian approach of portraying the transcendent and pan-human, rather than the particular and idiosyncratic, regained popularity. Speaking for his own era, Joshua Reynolds criticized Rembrandt's mimesis-inspired paintings because they sometimes showed mere commoners in mundane settings, using closely observed details to convey the uniqueness of each subject. Such art, the neoclassicists believed, could never serve art's highest purpose, which was to produce an uplifting effect on the audience.

FIGURE 10–3 Frans Hals (1581–1666), *Portrait of a Burgher.* Oil on canvas, 42" x 36" (106.7 x 91.4 cm). *(The Nelson-Atkins Museum of Art, Kansas City, Missouri [Nelson Fund] 31–90.)*

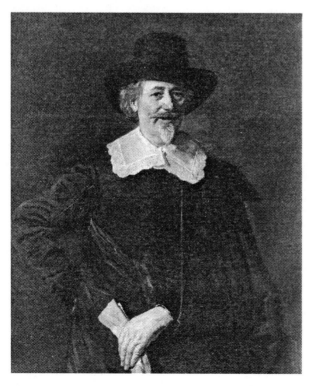

Mimetic theories have not been prevalent in serious aesthetic writing since the romantic rebellion against neo-classicism 200 years ago, but even if mimetic theorizing and criticism are passé in the fine arts, they remain a powerful force in popular thinking about the arts in the West. Consider, for example, the fate of *Star Thief,* a large painting by James Rosenquist. It portrays the vast reaches of outer space by setting against a black, starry background the images of modern machinery and architecture as well as fragments of a woman's face and floating slices of bacon. In 1981, a Florida arts committee proposed purchasing the work (for more than a quarter of a million dollars) to hang in the Eastern Airlines concourse in the Dade County Airport. The plan was vetoed, however, by the president of Eastern Airlines, Frank Borman. As a former astronaut, Borman had seen outer space firsthand, and he knew very well that it did not look anything like Rosenquist's painting! In Mr. Borman's opinion, the artwork was poor because there was "no correlation between the artist's depiction and the real thing" (quoted in Park 1986:22), a judgment that reflects the staunchly mimetic philosophy of a person outside the world of fine art.[6]

The aesthetic of mimesis is found in much popular art. The photograph on a bedroom dresser is treasured because it reminds its owners of their idyllic vacation trip to the mountains many years ago; a song about young romance becomes a favorite because it describes an experience sought for and shared by many people; or a movie about a World War II submarine crew has a forceful impact on the audience because of its portrayal of a heroic effort to survive a tragic, impersonal war. In each of these cases, art is valued because of its capacity to represent, either literally or ideally, some subject in our lives.

Popular art can be mimetic in unexpected ways, as revealed by an analysis of American songs (Anderson 2000:65–88). The study found that about a third of the 850 diverse songs examined made some descriptive (i.e., mimetic) reference to the arts. To cite just one subject area, overtly religious songs often portray art in a otherworldly setting, so that "heaven" is a place of singing angels, divine music, spotless robes, and shining crowns. The arts are found in "hell" as well, where the devil is a sharp dresser and mean fiddle player. American song lyrics also describe the arts as being in the spiritual realm. To cite just one of several examples from the sample, a song from 1965 that is still sometimes played on "oldies" radio stations says,

---

[6]Similarly, United States customs officials once seized a semiabstract sculpture entitled *Bird in Space* by Constantin Brancusi on grounds that it was not art and should therefore not enter the United States duty-free. At the trial, the government lawyer argued, "Mr. Brancusi claims that this object represents a bird. If you met such a bird out shooting, would you fire?" (quoted in Stolnitz 1960:135). Ultimately, the court decided that the work was indeed art, a ruling that reflected the ascendancy of formalism in the twentieth century.

The magic's in the music,
And the music's in me.

(Lovin' Spoonful,
"Do You Believe in Magic?")*

Finally, the arts are sometimes referred to in song lyrics as if they are an independent, animistic force, as in the case of musical instruments that positively
want to perform. Insofar as song lyrics paint a picture of American culture's
beliefs about art's transcendent dimension, they are mimetic.[7]

The mimetic tradition has been pervasive and enduring in the West.
Even the largely religious art of the Middle Ages relied on the assumption
that art's spiritual efficacy comes from its ability to depict sacred themes. Similarly, the emotionalist aesthetic of the romantic movement is based on the
belief that art's special capacity to provoke powerful feelings is due to its representing subject matter that is affecting.

Although one could force a great deal of Western aesthetic thought
into the mimetic mold, to do so would be misleading. For one thing, no matter how we try we cannot convincingly explain some sorts of art in mimetic
terms. Many art forms, including much instrumental music, most dance and
architecture, nonrepresentational visual art, and many popular arts such as
haute couture, do not depict a material subject outside the artwork itself.
That is, they are not mimetic in the way that, say, figurative painting is.

An even more compelling argument for a pluralistic model of Western
aesthetics is that some aestheticians and artists have defined art in terms that
are distinctly different from the mimetic ones discussed thus far. For a complete picture, then, we must look at other aesthetic paradigms that have been
important in Western culture.

Instrumental Theories

Instrumental theories of aesthetics are based on the belief that art should do
something worthwhile for the community that produces it. Art should serve
as a tool—an instrument—for human betterment. Specifically, art should
pave the way to a world that is socially, politically, or (most frequently) spiritually better.

Many varieties of art in the West find their justification in instrumental
aesthetic theories. For example, art made for purposes of political propa-
ganda is used in an effort to convince people to support a different, and ar-

---

*"Do You Believe In Magic," words and music by John Sebastian. Copyright © 1965 by
Alley Music Corporation and Trio Music Company, Inc. Copyright Renewed. International Copyright Secured. All Rights Reserved. Used by permission.

[7]The same chapter in *American Muse* also examines the lyrics' portrayal of metaphysical
themes, such as power, energy, and truth; the interplay between art and human emotions; and
art's role in society (cf. Anderson 2000:201–212).

guably better, political regime, and "art therapy" attempts to use artistic media to improve the mental health of individuals with psychological problems. But by far the most common type of instrumental art is made for religious (or "anagogic") purposes.

The roots of aesthetic pragmatism can be traced back to the Old Testament of the *Bible*. In contrast to the Greeks, who saw art's value as lying primarily in its intrinsic, formal qualities, the Hebrew tradition usually emphasized the effect art had on the percipient. It was not until the Middle Ages, however, that the anagogic potential of art was fully realized (see Figure 10–4). During that period the artist was expected to create beauty, but only as a means to as a end: Beautiful objects that symbolize heaven and the laws of the universe were believed to be the most effective teachers of God's ways (cf. Tatarkiewicz 1970b:291). Thus Suger, the twelfth-century abbot of the cathedral at St. Denis, wrote of his church, "I delighted in the beauty of the house of God; and the diverse colour and shapeliness of the gems detached me

FIGURE 10–4 *The Flagellation of Christ,* from Troyes Cathedral, 1220–1240, Chartres, France. Stained glass, lead, thirteenth century; 53.3 cm in diameter. *(Courtesy Denver Art Museum, Dora Porter Mason Collection. 1947.33 © Photo by Denver Art Museum. All right reserved.)*

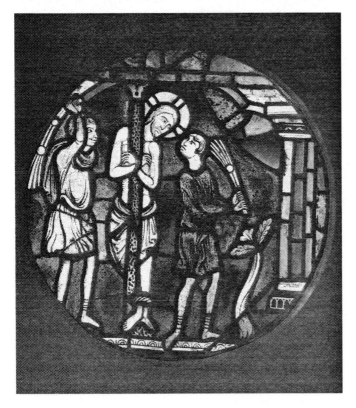

from my outward cares and, bearing me from the material to the non-material sphere, inclined me to reflect on the diversity of holy virtues" (quoted in Panofsky 1955:60). Not only was the subject matter of medieval art overtly Christian, but also an elaborate symbol system enlisted colors, flowers, and items of dress to convey additional messages (cf., e.g., Ferguson 1954).

The notion that art should have a higher purpose by no means died with the Middle Ages. As noted previously, neo-classicism represented a merging of mimetic means with instrumental ends. The resultant aesthetic is apparent in Sir Philip Sidney's *An Apologie for Poetry*, which, dating from the 1580s, is perhaps the first work of art criticism to be written in the English language. Sidney claimed that poetry "is an arte of imitation, for so Aristotle termeth it in the word *Mimesis,* that is to say, a representing, counterfeiting, or figuring foorth—to speak metaphorically, a speaking picture: with this end, *to teach and delight*" (quoted in Abrams 1953:14; emphasis added). Similarly, Dr. Johnson praised Shakespeare's works because, Johnson believed, "the end of writing is to instruct; the end of poetry is to instruct by pleasing" (Abrams 1953:19).[8]

Religious art is still produced in the modern era, of course. Some is in the form of popular art with, for example, gospel music enjoying a large audience. Colleen McDannell has given a remarkable inventory of "material Christianity," that is, the myriad popular art items, from mass-produced portraits of Christ to T-shirts carrying the printed message, "God ♥ You." Moreover, a few fine artists, such as Georges Rouault and Edward Elgar, have produced profoundly religious art.

The instrumental aesthetic also has come down to us in the form of political and utopian art, which are made in an effort to direct people toward a better way of life. Equally instrumental are authors who hope their writing will bring about social reform, a tradition that can be traced from Charles Dickens through Upton Sinclair and James Baldwin, to the plethora of self-help and New Age authors, all of whom attempt to reveal in order to instruct. Realism in photography (e.g., Riis's photographs of New York slums in the 1890s) and in cinema (e.g., Costa-Grava's films about political oppression in various countries) fit the same pattern.

Aesthetic theories based on instrumentalism were largely out of fashion through much of the twentieth century, with only the rare writer, such as Suzi Gablik, arguing that the visual arts should have a moral or ethical dimension, or John Gardner calling for a literature that "establishes models of human actions, casts nets toward the future, carefully judges our right and wrong directions" (J. Gardner 1978)—a remark that echo's Dostoevsky's hopeful prediction that "Beauty will save the world" (Zenkovsky 1962:136).

---

[8]The idea that art is both representational and a model for human behavior is supported by cross-cultural research that suggests that art generally *does* reflect a culture's fundamental themes, although the message tends to be structural and implicit rather than didactic and explicit (cf. Fischer 1971; Anderson 1979:46–48).

In the last decades of the twentieth century, however, the paradigm of postmodernism brought politics back into the fine arts, as seen, for example, in the work of artist Judy Chicago (cf. Lucie-Smith 2000). Her major installations have been overtly political, dealing with feminist issues such as women's place in Western civilization and art history (*Womanhouse* and *The Dinner Party*), birth and creation images (*The Birth Project*), her own Jewish heritage (*The Holocaust Project*), and the house, as seen from the perspective of residents of Kentucky (*At Home*). Chicago collaborated with others in these works and she has often used media, such as quilts, that traditionally have been more associated with popular art than fine art. Such methodological decisions reflect Chicago's fundamental goal, which is to use art to empower and educate women, a goal that does not seem unrealistic: *The Dinner Party* (Figure 10–5), her best known work, has been seen by a million people in six countries. On her website, Chicago affirms her "commitment to the power of art as a vehicle for intellectual transformation and social change and to

FIGURE 10–5   Judy Chicago, *The Dinner Party* (detail of Virginia Woolf and Georgia O'Keeffe place settings). Mixed media installation, 1979. *(© Judy Chicago, 1979. Collection of The Brooklyn Museum, Brooklyn, NY. Gift of the Elizabeth A. Sackler Foundation. Photo © Donald Woodman. Through the Flower.)*

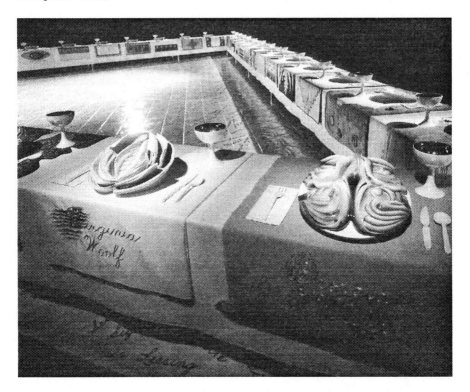

women's right to engage in the highest level of art production" (www.judychicago.com). In Judy Chicago and many other postmodern, politically aware individuals in the visual, performing, and literary arts, the instrumental aesthetic is alive and well in the contemporary Western world.

Emotionalist Theories

In the mid-eighteenth century, the dominant voice in the quartet of Western aesthetic traditions began to shift from the pragmatism that spawned neoclassical art to the emotionalist beliefs that fueled the romantic rebellion. It might be said that if the reality of mimetic art is found in the material and social world, and the truth of instrumental art lies in the moral, ethical, and spiritual realms, then emotionalist theories take as their domain the individual's feelings.

The historic roots of the emotionalist tradition antedate romanticism, however. As noted above, the ancient Hebrews were less interested in an artwork's external characteristics than they were in its effects on the inner experience of the percipient. Aristotle developed a similar concept in his theory of catharsis. Tragic poetry was valuable, he believed, because by engendering pity and fear it purged pent-up emotions of those who experienced it, emotions that otherwise could be harmful. Aristotle also noted that in the art of rhetoric, persuasion is accomplished by, among other things, stirring the audience members' feelings. The later Roman writer, Lucretius, also contributed to the emotionalist tradition by asserting that emotions are of fundamental human importance because they derive from a primordial past in which men were supposedly "endowed only with instinct, passions, and mere potentiality of reason" (Abrams 1953:83).

The voice of emotionalist aesthetics can even be heard during the Middle Ages, as a counterpoint to the prevailing instrumental thinking of the time. For example, some genres of oral literature, such as Goliardic verses and the fabliaux, were created principally for entertainment, and there was a widely held belief that a regular dose of "literary pleasure" helped sustain one's mental, and even physical, well-being (Olson 1982).

It was in the late eighteenth century, however, that a coherent and pervasive emotionalist theory appeared in the form of the romantic movement, which viewed art as an embodiment and expression of emotion. The creative process itself became a major focus of interest, and art's "subject matter," if it may still be called that, became the artist's personal thoughts, perceptions, and feelings. Even today we speak of artistic "expression," a term suggesting that something is "forced out by a pressure from within" (Abrams 1953:138); indeed, fine art was increasingly thought to be produced by individuals who, because of their exceptional sensitivity, possess an abnormally great measure of emotion and feeling, psychological states that well forth in the creation of art.

Because of its great popularity, and also because of the easy availability of writing, the tenets of emotionalist theory can be found in the words of modern artists themselves. For example, the mid-nineteenth century French painter Corot called explicitly for emotionalism, individuality, and sincerity in painters: "Be guided by feeling alone . . . [follow] your own convictions. It is better to be nothing than an echo of other painters. . . . If you have really been touched, you will convey to others the sincerity of your emotions" (quoted in Stolnitz 1960:158). Wordsworth, for his part, defined poetry very simply as "the spontaneous overflow of powerful feelings" (quoted in Abrams 1953:21).

Such thinking had interesting ramifications for art. Nature scenes and common people, both of which were portrayed in such a way as to emphasize their (or the artist's) feelings and passions, provided common subject matter (see Figures 10–6 and 10–7). Also, criticism in the visual arts placed less emphasis on the artist's skillfulness in representation (as mimetic aesthetics had dictated) or on the social and moral message of the subject matter (as prescribed by the aesthetic of instrumentalism). Instead, the first requisite of an art work was its uniqueness: Since every person's feelings are individual and inborn, no artwork should be a copy of another. One consequence of this was the ascendence of the belief that in making fine art, a forgery is considered unethical—indeed, not to be art at all, even though there may be no discernable difference between the fake and the real thing.[9]

Formalism later supplanted romanticism in most serious writing on the arts, but emotionalist aesthetic values remain alive and well today, providing a foundation for much Western popular art. However, whereas artists themselves are still commonly thought to possess heightened sensibilities, the greater emphasis today tends to be upon art's effects on the audience member's emotions.

Thus, emotionalist aesthetics provides a clear justification for most popular art forms. Rock concerts; recorded background music in stores, restaurants, and offices; and the interminable broadcast of music to home and car radios—all are intended to bring pleasure, diversion, and some degree of enjoyment to those who hear them. The same motives prompt Westerners to spend millions of dollars each year to go dancing and to the movies, and still more is spent by advertisers in an effort to sell their products through association with the comic and/or dramatic offerings of television.

---

[9]Ross Bowden [1999] has shown just how culture-specific this position is. In the course of his fieldwork in the Sepik, Bowden found that the Kwoma believe all art was originally brought into being by supernaturals. Mortals are in no way expected to be creative, and the best human carvers are those who can make the most accurate duplicates of sculptures and bark paintings when the old ones start showing their age and need to be replaced. So for the Kwoma, originality, far from being a definitive and necessary trait of art, is consciously avoided.

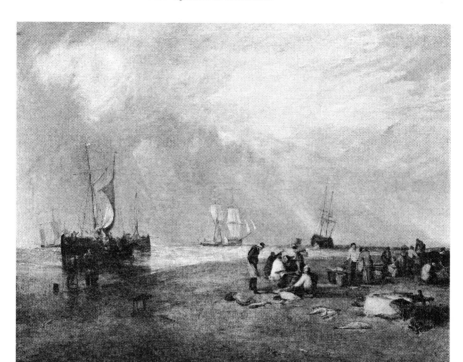

FIGURE 10-6 Joseph Mallord William Turner (English, 1775–1851), *Fish Market at Hastings Beach, 1810.* Oil on canvas, 47 1/2" x 35 3/4" (120.65 x 90.80 cm). *(The Nelson-Atkins Museum of Art, Kansas City, Missouri [Nelson Trust], 31–74.)*

An illustration of the importance of emotions in popular art is found in research conducted by Csikszentmihalyi and Rochberg-Halton (1981). They systematically asked a large sample of individuals, "What are the things in your home that are special to you?" They then went on to ask why the objects mentioned were "special," what life would be like in their absence, and so on. The objects people mentioned as being special can be sorted into forty-one categories, and of the ten most-mentioned categories, each one is either directly connected with art (e.g., "visual art" and "stereo") or else an object that typically gives aesthetic gratification (e.g., "plants" and "plates," both of the decorative variety). Many of the other, less frequently mentioned categories, such as jewelry, clothes, quilts, and silverware, also have aesthetic associations. Only rarely did people have feelings of specialness for nonaesthetic things such as sports equipment, telephones, or refrigerators.

The personal significance that their owners attach to these objects is even more interesting, revealing how often emotions make our favorite possessions special. Although one might expect art objects to be valued primarily for their aesthetic qualities, this was true only 16 percent of the time. Far more important were the sentiments that people attached to things, espe-

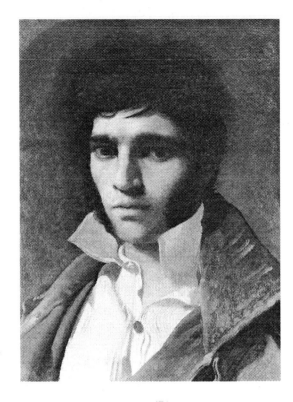

FIGURE 10-7   Jean Auguste Dominique Ingres (1780–1867), *Portrait of the Sculptor, Paul Lemoyne.* Oil on canvas, 1808–1820; 18 9/16" x 14 3/8" (47.14 cm x 36.50 cm. *(The Nelson-Atkins Museum of Art, Kansas City, Missouri [Nelson Trust] 32-54.)*

cially feelings that linked the owner to another person. A representative example is a woman who said, "I am going to keep this thing [a bust] forever. I wasn't even in school and me and my mother went to the store and I told her this looked like her, so she bought it. I'm going to keep this for life. It reminds me of my mother" (Csikszentmihalyi and Rochberg-Halton 1981:77).

Csikszentmihalyi and Rochberg-Halton's study shows that the most important art in people's day-to-day lives usually is not valued merely because of its subject matter (in compliance with mimetic theory), nor because it makes people more religious or ethical (as the instrumental paradigm calls for). Rather, art mostly matters because of the *feelings* it evokes. The emotions may not reflect the high romanticism of Wordsworth or Corot, but they are potent forces nonetheless.

Formalist Theories

An aversion to the supposedly harmful effects caused by art that "only" makes one happy can be found in the Old Testament, and it has appeared in Western thought periodically ever since. In the early twentieth century romanticism was largely replaced in serious writing on art by the aesthetic of formalism. This school of thought asserts that art is valuable because of its "formal" qualities—the painter's use of color and composition, the music composer's mastery of the sonata form, or the poet's choice of words to fit a rhyme scheme.

Like the other three aesthetic traditions of the West, the roots of formalism can be traced back to classical sources. Pythagoras (or one of his followers) said, "order and proportion are beautiful and useful, while disorder and lack of proportion are ugly and useless" (quoted in Tatarkiewicz 1970a:86); and several generations later Aristotle asserted in *The Metaphysics* (ibid.:31) that "the main species of beauty are order, symmetry, and definiteness." This outlook (which was later injected into Christian writings by Greek translators) led classical artists and aestheticians to seek harmony, proportion, and measure in artworks. Later, these goals were embraced by medieval and renaissance thinkers, but they were antithetical to subsequent baroque and romantic artists. By the late nineteenth century, however, the aesthetic pendulum had started to swing back toward the idea that formal qualities are what matter most. For example, the painting now popularly known as *Whistler's Mother* was actually named *Arrangement in Gray and Black* by its creator, James Abbott McNeill Whistler, because, he said, "That's what it is. To me it is interesting as a picture of my mother; but what can or ought the public to care about the identity of the portrait?" (quoted in Canaday 1981:214)

In the early twentieth century such notions coalesced in an influential school of criticism known as formalism. Roger Fry, Clive Bell, and others found perfection in the "significant form" of the finest of art, a quality that is identified by its capacity to provoke in the sensitive audience member a powerful and distinctive "aesthetic response." Bell asked,

> What quality is shared by all objects that provoke our aesthetic emotions? What quality is common to Santa Sophia and the windows at Chartres, Mexican sculpture, a Persian bowl, Chinese carpets, Giotto's frescoes at Padua, and the masterpieces of Poussin, Piero della Francesca, and Cezanne? Only one answer seems possible—significant form. In each, lines and colours combined in a particular way, certain forms and relations of forms, stir our aesthetic emotions. (Bell 1958:28)

Formalism's uniqueness becomes more apparent when it is contrasted with the other three aesthetic traditions of the West. Unlike mimetic theories, formalism does not emphasize art's ability to resemble some of extra-artistic subject matter. Thus Bell says, "Let no one imagine that representation is bad in itself; a realistic form may be as significant, in its place as part of the design, as an abstract. But if a representative form has value, it is as form, not as representation" (Bell 1958:42). Indeed, formalism can be seen as a natural consequence of twentieth-century artists' shift away from representationalism and toward abstract art (Figure 10–8), a trend that was to ultimately provoke such dictums as, "The meaning of painting is paint!" Formalism is equally distant from instrumental theories, and the "preachiness" of much religious and political art is considered by formalists to be a liability rather than an asset.

Finally, although formalism resembles emotionalist theories in its definition of art as that which evokes a powerfully affective response in the percipient, it is significantly different from emotionalism. Formalism claims that the psychological response to true art is unique. According to formalist thinking, gazing upon an abstract masterwork by Mondrian, for example, is an altogether different experience from, say, looking at a magazine illustration of a tow-headed boy digging a grave for his beloved but recently deceased dog, Rover. The latter picture might bring a tear to the viewer's eye, but a formalist would assert that such a sentimental response has no more to do with true art than the tear shed by a loyal sports fan whose team has just lost a pivotal game in its otherwise promising season. With formalism came the phrase, "art for art's sake."

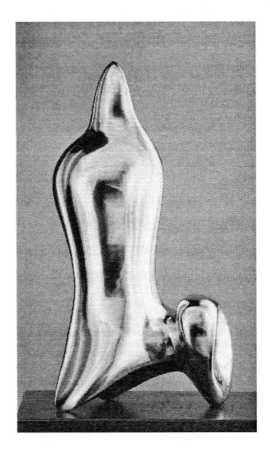

FIGURE 10–8 Hans Arp (French, 1887–1966), *Vue et Entendue* (Seen and Heard), 1942. Polished copper alloy H 13 1/4" (33.65 cm). *(The Nelson-Atkins Museum of Art, Kansas City, Missouri [Gift of the Friends of Art], F63-14.)*

Formalism has had particularly interesting implications for literary criticism, since the written word inevitably conveys some subject matter. Formalist critics, from the earlier era of "new criticism" to the more recent school associated with "deconstruction," have attempted to look at literature as an artifact that exists above and beyond its overt meaning. Formal analysis concentrates on such qualities as the work's conformance to its genre or its style of word use. The assumption behind such approaches is that the critic's proper goal is "to explore the concept of the poem as a heterocosm, a world of its own, independent of the world into which we are born, whose end is not to instruct or please but simply to exist" (Abrams 1953:27).

Almost all formalist writing from Aristotle's time to the present has focused on the fine arts. However, insofar as formalism focuses on the artist's consummate mastery of a medium, it corresponds to a fascination with artistic technique that the public at large has regarding all the arts, whether fine or popular. Artists possess levels of skill that far exceed those of nonartists, so in many people's minds the mere ability to perform a piano concerto, to dance *sur les pointes,* or to realistically draw a person's likeness insures that the maker is an "artist." Popular artists, too, are respected for their exceptional talent, training, and effort. Furthermore, the common tendency to define art as being nonutilitarian, to believe that art does not do anything (except bring some grace into one's life!)—this too resembles the formalist perspective on art.[10]

Formalism, both as narrowly applied to the fine arts and in its broad and enduring application to the popular arts, has played a significant role among Western aesthetic traditions. As native members of Western culture, many of us must admit that the basic premise of the formalist argument strikes a resonant note in our thinking about art. There *is* something very special about those things we consider to be art, a quality that somehow transcends art's mimetic, instrumental, and emotionalist potentialities.

Conclusion

The West has produced vast quantities of art as well as a correspondingly large amount of speculation about art's underlying purpose and nature. The long

---

[10]The study by Csikczentmihalyi and Rochberg-Halton of things that Americans consider to be "special" in their homes found that although emotional factors were given most commonly to explain people's attachment to their special things, formal qualities ("style" and "aesthetic considerations") were also mentioned for more than one-quarter of the items of visual art. Even the hope that a painting will "go with the drapes" is formalistic in a sense.

sweep of Western history has seen many permutations of abstract thought. Western aesthetics has been steadfastly pluralistic, a "quartet" of traditions composed of four related but distinctive voices.

These four paradigms also have had an impact on the evaluation of actual artworks. For example, George Boas's clever paper, "The Mona Lisa in the History of Taste" (1963/1940) traces the vicissitudes of critical thought regarding Leonardo da Vinci's portrait of a burgher's young wife. During the painter's lifetime, the work apparently was not considered to be particularly outstanding; however, later in the sixteenth century Vasari gave voice to the dominant mimetic standards of the Renaissance by praising Leonardo's uncanny accuracy in portraying his subject. With the passage of time, this view gradually changed, and comments on the painting increasingly emphasized the way in which it captured its quintessentially feminine subject, a view whose mimetic underpinnings were being influenced by neo-classical idealism. Critics of the romantic period continued to praise the *Mona Lisa* for its subject matter, but the face that had been seen as a paragon of sweetness and light became, by 1800, that of a *femme fatale,* about whom critics could embroider emotionalist fantasies of intuition, feeling, and all things unlike the stereotypical male rationality.[11] Thus did the popular evaluation of the *Mona Lisa* weather the aesthetic sea change as the mimetic and instrumental values of the neo-classical period were replaced by the emotionalist assumptions of romanticism.

Clearly, the artistic and aesthetic pluralism of the West reflects the complex currents and countercurrents of Western economic and political systems. For example, Karen Field (1982) has described art education in three distinctly different situations—an art college, an art department in a large university, and an amateur art club. In the course of a year's fieldwork, she collected information on, among other things, the criteria used by instructors and artists in evaluating artworks. Field found that critiques in the art college tended to emphasize artist-centered qualities (e.g., expression, confidence, and honesty) reflecting the spirit in which the work was created, whereas art club teachers were more concerned with the objective features of the artwork itself (e.g., beauty, economy, and rhythm). Instructors in university art departments tended to fall between these two extremes. Thus, Western aesthetics continues to be as pluralistic as ever.

---

[11]Boas observes that 300 years before the romantic rebellion, women in the West were stereotyped by most men as being "cruel, coquettish, vain, deceitful, gentle, fickle, tender, weak, but they had rarely been enigmatic. Men knew them only too well" (Boas 1963/1940:584). It was the much later notion of "woman-as-enigma" that prompted the romantics to praise the *Mona Lisa's* ambiguous smile.

Further Reading

The Western aesthetic tradition is as old as recorded Western history. Tatarkiewicz's three volumes (1970a, 1970b, 1974) provide a storehouse of primary sources, from early Greek and Hebrew roots to prominent thinkers of the early twentieth century. Two other useful reference works are Kelly (1998) and Cooper, Sartwell, and Margolis (1995).

An excellent overview of the field of aesthetics in the West, and one that addresses not only traditional fine art but also avant-garde and popular art, is Carroll (1999). Davies (1991) discusses at length various philosophers' attempts to define "art." Several anthologies (e.g., Feagin and Maynard 1997; Korsmeyer 1998; Ross 1994) provide access to numerous seminal texts in aesthetics.

A good place to find recent and current contributors to Western philosophy of art is *The Journal of Aesthetics and Art Criticism,* available in many academic libraries. (The periodical's contents since its inception in 1942 can also be found on the World Wide Web via the page for the American Society for Aesthetics at http://www.temple.edu/jaac/.)

The literature on American vernacular aesthetics is comparatively smaller. *American Muse* (Anderson 2000) is a broad treatment of the subject. Other interesting analyses of specific popular art forms are Forrest (1988) and Halle (1993) on art in domestic settings, Sartwell (1995) on country-western music and on vernacular aesthetics generally, McCloud (1994) on comics, and McDannell (1996) on "material Christianity." The *Journal of Popular Culture,* also found in many academic libraries, contains numerous analytic and descriptive essays, as well as reviews of recently published books.

PART TWO

11

INTRODUCTION TO PART TWO

> Aesthetic theory has often been pretentious. . . . Each theory has to do with a possibility of art, but not, as they have often claimed, to do with "Art." This is especially evident when the arts of non-western cultures are included in the art world, a not unreasonable request. (Deutsch 1975:x–xi)

The chapters of Part One have examined many "possibilities" (as Deutsch calls them above) of art, but the question remains, what conclusions can be drawn about "Art"? That is, what do the preceding accounts of aesthetics in ten societies tell us about the general phenomenon of art? Each culture we have looked at has had its own philosophy of art, its own Calliope. But how significant is the distinctiveness of each of the muses we have met? Is every one truly a unique entity, fundamentally unlike all others, or are the culture-specific idiosyncrasies of Calliope's sisters relatively superficial, masking a single genius of art? Part One attempted to bring each society's aesthetic system alive by calling attention to its coherence, its credibility—and ultimately its dignity. But for purposes of comparison, we must now examine them in terms that are abstract enough to allow cross-cultural similarities and differences to stand out.

The quest for aesthetic universals has engaged many Western thinkers since at least the fifth century B.C.E. Their efforts have often failed because they began with untestable axioms about art and proceeded to conclusions via deductive logic. I am adopting the opposite approach: Instead of beginning with premises assumed to be true about art *a priori*, I start with the hard-earned discoveries of the many fieldworkers who have studied the arts of other peoples in depth and at first hand. From this information, we can only hope that a logically consistent picture can be discerned, but the existence of such a pattern is not taken for granted. However, as the following chapters reveal, I believe that the information at hand does suggest a single Calliope and that it goes a long way toward revealing her fundamental nature.

The chapters of Part Two use the data from Part One for several specific purposes. First, Chapter 12 looks for systematic patterns of cross-cultural variation. That is, insofar as philosophies of art do differ from one place to another, to what extent are these differences linked to concomitant variations in other sociocultural factors? Then Chapters 13 and 14 discuss features of aesthetics that occur in all ten of Part One's societies and that may well be universal. Finally, as an epilogue, Chapter 15 compares Western aesthetics to the philosophies of art found in other cultures.

12

COMPARATIVE AESTHETICS

The Many Faces

of the Muse

Different strokes for different folks!

When a person walks through a museum's non-Western art collection, the likely reaction is that *it looks so different*, at least in comparison to the work of most Western artists. One might dismiss the differences as being no greater than those between, say, a Baroque painting by Rembrandt and a modern sculpture by Louise Nevelson. It's all striking, creative, and a pleasure to look at, so it must be "art." (After all, it *is* in an art museum, isn't it?[1]) This view may evaporate, however, as our hypothetical museum-goer reads the labels that accompany the non-Western art works: "Cult figures" stand next to "initiation masks," "lip ornaments," and a "chief's royal stools." Surely such uses set these artworks apart from the pieces by Rembrandt and Nevelson.

In Chapters 13 and 14, I will show that a common unity *is* shared by art throughout the world, with artists everywhere using their special skills to imbue sensuous media with potent meaning. In so doing, art seems to fill a need that is universal throughout the human race. This realization supports the legitimacy of housing the diverse objects of non-Western origin under the same roof as Baroque paintings and contemporary sculptures.

But it would be counterproductive to ignore the museum-goer's reaction to the apparent multiplicity of art. It does, after all, reflect a second characteristic of our species—our restless creativity, as manifest in the wide compass of cross-cultural diversity. The resident of Manhattan cannot ignore considerations of subsistence any more than can an Inuit. Nonetheless, hunting seals through winter sea ice to obtain food is quite different from working on the New York Stock Exchange to earn money to buy food in a restaurant

---

[1]Clifford Geertz (1983:119) has remarked, "Most people, I am convinced, see African sculpture as bush Picasso and hear Javanese music as noisy Dubussy." It is also worth noting that *museum* derives from the Latin term for "temple of the muses."

or grocery store. If the first goal of science is to uncover the fundamental unities that underlie our universe, the second objective, and the particular purpose of this chapter, is to search for patterns in our diversity.

Small-Scale versus Complex Societies: Contemporary Comparisons

Some of the more embarrassing skeletons in cultural anthropology's closet are the evolutionary theories that were constructed by the discipline's first generation of scholars in the late nineteenth century. At their worst, those writers assumed that the institutions found in their own complex, industrial societies of their day were perched atop an evolutionary ladder and that the practices found elsewhere could be assigned to lower rungs, representing stages through which our more "advanced" institutions had passed.

The notion that Western practices are necessarily more advanced or better than those found in other cultures is now rejected as an ethnocentrism with racist ramifications. Nevertheless, one should not dismiss the important differences among contemporary societies—not in their worth or their validity but rather in such unarguable areas as their demographic size, the complexity of their technology, and the degree to which the division of labor and other differentiating factors (such as social class or ethnic identity) create a relatively high degree of internal diversity. Indeed, these three factors—population, technology, and heterogeneity—generally vary with one another, and taken together they define a dimension that differentiates relatively *small-scale* from relatively *complex* societies.[2]

Because of their relatively simple technology and low level of social heterogeneity, the three nonagricultural societies discussed in Part One—the San, the Inuit, and the Aboriginal groups of north-central Australia—do indeed show certain similarities in their art production. Their nomadic lifestyle and their lack of draft animals prompt one obvious commonality: Their art is *portable*. Song, dance, and oral literature are the ultimate transportable art forms, and we have found them to be very important among nonsedentary groups.

Body decoration is important in small-scale societies for the same reason. Distinctive haircuts, tattoos, decorative scars, and body paint constitute negligible baggage for nomads (Figure 12–1). Jewelry and distinctive clothing weigh only a little more, and they also have the advantage of leaving the hands free for carrying objects, tending children, or food-collecting while on the move.

---

[2]Elsewhere (Anderson 1979:2–8) I have discussed the hazards of using the word "primitive" to refer to those societies that are here designated "small-scale" (see also footnote 1, p. 4).

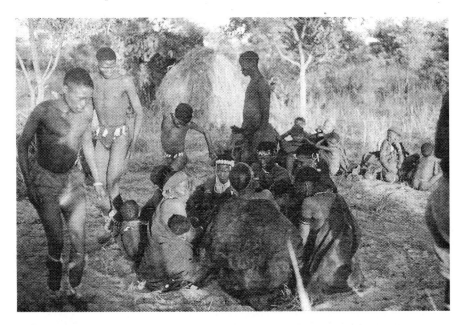

FIGURE 12-1   The nomadic San carry some of their art with them on their decorated bodies. *(Photo courtesy of Documentary Educational Resources.)*

The decorations on utilitarian items—the San's ostrich eggshell canteens, Inuit harpoons and needle-cases, and Australian boomerangs—exemplify another solution to the nomad's problem.[3] Among these necessities are artistic objects used for religious purposes, such as Inuit amulets, Australian tjurungas, and San oracle disks. But the dearth of secular, three-dimensional art suggests that aesthetic considerations are secondary to religious ones in objects such as these. That is, hunters and gatherers probably carry "religious art" with them because it is religious rather than because it is art.

Of course, small-scale societies are not alone in producing easily portable art. Complex societies also practice the performing arts, lavish attention on the appearance of the individual, and decorate some of their tools. It is the *absence* of bulky art (e.g., the "permanent collections" that are stored in stately museums) that sets nomadic groups apart—that, and the great importance of the transportable art that is produced. Recall the picture of a San encampment: At any given time, someone is making music, stories are being

---

[3]As noted in the chapters on San and Australian Aboriginal aesthetics, nomadic peoples sometimes paint on caves and on other permanent stone faces. Such groups rarely wander randomly; instead, they typically visit the same sites, one after the other, with the passing of the seasons. Thus, the labor-intensive art is only temporarily left behind, to be seen and used on subsequent visits to the same site.

told, and the bodies of young and old alike are adorned with tattoos, beads, and other decorations. Thus, restricting art to easily portable media obviously does not nullify its importance.

The forgoing remarks concern the production of art rather than the philosophy that underlies it. Regarding aesthetics, the most obvious difference between small- and large-scale societies is the explicitness with which aesthetic ideas are articulated, a fact that has important consequences. If the predominantly mobile nature of art in hunting-gathering-fishing groups is a consequence of the nomadic lifestyle of those societies, then the explicitness with which art is discussed in complex societies results from another characteristic difference between the smallest and largest of societies—namely, the more elaborate division of labor that characterizes complex cultures.

All societies, even the smallest in scale, have their native philosophers, but in small-scale societies, such intellectuals must perforce engage in subsistence activities along with the other adult members of their sex. But agriculture, especially as it becomes more intensified, typically brings with it a class of part- or full-time specialists who, freed of manual labor, have time to devote to the skills of the mind. Historically, most members of this class were probably no more than priests, bureaucrats, and tyrants, but the speculative thinkers among them did produce such things as cosmologies to accompany calendrical systems, ideologies to justify increased political centralization, and, significantly, aesthetic theories to explain new art and craft techniques.

Despite the lack of such specialists, hunter-gatherer-fishers have definite ideas about the meaning and value of art, just as their belief systems include many cosmological and ideological propositions. But in small-scale societies, such concepts are either implicit and couched in the matrix of folklore, myth, and world view, or else are only narrow statements about why one thing is preferred over another. But this picture changes dramatically as the division of labor increases and intellectuals become part-time and then full-time specialists in speculative thought. For example, the Aztec *tlamatinime* defined themselves as men whose mission was to "shine their light on the world, to inquire into the region of the gods above and into the region of the dead below" (León-Portilla 1971:448) (Figure 12–2). Similarly, classical India had its Hindu *rasikas*, whose exceptional sensitivity and enlightenment allowed them to experience the complex emotions associated with *rasa*. For Japan, we repeatedly read of individuals, primarily priests, who made pronouncements about the role of art in the various sects of Buddhism. In the West, intellectuals going back at least to Pythagoras have analyzed art in great depth and detail, either in conjunction with broader philosophical arguments or else as an intellectual challenge in itself.

If aesthetic ideas are generally implicit in small-scale societies and explicit in complex societies, then agricultural societies fall between these two

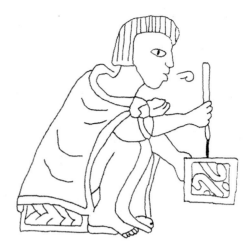

FIGURE 12-2 Figure from Aztec codex representing the scribe, or tlacuilo. *(Courtesy of John F. Chuckiak, Southwest Missouri State University.)*

extremes. For example, the Yoruba language contains two words—*amewa* and *mewa*—that refer to individuals who are known for their ability to judge beauty. A *mewa* is a true specialist, whereas an *amewa* is not a full-time aesthetician but a farmer, a village chief, or a practicing artist who is particularly skilled at judging and discussing art. Further, the expertise of these connoisseurs is in verbalizing the stylistic strengths and weaknesses of specific art works; more fundamental and general aesthetic beliefs are, for the most part, implicit.

Not *all* of the aesthetic ideas in complex societies are explicitly formulated by professional theoreticians. To the contrary, such societies have their share of aesthetic notions that are never more than implied within the general fabric of the culture. For example, the popular arts in the West have only occasionally caught the attention of aestheticians. Likewise, in Japan, the aesthetic principles that derive from Shintoism never seem to have been overtly articulated, despite their importance for the Japanese aesthetic tradition generally. (This is not surprising since Shintoism's roots go back to pre-Neolithic Japan, and its aesthetic premises were thoroughly integrated into Japanese aesthetic thought before the arrival of Buddhism.)

Such exceptions notwithstanding, if much aesthetic thought in complex societies is available via the explicitly written and spoken word, aesthetic principles in small-scale societies may be equally accessible, but in a different way, being straightforward enough that all members of the society find it easy to understand them. In small-scale societies, normal processes of socialization suffice for transmitting ideas about art from one generation to the next. Courses in "art appreciation" are unnecessary, no arcane and specialized vocabulary is needed, and elaborate metaphysical argument is absent.

The self-conscious nature of aesthetics in complex societies leads them to cover the same general territory as those in small-scale societies, but to do so in more detail. For example, all societies have ideas about beauty, but in small-scale societies, such standards are fairly general and are applied primarily to the appearance of humans and their close associates, such as the pastoralist's cattle. By contrast, complex societies typically have an intricate canon of beauty or, more generally, of formal appropriateness (see Figure 12–3). For example, the West and India both developed complicated mathematical formulae for the optimal proportions not only for the ideal human body (Figure 12–3) but also for architecture, music, and calligraphy. No doubt, Inuit distinguish between the smoothly curving arc of a well-made igloo and the ungainly shape of an ill-made one, but their standards of archi-

FIGURE 12-3 Leonardo De Vinci (1452–1519), *Study of Human Proportion: The Vitruvian Man,* ca. 1492, pen and ink drawing. *(Photo credit: Cameraphoto Arte, Venice / Art Resource, NY, Academia, Venice, Italy)*

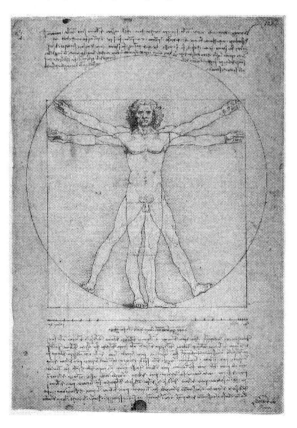

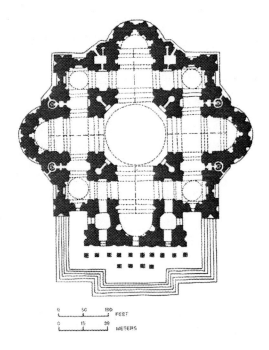

FIGURE 12–4 Floor plan of St. Peter's Basilica, Vatican City. *(From Art Thru the Ages HSIE 9th editionby de la Croix.© 1991. Reprinted with permission of the Wadsworth, a division of Thomson Learning: www.thomson-rights.com. Fax 800 730-2215)*

tectural beauty are far less elaborate than, for example, the calculations Michelangelo used in planning the dome for St. Peter's Basilica (Figure 12–4), where he was challenged to design an edifice that was not only structurally sound but also would comply with the complex, classical norms of correct proportion.

As aesthetics in complex societies is the province of an intellectual (and, generally, socioeconomic) elite, it also becomes more densely textured in its ideas about the emotional response that art can provoke. Again, the development is not so much a matter of exploring new aesthetic domains but rather is a movement toward mapping known territory in ever greater detail. Presumably, Greeks before Aristotle and Indians before Abhinavagupta experienced the whole gamut of aesthetic feelings, but it remained for these two seminal thinkers, writing in their respective traditions, to set down typologies of emotions. Thereafter artist and audience alike could approach art with a conscious awareness of the potentialities of the aesthetic response, aided by the aesthetic vocabularies that Aristotle and Abhinava formalized.

But "intricate" is not the same as "profound," and we would be mistaken to assume that aesthetics in small-scale societies is on the whole less intellectually compelling than in complex societies. Recall, for example, the Inuit, with their premise that art has the capacity to transmute things between the realms of the natural, the human, and the supernatural. Surely the insight of this theory equals that of, say, the four traditions that Western aestheticians have developed.

Nor do large and small societies differ in the pragmatism of their aesthetic ideas. In all societies, it is common to view art as a means to an end, often a supernatural end. Australian Aboriginal concern with the Dreamtime and Navajo ideas about nature's harmony and beauty, as embodied in *hózhǫ́*: Neither one is less advanced than religious aesthetic thought in Aztec, Indian, Japanese, and Western culture.

The theories of the elite class in complex societies are not only explicit, they are also often self-serving, extolling the virtue and refinement of the aristocracy. In *rasa* theory, only those brahmins who had attained a high level of spiritual consciousness could relish genuine aesthetic delight. For their part, Aztec wise men believed that only the enlightened ones, those with "deified hearts," would have their flowers and songs accepted by the gods.

Matters are more complex in Japan and the West, where the shifting tides of political ascendancy have caused periodic changes in the makeup of the elite. In Japan, both Esoteric Buddhism and Zen Buddhism claimed that salvation and enlightenment would come only to the select few—specifically those who could grasp the ineluctable core of art's message. Amida Buddhism, a far more popular religious movement, had a correspondingly more egalitarian aesthetic; however, the Confucian influence on Japanese aesthetics emphasized stability of the state and the use of the arts to perpetuate the status quo.

Intellectual (and sometimes sociopolitical) elitism is a recurrent feature in the West also, as seen in the classical and neo-classical tendency to equate beauty with perfect form; in the claim that in art the ideal can be known with certainty only by the privileged arbiters of taste; the claims by religious thinkers that the anagogic glories of art are available solely to the elect; in the assertion by Romantic theorists that the emotional response to art is confined to those with heightened emotional sensitivity; and in the formalist modification of this last tenet that substitutes formal for emotional sensitivity. All of these are ways of saying that only superior people can recognize or appreciate "true" art.

The elitism common to aesthetics in complex societies is predictable when one considers the methods of art production. The technical subtleties of a "fine" art style may well be lost on individuals who have limited experience with the medium; they can be appreciated only by the artists themselves (hence the "artist's artist") or by individuals who have had the luxury of free time to study the medium, acquiring a refinement of taste that the less privileged never know (hence the "critical success but popular failure"). Also, complex societies may include not only the hierarchy of social class but also gradients of ethnic and regional diversity, with each sector practicing its own art forms. Thus, when the Aztec philosophers praised the art of the "true Toltecs," they were elevating their fellow Nahua-speakers above the many other ethnic groups under their control.

As we have just noted, the art and aesthetics of small-scale societies may differ from those in complex societies in terms of *structural* attributes such as explicitness and intricacy, but what about the *content* of their aesthetic systems? One might ask, Is the art of hunter-gatherers more oriented toward the supernatural than art in complex societies? A comparative study of contemporary societies reveals only that art in *all* societies embodies culturally significant meaning, and small-scale societies seem to have at least as great an interest in the secular significance of art as do complex societies.

Nor does symbolism appear to differ systematically between small- and large-scale societies. In both, some art is iconographic while other art is genuinely symbolic in that its resemblance to its referent is wholly conventional and not based on any apparent similarity. Perhaps the iconographic repertoire increases in size as societies become more complex—a larger array of gods, spirits, ancestors, mortals, and natural objects potentially provide the artist with a greater abundance of subject matter. Also, the emergence of a class of religious specialists may permit the development of a larger pantheon, although one should not underestimate the complexity of oral traditions of myth in small-scale societies.

Evolutionary Aesthetics?

The forgoing comparison of aesthetics in small-scale versus complex societies largely has focused on contemporary and relatively recent cultures, but this question suggests a companion query, one concerning gradual cultural change. After all, every civilization is the culmination of a long historical development. Given sufficient archaeological effort, every state-level society's roots can be traced back thousands of years to pre-Neolithic bands of nomadic hunter-gatherers that, with the passage of time, slowly changed into the formidable empires of history.

How have philosophies of art changed during this process? There are serious obstacles to using evidence from contemporary or recent societies to construct evolutionary theories of change, not the least of which is that modern-day small-scale societies cannot be equated with the societies of the distant past. At most, they are only suggestive, providing clues about what people did and thought during distant times.

Some of these clues can never lead to anything more than untestable speculations, but others lend themselves to empirical study and may eventually receive sufficient archaeological support to become accepted as fact. For example, we know that the literate societies of the historic era are descended from prior, nonliterate societies. Thus, it is altogether plausible that the aesthetic differences between small-scale contemporary societies versus complex societies parallel changes in aesthetics that have occurred in those parts of the world where the Neolithic Revolution has run its course. Thus, I would posit the existence of what might be called "meso-evolutionary"[4] aesthetic change: Until 10,000 years ago or so, all human societies possessed aesthetic systems that, though they may well have been quite profound, were implicit, relatively nonintricate, and pervasive throughout their respective cultures. Then in those locations where the domestication of plants or animals brought about increasing specialization in the division of labor and social stratification, aesthetics tended to change into more explicit and intricate systems of thought that were largely the concern of small, specialized groups of people.

It remains to be seen what the implications of aesthetic meso-evolution are for art, artists, and audiences. (For example, the invention of writing and the cultural pluralism that appeared during the process of state-formation might be expected to have led to fertile cross-pollination between aesthetic thinkers of different times and places.) But the picture of aesthetics in the ten societies presented in Part One leaves little doubt that there *are* systematic differences between aesthetics in complex versus small-scale societies in the contemporary world, and these seem directly related to the increased specialization and stratification that is known to have occurred during the long course of development that led some small-scale societies to gradually change into complex cultures. Nevertheless, the changes in art that come about as a result of aesthetic meso-evolution seem far less significant than other kinds of sociocultural variation. If one considers our urban mode of living, the industrialized economies our subsistence is based upon, or our capacity to destroy the world through nuclear holocaust, the gulf between ourselves and people in small-scale societies seems enormous. In matters of art, the distance is small indeed.

Aesthetic Milieu

In one way or another, several of the aesthetic systems described in Part One contain the premise that human well-being depends upon artistic activity. Examples are the Western concern with the anagogic capacity of art during the Middle Ages, Indian *rasa* theory, Aztec fears that the world would suffer its final destruction unless the gods were supplicated with flower and song, Navajo efforts to maintain *hózhǫ* via the creation of art, and Australian Aboriginal uses of art to sustain the fertile and harmonious conditions of the Eternal Dreamtime. Each of these represents an effort by the society to survive by means of art production.

Interestingly, in each of these cases, the society in question existed in a state of duress, where people lived under prolonged attack by outsiders or

---

[4]"*Meso*-evolution," because the process emerges due to processes primarily within the culture itself, in contrast to the "*peri*-evolution" defined later.

else, as in the case of the Navajo, they inhabited an ecologically marginal environment. The Aztecs were successful in overcoming the inhospitable setting of their rocky island in Lake Texcoco, but this hazard was replaced by hostile neighbors, over whom the Aztecs had only tenuous control.

It is easy to speculate that people redouble their artistic efforts when times are hard and nothing else seems to work, but proof of such a hypothesis is elusive. One might conjecture, for instance, that the emphasis on health and fertility found in Yoruba aesthetics reflects a need to stimulate birth rates in an area of the world where the introduction of slash and burn horticulture some centuries ago caused a rise in malaria. Testing such a thesis, however, would be a difficult undertaking.

Limited support for this hypothesis can be found in some places, however. For example, Dorset culture prevailed across the North American arctic for about 2,000 years, but art production in the region did not remain constant. Late Dorset peoples faced two growing threats—changing climatic conditions and Thule invaders from the west. Taçon (1983) has shown that increases in these challenges coincided with dramatic increases in the production of Dorset art.[5]

Powerful and acquisitive neighbors and poor luck with climatic and environmental conditions are threats that societies rarely have effective defenses against. In such difficult circumstances, it seems reasonable that people might turn to symbolic means of trying to protect themselves.

Intercultural Influences: Hybrid Art on the Global Stage

A society's ideas about art are often affected by the societies it interacts with. Often the aesthetic influence of neighbors is a result of factors far removed from art. For example, when Napoleon Chagnon first visited the Yanomami village of Momaribowei-teri in Venezuela, the residents told him that long ago they had forgotten how to make pots, that the local clay was unsatisfactory for pottery, and that in any case their allies in the village of Mowaraoba-teri made enough pots for everyone. Later, when the alliance between Momaribowei-teri and Mowaraoba-teri became strained, the people of Momaribowei-teri "remembered" how to manufacture clay pots, and Chagnon realized that their earlier statements had only been a rationalization for their desire to trade and socialize with their neighbors (Chagnon 1983:150). The Yanomami case is by no means unique. Intergroup exchanges of art works often "lubricate" the trade of goods, ideas, and people between neighboring groups. The ostrich

---

[5]Mimbres culture, discussed later, may be another instance of people reacting to an environmental crisis by expanding their artistic efforts. J. J. Brody (1977:210) has suggested that a crisis in food production stimulated the novel pottery style of the Mimbres people.

eggshell beads made by the San and the decorative feathers and shells of the New Guinea Tsembaga, both mentioned in Part One, follow this pattern.

Sometimes intercultural interactions reach across the globe. For example, consider the "traditional" Navajo blanket. It is made of wool from sheep descended from those that the Spanish brought to the Americas. (Indeed, sheep came into Spain only after having been domesticated in the Near East or central Asia.) It is woven using techniques acquired from Indian groups to the Navajos' south. By one account, rugs with zigzag patterns have even more remote sources, being based on Mexican sheepherders' serapes, which originated in Spain, the zigzag design having been brought to Spain by North African Moors (Cowen 2002:43-46).

Or to cite an example closer at hand, consider the diverse intercultural ancestry of the pages of an American book. They are made of paper, a Chinese invention, and are numbered using a system that came from India by way of the Arabs. They bear a text written in an alphabet that goes back to ancient Phoenicia, printed by means of a device invented by a German, who borrowed ideas that again take us back to China (ibid.:6).

During the last 500 years, the process of culture exchange has accelerated as a result of technologies that facilitate movement from one part of the globe to another, and since World War II, the rate of change has accelerated ever more. In recent years the process whereby societies near and far affect each other has come to be called "globalization," defined as "the interconnectedness of the world, by way of interactions, exchanges and related developments, affecting not least the organization of culture" (Hannerz 1996:7).

Globalization presents a challenge to the social sciences, most of whose theories and methods were first developed to study less-than-global entities, from the nation-state (in the case of political science), through small, traditional, face-to-face societies (cultural anthropology), to the individual human mind (psychology). Only economists have much experience examining transnational interactions, which probably accounts for their having contributed the greatest share to the growing literature on globalization.

The topic of globalization often evokes strong feelings. Some people foresee a new and exciting age of dynamic interaction that will bring sweeping benefits to humankind as a whole; others decry the loss of local distinctiveness and self-determination. As Ulf Hannerz (1996:5) has remarked, "One almost expects any mention of globalization now to be accompanied by either booing or cheering." Both sides of the debate are in some measure correct. Unquestionably, there is less intercultural diversity in the world today than there was 500 years ago. Every continent once had societies that are now utterly extinct, and of those cultures that still do exist, all bear evidence of having been greatly impacted by others.

However, the prediction that the world is rapidly on its way to total homogenization (and specifically, Westernization) is seriously thrown into question by several observations. For one thing, as cultural items move from one place to another, they are inevitably reinterpreted and modified in light of the destination culture. Thus, for example, although there are McDonalds restaurants in more than a hundred countries, in many places they differ from the McDonalds in the Unites States, having been modified in accord with local tastes. In India, for example, beef and pork have been removed from McDonalds' menu to avoid giving offence to Hindus and Muslims. Instead, one finds Mutton Kabobs and the Maharaja Mac, the latter being "two all lamb patties, special sauce, lettuce, cheese, pickles, onions on a sesame seed bun" (http://www.media.mcdonalds.com/secured/products/international/maharajamac.html). (McDonalds' marketing strategy would seem to have been a success inasmuch as 350,000 Maharaja Macs were sold in India during the first year they were available [ibid.].)

Another factor that opposes the trend toward global homogenization is that, in dialectical fashion, when alien influences begin to affect traditional cultures, powerful popular reactions may come about, opposing change and seeking to revive prior ways of doing things. The conservative, fundamentalist movements that so dominate today's world news exemplify this process (Lechner and Boli 2000:2).

Tyler Cowen, an economist, has added another dimension to the debate on globalization by pointing out that, contradictory though it may seem, one sort of *increased* cultural homogeneity inevitably is accompanied by a different sort of *decreased* cultural homogeneity. For example, consider what happens when a carver in New Guinea sells a mask to an American tourist and then uses the money from the sale to buy a t-shirt that displays an American logo. Through these transactions America and New Guinea have become a bit more alike: Now in both places there are Sepik masks and logo-printed t-shirts. But at the same time, the heterogeneity *within* each of the societies is increased in that Americans now have the opportunity to see an art form (the mask) that previously was confined to New Guinea, and the mask carver's clothing options have been broadened by his having the t-shirt. As Cowen puts it, "Individuals become more diverse as their societies become more alike" (2002:129).[6]

Such countervailing processes are not trivial. For example, with the development of music recording technologies, especially the cassette tape recorder, as well as the increase in international trade in recorded music, countless new music genres are now thriving, each a distinctive blend of traditional and introduced instruments and styles. Latin America and the Caribbean; North, West, and Central Africa; Southeast and South Asia; the

---

[6]Although Cowen calls attention to the current positive benefits of cultural exchange (e.g., "the poorer countries in the world have virtually exploded with creative art, music, and literature in the twentieth century," p. 33), he also warns of a long-term danger. When culture exchange increases beyond a certain point, he fears, the ethos of a traditional society may die and with it the fertile setting that gives birth to new, hybrid art forms.

Middle East—all have spawned numerous hybrid musics. Meanwhile, in Europe and North America new music genres are constantly emerging that combine elements from all of these sources. In recent decades, many genres of traditional music have indeed disappeared, but fears of the total Americanization of other countries' musical markets have not come true. In India, for example, 96 percent of the music sold is produced domestically (Cowen 2002:8).

The "Epilogue" sections of Chapters 1 through 7 illustrate the dynamic effects of culture exchange. In every instance, great numbers of people suffered unmercifully the effects of colonization. The residents of the New World were decimated, and those who did not die lost much or all of their land. Africans were enslaved or reduced to subject populations. The native inhabitants of the Pacific islands endured both those fates, and in the bargain the survivors were denied the profits made from the exploitation of their valuable natural resources.

It is not surprising that the cataclysmic changes occasioned by colonization were accompanied by dramatic changes in art and aesthetics. Some of the culture exchanges could never have been predicted. We saw in Chapter 1, for example, that the "billikin," invented in the American Midwest, became a popular subject for Alaskan Eskimo sculptures. From Alaska it traveled to Japan, ending up in, among other places, a shrine. Meanwhile, a Japanese printmaking technique, *ukiyo-e,* migrated in the opposite direction, arriving (via artist James Houston) in northern Canada, where it was adopted by Inuit printmakers.[7]

Such unlikely events notwithstanding, the artistic outcomes of the colonial experience are not random. One frequent result is the emergence of "hybrid" art forms that combine elements of the indigenous with the foreign. Consider a few of the many examples noted in the Epilogues:

- The Botswana San who work at the Kuru Art Center use both traditional and imported pigments not only to illustrate some of their own age-old oral literature but also to address such contemporary topics as AIDS, all in the new (for them) medium of easel painting.
- In northern Canada, Inuit had long carved utilitarian items out of soapstone as well as small figurative sculptures out of ivory. Today, thanks to marketing skills imported from the south, these older techniques have been supplanted by the new art form of representational soapstone carving.

---

[7]For a general anthropological treatment of change in art in small-scale societies, see Anderson 1989:156-184. Nelson Graburn (1976) pioneered the anthropological study of "hybrid" art (Graburn 1999:344)—that is, art engendered by traditional societies' confrontation with the West.

- Aboriginal Australian fine art painters, such as Banduk Marika, likewise combine indigenous sensibilities with newly introduced media. Also, the very fact that she, a woman, is a visual artist represents a major change in gender definition inasmuch as all traditional Aboriginal painters were males.
- With regard to the Sepik, recall the alligator-shaped napkin rings mentioned by Silverman as well as the tambaran-like architecture of the Papua New Guinea Parliament House. Both combine the traditional with the introduced.
- Artists living in the African Diaspora have creatively combined Yoruba *orisha* with Catholic saints to produce powerful icons for alters in the New World.

To call such work "hybrid" art is, I think, altogether appropriate. Every example is a product of cross-fertilization between distinctly different cultural traditions. In retrospect, we can see that some efforts at hybridization (e.g., Inuit oil painting) were unsuccessful, others (e.g., ivory cribbage boards from Alaska) have come and gone, and still others would seem to carry little cultural significance. But sometimes the outcomes parallel the biological phenomenon known as "hybrid vigor," that is, the efficacious crossbreeding of animals, the common example being the mule, which is generally stronger, taller, and longer-lived than either its horse dam or its donkey sire.

Contemporary Mexico provides countless instances of culture exchange that are striking examples of hybrid vigor.

The Mexican Day of the Dead as Hybrid Art

The most important celebration of the year in Mexico takes place on the first days of November.[8] Called the Day of the Dead, it is grounded in religion—specifically, the belief that during certain times in the autumn, departed family members should be remembered and activities should be undertaken to bring their spirits back, at least for a while. Previously, graves will have been swept and adorned with flowers and paper cut-outs. In their homes, people will have constructed commemorative altars that may include candles, incense, photographs, keepsakes and other personal items of the deceased, as well as such things as special breads, small skulls made of white sugar and in-

---

[8]What follows is a very generalized account of the Day of the Dead in Mexico. Except for the fundamental concept of commemorating the spirits of deceased family members, all of the details of the celebration, even the dates of observation, differ from place to place. Day of the Dead activities occur with even greater variation in other parts of Latin America and in Mexican American communities in the United States.

scribed with the name of the person being remembered—even, perhaps, a basin of water and hand towel so that the visiting souls can wash before (spiritually) consuming the foods and beverages presented to them on the altar.

Like ritual celebrations in many other places, the Day of the Dead incorporates many kinds of art.[9] The home altars and the decorated graves are, in effect, art installations: The food is created and set out as beautifully as possible; celebrants wear their finest (and if possible, new) clothes; in the evening, mariachi bands perform in some cemeteries; and the night's activities may conclude with a fireworks display. In recent years, it has become common for urban artists to construct Day of the Dead altars in museums and galleries. On an individual level, Day of the Dead enhances family solidarity: The deceased are brought back to the minds of the living, and surviving family members, some of whom return home from distant places for the event, feast on tamales and other traditional foods and renew old bonds of affection. (The social integration occasioned by the Day of the Dead also extends beyond the family inasmuch as special gifts of food are presented to neighbors and others in the community.)

Today, Day of the Dead celebrations in Mexico constitute a powerful, integrated cultural event, but an examination of their history reveals that they are in fact an example of aesthetic hybrid vigor wherein selected arts and ideas from disparate traditions merge and intermingle to produce compelling and viable new art forms. In the case of the Day of the Dead, some elements echo pre-Hispanic practices. Celebrating the theme of death has a long history in Mesoamerica, reaching back at least to 800 B.C.E. and becoming even more prominent from about 900 C.E. onward. In the early 1500s, Sahagún described several pre-Hispanic Aztec festivals that were held specifically to honor the dead. For example, during a celebration called Izcalli women made special tamales, some of which were given to friends, others consumed in a family feast, the remainder being an "offering for the dead, where they laid buried" (Charmichael and Sayer 1991:31), and all of these activities have counterparts in contemporary Day of the Dead activities. Other passages of Sahagún's account mention propitiating the dead with flowers. (Then, as now, the most commonly used variety being *cempasúchil*, "flowers of the dead," called marigolds in the United States.) Copal incense and ornaments made of bark paper were also part of pre-Hispanic gifts to the departed, just as today. In other annual ceremonies of the Aztecs, houses were ritually swept clean, paralleling the contemporary Day of the Dead custom of sweeping clean family graves.

In addition to these specific details, the fundamental idea that underlies the celebration of the Day of the Dead has indigenous roots.

---

[9]See Anderson (2000:41–58) for an analysis of the lavish arts that accompany rites of passage, such as weddings, in the United States.

Charmichael and Sayer (1991) observe, "The pre-Hispanic idea of life arising out of death is very clear. . . . In Aztec religion (and indeed all Mesoamerican religions) this is the recurrent theme: the interdependency and interaction between humanity and the gods" (ibid.:25). The Aztecs believed that people's fate after death was influenced by their memory being ceremonially honored by their survivors, and their afterlives also were affected by the circumstances of their death, rather than their conduct while living. In similar fashion, celebrants of the Day of the Dead believe that the spirits of loved ones return in an order determined by time and nature of their death. (The most widely held belief is that the souls of those who died as children return on November 1; adults, on November 2. In some communities, special days are set aside for those who died in accidents or who suffered violent deaths [ibid.:16].)

Other elements of contemporary Day of the Dead celebrations come not from indigenous traditions but rather have their roots in Europe. For example, when the dead are depicted today in Mexico, they sometimes appear as skulls, and skulls were indeed common in pre-Hispanic Mesoamerican art: Many archeological sites include a low, flat-topped structure that is now generally referred to by its Nahuatl name of *tzompantli,* or skull rack, on the top of which were displayed the skulls of slain enemies and whose sides were decorated with row after row of low-relief skulls.

Depictions of skulls appear in today's Day of the Dead activities, but most skeletal imagery—in bread sculptures, in two-dimensional graphic images such as the prints of José Guadalupe Posada, and so on—depicts *entire* skeletons, and this image of death goes back to sixteenth-century Spain and beyond that to medieval Catholic Western Europe in general. In fact, the geographic distribution of full skeleton images today reflects the extent of Spanish influence in the past: They appear more in Mexico City and other urban centers (where Spanish influence was greatest) than in rural, less Hispanicized areas, and they are seen more often in the states north of Mexico City (where Spanish settlement was greater) than in southern Mexico and the Yucatán (ibid.:22).

Other elements of contemporary Day of the Dead activities also come from Europe. A special mass, obviously foreign in origin, is part of the occasion. In the church (as well on home altars) one may see paintings and sculptures that ostensibly depict Catholic saints, although in many cases they may also be identified with pre-Hispanic deities, examples being Saint Thomas the Apostle, who is associated with the Plumed Serpent, Quetzalcoatle, and Saint John the Baptist, who is syncretized with the rain god, Tlaloc (ibid.:41).

Also, the dates of Day of the Dead celebrations are derived from the European cycle of Catholic holidays, in which November 1 is All Saints' Day and November 2, All Souls' Day. These dates were originally selected in an effort to displace a Celtic festival called Samhain, which marked the end of the autumn harvest.[10] Samhain was believed to be a time when the souls of people who had died during the previous year returned and wandered the earth. Masked revelers, sometimes costumed as skeletons, celebrated the night before November first—that is to say, on the Eve of All Saints' Day, also called Eve of All Hallows or Hallow Even, and known in the United States today as Halloween.

Today, in the era of NAFTA and globalization, early November celebrations in Mexico are expanding to include elements from a third source: The United States. Plastic pumpkins, cardboard witches, and fanciful costumes for the playful diversions of children now are sold in markets in addition to sugar skulls and marigolds for the more serious Day of the Dead activities. Thus, the Day of the Dead is an excellent example of the ways in which diverse traditions cross-fertilize one another to give birth to things that are at once new, old, and changing.

Artistic and aesthetic hybridization inevitably affect the traditional cultures of the colonized, but the same is true of the cultures of the colonizers, and the impact of non-Western art traditions on modern Western culture is neither hypothetical nor inconsequential. Since the nineteenth century, there have been many cases in which East Asian, sub-Saharan African, Native American, and Mesoamerican motifs migrated into Western culture. In some cases, they were short-lived fads, but in others, they permanently altered Western arts.

Certainly, this has been true in the fine arts. What would Euro-American painting be like if Picasso and Braque had never seen the visual arts of Africa, Oceania, and the American Northwest Coast? If Gaugan had never gone to Tahiti? If Matisse had not looked at Islamic and North African work? The same question could be asked about other fine art media such as music (e.g., Stravinsky's use of African rhythms), architecture (Japan's influence on the work of Frank Lloyd Wright), and so on.

Non-Western sources have had a major effect on Western popular culture, as well. The African roots of blues, jazz, and rock music is an obvious example, but many other imported elements have become so intrinsic to the Western art form that we forget their cultures of origin. The commonplace fabric known as calico is as marginally American as apple pie, the former having originated in the city of Calicut, India, the latter being made with a fruit that was first domesticated in central Asia. Countless other items have equally distant places of origin. The fashion of wearing heavy silver jewelry came from the American Southwest and was given a healthy boost by a cover photo

---

[10]According to Charmichael and Sayer (1991:14), All Saints' Day and All Souls' Day actually may have begun in the seventh century as a springtime celebrations, created to supplant pagan festivals of the dead at that time of the year. By the eighth century, however, their dates had been moved to the first two days of November.

on *Vogue Magazine* of the Mexican painter, Frida Kahlo, wearing what she took to be pre-Hispanic jewelry. One probably associates tango with Latin America, especially Argentina, although some have speculated that tango movements, rhythms, and the name "tango" itself may have Africa as one of their points of origin. The painters of graffiti art (the name of which comes from wall markings in classical Rome) have been influenced by Mexican muralists, and so on.

Artworks from elsewhere that end up in Western stores and galleries often have been created with either fine art or popular art buyers in mind. For example:

- Two categories of Inuit soapstone carving are produced in the Canadian arctic, namely, the few special pieces that are sold to collectors for prices in the thousands of dollars, and the more numerous and relatively less expensive pieces that are made for sale to tourists and the general public.
- Countless shopping malls in the United States have stores specializing in Native American art, often selling Navajo commercial sandpaintings, jewelry, ceramics, music, and other items of Navajo creation. Meanwhile, art galleries in places such as Santa Fe and Scottsdale (and, for that matter, the internet) offer their affluent clienteles very expensive paintings and sculptures by Navajo fine artists.
- The foreign market for contemporary Yoruba artists has also bifurcated, one branch being represented by fine art painters such as Adebisi Fabunmi, Muraina Oyelami, Jimoh Buraimoh, and Twins Seven-Seven; the other, by carvers and musicians whose work fits a market niche composed of people who simply appreciate West African culture and its arts.[11]

Whatever their popular and fine art destinations in the West, however, artworks in other cultures may continue to serve important functions at home. For example, besides being sold to outsiders, Aboriginal bark paintings still fulfill a domestic pedagogical function, helping elders pass down knowledge of the Dreamtime to members of the younger generation.

When smaller-scale societies collide with larger, colonizing states, it may seem to be an impersonal confrontation. The Epilogues of Part One, however, help put a human face on the process. The succession of changes that take place in the arts of the colonized peoples often are initiated or facili-

---

[11]Besides contemporary Navajo and Yoruba fine art, some old pieces—typically early Navajo textiles and old Yoruba wood carvings—now command four-figure prices because of their age, rarity, and visual appeal to specialist collectors.

tated by a single, or at most a few, outsiders, individuals who have a personal affinity for the culture and for the people who embody it. James Houston's fateful trip to Inukjuak (then Port Harrison) in 1948 and the subsequent dramatic emergence of Inuit soapstone carving is a good example, but it is far from unique. Others are Baldwin Spencer's early collecting of Australian Aboriginal bark paintings, Chuck and Jan Rosenak's role in transforming Navajo figurative wood carvings from children's toys to commercially viable "folk art," and the involvement of Suzanne Wenger and Ulli and Georgina Beier with the nascent fine art movement Yorubaland. Missionaries and church groups also played important roles, as in the case of the Botswana Reformed Church's sponsorship of the Kuru Art Center for the San. Similarly, mission shops in Australia and New Guinea provided the first outlets for commercial indigenous art.

The forgoing remarks have been more about artworks than about art ideas; however, evidence suggests that the colonial process brings about very important changes for aesthetic systems, too. For one thing, as traditional arts become commercial undertakings, concerns about technical skill of execution often increase in importance while interest in religious efficacy diminishes. Recall, for example, the modern Aztec village where Peggy Golde (1963; Golde and Kraemer 1973) found that only technical mastery, not spiritual significance, was thought to differentiate good from mediocre ceramic vessels. That is, whereas the potter in pre-Hispanic times had to have a "deified heart," his modern descendant needs only a steady hand. Kearney similarly found that among the Zapotec villagers of Ixtepeji, "aesthetic criteria are based on functional utility and materialized worth rather than on some abstract notion of beauty. In Ixtepeji things are 'beautiful' because they are well-made and wear well" (Kearney 1972:68). All of the foraging and horticultural societies of Part One experienced a similar shift of emphasis from the spiritual to the technical.

A second common change in traditional thinking about art involves market value. In some communities, the production of art is a major component of the local economy. (As we saw for the Inuit of northern Canada, it is *the* major source of income.) The new focus on market value often is linked to the aforementioned concern with technical skill, with resultant aesthetic ramifications. For example, Betty LeFree's (1975) study of modern Pueblo pottery, especially at Santa Clara, revealed that a pot's quality is judged primarily by the maker's skill as reflected in smooth surfaces and evenly spaced designs. Such standards are obviously well-suited for intercultural appreciation: One need not understand the subtleties of Pueblo religious and aesthetic thought to recognize a well-crafted pot. Since relative degrees of manual skill can be distinguished by buyers and sellers, there is a relatively unambiguous basis for differentiating the pottery of the "best" artists from lesser work (Figure 12–5). Thus, considerations of the marketplace have displaced older, deeper beliefs about the role of art in human life.

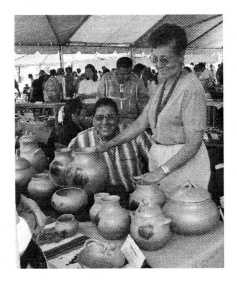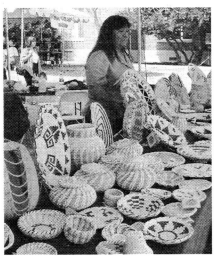

FIGURE 12–5 Exhibitors at the Southwest Indian Art Fair. Held every February in Tucson, the fair is one of the region's most prestigious competitions. *(Photo courtesy of Marnie Sharp, University of Arizona, the Arizona State Museum.)*

In addition to skill of execution and market value, a third factor often appears with regard to art in the culture contact situation: Producers and consumers alike may view artworks as symbolizing the identity of the people who made them. Thus, even though Canadian carvers only started working in soapstone in the late 1940s and now incorporate many features that pre-contact Inuit culture lacked, both they and those who buy the carvings see the soapstone carvings as an effective channel whereby the proud identity of traditional Inuit society can be communicated to non-Inuit people who, in fact, have a powerful influence over contemporary Inuit lives and welfare. And when Qantas airliners are decorated with Aboriginal designs and British Airway planes are painted with images from the Kuru Art Center of the San, the cultural identity of the artists is displayed globally.

Thus, although the culture contact situation is as volatile as it is varied, for all its complexity, a distinct pattern may be discerned with regard to aesthetics. It might be labeled aesthetic "peri-evolution," and it occurs in the course of culture contact when traditional, indigenous aesthetic systems, which inevitably view art as conveying significant cultural meaning, are supplanted by values that emphasize the maker's technical skill, the trade value of the artwork in the context of a larger, state or global economy, and considerations of ethnic identity or cultural pride.

Given the multiple dimensions of perievolution and of the globalization of art in general, most people probably find it difficult to label such changes altogether good or bad. Value judgments about art and aesthetics derive from broadly felt values, of course, but there are certainly aspects of these things that I myself like very much, such as the ways in which today's dizzying cross-currents of art give birth to exciting new means of aesthetic expression. By using art to help a people remember who they are and to proudly proclaim their identity to the larger world, a traditional sociocultural function of art is being valuably adapted to the world we now live in. Further, when artists hone their techniques to high levels, the results can provide a delightful— even an awesome—experience for others fortunate enough to see, hear, or otherwise be exposed to the art.

On the other hand, although commercialization is not, in my opinion, intrinsically or necessarily evil, when the profit motive for making art replaces other, more human and spiritual motives, the loss is unfortunate.[12] As we shall see in Chapter 13, art has a tremendous ability to convey significant cultural meaning, and insofar as that potential is not fulfilled, artists and their audiences are the losers.

Conclusion

Cross-cultural differences between philosophies of art can easily be found, but the question remains, How fundamental are they? On close examination, many dissimilarities turn out to be fairly superficial. In several societies, for example, it is thought that art can perpetuate the conditions that are necessary for life itself, but this axiom takes varying guises in those cultures in which it occurs.

Other differences are deeper, however. The most important of them become apparent when societies are arrayed along a continuum that ranges from small-scale to complex. The aesthetic systems of complex societies are explicit, intricate, and the domain of a small cadre of specialists; philosophies of art in small-scale societies tend to be relatively less so. These differences have more to do with the structure of aesthetic systems than their content, and they probably parallel historical patterns whereby complex, class-structured societies have developed out of small-scale, relatively homogeneous bands, a process I have called aesthetic meso-evolution.

In the culture-contact situation, aesthetic peri-evolution occurs when the cross-culturally diverse and individually profound aesthetic systems of traditional societies decline in importance, replaced by art that is made and esteemed for its display of craftsmanship, its trade value, and its ability to proudly convey the makers social identity.

---

[12]Before dismissing art that emerges from the culture-contact situation because of its commercial dimension, however, one should remember that in the West, there is a long tradition of being concerned with both craftsmanship and the commercial value of artworks. It is hypocritical to scorn these factors when they appear in cultures that we have impinged upon.

13

ART AS CULTURALLY
SIGNIFICANT MEANING

All art is quite useless.

(Oscar Wilde)

Art . . . is necessary only in that
without it life would be unbearable.

Richard Seizer 1979:196)

Some philosophers have given up the search for an absolute and eternal definition of art. Several years ago in an influential article, Morris Weitz
(1967/1957) argued that although there may be agreement on defining art
at any particular place and time, even a cursory look at the history of intellectual thought reveals that people have held quite different views elsewhere
and in other periods. Perhaps, said Weitz, the only constant lies in art's always
being creative, always evolving in style, in purpose, and, significantly, in definition. This being the case, art can only have an "open" definition that speci-
fies the traits that are *usually* present in those things commonly designated as
art, even though no single trait is definitively present in *all* art. Using a line of
reasoning developed by Wittgenstein, Weitz claimed that art is like a large
family, the members of which share a genuine resemblance with one another
even though no single feature is found in every individual.

Having surveyed aesthetic systems in ten largely separate and varied
societies, we can now ask whether any open definition can subsume art
cross-culturally. The answer, I believe, is yes, and I propose the following
open definition: *Art is culturally significant meaning, skillfully encoded in an affecting, sensuous medium.* Although this definition reads syntactically as a sen-
tence, it is in fact a list of qualities—"culturally significant meaning," "skill,"
"code," and "affecting, sensuous medium"—and I believe it can be shown

that each of the diverse congeries of "arts" that were described in the chapters of Part One have most or all of these qualities.[1]

Granted, art traditions and individual artworks vary in the relative emphasis placed upon each of these qualities. Australian Aboriginal groups, for example, think of their *tjurungas* as embodying the deepest of spiritual meanings, whereas the manual skill of the *tjurunga*-maker may be no greater than others. Or to cite another case, the sensuousness of most types of San and Inuit body decorations is paramount in native thought, whereas the cultural significance of the decorations is limited to ideas about social status and personal beauty, values that may be somewhat removed from the cores of both of the cultures. But despite such variations (which, after all, are permitted by an open definition), most or all of these qualities seem inevitably to be present in those things that we consider to be art.

Moreover, things that are not commonly considered to be art rarely have all of the qualities listed above. (That is to say, the traits specified in the definition are not only *necessarily* present in art, but their absence is *sufficient* to set art apart from non-art.) For example, although Western religion embodies cultural meaning of considerable significance and the execution of religious ritual typically requires a trained (i.e., skilled) specialist, only those things that are executed in such a way as to capitalize on the affecting qualities of a sensuous medium are considered to be religious "art." For example, a passage from the Bible is not generally considered to be art unless its aural delivery is enhanced by setting it to music or its literary qualities are heightened by poetic techniques, as in the case of *Psalms* or the *Song of Songs*.

Although most things can unequivocally be classed as either "art" or "non-art" by the proposed definition, some fall in the gray area between the two categories. The traits that make up the definition obviously do not lend themselves to quantification, and we cannot specify precisely *how much* of the traits qualify something as being art. Such a situation is inelegant (and for that matter, aesthetically unpleasing), but it reflects disagreements in the real world, where consensus sometimes gives way to heated debate about whether a particular thing is "really" art or not.

Each of the qualities that constitute the open definition of art requires extended discussion. The first—culturally significant meaning—is the most

---

[1]Weitz's own tentative definition is that art implies "there being present some sort of artifact, made by human skill, ingenuity, and imagination, which it embodies in a sensuous, public medium [with] . . . certain distinguishable elements and relations" (1967:9). If my proposed definition resembles that of Weitz, this may, of course, be because I read Weitz's definition some time before I began the present study. However, it was *after* I had formulated the above definition that I found one that Clifford Geertz similarly proposed: "If there is a commonality in art, it lies in the fact that certain activities everywhere seem specifically designed to demonstrate that ideas are visible, audible, and—one needs to make up a word here—tactible, that they can be cast in form where the senses, and through the senses the emotions, can reflectively address them" (Geertz 1983:120). Osborne (1974) and Cohen (1983/1962) have discussed kindred issues.

complex and will be the sole concern of the remainder of the present chapter. The other issues—code, skill, and sensuous medium—will be dealt with in the next chapter. When this discussion is completed, we will, in effect, have revealed Calliope. In keeping with the nature of an open definition, we must be prepared to see Calliope take on differing guises in varied cultural contexts, and there is every likelihood that she, like art styles themselves, will evolve with the passage of time. Nevertheless, we have a cross-cultural definition of art that derives not from *a priori* assumptions about art but rather from a systematic examination of the empirical world of the makers and users of art.

Meaning in Art

Human existence is intrinsically linked to meaning—to comprehend meaning, to communicate meaning, and, in our most distinctively human capacity, to create meaning. Within the genus *homo,* we have designated ourselves the species *sapiens:* Our highly developed ability to be sapient—to think, to understand—distinguishes us from our hominid ancestors and relatives.[2]

Sometimes nature dictates meaning ("that fruit's redness means it is ripe enough to eat"), and the possibility of a fundamental, manifest meaning in the cosmos cannot be ruled out. Much of our environment, however, is surely devoid of intrinsic meaning and indifferent to human concern. Nevertheless, humans do *create* meaning, postulating that the fruit's redness is "beautiful," and that, perhaps, a man from the "red" clan may not marry a woman from the same "red" kin group. The result, of course, is a "logicomeaningful system of symbolic relationships" (Fernandez 1973:194)—that is, the vast and remarkable artifact we call human culture. In our eternal drive to create meaning, we have generated social structure, systems of myth and religion—and art. To paraphrase the previously quoted remark (p. 36) by the Inuit, Orpingalik, culture is as necessary for us as our breath.

All the societies examined in Part One invest art with significant cultural meaning. That is, in addition to an artwork's being "about" its own stylistic conventions and the emotional response that its embodiment in a sensuous medium can evoke, it is also "about" some subject in the sociocultural matrix of which it is a part.[3]

---

[2]Several of the themes discussed below are also dealt with, albeit from quite a different perspective, by Robert Plant Armstrong (1971, 1975, 1981).

[3]One might simply say that art everywhere tends to be "symbolic," but I intend here to suggest a more multidimensional quality in art. Art may be narrowly symbolic (by referring to something outside itself that it does not resemble), iconically representational, or even reflexive (by making statements about itself or the stylistic conventions it manifests). For that reason, I shall speak of art as conveying significant meaning, rather than being symbolic.

Means as Meaning

Art's cultural significance may lie in its capacity to bring about some desired end—that is, one meaning of art lies in its being a *means* to some goal. In the same way that the most salient meaning of "hammer" is "tool for driving a nail," the meaning of an artwork may be the means it provides to attain an extra-artistic end.

In such cases, religious meanings are often involved. For example, an item of sacred Australian Aboriginal art, such as a bullroarer, is not so much an embodiment of transcendent meaning in itself but is a means of influencing the sacred realm—ensuring the eternal order of things, including fertility, the perpetuation of human life and culture, and so on. Inuit art is also made for purposes that are both utilitarian and sacred—namely, assuring personal well-being in this life and the next. Similarly, art *cognoscenti* among the Yoruba, the Navajo, the Aztecs, and the Japanese sect of Shintoism believe that art induces supernatural spirits to aid mortals. Art in classical India and medieval Europe was equally purposeful, yielding desirable spiritual results by bringing people closer to the supernatural realm.

Means-as-meaning is widespread, but it varies in the form it takes. Sometimes the end is thoroughly concrete and definable. Certain tattoos on Inuit women are intended to ease their labor pains during childbirth, and a perfect mirror was used to lure the fearful Shinto Sun goddess, Amaterasu-ô-mi-kami, out of the Rock Cave of Heaven (Figure 13–1). Or else the end may be abstract in nature. A Navajo sandpainting, for example, insures a continuation of the world's natural state of goodness and harmony. Art's ends may be sacred, as in these cases, or wholly secular, as with the sensuous pleasure and

FIGURE 13-1   Utagwa Kunisada (1787–1865) *Amaterasu Emerges from the light. (Courtesy of Victoria and Albert Museum, London, Great Britain/Art Resource, NY, Woodblock print CT 21443.)*

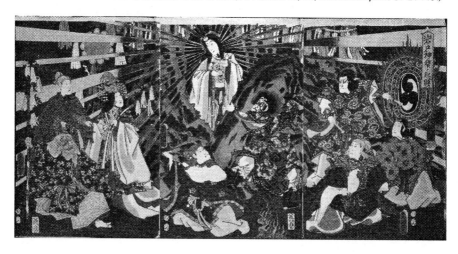

aesthetic delight that San and Inuit art inspire in their percipients. Moreover, the sacred and the sensuous are not mutually exclusive, and in actual practice the two qualities often complement each other.

There is ample evidence that art conveys significant cultural meaning not only in the societies discussed in Part One but in other groups as well. Bohannan, for example, observes that the West African Tiv "are more interested in the ideas conveyed by a piece of art than they are by its manufacture" (Bohannan 1971:175). Similarly, Graburn (1978) found that California museumgoers preferred Inuit carvings to objects made by Naskapi-Cree, probably because they misunderstood the works' meanings, erroneously assuming that Cree Craft objects represented a greater degree of commercialism than did the Inuit carvings. Since this motivation was antithetical to the meaning of "art" for them, they placed a lower value on the Cree works.

Sacramental Meanings in Art

Not only does art typically convey culturally significant meaning, but it often communicates several such meanings simultaneously. When the messages reinforce each other, the effect is particularly powerful, transcending normal modes of discourse. Gregory Bateson has called such communication "sacramental," as in this hypothetical dialogue between a father and his precocious daughter about the ways in which the ballet *Swan Lake* has a meaning beyond the merely rational:

Father: The swan figure is not a real swan but a pretend swan. It is also a pretend-not human being. It is also "really" a young lady wearing a white dress. And a real swan would resemble a young lady in certain ways.
Daughter: But which of these is sacramental?
Father: Oh Lord, here we go again. I can only say this: that it is not one of these statements but their combination which constitutes a sacrament. The "pretend" and the "pretend-not" and the "really" somehow get fused together in a single meaning. (Bateson 1972:37)

A similar idea can be seen in a remark attributed to Isadora Duncan, who was instrumental in developing modern dance in the early twentieth century. When asked what her choreography meant, she reputedly replied, "I can't explain dance to you. If I could say it, I wouldn't have to dance it!" Not all art is sacramental, but a distinctive property of art is its capacity to ineffably convey meanings in a way that transcends the rational, the explicit, the unambiguous.

The phallic meaning of Sepik art is a good example of the sacramental dimension of art (Figure 13–2). The wood, fiber, paint, and shells that make a mask, shrine object, or tambaran house decoration are recognized as such, but at the same time they are ardently believed to be embodiments

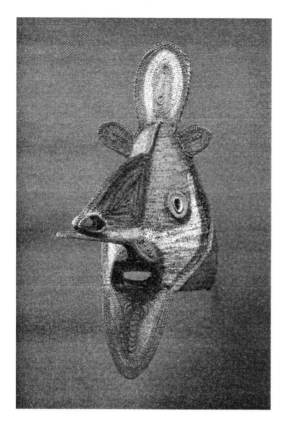

FIGURE 13–2   Karpiman or Kani-gara people, Mask, collected before 1932, painted cane. H: 69 cm. *(Courtesy of Museo Missionario Etnologico, Vatican Museums.* © *Scala/Art Resource, NY.)*

of spirit beings. As with the sacraments of communion, where bread and wine are presented not only as food and drink but also as the body and blood of Christ, the Sepik art objects convey a potent message. Surely this must result from both the synergistic effect of uniting sensuous medium with spiritual meaning, as well as the nature of the abstract message itself. The Sepik spirits *are* powerful, but they rarely, if ever, exist in a tangible, non-art form. In art, however, they become palpable, dynamic beings.

Art and Beauty

Often art's central meaning lies in its being a tangible embodiment of abstract norms of beauty and social goodness. For example, we began our search for the root of Yoruba aesthetics by examining standards of sensuous beauty as they apply to art objects, but these were clearly derived from the criteria of human beauty. Looking more deeply for the source of these standards, we came to the generalized principles of harmony and energy, two core values that hold sway in Yoruba culture at large. In Yoruba, the words for "beauty" and "goodness" are synonymous, and the same is true in many other African languages. Similarly, Navajos use *hózhǫ́* to mean not only "beauty" but also "goodness" and other positive qualities.

Since art is often related to beauty, we would do well to ask about the source of human standards of beauty. Beauty criteria vary from one society to another, of course, but they generally do so within restricted limits, and at least some of these are rooted in practical considerations. "Beautiful" skin is usually healthy skin, free of the blemishes of disease and the wrinkles of advanced age (cf. Symonds 1995). It is surely no coincidence that sound, white teeth are both attractive and practical (Figure 13–3). The female breast is often a focus of interest, the ideal being either young, firm breasts that show the promise of nurturing many children (as in Yoruba and north-central Australian cultures) or else pendulous breasts that have already done so (as among the Mountain Arapesh of New Guinea and Anang of West Africa). The standards of male beauty found in many societies may be at least as rigor-

FIGURE 13–3 Men among the Wodaabe, a pastoralist Fulani group in Niger, West Africa, display their physical beauty during the *yaake* dance performance. They pride themselves not only on their facial attractiveness, especially on their bright eyes and shinning teeth, but also on their hair and body decorations, as well as their charm and charisma. *(Photo courtesy of Carol Beckwith, Robert Estall Photo Agency.)*

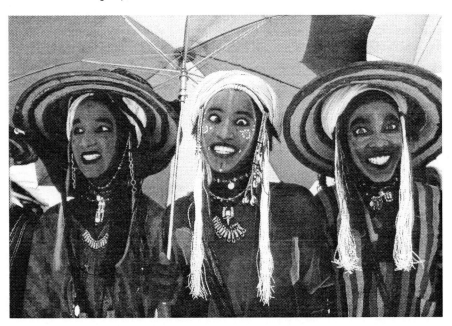

ous as those for women and often derive from considerations of health, strength, and vigor (cf. van Offelen 1983).[4]

Beauty standards may be unrelated to subsistence and procreation but still serve a practical purpose. Shintoists, for example, find beauty in cleanliness and purity—perhaps because these qualities enhance healthiness. Even in the Western aesthetic tradition, Dostoevsky writes, "Beauty inheres in everything healthy. . . . It is harmony, and it contains a guarantee of tranquility" (quoted in Zenkovsky 1962:141).

The East African Pakot show how beauty may be found in places not expected by Westerners. Pakot women are gardeners, and they find beauty in "a healthy, green field of eleusine plants" (Schneider 1956:105). On the other hand, Pakot men, who are cattle herders and who have little to do with gardening, see no beauty in eleusine plants. They do, however, wax rhapsodic about the beauty of certain types of steers, a passion beyond the ken not only of most Westerners but of Pakot women as well.

Evidence of an appreciation of the practical value of beauty comes from many places. The Yanomami of South America, for example, believe that their material welfare requires the blessings of supernatural spirits called *hekura*, to whom the men chant while under the influence of a powerful hallucinogen called *ebene*. On one occasion during his fieldwork with the Yanomami, Napoleon Chagnon participated in the chanting:

> We walked silently over to Kaobawa's house for that is where the daily activities were to begin. "Let me decorate you, my dear brother!" said Rerebawa softly, and I knelt on the ground while all my friends generously made their special feathers and decorations available to me so that I might become more beautiful and therefore more worthy to the hekura. (Chagnon 1983:208)

For the Yanomami, members of the spirit world are not only beautiful in themselves; they are summoned by beautifully decorated mortals. And in this case, the decorations were efficacious for Chagnon. After inhaling powdered *ebene*, he did experience seeing the *hekura*.

---

[4]Freud wrote, "The love of beauty is a perfect example of a sentiment whose aim is inhibited. It is remarkable that the genitalia themselves, the sight of which is always sexually exciting, are hardly ever regarded as beautiful; beauty seems to accrue rather to certain secondary sexual characteristics" (quoted in Comfort 1962:100). Inhibition or no, it appears that most societies do attach more importance to the appearance of secondary sexual traits than to genitals; however, these secondary traits—men's legs and torsos, women's buttocks and breasts, and so forth—are also of practical importance. And where genital preferences are stated, as among the Anang (Messenger 1981), they are often emblems of gender rather than marks of beauty.

Art and Social Values

If art often embodies messages about beauty, it also frequently suggests ideas of social goodness. Since ancient Greece, for example, Westerners have equated certain "attractive" facial features with desirable qualities of character, while others are "ugly" and found only in unsavory individuals, as in Aristotle's claim that straight eyebrows indicate an undesirable "softness of disposition" (cf. Liggett 1974:181–215).

The most pervasive pattern linking beauty and goodness focuses not on qualities intrinsic to the individual but rather on those that have a social dimension. Terence S. Turner has observed that among the central Brazilian Kayapo, to be dirty is to be actively antisocial because personal dirtiness contravenes a primary value of social life. Beauty is thought by the Kayapo to be a quintessential expression of society itself (Turner 1980:115, 135).

Or, to take a different example, consider the traditional conception of the artist in Chinese culture: He is a man "who is at peace with nature. . . . Above all, his breast must brood no ill passions, for a good artist, we strongly believe, must be a good man" (Lin Yutang 1935:288). Harold K. Osborne observes, "While the Western artist typically aimed to produce a replica of reality, actual, imagined, or ideal, the Chinese artist—although he might in fact do this—made his first aim to bring his own personality into keeping with the cosmic principle so that the Tao would be expressed through him" (Osborne 1968:107). The Chinese artist can only create beauty if he himself is a paragon of goodness, a model for others to emulate and revere.

Art and Truth

Two common value-meaning associations of art have already been noted—namely, art's link with human health and physical well-being and its relation to social goodness. But art's value dimension has a third component. Art may also be conceived as a manifestation of *truth*. One is reminded of John Keats's dictum,

> 'Beauty is truth, truth beauty,'—that is all
> Ye know on earth, and all ye need to know.

These lines express the popular belief that the great verities provide a foundation not only for society but for art as well. For example, among the central African Lega, the vocabulary of aesthetic values is isomorphic with Lega sociocultural values (Figure 13–4). Only those Lega individuals who have attained the state of *bugosa* are admitted to the highest levels of society. This term refers not only to beauty but also to goodness; and *bugosa* is goodness of

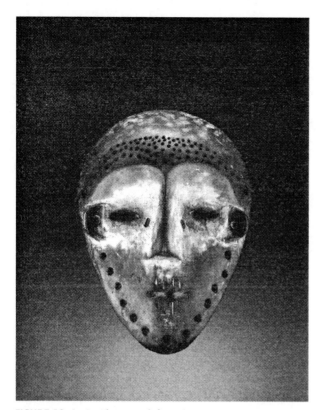

FIGURE 13-4 An *idumu* mask from the Lega peoples, Democratic Republic of the Congo. Wood, pigment fiber; 29.5 cm H x 22 cm W x 10.5 cm D; late 19th—mid 20th century. *Idumu* masks were used to illustrate proverbs about proper behavior. *(Photo courtesy Franko Khoury, National Museum of African Art/Smithsonian Institution.)*

a fundamental sort, implying, among other things, *izu,* or "deep insight and wisdom, as opposed to *kizio,* simple knowledge" (Biebuyck 1973:129).

Or consider a different Black art form, the idiom of blues music:

> The main aesthetic standard . . . for early folk blues was truth. But it was a truth based in universal human experience or at least a kind of experience that was known to the singer and audience. Unlike other major forms of black folklore, the blues did not deal with the imaginary animal world of Br'er Rabbit or the deeds of legendary heroes like John Genry or Stacker Lee. . . . Along with this went traditional melodies and instrumental patterns and techniques. These too had to be delivered by the performers with conviction and "truth." (Evans 1982:52f)

Thus, blues music, like the sculpture of the Lega, is a public and tangible statement of important verities. The maxim of Navajo aesthetics, "If it's worthwhile, it's beautiful" (McAllester 1954:71), is embraced by people from all points of the compass.

Art and Religion: Transformation and Communion

Whereas the metaphysical messages of art are sometimes implicit, the meanings of religious art can be explicit and concrete. The performance of the San Ritual Healing dance; the amulets and some of the tattoos made by Inuits; Australian Aboriginal dance, song, and drawings of the Eternal Dreamtime; Sepik art made for the tambaran cult and other ceremonial uses; Navajo sandpaintings intended to maintain or reestablish *hózhó;* cult usages of Yoruba sculpture, costumery, dance, and song; Aztec art dedicated to the gods with the hope of forestalling the final destruction of our earth and all who live here; Indian art's embodiment of *rasa,* with its capacity to elevate one to a higher spiritual plane; and Japanese art, with its close ties to Shinto spirits and the various sects of Buddhism—each is an example of art conveying a specifically religious meaning.

Needless to say, the combined issues of religion, morality, and ethics have been dominant themes in the secular West, as well. Besides the obviously religious art of the Middle Ages, Western mimetic works often have had as an ulterior motive the moral and spiritual betterment of the viewer (Figure 13–5). Also, the tenets of romanticism and formalism frequently have been advocated with a religious fervor (Beethoven once remarked, "Music is a moral force"), and they may present art as a means whereby the sensitive individual can be transported to the high realms of aesthetic bliss.

The religious functions of art may involve art bringing about miraculous, qualitative transformations. Inuit art affects a metamorphosis between the natural world, the human world, and the world of the supernatural. Similarly, Australian Aboriginal groups believe that art transmutes mortals and mundane objects such as painted pieces of wood into the spiritual realm of the Eternal Dreamtime. In the Sepik, the tambaran and long yam spirits reside in the objects that are painted and decorated in their honor, and Yoruba dancers, when they don mask and costume, actually become the *orisha* in whose praise they are dancing.

In cases where art is not an actual manifestation of the supernatural, it may provide the prime means whereby mortals come in intimate contact with the sacred. Navajo sandpaintings embody *hózhó,* and Aztec art, made as a gift to the gods, came from the gods in the first place. Indian *rasa* is the primary tangible means whereby mortals apprehend higher spiritual principles of religious belief, and the same could be said of the anagogic art of the Middle Ages in the West. Finally, regarding Japanese aesthetics, one is reminded of the Shinto creation myth in which it was the arts—music, dance, and the perfect mirror—that lured the Sun Goddess out of the Rock Cave of Heaven.

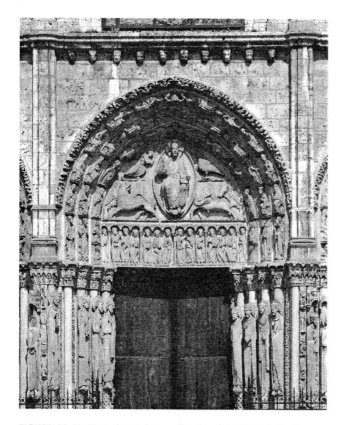

FIGURE 13-5 Central portal, west façade, of the Cathedral of Notre-Dame, Chartres, France. Created in the mid-twelfth century, the high relief sculpture on the building's exterior is full of Biblical references. Above the door can be seen Christ, surrounded by symbols for the four evangelists, while the lintel depicts the tweve apostles, plus two additional figures—probably Elijah and Enoch. *(Photo courtesy of Erich Lessing, Art Resource, NY.)*

Thus, at least some of the art produced in each of the cultures discussed in Part One is an embodiment of the spirit world or, at least, serves as a medium through which mortals can communicate with that world. In a word, a pervasive and significant meaning of art is as a "transformer," permitting communication between the sacred and profane levels of existence.[5]

---

[5]On the other hand, we must remember that not all art is religiously oriented. As Part One revealed, societies at all levels of complexity make art for distinctly secular purposes.

Compelling Action

Art not only provides communication with the spiritual realm, it may also *compel* spirits to act. Robert Horton (1965) has described such a process for the Kalabari of southern Nigeria. Kalabari religious belief includes many spirits—ancestor spirits, water spirits, and the spirits of village heroes. These are all potentially powerful beings, but their strength is contingent upon human intervention. Intensive worship makes a spirit strong, giving it the power either to benefit or harm its devotees; neglect, on the other hand, reduces the spirit to insignificance. This is what Kalabari mean when they say, *tomi, ani oru beremara*—"it is men who make the gods important" (Horton 1965:6; cf. also Barbar 1981 and Reichard 1944).

Significantly, the praise given to Kalabari spirits generally takes the form of art—praise song, drama, dance, or sculpture (see Figure 13–6). Thus, in a sense the Kalabari spirits are controlled by art. When a man acts arrogantly, Horton observes, he may be asked,

FIGURE 13–6 Carved and painted wooden figure made by the Kalabari in western Ijo, Nigeria. 64.4 cm. high. *(The Metropolitan Museum of Art, The Michael G. Rockefeller Memorial Collection, Gift of the Matthew T. Mellon Foundation, 1960 [1978.412.404].)*

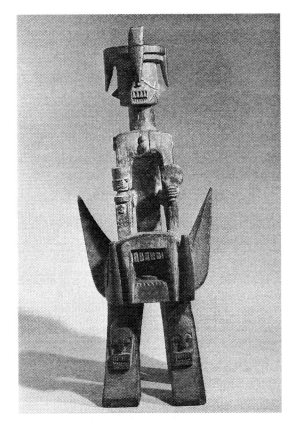

"Are you a spirit without a sculpture?"—meaning, "Do you think we have nothing through which we can control you?" Behind these figures of speech is a serious feeling that sculpture is a necessary instrument for controlling the spirits,
and that any spirit without a sculpture to represent it is dangerous because it
cannot be adequately controlled. (Horton 1965:8).

Art's role in compelling Kalabari spirits to action is all the more dramatic in light of the fact that, besides the spirits, the Kalabari also believe in a
supreme being, Tamuno, who is totally independent and who does as he
wishes with no concern for human activities. Mortals can only express submis-
sion to Tamuno; as the Kalabari say in moments of resignation, "*Tamuno*
never loses a case" (Horton 1965:7). Consequently, the Kalabari make no art
for Tamuno. Tamuno cannot be compelled to action, and making art in his
name would be futile.

As the Kalabari example illustrates, in addition to art's being a means
of religious communication, art can also be used as a means of *controlling*
the supernatural. This is true in several of the cultures discussed in Part
One. Navajo sings, if carried out properly, will guarantee the desired result
of creating and maintaining *hózhǫ́*; Shinto annual ceremonies influence the
kami for human good; Australian Aboriginal ceremonies compel the representatives of the Eternal Dreamtime to renew and sustain the blessings that
existed at the time of creation; and San healers use the heightened consciousness of *kia* to fend off the invisible but dangerous spirit-arrows that
harm people.

The claim that art embodies messages about supernatural power
should not be dismissed as mere superstition. While living with a Navajo
family in the summer of 1969, Gary Witherspoon witnessed a series of events
centering around an 82-year-old woman who had suddenly become ill and
fallen into a coma. She was taken to a hospital where doctors believed she
could only be kept alive by intravenous feeding. However, a diviner diag-
nosed her problem as having a supernatural cause and prescribed a particular Sing. Although her doctors said she would die if not given intravenous
food, her family took her home and quickly arranged a performance of
Enemyway. According to Witherspoon, "When she arrived at home, she
seemed to me to be in a deep coma, totally unconscious, and nearly dead. By
the conclusion of the rite she was walking around almost normally. Several
non-Navajos working at the local school were amazed; most Navajos were not
amazed but were gratefully serene. I last saw her, alive and well, in 1973"
(Witherspoon 1977:13f).

Before we attribute this and similar cases to "spontaneous remission"
(i.e., coincidence) or "merely" the power of suggestion, we should recall the
potential power of artistic activity. Art conveys meaning and its effects can be
powerful. Humans live in a world constrained by the laws of the mind no less
than the laws of physics. A lifetime of exposure to, and belief in, the world of

meaning conveyed through art influences an individual's social and psychological well-being as surely as biology influences one's physical health.

A final dimension of art's role in conveying religious meaning should be noted. In some societies, art not only transmits religious meaning, it also carries messages of a particularly deep and obscure nature. When religious concepts are so abstract that even initiates grasp them only with difficulty, art can serve as a means whereby the people at large can gain some grasp of religious principles. Medieval Christianity, with its mysteries and miracles, is an example, as is classical India with its concept of *rasa*. Steven J. Lansing has remarked regarding the syncretic religion of contemporary Bali, "For the Balinese, art is not merely ornamental but a way—perhaps the best way—to understand the true nature of reality. . . . The arts provide a way to understand and experience the divine essence" (Lansing 1981:36–37).

The Importance of Meaning in Art

I have claimed that the elusive Calliope thrives in all ten of the societies examined in Part One—that is, that each society produces art, where "art" is defined as being culturally significant meaning, skillfully encoded in an affecting, sensuous medium. This definition isolates several dimensions that are typically present in art, but in any particular cultural context we may find one dimension of art to be emphasized more than others. Like a mortal, one particular component of Calliope's personality may or less be dominant, depending on where she is. She may be the beautiful, sensuous Calliope, the belle of the ball, who entertains and excites all who meet her, but she can also present a serious side, concerned with matters of deep philosophical import. The information in Part One shows that the aspect of significant meaning in art can rise to such importance that it overshadows all else.

Recall San oracle disks (Figure 1–8, p. 26), for example. Little skill is required in creating them, and we find no evidence that the San value them for their sensuous beauty. Yet they convey important *meaning*. They are tools for learning about and influencing what is otherwise unknown and independent of human control. Carved amulets probably play a parallel role in traditional Inuit thought. Since my definition of art is "open," composed of several traits that constitute a generalized "family resemblance," we cannot authoritatively determine whether San oracle disks are indeed "art." With regard to meaning and their conformity to a traditional style, they are, but with respect to skill and sensuous appeal, they fall only marginally into the category of art.

The history of Judeo-Christian ambivalence toward representational art is interesting in this context. Although Western art has produced some of its greatest achievements in service to religious belief, sometimes there has also been a fear of art leading the faithful to worship something other than one god. The ancient Jews even included in the Ten Commandments a taboo against making and worshiping "graven" images. Jewish scholars have suggested (cf. Bacon 1971) that the prohibition probably began as a fear that people would worship an idol for its own sake, or that they might come to believe that it held a supernatural spirit other than the Hebrew god, apparently a not-unfounded fear since other Near Eastern groups believed that spirits did control natural phenomena such as rain, health, and human well-being, that they could inhabit inanimate figures, and that worshiping the figures would propitiate the resident spirits.

Symbol and Icon

Humans make meaning. We view the cold, indifferent universe as being alive with spirits and forces that, though not wholly human, are somehow our kin. It is not surprising that we do so. Consider the Inuit seal hunter standing alone, hour after hour, on the windswept sea ice of an arctic winter, waiting for a sign that a seal has come to breathe through the hole that he is watching in the ice. The seal comes; the hunter strikes. After he has dispatched the seal and pulled it up through the ice, the hunter makes a cut in its body. As he carves out a piece of the seal's liver to eat, both as a memorial and as food, the hunter recognizes his kinship with the seal, the only other warm thing in the arctic panorama that surrounds him. He owes his own life to the seal. The seal has spirit; the seal has meaning. The hunter knows these things and expresses them in his carvings of seals, of men, and other living things.

Our penchant for constructing meaning and vesting it in our art has implications for some long-standing debates, such as the question of Paleolithic art. As far back as 60,000 years ago, *Homo sapiens* were making geometric designs, and figurative painting, engraving, and sculpture goes back at least 30,000 years. Animals provided the most common subjects for European artists during the Upper Paleolithic, and although some of the species portrayed were hunted as food, others were not.

Several explanatory hypotheses have been suggested, but disagreement persists among pre-historians regarding the meaning of Paleolithic art. Perhaps the motive was "sympathetic magic," whereby artists hoped to gain some measure of control over the beasts they depicted, or maybe the figures reveal a structural interplay between masculine and feminine principles, or the pictures could merely illustrate scenes from their makers' myths, or even their day-to-day activities. Whatever the explanation, our present analysis of aesthetics in contemporary societies strongly suggests that the animals must have had great significance for the communities that produced them. The same must be true for the many pre-historic figures, explicit or stylized, executed in either two or three dimensions, that portray the (usually female) sexual anatomy. Whether they symbolized human reproduction, eroticism, or generalized "fertility magic," we have, I feel, no sure way of knowing. But the drawings surely were vessels of potent meaning, and not just trivial graffiti.

Another old debate concerns the relative ages of representational and nonrepresentational art. In the late nineteenth and early twentieth centuries, some scholars believed that representational art came first and that some pictorial subjects gradually became so stylized that they lost their original meanings and were eventually treated as purely nonrepresentational figures. By contrast, other prehistorians claimed that the pleasure of design prompted people first to make meaningless patterns, and representational interpretations were read into them at a later time. Like many debates of the day, this one was fought more with polemic and deductive reasoning than with empirical evidence.

Franz Boas was the first to systematically evaluate the cross-cultural and archaeological data bearing on this issue, and he concluded that "it seems futile to discuss the question of whether representative decorative art is older than geometrical decorative art, but that it rather appears that we are dealing here with two different sources of artistic activity, which tend to merge into the development of graphic and plastic arts" (Boas 1963/1940:236–237).

To consider the question of representationalism cross-culturally, rather than historically, we may start with the end of the continuum at which we find explicitly figurative art. Boas rightly observed that an absence of realism in most non-Western cultures is not due to a lack of skill. Some modern Yoruba carving illustrates the accuracy with which the human figure can be portrayed; and the pre-historic antecedents of Yoruba art prove that such skill is not limited to the modern era: Benin bronzes (Figure 13–7) made before the 1700s, Ife bronzes and terracottas that date before 1200, and Nok terracottas going back to the fourth century B.C.—all show such consummate artistry in sculptural rendering that the first Europeans to see them believed ethnocentrically (and erroneously, of course) that they must have been produced by migrant Europeans rather than by Africans.

Moreover, Westerners have no more of a monopoly on skill of representation than they do on *appreciating* such skill. The Yoruba's neighbors, the Kalabari, may refuse to pay for a commissioned sculpture because it is not true enough to its model. However, the Kalabari case raises an important issue on the subject of representational versus nonrepresentational art. The model for a Kalabari carved figure is not any specific person but an old, often-used cult object that has fallen into disrepair. The carver's success is measured solely by his replication of this model, itself a highly stylized depiction of the human face and form; all other standards of representational accuracy are irrelevant (Horton 1965:23).

The situation becomes more intriguing when we consider the Fang, who live southeast of the Yoruba. James Fernandez, who has written extensively on Fang art and aesthetics says, "The Fang often argue that their figures and masks constitute traditional photographs" (Fernandez 1973:204). The

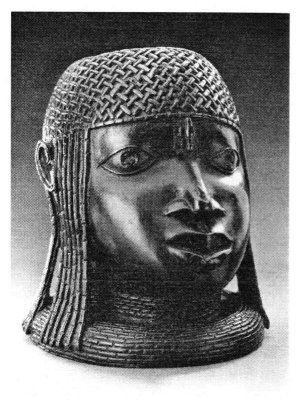

FIGURE 13-7   African, Nigerian, Benin peoples, "Memorial head of an Oba," 16th century, brass, 9 1/8" H. The Nelson-Atkins Museum of Art, Kansas City, Missouri. *(Nelson Trust through the generosity of Donald J. & Adele C. Hall, Mr. & Mrs. Herman Robert Sutherland, an anonymous donor and the exchange of Nelson Gallery Foundation properties. Photograph by E.G. Schempf (7/1987)-*

fact that the mask illustrated in Figure 13–8 would be identified as a portrait of either Franco or DeGaulle reveals the great influence of culture on conceptions of realism. For contemporary Westerners, a photograph shows a particular individual, but for the Fang,

> what the statue represents is not necessarily the truth, physically speaking, of a human body, but a vital truth about human beings symbolically stated. This symbolic intelligence seems to arise from the way the statue holds opposites in balance—old age and infancy, somber passive inscrutability of visage and muscular tension of torso and legs, etc. What is expressed in these statues, then, is the essence of maturity. (Fernandez 1973:205)

Similarly, the contemporary British painter, Francis Bacon, has said, "Isn't it that one wants a thing to be as factual as possible, and yet at the same time as deeply suggestive or deeply unlocking of areas of sensation other

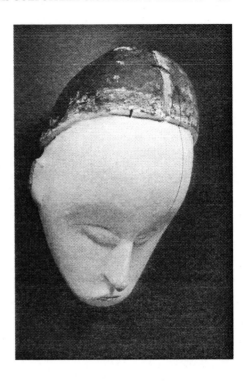

FIGURE 13-8 Fang dance mask, said to depict either Franco or DeGaulle. Made by Mvole Mo Ze in the early 1950s. *(Photo courtesy James W. Fernandez)*

than simple illustrating of the object that you set out to do? Isn't that what art is all about?" (quoted in Berger 1980:112). A comparable belief was expressed in Classical Chinese aesthetics. Su Tungp'o wrote, "If one criticizes painting by its verisimilitude, one's understanding is similar to that of a child" (quoted in Lin Yutang 1935:309); according to this aesthetic, mature painting should express the subject's *spirit.*

But probably nobody would mistake the Fang mask in Figure 13–8 for an abstract form with no meaningful referent: It clearly represents a human head. However, some artworks that appear to be totally abstract turn out, on closer inspection (Figure 13–9), to actually be representational. The fine rugs woven by women in the Georgian Caucasus (Figure 13–10) appear to be decorated with purely geometric designs. Research has revealed, however, that some of these patterns are intended to portray a specific and culturally important subject—namely, one of the four traditional floor plans found in Armenian churches (Sassouni 1981).

We can move one step further in the direction of abstraction by considering Tantric mandalas, the seemingly nonrepresentational paintings used by devotees in India and Tibet (see Figure 13–11). Although many of the paintings do not portray specific subjects found in the sensible world, they are not meaningless. They represent the highest spiritual principles of Tantric belief.

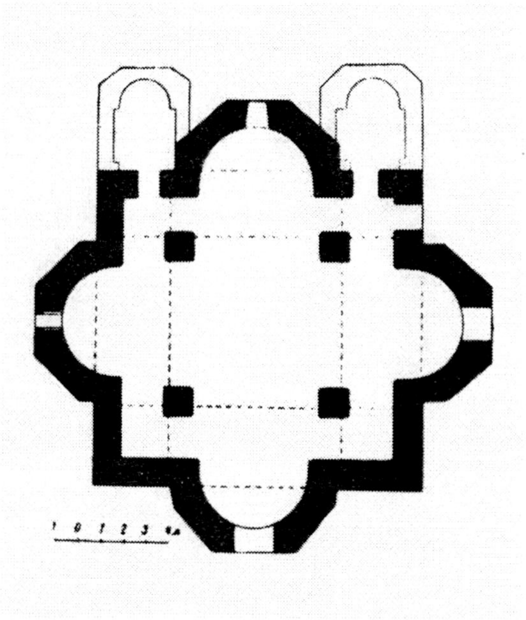

FIGURE 13–9 Baragan, a 7th century Armenian church with a radiating-on-a-square floor plan.*(Courtesy of The Hali Archive, London.)*

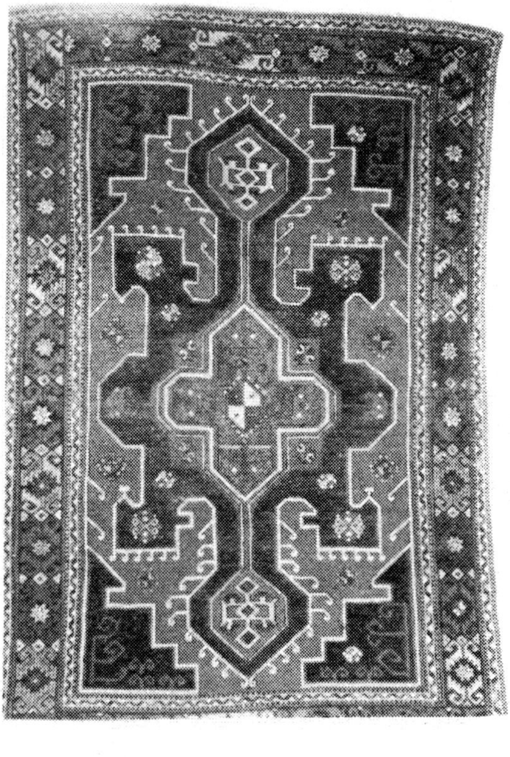

FIGURE 13–10 An Ushak rug, the central area of which is a radiating-on-a-square design. *(Courtesy of The Hali Archive, London.)*

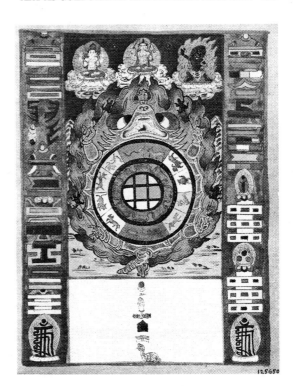

FIGURE 13-11 Tibetan Mandala representing Par-ka, Mewa, the signs of the zodiac, and the days of the week. *(Courtesy, Field Museum of Natural History, Chicago, neg. no. 100383.)*

They are meant "to stimulate radiant inner icons, whose bodies and features would be quite unrealistic in any ordinary sense of the word" (Rawson 1973:25).

Body decoration is another notable genre of apparently nonrepresentational art. Consider the Nuba, a group of farmer-pastoralists who live in the Kordofan Province of Sudan. James Faris has described in detail several specific ways in which Nuba men decorate themselves (Faris 1972). One category of geometric design appears to be devoid of referential meaning—for instance, a band of three or more black diamond figures connected point to point and bordered by two black lines. (see Figure 13–12). Although one might assume that this is merely a geometric design prompted by the pleasure of pattern, the Nuba call it *ŋōrā* and recognize it as representing cowrie shells on a strip of leather. Alternatively, if the diamonds had not been filled in with black, the design would have been *deŋa-kwa,* a poisonous snake. Other Nuba body decorations convey different, and more abstract, meanings in a different way. For example, a person's haircut indicates membership in a patrilineal clan.

But Nuba body decoration has another level of meaning, and this reveals a second way in which the art is in some sense representational. To shave one's body hair, to tattoo oneself, and to apply oil and pigment to the

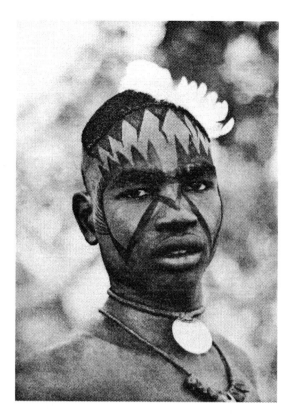

FIGURE 13–12 Nuba man, with painted decorations, hair and neck ornaments. *(Photo courtesy James Faris.)*

skin is to display one's humanity, one's maturity, one's beauty. Faris notes that in Nuba thought, "It is not language (which monkeys, in Southeastern Nuba myths, once shared with man), but shaving—the *choice* to have or not to have hair—that distinguishes humans from other 'moving species'" (Faris 1972:56). Nuba body decoration is a conscious and explicit recognition of a belief found in many other societies—namely, that body decoration signifies both the unique identity of the wearer as well as membership in a larger social entity. Be it the style of fur and leatherwork characteristic of an Inuit group, the medieval European coat of arms, or the designer clothes of contemporary America, the seemingly nonrepresentational art of body decoration is rich with meaning.

All art represents meaning, whether it is figuratively representational or not. The meaning may, following C. S. Peirce, be called iconographic, with the artwork resembling the subject it represents, as in the lines, circles, and dots that some Aboriginal Australians draw to represent the travels of mythic creatures during the Eternal Dreamtime (cf. Munn 1973). Or the meaning may be symbolic, like Tantric paintings and much body decoration.

To return to the debate about whether art was born from a decorative or a symbolic impulse, I would argue that a meaning component (either symbolic or iconographic) is *always* present, even in artifacts that appear to be only decorative in nature. The importance of aesthetic playfulness will be considered later, but for now we can see that Boas was probably correct in admitting the futility of the search for the representational versus nonrepresentational origin of art. This is not because there were separate sources of artistic activity, however, but rather because in this context the distinction between representational and nonrepresentational art is spurious. *All* art represents; the only difference is the degree to which an artifact's referent is known to those outside the tradition that produced it and the degree to which the represented subject itself is either concrete or abstract.[6]

Difficult Meanings

That the meaning conveyed by art is not necessarily easily accessible comes as no surprise. Art is often accorded the honor of being the medium through which deep philosophical issues are conveyed. This has been the case historically in Western art and it remains so today. Getzels and Csikszentmihalyi (1976) interviewed a large sample of painting and sculpture students enrolled in American art colleges, asking why they wanted to become artists. The researchers found that

> practically none mentioned the creation of "beauty," "harmony," "order," or any other such aesthetic goal. Most responses centered instead on cognitive goals: The young artists said they painted in order to get a better understanding of reality. The kind of understanding they sought referred to areas of experience that were highly ambiguous, like life and death, or were very personal and complex. They wanted a better understanding of problems for which no rational solution is available. (Csikszentmihalyi 1978:118)

We can only speculate about the psychological basis of this phenomenon. Peckham has claimed that humans have a natural drive to order and certainty, which is adaptive under many conditions, but perhaps we also need an arena in which we can experience doubt and disorientation because only in such a flux can we forge new life ways to cope with a changing world (Peckham 1965). Art, in this view, serves such a need by providing a domain in which chaos and mystery can be experienced without endangering survival.

---

[6]I refer here not only to material artifacts but also to such "behavioral artifacts" (or, as Keali'inohomoku has dubbed them, "phenomifacts") as songs, dances, and stories. These also generally convey meanings in ways that are both obvious and obscure. Music, for example, often has a text, and the melody may imitate sounds of nature—animal calls, weather noises, or whatever. In addition, music may symbolically convey messages of group identity.

George Devereux has made a similar proposal, although he turns the matter around by asking why the significant truths conveyed by art "should have to be beautified, or why the lily gilded. The only reasonable answer to this question is that only painful or upsetting truth needs to be 'varnished'" (Devereux 1961:373). Art can provide an avenue for expressing emotionally and philosophically wrenching ideas because, in the first place, it embodies the idiom of cultural tradition, and in the second place, being symbolic, it is always repudiable.

The societies of Part One provide concrete examples of art conveying difficult and complex messages. Often the problem lies not in the content of the art's subject matter, but rather in its embodiment of concepts that are themselves contradictory. Yoruba aesthetics provides an excellent example. On a stylistic level, as well as in its manifest meaning, Yoruba sculpture, music, and dance convey a message of "harmonious energy"; but, as noted, the individual goals of harmony and energy fundamentally contradict each other.

The capacity of art to encapsulate conflicting messages takes several forms. One possibility is that a particular society may sustain two or more distinctly different art styles, each with its own particular meaning and message. Thompson describes (1973) the elegant aesthetic criteria that Yoruba art connoisseurs apply to most sculptures, but he also notes that they are intentionally contravened in art created for satire, social criticism, or psychological harassment. Similarly, among the Bamana (Bambara), McNaughton found that most art reflects such values as "clarity, purity, straightforwardness, and discernibility" (McNaughton 1979:42). However, masks made for use by the powerful *Komo* society of the Bamana (Figures 13–13 and 13–14) purposely contradict these values. For example,

> large and small horns may well appear together with the tusks of pigs, the small ones often lashed to the mask with rag or twine so that they wobble slightly when the mask is in motion. . . . This composite imagery is anything but clear (in terms of representation), nor does it produce the impression of economy or harmony. . . . The message is unmistakable. The power of *Komo* is secret; it is unknown and all the more dangerous because of it. (McNaughton 1979:43f)[7]

To take yet another example of art's peculiar capacity to embody opposites, consider the Afikpo of Nigeria. Simon Ottenberg (1982) has described the ways in which Afikpo masked dancers simultaneously embody two contradictory messages. The masks, costumes, movements, and music of the

---

[7]An even more complex situation occurs when contradictory messages coexist within a single, unified stylistic tradition. Navajo art, as noted earlier, holds in balance the opposite poles of activity and passivity, symmetry and asymmetry, inner and outer, and masculinity and femininity.

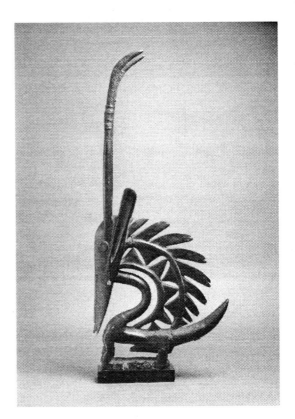

FIGURE 13-13 Bamana peoples of Mali, Crest mask headdress (chi wara kun), wood fiber, cowrie shell, hide and metal, 112.4 cm (44 1/4"). Bequest of Eliot Elisofon, 73-7-56. *(National Museum of African Art, Smithsonian Institution. Photo courtesy of Aldo Tutino/Art Resource, N.Y.)*

dancers embody fundamental cultural principles; but on a different level, the dancers also present a counter-reality: After all, the dancers are not mortals but spirits and as such they wear not everyday clothing but extraordinarily beautiful (or grotesque) clothing and masks; their voices, through the use of falsetto or other vocal techniques, are made to sound different from normal voices; and by dancing, walking on stilts, or even attacking children and other bystanders, they move their bodies in ways foreign to mundane life (Figure 13–15).

Although there is no direct evidence to support it, Ottenberg offers the interesting conjecture that the double reality of West African masquerades serves several important psychological functions. For children, the maskers may be larger-than-life embodiments of parents, older siblings, and other authority figures, whom children inevitably see as being alternately wise and funny, entertaining and threatening, and always looking and acting differently from the children themselves. Ottenberg says, "Children may fear these maskers as powerful figures but they also learn that there are limits to how far the maskers (as their parents) will go. Then the children may still be afraid of

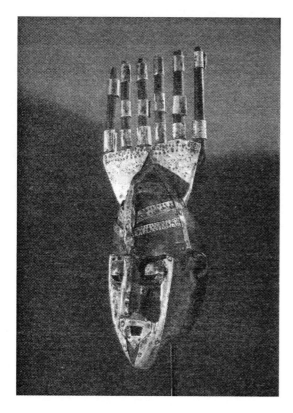

FIGURE 13-14   Helmet mask of the Bamana Komo society, made of wood quills, tusks, a bird skull, and other organic materials. 19th-20th century. 33 1/2 inches long. *(Werner Forman / Art Resource, N.Y.))*

them, but now it is also a game of play—to run and return, run and return" (Ottenberg 1982:172).

The contradictions embodied in these complex West African masquerades also may strike another psychological chord:

> The masquerade touches on a panhuman illusion. We act toward one another in our roles *as if* we were open and relatively free, yet we are generally guarded, withholding, secretive, having private wishes and fantasies. . . . The performances expose this game, commenting on people's private worlds in a public way. . . . This may be amusing or anxiety producing for those involved, but allows persons to deal with a range of repressed associations. (Ottenberg 1982:176)

Not all art mediates opposing ideas, forces, or groups of people, but the art that does accomplish this feat makes an invaluable contribution to its community. It is not surprising that art can do this, since such meanings are, after all, conveyed symbolically. The laws of noncontradiction that we assume to apply to the tangible world are not required by the subjective realm. An electrical charge cannot be both positive and negative, but it is altogether possible to both love and hate someone, to feel dread and relish at the same

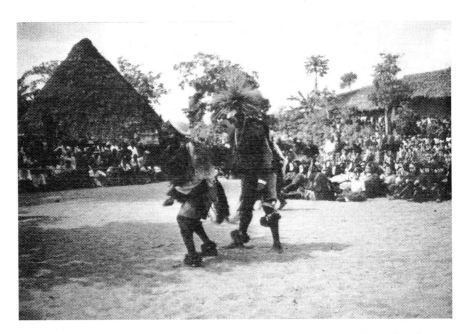

FIGURE 13-15 Two dancing Afikpo Ibo men. McNaughton (1972:106) says that such perfor-mances "are allowed great freedom to dance in any style they wish, and somteimes, as here, do so grotesquely." *(Photo by Dr. Simon Ottenberg, 1960. Courtesy of Eliot Elisofon Photographic Archives, National Museum of African Art, Smithsonian Institution. EEPA 2000 070587)*

time, or to experience bafflement and awe while simultaneously feeling com-prehension and acceptance. An analysis of the style and symbolic content of art reveals how such contradictions can be embedded in art objects.

Conclusion

For all the diverse aspects of meaning in art, the central conclusion remains. In very many cases, if not all cases, *art has meaning*—and usually meaning of considerable significance in the culture it comes from. Cultures vary in their definition of what is and what is not significant; and there are differences in the overtness with which the meaning is manifest in the artwork. Neverthe-less, art does typically convey culturally significant meaning.

14

STYLE, FEELING,

AND SKILL

Art is the straining of pure affect
against pure. . . discipline.

(Devereux 1961:362)

Part One's survey of ten societies' aesthetic systems revealed that art typically conveys meaning of considerable cultural significance, and numerous aspects of that dimension were explored in the preceding chapter. But Calliope has other widespread and enduring traits: Art everywhere tends to be executed in a style and a medium that is characteristic of its place and time; art usually makes a notable impact on the feelings of those who experience it; and art is typically executed with exceptional skill. This chapter will examine these three additional characteristics of Calliope.

Style: The Codification of Meaning

Information theorists have pointed out that meaning must be encoded in a medium. The telegrapher's message, for example, is transmitted via the Morse Code; and in parallel fashion, one can think of artistic style as being the medium through which art's meaning is communicated. It is possible, of course, to discuss style apart from the meaning it conveys. For instance, there is a striking contrast between the high level of graphic complexity found in Western Apache art from the American Southwest in comparison to the relatively less complex design of Comanche art from the Southern Plains. Visual differences between these two art styles are obvious, and one could undertake a description of the exact nature of this stylistic contrast, its historical background as seen in the archaeological record, and the transition in style as one goes from Comanche to Western Apache via intervening groups in the region such as the Puebloans.

On the other hand, the stylistic contrast between Western Apache and Comanche art could serve as a starting point for an explanation of the *significance* of this stylistic difference between the two cultures. Unfortunately, we do not have anything resembling a complete picture of the traditional aesthetic systems of either of the two groups in question, but there is a clue about the reason for the stylistic differences of their visual arts. Herbert Barry has examined the cross-cultural relationship between art style and several personality variables and has found statistically significant data to support his hypothesis that nonliterate societies in which child socialization is severe tend to produce art that is more graphically complex than do societies in which socialization is less severe (Barry 1971). Interestingly, available ethnographic information suggests that the Western Apache and the Comanche fit this pattern quite well. Of course, this leaves many questions unanswered, but it can guide research in a direction that may prove profitable—namely, to explore the psychological meaning of the respective styles of Western Apache and Comanche art.

Style is not a completely independent variable, and practical considerations often restrict the expressive freedom available to artists. For example, the parameters of clay and firing technology limit the shape of ceramics, and their utilitarian purpose places still further restraints on the shapes of pots (cf. Hendrickson and McDonald 1983). But within the boundaries set by such factors, style can be thought of as a manifestation of meaning in art. At the very least, the conventions that characterize the art of a particular place and time convey tacit messages regarding the identity of the makers. Other stylistic features can convey more narrow and explicit messages. For example, to those who can "read" Yoruba style, the smooth surface and symmetrical posture of a wooden statuette convey information regarding human beauty and personal demeanor. Even more overtly, Yoruba iconography tells the viewer (or, at least, the informed viewer) which specific *orisha* cult a given dance mask is made for.

Although artifacts convey information through style, H. Martin Wobst (1977) has asserted that they do this somewhat differently than do other modes of communication, such as language. Part One's survey of native systems of aesthetics gives us a chance to test—and extend—this claim.

Wobst noted that an artifact "stores" information so that it can be "sent" to people who are temporally and spatially distant. Although all information degrades with the passage of time, the inevitable process of deterioration occurs more slowly in artifacts than it does with most other modes of communication. So, according to Wobst's reasoning, although the initial production of the artifact may be "expensive" in terms of energy and materials, sending the message to large numbers of people is inexpensive. For example, the carving of a mask for the Yoruba Gęlędę dance requires intensive work by the carver, but during its lifetime the completed mask conveys a potent message to thousands of viewers of Gęlędę festivities, year after year, with little additional input of energy (Figure 14–1).

Wobst goes on to note that the benefits of disseminating complicated or short-lived messages may not justify the effort required. Therefore, although

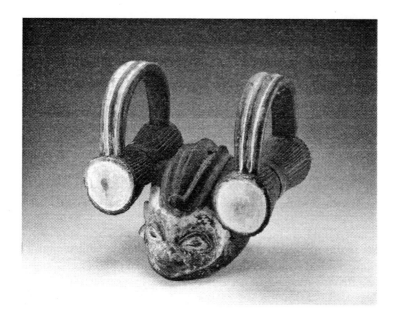

FIGURE 14-1   Cap mask of the Yoruba Gelede society. Above the carved wooden
head are two carved drums, their suspension straps forming arches above them.
Nigeria, mid-late 20th century, wood, pigment, 33.7 cmH x 34.6 cm W x 27.9 cm
D. Museum purchase, 79-13-36. *(National Museum of African Art. Photo courtesy
of Franko Khoury, National Museum of African Art, Smithsonian Institution.)*

any message might in theory be conveyed via artifacts, style is a practical
medium only for communicating such simple and recurrent messages as
those of emotional state, identification with a particular group, and owner-
ship (Wobst 1977:323; cf. also Rice 1983). Messages such as these are indeed
often communicated by art. Body decoration typically conveys information
about sexual identity and status, and art used by cults frequently objectifies
the attributes associated with the group's particular deity.

As we saw in the preceding chapter, however, some art conveys meanings that are ambiguous, and much of the artist's skill lies in the ability to
bind together meanings that contradict each other (as in Yoruba carvings
and Navajo sandpaintings), that are metaphysically elusive (e.g., the trans-
muting aesthetics of the Inuit), or that are so complex and subtle that their
full meaning may be grasped only after years of study (exemplified by the
mandalas of Esoteric Buddhism).

Art that conveys complex and obscure meaning resists simplistic interpretation, especially when its cultural context is unavailable, as is generally
the case in archaeology. Consider, for example, the distinctive visual style of
Mimbres painted pottery (see Figure 14–2). It was made between 1000 and
1200 C.E. in hundreds of villages scattered along the Mimbres River valley in
what is now southern New Mexico. Geometric and representational designs
were used to decorate the insides of many shallow Mimbres bowls. Scratch

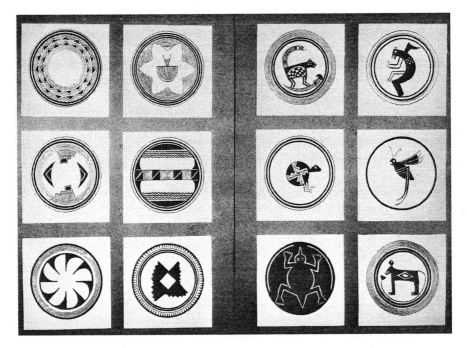

FIGURE 14–2 Twelve Mimbres pot designs. *(Courtesy National Anthropological Archives, Smithsonian Institution.)*

marks indicate that most of the bowls served practical purposes, but many of these ultimately were placed in graves along with other burial items, usually after a hole had been punched in the bottoms of the bowls. This was almost always the fate of bowls that bore representational drawings, some of which seem to have been made solely for funerary purposes.

What is the meaning of Mimbres bowls? What information do they convey? In a definitive study, J. J. Brody has argued that the distinctive Mimbres ceramic style must have been a self-conscious symbol of the identity of the Mimbres culture. Beyond that, it may represent an effort to metaphysically "classify the universe" (Brody 1977:212–213).

We can only speculate about more concrete interpretations of Mimbres designs. Consider for instance the intended meaning of two bowls that seem to clearly portray one individual decapitating another (cf. Brody 1977:Plate 11). The bowls come from different localities, so their message probably was widely known in Mimbres culture. Do they represent a priest sacrificing a man in hopes of bringing an end to a drought, as was done among the Hopi and Zuni as recently as the nineteenth century? Do they portray ritual decapitation, as occurred in Casa Grandes and other cultures to the south? Or might they illustrate "the Mimbres version of a Classic Mayan myth in which one twin culture hero decapitates his brother as part of a scheme to trap and slay the Lords of the Underworld" (Brody 1977:206)? Art style alone may not reveal which (if any) of these complex messages Mimbres potters meant to convey. If any of these interpretations is correct, then Mimbres pottery, like much of the art discussed in Part One, carries subtle and complex information and thus is yet another exception to Wobst's general claim that artifacts do not encode complicated messages.

What about Wobst's assertion that artifacts, once produced, tend to convey information that is not subject to rapid change? Clearly, this is not true for the "behavioral artifacts" produced in the performing arts, but neither does it hold true for the objects that have been called "ephemeral art," that is, "visual phenomena created or assembled with the conscious knowledge that they will be destroyed, dismantled, or permitted to decompose within hours, days, or at the most several months" (Ravicz 1976:1). Ephemeral art includes such obvious things as masks that are made for a single use but also items that Westerners might tend to overlook, such as fireworks, food decoration, and mud sculpture.

The 155 cross-cultural instances of ephemeral art studied by Ravicz shed additional light on Wobst's claim that artifacts tend to convey stable, unchanging messages. Ninety-six percent of the examples, Ravicz found, occur in ritual contexts. Ravicz reasons that although ephemeral art objects are necessarily made from easily accessible materials, they take on a special, heightened status because aesthetic manipulation raises them above the level of the mundane and common.

Navajo sandpaintings provide an excellent example of ephemeral art, the value of which lies in the very act of creation and in their ability to elevate humble materials to a special, sacred state.

These factors suggest that Wobst draws the right conclusion but for the wrong reasons. It is true that art rarely conveys short-lived and changing information, but this is not because novelty requires extra work—in fact, it takes more effort to doggedly replicate pre-existing designs than to change them. Instead, innovation is limited by the inertia of tradition, a powerfully conservative force in most cultures. The symbolic associations of a given genre and medium cannot easily be exchanged for meanings that are altogether fresh and new.

Thus style, as the embodiment of meaning, can be seen as setting limits on creativity in art. Granted, some societies prize innovation. For example, the frequent presence of Changing Woman in Navajo myth indicates the high value placed on the creative impulse.[1] Similarly, the basketry of the California Yorok-Karok (cf. O'Neale 1932) and the Mimbres pottery of the

---

[1]But one must remember that "creativity" in a Navajo context means something quite different from what, say, a Western avant-garde artist might mean by the word. Sandpaintings are actually *re*created, and even in the Navajo secular arts of weaving and silversmithing, there are many restraints on innovativeness.

pre-historic Southwest both display such exceptional degrees of diversity as to suggest that their makers took positive pride in producing unique designs.

Such societies are exceptional, however. More typically, creativity is not sought as an end in itself, and some cultures have an explicit proscription against it. For example, in striving to produce art informed by accord with *rasa,* the classical artists of India took the ancient Vedas as their law and all of their art strictly conformed to Vedic principles. Similarly, Aboriginal Australians traditionally avoided innovation because their artworks embodied the unchanging Eternal Dreamtime. The Sepik River peoples also shun innovation because their art products serve as habitations for spirits: If these dwellings are altered, the spirits may not come to live in them—a situation in which mortals would be the losers. Granted, the archaeological record always reveals that as the decades and centuries recede into the past, change has indeed occurred; but in most cases this is a result of accident and "aesthetic drift" (cf. Anderson 1979:159–162) and takes place despite a reluctance to innovate.

Even in the supposedly dynamic Western tradition, innovation in art has not been as continuous as modern fine art might lead us to believe. Not only has Western fine art gone through conservative periods, as during the Middle Ages, but the popular arts too have tended to resist change. For example, the history of some Western folk melodies and folktales can be traced back many centuries, and contemporary standards of personal beauty have changed surprisingly little since Roman times.[2]

Whereas stylistic conventions limit variation in art objects on the societal level, for the individual artist they control the extent to which art can serve as a personal statement. But again, total conformity is as impossible as total nonconformity. George Devereux summarizes the situation well:

> If mere "expressiveness" and/or "projection" were the criteria whereby one determines whether a given product is art or something else, then the bellowing of an agitated catatonic would be the most genuine of arts. Conversely, were style and other conventions the true criteria of art, then classroom exercises in strict counterpoint would represent the summit of artistic behavior. Ideally, the dynamic criterion of art is the straining of pure affect against pure (culturally structured) discipline. (Devereux 1961:362)

Art has meaning, and its messages are conveyed via the code that we call style. Far from being simple and redundant, the messages are typically of con-

---

[2]"A fashionable, desirable Roman girl at the beginning of the Christian era would . . . have been tall and blond (rather than brunette), worn a plain robe, and had bright red cheeks and eyes shaded with kohl or painted with saffron. Her brows would have been penciled, and she would have had a patch or two on her cheek or neck, or, perhaps, even more daringly, on her bare shoulder or arm" (Liggett 1974:61).

siderable consequence (as in art that embodies fundamental metaphysical and religious principles) or else of great individual importance (as with body decorations that convey information about sexual availability, status, and affiliation). Both possibilities lead us to address two further questions regarding style in art: Are there any pan-cultural criteria for art criticism? And what is the basis of the sensuous art object's psychological effect?

Accounting for Taste: The Bases of Stylistic Criticism

Humans often seem unable to resist passing judgment, not only on people but also on the things people make. Needless to say, we do not always agree among ourselves in our judgments. In Western culture, even individuals with the most refined of tastes often have different opinions. Emerson did not like the work of Jane Austen; Carlyle hated Keats; and Turgenev could not abide either Dostoyevsky or Tolstoy (cf. M. Gardner 1983:76). Or recall George Boas's essay, "Mona Lisa in the History of Taste" (1963/1940), which describes people's changing responses to the famous painting since Leonardo created it. Even something as supposedly free of cultural associations as the "golden mean," which has been a favored geometric proportion in the West since the time of classical Greece, may not have universal appeal: In one controlled experiment a group of Japanese subjects tended to choose rectangles that were nearly square in preference to ones whose dimensions were based on the golden mean (Berlyne 1970; 1980:344).

Information theorists have pointed out that questions generally have countless wrong answers but only one or a few right ones. This principle suggests that whereas a system of aesthetics may provide a handful of general principles prescribing what good art *should* be, there is a much larger residual category composed of what good art *should not* be. Thus, there are more ways to be ugly than to be beautiful; discord is unnervingly simple to produce whereas sweet harmony is always elusive; and proper steps are few although the ways to stumble seem boundless. Sometimes this situation is reflected in traditional philosophies of art. For example, John and Betty Messenger (1981:35f) report that the Nigerian Anang possess more criteria for personal ugliness than they do for personal beauty, and for most of us, it is far easier to document the flaws in an artwork than it is to specify precisely its fundamental qualities of excellence.

Most attempts to uncover cross-cultural similarities of aesthetic judgment have been unproductive. For example, Frances and Tamba (1973) asked Japanese musicology students to rank ten excerpts of Japanese music in order of preference. They then compared these choices to the preferences of three French groups—professional musicians, music students, and non-music students. Not only did the researchers find no correlation between Japanese and French preferences, but the choices of the French professional musicians actually tended to be just the opposite of the Japanese subjects.

If there are universals of artistic taste, they would seem to be manifest in underlying structure rather than in superficial style. For example, Robbins Burling (1966) has found that the rhyme and meter pattern found in the popular English nursery rhyme "Humpty Dumpty" appears in children's verses in Chinese, Arabic, Serrano (a language indigenous to southern California), Benkula (spoken in Sumatra, Indonesia), Yoruba (Nigeria), and Trukese (South Pacific).

Similarly, cross-cultural studies have uncovered only the most generalized sorts of agreement in the visual art styles. Rhoda Kellog once postulated a series of well-defined developmental stages in children's drawing style (see, e.g., Kellog 1969); but her non-Western data were gathered somewhat haphazardly. When Alexander Alland (1983) carried out a more systematic study of the question, collecting drawings from children in six diverse societies under controlled conditions, he found that after an early stage of "kinetic scribbles," no universal patterns of development in style or content of drawing were apparent. However, on a deeper level, the drawings Alland collected did seem to support claims by Jacqueline Goodnow that children's drawings conform to certain structural rules such as being thrifty in the use of units and tending to experiment only with a basic vocabulary (cf. Goodnow 1979:141–145).[3]

To extrapolate from these findings about children's drawings to sophisticated artworks of adults living in various societies may not be warranted, but the findings of Alland (and of other scholars such as the psychologist Howard Gardner [1980] and the art historian E. H. Gombrich [1979]) suggest that preferences for details of art styles are no more instinctive than are the vocabularies of the world's languages, even though some formal features of language may indeed be pan-human.

A similar situation prevails regarding color. Humans have gone to great effort to obtain colored pigments since the most distant antiquity (cf. Wreschner 1976, 1980), but psychological studies of *preferences* of certain colors have often yielded ambiguous results, even with Western subjects. Within a particular society, however, people are often unequivocal with regard to the meanings they attribute to specific colors. The Navajo, for example, associate certain colors with the four cardinal directions, and a convincing illustration of the diffusion of Mesoamerican customs into the Southwest is provided by comparing modern Navajo color symbolism with that of the pre-Columbian Toltecs in the Valley of Mexico (cf. Witherspoon 1977:145–146; Nicholson 1976):

---

[3]Interestingly, studies of drawings by non-human primates suggest that chimpanzees also produce patterns that are consistent with those postulated by Alland (cf. Schiller 1951; Morris 1962; Whiten 1976.)

Direction	Navajo Color	Toltec Color
East	White	White
South	Blue	Blue
West	Red	Yellow
North	Black	Black

That such associations are at least in part arbitrary is illustrated by the color symbolism of the Navajos' neighbors, the Pueblo groups. Ortiz (1972) reports that among the Tewa-speaking Puebloans, blue is associated with north and yellow with the west, although exactly the opposite is true in the Keres-speaking Pueblos.

Although there is no consensus among world cultures regarding color symbolism in general, tentative evidence suggests that there is limited agreement regarding some colors. Victor Turner (1966) has argued convincingly that red, white, and black play important symbolic roles not only among the East African Ndembu, whom he studied in depth, but also in many other of the world's societies. This, Turner suggests, is because blood is everywhere red, milk and semen white, excreta and rot black. Adams and Osgood (1973) used the Semantic Differential test with subjects from twenty-three countries to study the connotations of color terms; and they found significant cross-cultural agreement on several points, most of which lend support to Turner's hypothesis about red, white, and black. If black's significance derives primarily from its association with excreta, and white with milk and semen, then one would typically expect black to be viewed as bad and white as good. It would likewise make sense to expect red, associated with blood, to be strong and active; and black to be passive. And, in fact, Adams and Osgood found all of these correlations to exist.[4]

Art Media

The very existence of an art style presupposes the existence of a medium in which artworks are executed, and cultures inevitably have explicit or (more often) implicit guidelines about the media that are appropriate for artistic activities. In early India, for example, only poetry, architecture, and music were considered to be genuine art; dance and the visual arts were secondary; and

---

[4]Cross-cultural patterns have also been found in language. For example, linguists assumed for decades that color vocabularies were culture-specific, with each language selecting and naming its own distinctive handful of colors from among the millions that can be distinguished by the human eye. But in 1969, Brent Berlin and Paul Kay published their unexpected finding that "basic color terms" are not arbitrary, but that they occur cross-culturally according to a relatively simple pattern.

the senses of touch, taste, and smell were considered to be void of artistic potential. The West, too, has singled out the visual and auditory senses as the media for genuine art. There is clear evidence, however, that other sensory modes can serve as the basis of art. In Japan, for example, the tea ceremony calls into play the gustatory sense in the participants' appreciation of the flavor of unsweetened tea, and the sense of smell is used in response to incense. Indeed, it would not be stretching matters to say that Japanese *sumo* wrestling elevates the kinesthetic and tactile sensations to the level of art, certainly for the performers and, through identification, for the spectators as well.

Taste and smell are raised to central importance in some artistic activities. Consider, for example, the aesthetic accouterments of the *fualah*, an informal, though highly ritualized, get-together that takes place when a traditional woman in the United Arab Emirates entertains morning or afternoon guests (see Figures 14–3 and 14–4). The hostess first offers her friends a carefully prepared tray of food that presents a selection of bananas, pomegranates, dark brown sweetmeats, salted pistachios, pumpkin seeds, Danish butter cookies, and imported toffee, an array that fulfills the formal requirement of satisfying sweet, sour, salty, and bitter tastes (Kanafani 1983:1, 21). Coffee follows the food, and then the hostess brings in her *shandug*, a glass-lidded box that holds as many as eight small bottles of perfume oils, several varieties of incense, and one or two bodkins for applying the perfumes. The hostess opens one perfume bottle after another, passing each one around the circle of seated women:

> Each woman dips the bodkin in the bottle and depending on the nature of the perfume places it either on her hair, behind her ears, on the neck and nape, on her hair-veil or on her cloak where it covers her chest, shoulders, and armpits. She repeats her gestures several times, dipping and anointing at length. . . . I have never heard any woman ask her hostess about the kind of perfume offered. Women have developed such a remarkable sensitivity to scents that however different the oil or mixture may be, all are familiar with the basic ingredients and are able to detect them individually. (Kanafani 1983:23, 25)

When everyone has used the oils, the hostess lights perfumed incense or aloewood, and each woman in turn wafts the dense smoke over her hair, lifts her veil a bit to scent her face and, because incense dispels tension and aches, inhales the smoke. Then she places the censor under her dress and, wrapping herself with a cloak, allows the dense fumes to permeate all of her body and clothing. Like most serious aesthetic endeavors, these Arab women practice their gustatory and olfactory arts for several important reasons, some involving purification and local Islamic belief, others prompted by the sensuous (and sensual) pleasures they afford themselves and their husbands.

Such ethnographic cases prove that the arts need not be confined to the senses of vision and hearing (cf. Herring 1949). The only discernable pattern is that the relatively more intricate aesthetic systems of complex societies

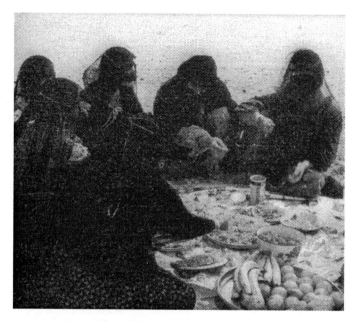

FIGURE 14–3 A women's *fualah* in the United Arab Emirates. *(Photo courtesy Aida Sami Kalafani.)*

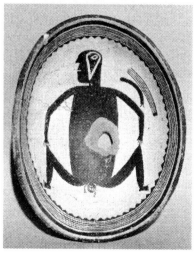

FIGURE 14–4 Mimbres pottery bowl with drawing representing childbirth. *(Courtesy of Peabody Museum of Archaeology & Ethnology, Harvard University. © Werner Forman/Art Resource, NY.)*

tend to isolate a few sensory modes for extended consideration while others are ignored or else dealt with only by analogy. By contrast, aesthetic preferences in small-scale societies are implicit, making them as applicable to one medium as another.

Not only are some senses favored in complex societies, but some materials are too. Aztec art is revealing in this regard. All the media that served as bases for artistic activity in the Old World—ceramics, loom weaving, large-scale sculpture, monumental architecture, and metallurgy, as well as music, dance, and poetry—had their counterparts in the New World as well.

This is significant in that some contemporary Western theories suggest or assume that any medium can serve as the basis for aesthetic expression. Although there is no logical argument against such propositions, artists have had a strong tendency to specialize in a small number of media. By most definitions, art production reflects an especially high degree of skill in the artist, and it is the nature of things that whereas some media lend themselves to high virtuosity, others present little challenge. Thus in far-flung parts of the world where artists are full-time professionals, great craftsmanship has been displayed in subtly carved hard, brittle stone (jade or obsidian rather than the softer sandstone or soapstone); weaving has shown an elaboration of pattern, color, and design; smiths have mastered exacting metallurgical skills; and so on.

This conclusion is difficult to prove conclusively. Some aesthetic paradigms downplay manual skill, and the degree of skill demanded by an art form may not be apparent to outsiders. Further, with a little imagination one may find challenges in *any* medium: Perceptual and conceptual skills might be emphasized and the requisite oculomotor skills unexceptional, or the specialness of art may depend less on the rarity of the artist's skills than on the scarcity of the medium itself—gem stones or precious metals, for example. But although such factors *might* be important (and instances of each do exist), the general cross-cultural pattern is toward specialization in a limited repertoire of difficult media. This regularity would seem to derive from the physical properties of the things we find in the world around us.

The Affective Aspects of Art

In each of the societies discussed in Part One, art is appreciated for, among other things, the pleasure it brings to those who perceive it. Even the few studies of "art" production by non-human primates suggest that apes apparently enjoy drawing.[5]

What common denominators can be found in the affective response to art cross-culturally? A theme running throughout Part One is that people everywhere savor the beautiful, tastefully adorned human body. As observed

---

[5]Desmond Morris (1962:44) recounts the following anecdote about a chimpanzee named Bella, who was given paper and colored pencils daily: "The most striking thing about Bella, when she was in a good drawing mood, was her high level of motivation. Miss Hylkema (her caretaker) once made the mistake of interfering when Bella was in the middle of a drawing, with the result that she was bitten by the animal. Bella would never bite when Miss Hylkema interfered with any other activity, not even when taking attractive food away from her."

earlier, standards of personal beauty are not altogether arbitrary. The attractiveness of healthy skin, strong bodies, good teeth, and indications of sexual competence rest on natural values for survival. Body decorations often enhance and call attention to such features as these.

Although the strong feelings that art evokes typically go far beyond the sensual, they sometimes seem to have evolved from a sexual matrix. For example, the classical Indian concept of *rasa* is an elegant, complex, and subtle theory of aesthetic emotion, and although it is usually associated with Hindu art, the pre-eminent *rasa* theorist, Kasmiri Abhinavagupta, was an initiate in Kula Tantra. Tantrism, we know, is unusual among religions for its emphasis on sexuality. Tantrism equates sexual libido with essential, beneficial, and creative energy (cf. Rawson 1973:32), and Tantric art is highly charged with sexual and erotic energy, which is meant to enhance the vital forces of the universe (see Figure 14–5). Hindu aesthetics has a similar impulse, but in a

FIGURE 14–5 Tibetan god, *Hayagriva*, embracing his consort. *(Courtesy, Field Museum of Natural History, Chicago, neg. no. 99646.)*

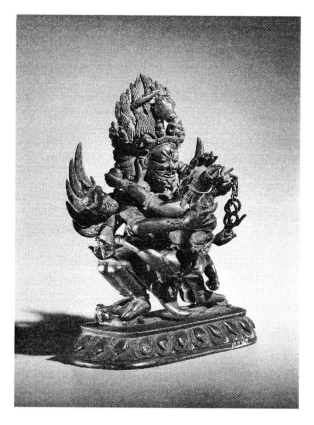

weakened form: Only one of the nine rasas, *kama*, is erotic; the others correspond to a wide variety of other emotions.

A similar situation prevails cross-culturally, where a not insignificant portion of the sensuous and emotional potential of art is realized in sensual delight derived from the beauty of the human body. But for the remaining (and larger) part of art's affective function, the best we can do is merely catalog the varieties of aesthetic feeling—and here we Westerners have progressed little beyond the work of Aristotle two and a half millennia ago, except that now we realize that the breadth of cross-cultural variation is greater than had thought possible.

The "Aesthetic Response"

Since the rise of the Western aesthetic theory of formalism (pp. 247–250), some aestheticians have asserted that the definitive feature of art is its capacity to prompt not just an affective reaction but a unique and distinctive "aesthetic response," a state of positive, focused, disinterested attention to the work's *aesthetic* component, as opposed to its subject matter or the artist's technical skill.

This approach prompts us to ask, Do art-attuned audiences in *all* societies experience the refined aesthetic reaction that formalists speak of? Jacques Maquet (1986:64) has answered unequivocally in the affirmative, stating that "many societies—all known societies, I dare say—recognize and actualize the human potentiality for aesthetic [in the narrow, formalistic sense] perception and appreciation." But as I have shown elsewhere (Anderson 1989), Maquet's argument rests on both flawed logic and a dubious reading of the secondary literature.

In fact, when one focuses on societies for which there is ample, field-work-based data, there is virtually no empirical evidence for the existence of the formalist's "affective response" in most other societies. Of the ten cultures discussed in Part One, only in early Indian aesthetics do we find a non-Western philosophy that attaches significance to a distinctive aesthetic reaction, and in that case there is an important difference between the *rasika's* affective response to an artwork and the far more personal and idiosyncratic response specified by Western formalism.

Certainly, artworks everywhere are associated with feelings—with the delight stimulated by a sensuous medium, with the many emotions engendered by diverse subject matter, with awe in craftsmanship, and so on. But such feelings vary considerably from one society to another, just as they differ from one person to another. For example, art inspires feelings, often quite strong feelings, among the Navajo, who find pleasure in sacred sandpaintings, secular silver jewelry, or the spontaneous singing of a song. But the deepest and most gratifying feelings for Navajos lie in the act of creation, not in the contemplation of the finished artwork, as called for by formalist dogma.

Art is nothing if it inspires no feeling, but to equate art with a narrowly defined aesthetic response is to ignore the other powerful sources of art's impact on the human psyche. Art for art's sake alone may be the least important reason for art's existence. To the contrary, art seems to inspire an emotional reaction by encoding significant cultural meaning while sensuously embodying special skill. This is not a contribution to be taken lightly and may well be a major reason for the universality of art as well as the apparent unity of Calliope. Art brings together meaning, feeling, and skill to produce a powerful experience, a product that, like kinship and language, seems to be an indispensable component of human existence.

Skill in Art

The third trait commonly found in art is the special *skill* with which it is produced. As with art's meaning and the affective response to art, skill alone does not define art, and it is futile to seek an unequivocal boundary between those things that represent special skill and those that do not. But the skill required to produce art is usually special, raised above the level of the ordinary in the eyes of the audience.

The artist's special skill is generally taken for granted in Western society, but how widely is it recognized elsewhere? With respect specifically to the three complex societies discussed in Part One, all clearly appreciate the uncommon abilities of their artists. Recall, for example, the qualities the Aztecs attributed to true artists: "capable, practicing, skillful; maintains dialogue with his heart, meets things with his mind" (quoted in León-Portilla 1963:168). By contrast, "The carrion artist works at random; sneers at people; makes things opaque; brushes across the surface of the face of things; works without care; defrauds people; is a thief" (León-Portilla 1963:168).

Likewise, in all three of Part One's horticultural and herding societies, artists are recognized as having abilities that are out of the ordinary. All Sepik men carve wood with a facility that most Westerners would find difficult to match, but only the most accomplished Sepik carver is commissioned to produce the masks and other objects needed for cult activities. As a reward for his abilities, he receives both goods and prestige. Sepik artists themselves are aware of various evaluative criteria. Similarly, there is ample evidence that the Yoruba have demanding standards of excellence for statuette carving and the performing arts. For example, Abiodun reports that a sensitivity to the arts is something one acquires only through effort, citing a proverb that says, "Only the wise can dance to *Ogidigbo* [drumming], and only the discerning are able to understand and interpret it" (Abiodun 1987:270).

The Navajo illustrate why a clear demarcation is not possible between activities that embody special skill and those that do not. Given the Navajo concept of *hózhǫ́*, which attributes beauty, harmony, and positive value to all things as a natural potentiality of their existence, it is not surprising to read that "nearly all Navajos are artists and spend a large part of their time in artistic creation" (Witherspoon 1977:152). In one sense this is true, but it is also true that those Navajos who possess exceptional skills—Singers, with their prodigious memories, for example—are recognized and rewarded for their abilities. The situation is analogous to Western culture, where most individuals can produce handwriting, a skill whose acquisition requires years of training.[6] But those few people with exceptional handwriting ability are considered to be artists—calligraphers. Their capabilities are praised, and they may be hired to produce announcements for special occasions. (Of course, calligraphy differs from normal handwriting not only in the level of the skill of the person who creates it but also in the attention to style and attractiveness that are apparent in the result.)

Even small-scale, hunter-gatherer societies, with their distinctively low degree of labor specialization, recognize the singular talents of artists. At least, such was the case in all three of the foraging groups discussed in Part One.[7] Indeed, skill and art seem to go hand in hand in all societies.[8] Moreover, the artist's special abilities seem to appear at an early age: Alland's study (1983) of drawings made by children in six diverse cultures revealed that usually one or two children from each group of subjects showed exceptional artistic ability.

The Maroon, a Black African society living in the rain forests of Suriname, South America, are interesting with regard to artistic skill. Although the Maroon assume that *"all* adults will be active artists and assertive critics,"

---

[6]Leach (1961:29) has made a similar point regarding carvers among the Borneo Dyak.

[7]Lorna Marshall has written that some San "are more talented as musicians than others, and some take more interest in playing and singing well" (Marshall 1976:363; see also Kaufmann 1910:151); and Shostak reports that "a term of respect—the suffix *n/a* attached to a name—acknowledges the attainment of full adulthood. It may occasionally be applied to a younger person to applaud high achievement (in hunting, trancing, or *playing a musical instrument*, for example), but it is usually given to people in their forties" (Shostak 1981:321, emphasis added). Similarly, Mountford says that although all Australian Aborigines are potential artists, "some are more skilled than others and take more care" (Mountford 1961:7; see also Berndt and Berndt 1964:329; Elkin, Berndt, and Berndt 1950:110; McCarthy 1957a:13-14; and Spencer and Gillan 1938:575). Finally, traditional Inuit also recognized special abilities, certainly in song, dance, and dress, and probably in carving, although gauging differential skill is difficult because such differences fly in the face of the cooperative ideal that pervades Inuit culture.

[8]For example, Kaeppler (1971) describes the importance of skill in evaluating dance performance among Polynesian Tongans; Bohannan (1971) reports that although the Nigerian Tiv know that most men can carve well enough to make common items, they appreciate exceptional carving and regard as specialists those few carvers who work alone and consciously attempt to excel in their carving. Finally, Harry Silver found that the Ashanti believe that "the gifted are not simply keener of eye or hand; they also possess a facility for concentration which far exceeds their peers. They claim to think deeply about their work, constantly searching for more effective ways to 'tease out' messages from the wood" (Silver 1981:105).

it remains the case that "the work of certain individuals is generally considered especially beautiful. . . . They are rewarded by the admiration of their fellows and occasionally asked to help design an object which a friend or kinsman is preparing to execute" (Price and Price 1981:36).

That the most adept of Maroon artists are sometimes asked to "help design" others' objects reveals an important aspect of skill in artistry: The artist's special abilities may be mental rather than manual. The technical capacity of the artist may be no greater than that of others, especially in societies where the division of labor is not complex, but the person's conceptual skills are often outstanding. The ability to innovate, to manipulate visual (or auditory, choreographic, or whatever) images and ideas, to concentrate on a specific task for long periods of time, to recall and play with traditional aesthetic material—these are the hallmarks of the artist.

The West has recognized the artist's special conceptual skills since at least the time of Plato, who observed that poetic inspiration is "a thing ethereally light-winged and sacred, nor can one compose anything worth calling poetry until he becomes inspired and, as it were, mad" (quoted in Hatterer 1965:17). Such views explain the long-standing tradition of Western master artists assigning to apprentices or technicians those components of their work that require mere craft, and it plays an important role in the rationale of many schools of modern art, from Cubism and Surrealism, through Abstract Expressionism, to Conceptual Art, each of which attaches great importance to the artist's personal vision. Given the significance of meaning in art, it comes as no surprise that artists' cognitive skills are of vital importance. For most societies, it is in the mind, rather than the hand, where true artistic genius is to be found.[9]

Connoisseurship is another special cognitive skill associated with art. Often artists themselves are among the most sophisticated and articulate judges of art, as was shown in Forge's (1967) account of Abelam artists, who discuss carvings more perceptively and incisively than do others. But non-artists may also develop special artistic sensibilities and be considered connoisseurs. Of the many art critics among the Yoruba interviewed by Thompson, some were artists but the majority came from a variety of occupations, from village chief, to trader, to farmer. Furthermore, genuine connoisseurs among the Yoruba are different from those who merely appreciate art: Thompson (1973:23) tells of an occasion on which one young man's efforts at evaluating a statuette were explicitly disparaged by another man of far greater critical ability.

---

[9]Thus, the tenth-century Chinese landscape painter Ching Hau distinguished four kinds of painters, ranging from the lowly *ch'iao*, who is merely skillful in imitating nature; through the *chi* and the *miao*, or "clever," who "penetrates with his thoughts the nature of everything in heaven and earth"; to the *shen*, the "divine, . . . who makes no effort but achieves the forms spontaneously by following the transformations of Nature" (quoted in Deutsch 1975:39).

Why do some individuals go to the trouble of mastering the multifarious mental skills required by art? Western psychologists, with their emphasis on behaviors that become habitual as a result of extrinsic rewards, often ignore "autotelic activities"—that is, those that require concentration and energy but provide little in the way of material compensation. In at least some cultural settings art is an autotelic activity, and Csikszentmihalyi (1975) has argued convincingly that individuals may obtain great satisfaction by carrying out tasks that are too challenging to be boring yet not so difficult as to produce an unacceptably high level of anxiety. The gratification involved may well account for the fact that some individuals, past and present, have mastered the difficult skills that art media inevitably demand.

Skill alone does not make art, but societies inevitably recognize the exceptional capacities of the artist. The extent to which the artist's heightened abilities are inborn is unknown, but it is clear that art's specialness, its ability to convey potent meaning, and its capacity to affect the emotions of the percipient, must in part result from the artist's exceptional skill of execution.

Conclusion

The available information about aesthetics in the world's societies is still too scant for us to draw many detailed or certain conclusions. Based on this chapter and the preceding one, however, a few findings are clear.

First, *art* is a legitimate and meaningful cultural category. The generalized relativism that informs modern cultural anthropology, as well as the avoidance of stylistic dogmatism that, at least in theory, was a major tenet of Western thinking about the fine arts during the last hundred years make this conclusion significant. The premise that "anything can be art" may wrongly lead one to expect that "everything is art" and that nothing distinguishes art from non-art, especially when non-Western societies are included for consideration.

Art generally embodies culturally significant meaning that is encoded with uncommon skill in a traditional style and sensuous medium. After conceding that these traits may be present in different degrees and that a clear dividing line cannot be drawn to separate art from non-art, we nevertheless have seen that art does exist in all ten of the societies surveyed in Part One. Each culture has principles that account for the fundamental nature and purpose of art. As in the domain of kinship, the principles that a given culture uses to define art's meanings and purposes are unique and may be largely implicit. But art is clearly universal, and, as with kinship, the lack of a generic native name for art does not mean that art is a trivial component of culture.

To the contrary, art is usually accorded a vital role in traditional thought, conveying meanings that are fundamental to the culture. The artist's skill may be taken for granted, and stylistic conventions may serve only as a basis of criticism, but meaning is vital. One might even ask, how could so much time and effort be spent in the demanding work that art entails in the absence of a compelling justification for doing so?

A second conclusion is that a knowledge of comparative aesthetics deepens one's capacity for responding to alien artworks in ways that their makers intend. There is nothing to prevent a person from treating another society's artworks as just so many instances of found art—objects to read one's own interpretations into with no regard for their original meaning. The creator's intentions are not the *only* basis for reacting to art, and indeed artworks from other societies provide a very rich storehouse of ideas for stimulating the imagination. The development of Cubism by Western artists who had seen art works from Africa, the Northwest Coast, and Oceania is a testament to how productive such cross-fertilization can be for art (cf. Goldwater 1967).

If one's aim is to appreciate art of foreign origin (or, indeed, of domestic origin) on its own terms, however, then obviously an understanding of the theoretical basis of that art is necessary. Clearly, the more distant the aesthetic system is from our own, the more such information is needed. Eliot Deutsch (1975:37–86) has described several levels of meaning that one must possess in order to fully appreciate a given society's art: the worldview of the artist's culture, the stylistic and formal options available to the artist, and the symbolic meaning conveyed by the work. The desirability of such knowledge can hardly be questioned; getting it is another matter. (Deutsch's call for an understanding of "cultural-authorial *Weltanschauung* [worldview]," though a mouthful, is more easily said than done!)

Although the relative proportions of the factors that are involved in art vary from place to place, they everywhere complement each other to produce something that is vital to human existence—or so art's universality suggests. In *The Picture of Dorian Gray,* Oscar Wilde says that "All art is quite useless." The claim is true if one considers only practical usefulness, the sort of instrumentality that puts food in our mouths and roofs over our heads. But when our existence is viewed in humanistic terms and we think of ourselves as more than just another animal species stalking the land, then Wilde's homily must be replaced by a remark by the surgeon Richard Seizer (1979), who, writing on life, death, and the nature of being human, says that art "is necessary only in that without it life would be unbearable." The portrait of Calliope that has emerged should prove that art weds sensuousness and intellectuality, play and necessity, shared experience and rare virtuosity, giving us a means to live not as brutes but as human beings.

15

AFTERWORD

Western Aesthetics in Cross-Cultural Perspective

No doubt people everywhere have particularly strong feelings about the cultural system they are a part of; one inevitably has a visceral identification with the art traditions that have constituted one's own milieu since birth. Westerners are no exception to this rule. Western aesthetics necessarily occupies a special place in our thinking about art, and we often assume that our own art is *natural,* the standard from which all other possibilities are variants.[1]

And indeed, Western aesthetic traditions are in some respects unique. One of the most distinctive features of the West is our resolute pluralism regarding art, with four theories that emphasize distinctly different qualities in art. (The several Japanese aesthetic themes are, by comparison, far more complementary to each other.) This has meant that although a gradual homogenization has taken place in Western culture as regional and ethnic differences become smaller, a Westerner has an exceptionally broad array of possible ways of thinking about art.[2] Not only have there been four aesthetic systems within our own culture, but modern communications and commerce have given us an opportunity to experience art from much of the rest of the world, a situation unique in the history of the human race.

Western culture also is distinctive in its technology, and this too has given our art and aesthetics a distinctive coloration. In many media, even the most virtuoso of artists cannot hope to match the skill of technical produc-

---

[1]In referring to the West as "our" culture, I ask the forbearance of readers who are not Westerners. Whether this entire Afterword is "ethnocentric," or merely "reflexive," I leave to those readers to say.

[2]Even though the West is aesthetically pluralistic, the diversity found here is still not proportional to the size of our population. Although quantification in such matters obviously is impossible, if Western culture is, say, ten times more heterogeneous than a small-scale society, our population is hundreds of thousands of times larger in numbers.

tion easily attained by mechanical devices such as the camera, computer-controlled robot welders, and electronic sound production equipment. As a result, modern Western artists are more often praised for their conceptual and expressive abilities than for their manual skills. Similarly, the availability of mass production has led to a compensatory nurturing of artistic innovation. Since machines can easily turn out duplicates of almost any object *ad nauseam,* artists are expected to produce a never-ending stream of original creations.

The content of some of the Western aesthetic traditions is also unique. The tradition of mimesis, for example, has rarely been carried to such extremes of literalness as in the West. And the glorification of individual expression that characterizes romanticism is developed to a higher level in the West than elsewhere. Granted, the *rasa*-theorists of India talked at length about the percipient's emotional response to art, and the Japanese find delight in the melancholy expression of *mono no aware.* Nevertheless, the individualized and powerful feelings that moved the apostles of romanticism find little parallel in other cultures.

Of all Western aesthetic theories, formalism is the most exceptional. Its assertion that art exists solely for aesthetic satisfaction and its claim that any social, cultural, or even representational message is a distraction from art's higher purpose is, so far as I know, unprecedented in comparative aesthetics. The art-for-art's-sake premise of formalism stands in marked contrast to the various art-for-life's-sake themes found in other aesthetic traditions.

A final question may be asked regarding the comparative standing of Western aesthetics: What is its *merit* as compared to those in other societies' philosophies of art? The answer, of course, depends on how one measures merit. As in other complex societies, the West has had explicit theories of art for a very long time, and the accumulated body of Western aesthetic thought has examined art from many perspectives and in great detail. So if explicitness and intricateness are thought to be virtues, then Western aesthetics unquestionably gets high marks.

But two other criteria may come to mind when one tries to think qualitatively about aesthetic systems. The first concerns the *pervasiveness* of the beliefs in the context of the society at large. Thus, Australian Aboriginal and Navajo philosophies of art not only motivate artistic production but inform a very wide range of other activities as well. The fabric of life in these societies seems to be permeated by an aesthetic sensibility. Again, one hesitates to pass final judgment for lack of exhaustive information, but in, say, Sepik River cultures and in early India, the aesthetic enterprise seems clearly to be demarcated from other endeavors such as subsistence activities, social interaction, and political affairs, except where art objects are called upon as tools, as it were, for carrying out these projects. Another aspect of the issue of aesthetic pervasiveness is revealed by asking, Does the population at large identify with the aesthetic principles in

question, or is aesthetics the domain of specialists who make public pronouncements about art, at some social and cognitive distance from the mass of
people—and even, perhaps, removed from artists themselves?

Besides pervasiveness, another issue one might consider regarding the
merit of an aesthetic system is its *depth*. One can plausibly argue, I believe,
that the several components of art (that is, its communication of cultural
meaning by means of a conventional style through the skillful, affecting manipulation of a sensuous medium) are not of equal value or importance. In
my opinion, art reaches its highest purpose when it conveys meanings of significance for a culture's spiritual, philosophical, or ethical traditions. I certainly enjoy the sensuous satisfaction that artistic media can inspire, and I
have boundless respect for the consummate skill of the master artist, but all
else being equal, I somehow feel that it is a lesser art that embodies primarily
sensuousness and skill and has little social or philosophical meaning. If one
accepts this premise, then Inuit aesthetics, with its concept of using art to
transmute things between the natural, human, and supernatural realms,
would score higher than the relatively secular aesthetics of the San.

Also, an aesthetic system that taps several of art's dimensions would seem
to be more praiseworthy than one that touches fewer levels. For example,
much of the appeal for me of Yoruba aesthetics lies in its amazing capacity simultaneously to challenge the creator's skill, to embody principles of sensuous
beauty, to express important social and ethical principles, to mediate the di-
alectically opposed principles of harmony and dynamism, and to base all this
on a compelling metaphysical foundation. By comparison, the Aztec philosophy of immortality via flower and song seems rather one-dimensional.[3]

Using these two standards, pervasiveness and depth, how does Western
aesthetics compare to other societies' philosophies of art? Regarding pervasiveness, the picture may at first look unpromising. Aesthetics, after all, is a
highly esoteric specialty—indeed, subspecialty—and as such it has been a
subject of conscious interest to a small circle of people, usually discussed only
in academic monographs and professional periodicals.

But as the chapter on Western aesthetics noted, although our theories
were created to address the fine arts, the popular arts implicitly accept the
same assumptions. So Western aesthetics, by influencing both fine and popular art, does pervade all sectors of our population.

Nevertheless, the pervasiveness of Western aesthetics is severely restricted in a different way: It applies only to art and not, generally, to the vast

---

[3]Clearly, this judgment would be mistaken if we were to somehow learn that, contrary to
the picture we receive from the codexes, the *tlamatinime* speculated at length not only about art's
ability to prevent the final destruction of the world, but also about issues such as connoisseurship
and the secular pleasures of art.

congeries of things and actions that we deem not to be art. Among the Navajos, "one is admonished to walk in beauty, speak in beauty, act in beauty, sing in beauty, and live in beauty" (Witherspoon 1977:153). In contrast, the West makes as firm a distinction between the aesthetic and the (far greater) non-aesthetic world as it does between the realms of the sacred and the secular. Aesthetic considerations play little role in most of our subsistence activities (i.e., our technology, our industrial production, and our system of commerce). They play an even smaller part in the political arena, formal education, and most components of family life. And in the area of speculative thought, we are admonished merely to seek parsimony (but, as Whitehead says, not necessarily to trust it!). Most Westerners do not live particularly aesthetic lives, although the evidence is clear that other peoples such as the Navajo and Aboriginal Australians do.[4] Viewed in this way, the West scores low regarding the pervasiveness of its aesthetic system.

The second criterion for evaluating aesthetic systems, depth, concerns the contributions art makes to spiritual, philosophical, or ethical areas of life, and the West hardly excels in this area either. Aesthetics seems to have played a secondary role during most periods of Western intellectual history. Granted, the promulgators of instrumental theories of aesthetics, whether Christian, neo-classical, or utopian, have seen art as a means to their own desired ends. But even here art has not been as important as it was, say, to Aztec thinkers, who believed that flower and song, the only genuine and enduring things on the face of the earth, were the sole offerings (other than blood sacrifice) that could postpone the final destruction of the world. In Japan and India, as well as in the cultures of the Yoruba, Navajo, and aboriginal Australians, art was thought to be the sole means by which human well-being could be attained or maintained. The Western predilection for mimetic representation, romantic expression, or art for art's sake all pale by comparison to such powerful philosophies of art. Other cultures demonstrate unequivocally that art can play a pivotal role in a people's worldview, and Western culture has rarely tapped that potential.

I suspect that this is not the result of an innate insensitivity to art on our part but is a consequence of other components of Western culture. Since the time of the pre-Socratic philosophers, and especially since the Enlightenment, many Westerners have looked to science for answers to the questions of philosophy and religion. Thus, we expect astronomers to provide us with origin stories and biologists and social scientists to explain our basic human na-

---

[4]However, as noted at the beginning of the chapter on Western aesthetics, if one considers not just fine art but also popular art in the West, the extent to which most of us aesthetically enhance our experience is surprising. And it is not just the full-time members of the art world for whom art is an all-pervasive concern. For example, as Keali'inohomoku (personal communication) has rightly pointed out, for some fans of Music Television, MTV is a way of life!

ture, and we employ members of the medical profession, rather than shamans, to protect our fertility, health, and peace of mind. For most people, little is left that inspires true awe, and art rarely impinges upon this small preserve of the sacred. Little is left for art to theorize about—except art itself.

Likewise, in such practical matters as subsistence, defense, and communication, we have, especially since the Renaissance, relied on technology; the possible efficacy of art in these areas has been generally ignored. We produce no counterparts to Navajo sandpaintings and songs, Eskimo and Australian Aboriginal amulets, Indian drama, or Aztec architecture—each of which was made for practical and life-sustaining purposes.

Furthermore, the domain of ethics is subsumed in the Judeo-Christian religious tradition, whereas in many other societies art makes a significant contribution to both ethical training and the administration of justice. In the West, bureaucratic governments are expected to enforce ethical codes; no clowns or tricksters, artfully disguised by mask and costume, are seen here—except at Halloween. Finally, much of the human need for sensuous satisfaction also tends to be met in the West by technology, rather than by art.[5]

Thus, although humans seem innately to need larger meanings, in the West we have tended to seek them not in art but in science, technology, government, and so on. In my view, we have some reason to envy the Navajo with their faith in *hózhǫ́* and their belief that the inevitable evils of the world can be held at bay and that goodness and harmony will be restored if artistic activities are properly carried out. We are likewise justified in longing for the certainty of ethical precepts that is condensed in a Yoruba statuette. Some of us might even trade a few of the blessings of technology for an unequivocal grasp of our human past, present, and future comparable to that which is implicit in Australian Aboriginal art's embodiment of the Eternal Dreamtime. Western art does provide an antidote to the highly structured pattern of life in the West, and it encourages a liminal state in which anti-structure and counter-structure are permitted. But beyond that, most Western art, in theory and practice, seems to provide little succor for our deeper human needs.

For many Western individual artists themselves, life would be unbearable without the production of art, and this is as true of untutored "folk artists" as it is of fine artists. There are even sectors of Western society in which art has great social and political significance. The ideology of Jamaican Rastafarians is conveyed effectively through their arts such as reggae music. A

---

[5]Such, as least, is true of Western fine arts. However, as Keali'inohomoku (personal communication) has observed, we do live in a world where some individuals mutilate and decorate their physical appearance to a degree that might be the envy of the most ornamented of New Guineans, where pets wear rhinestone collars, where advertisements continually promise to enhance our "sex appeal," and where politicians and newscasters alike (our tricksters?) commonly put on makeup before appearing in public (see also Anderson 2000).

Rastafarian painter-poet, Ras "T," has said, "Art to me is the integrator of all mankind. . . . My main theme in art is not only the portrayal of oppression in the daily experience of the ghetto-man, but there is also joy. I do not only portray oppression, I try to point the way out" (Barrett 1977:187). Given the ecological, economic, and political impasses the West now faces, one may well applaud Ras "T's" strategy.

REFERENCES

Abiodun, Rowland
    1987   Verbal and Visual Metaphors: Mythical Allusion in Yoruba Ritualistic Art of Orí. Word Image 3(3):252–270.
——, Henry J. Drewal, and John Pemberton III, eds.
    1990   The Future of African Art Studies: An African Perspective. In African Art Studies: The State of the Discipline. Washington, D.C.: National Museum of African Art. Pp. 63–88.
    1994   The Yoruba Artist: New Theoretical Perspectives on African Arts. Washington, D.C.: Smithsonian Institution Press.

Abrams, Meyer Howard
    1953   The Mirror and the Lamp. New York: Norton.

Adair, John
    1944   Navajo and Pueblo Silversmiths. Norman: University of Oklahoma Press.

Adams, Francis M. and Charles E. Osgood.
    1973   A Cross-cultural Study of the Affective Meanings of Color. Journal of Cross-cultural Psychology 4(2):135–157.

Alland, Alexander
    1983   Playing with Form: Children Draw in Six Cultures. New York: Columbia University Press.

Anderson, Richard L.
    1979   Art in Primitive Societies. Englewood Cliffs, N.J.: Prentice Hall.
    1989   Art in Small-Scale Societies (second edition of Art in Primitive Societies). Englewood Cliffs, N.J.: Prentice Hall.
    2000   American Muse: Anthropological Excursions into Art and Aesthetics. Upper Saddle River, N.J.: Prentice Hall.

Anesaki, Masaharu
    1915   Buddhist Art: In Its Relation to Buddhist Ideals, with Special Reference to Buddhism in Japan. Boston: Houghton Miflin.
    1933   Art, Life, and Nature in Japan. Boston: Marshall Jones.
    1963   History of Japanese Religion. Rutland, Vt.: Charles E. Tuttle Company.

Anonymous
    1990   Marriage Today: Facts and Figures. Bride's Magazine.
    1991   Modern Bride Facts. Modern Bride Magazine.

Armstrong, Robert Plant
    1971   The Affecting Presence: An Essay in Humanistic Anthropology. Urbana: University of Illinois Press.

1975   Wellspring on the Myth and Source of Culture. Berkeley: University of California Press.

Aristotle
1969   The Poetics. In Robert Paul Wolff, ed., Ten Great Works of Philosophy. New York: New American Library. Pp. 63–96.
1981   The Powers of Presence: Consciousness, Myth, and the Affecting Presence. Philadelphia: University of Pennsylvania Press.

Australian Council of Tourism, http://www.aus

Bacon, Gershon
1971   Idolatry. Encyclopaedia Judaica. Vol. 8, pp. 1227–1234. New York: Macmillan.

Balikci, Asen
1970   The Netsilik Eskimo. Garden City, N.Y.: Natural History Press.

Barbar, Karin
1981   How Man Makes God in West Africa: Yoruba Attitudes Toward the Orisa. Africa 51(3):724–745.

Barrett, Leonard
1977   The Rastafarians: Sounds of Cultural Dissonance. Boston: Beacon Press.

Barry, Herbert, III
1971   [orig. 1957] Relationships between Child Training and the Pictorial Arts. In Carol F. Jopling, ed., Art and Aesthetics in Primitive Societies. New York: Ducton. Pp. 64–72. Orig. in Journal of Abnormal and Social Psychology 54:380–383.

Bartlett, Katherine
1950   Present Trends in Weaving on the Western Navajo Reservation. Plateau 23:1–6.

Bascom, William R.
1969   The Yoruba of Southwestern Nigeria. Case Studies in Cultural Anthropology. New York: Holt, Rinehart and Winston.
1973a   A Yoruba Master Carver: Duga of Meko. In Warren L D'Azevedo, ed., The Traditional Artist in African Societies. Bloomington: Indiana University Press. Pp. 62–78.
1973b   African Art in Cultural Perspective. New York: Norton.
1991   Ifa Divination: Communication Between Gods and Men in West Africa (reprint edition; orig. 1969). Bloomington: Indiana University Press.

Bateson, Gregory
1946   Arts of the South Seas. Arts Bulletin 2:119–123.
1958   [orig. 1936] Naven. Second edition. Stanford: Stanford University Press.
1972   Metalogue: Why a Swan? In Gregory Bateson, Steps to an Ecology of the Mind. New York: Ballantine. Pp. 33–37.

Beardsley, Monroe C.
1981   [orig. 1958] Aesthetics: Problems in the Philosophy of Criticism. Indianapolis: Hackett Publishing Company.
Bell, Clive
1958   Art. New York: Putnam.
Benedek, Emily
1999   The Wind Won't Know Me: A History of the Navajo-Hopi Land Dispute. Norman: University of Oklahoma Press.
Bennett, Noel
1974   The Weaver's Pathway: A Clarification of the Spirit Trail in Navajo Weaving. Flagstaff, Ariz.: Northland Press.
Berger, John
1980   About Looking. New York: Pantheon.
Bergman, Robert
1971   Navajo Peyote Use: Its Apparent Safety. American Journal of Psychiatry 128(6):51–55/695–699.
Berlin, Brent and Paul Kay
1969   Basic Color Terms. Berkeley: University of California Press.
Berlo, Janet Catherine and Ruth B. Phillips
1998   Native North American Art. New York: Oxford University Press.
Berlyne, David E.
1970   The Golden Section and Hedonic Judgments of Rectangles. Sciences de l'Art/ Scientific Aesthetics 7:1–6.
1980   Psychological Aesthetics. In Harry C. Triandis and Walter Lonner, eds., Handbook of Cross-cultural Psychology. Boston: Allyn and Bacon. Pp. 323–361.
Berndt, Ronald
1976   Love Songs of Arnhem Land. Chicago: University of Chicago Press.
—— and Catherine H. Berndt
1964   The World of the First Australians. Chicago: University of Chicago Press.
1970   Man, Land and Myth in Northern Australia: The Gunwinggu People. East Lansing: Michigan State University Press.
Biebuyck, Daniel P.
1973   Lega Culture: Art, Initiation, and Moral Philosophy among a Central African People. Berkeley: University of California Press.
Biesele, Megan
1976   Aspects of !Kung Folklore. In Richard B. Lee and Irven DeVore, eds., Kalahari Hunter-Gatherers. Cambridge, Mass.: Harvard University Press. Pp. 303–324.
Birket-Smith, Kaj
1924   Ethnography of the Egedesminde District. Copenhagen: B. Lunos Bogtrykkeri.
1929   The Caribou Eskimos. Copenhagen: Gyldendal.

1933   The Chugach Eskimo. Copenhagen: Nationalmuseets Skrifter, Etnografisk Raekhe, 6 København, Nationalmuseets Publikationsfond.

1959   The Eskimos. Second edition. London: Methuen.

Bleek, D.F.

1928   The Naron, A Bushman Tribe of the Central Kalahari. Cambridge, England: Cambridge University Press.

Bleek, Wilhelm H. and Lucy C. Lloyd, eds.

1911   Specimens of Bushman Folklore. Cape Town, South Africa: Struik.

Black Arts and Culture: Visual Arts

http://abc.net.au/message/blackarts/visual/banduk_marika.htm)

Boas, Franz

1940   [orig. 1916] Representative Art of Primitive People. In Franz Boas, Race, Language, and Culture. New York: The Free Press. Pp. 535–540.

1964   [orig. 1888] The Central Eskimo. Lincoln: University of Nebraska Press. Originally published as Report of the Bureau of Ethnology 1884-1885. Washington, D.C.: Smithsonian Institution, 399–669.

Boas, George

1963   [orig. 1940] The Mona Lisa in the History of Taste. In Marvin Levich, ed., Aesthetics and the Philosophy of Criticism. New York: Random House. Pp. 576–594.

Bohannan, Paul

1971   Artist and Critic in an African Society. In Charlotte M. Otten, ed., Anthropology and Art. Garden City, N.Y.: Natural History Press. Pp. 172–181.

Borgatti, Jean M.

1982   Okpella Masks: In Search of the Parameters of the Beautiful and the Grotesque. Studies in Visual Communication 8(3):28–40.

Bowden, Ross

1983   Yena: Art and Ceremony in a Sepik Society. Oxford, England: Pitt-Rivers Museum, University of Oxford.

1984   Art and Gender Ideology in the Sepik. Man 19(3):445–458.

1999   What Is Wrong with an Art Forgery: An Anthropological Perspective. Journal of Aesthetics and Art Criticism 57(3):333–344.

Bradley, Ian L.

1977   A Bibliography of Canadian Native Arts: Indian and Eskimo Arts, Craft, Dance and Music. Victoria, British Columbia: GLC Publishers.

Brain, Robert

1979   The Decorated Body. New York: Harper & Row.

Bray, Warwick

1968   Everyday Life of the Aztecs. London: B. T. Batsford.

Brody, J.J.
  1977 Mimbres Painted Pottery. Albuquerque: University of New Mexico Press.
  1983 The Paintings of Jimmy Toddy (Beatien Yazz). In Sallie R. Wagner, ed., Yazz: Navajo Painter. Pp. 25–56. Flagstaff: Northland Press.
Brugge, David M.
  1999 The Navajo-Hopi Land Dispute: An American Tragedy. Albuquerque: University of New Mexico Press.
Brumfiel, Elizabeth M.
  1987 Elite and Utilitarian Crafts in the Aztec State. In Elizabeth M. Brumfiel and Timothy K. Earle, eds., Specialization, Exchange, and Complex Societies. London: Cambridge University Press. Pp. 102–118.
Burling, Robbins
  1966 The Metrics of Children's Verse: A Cross-linguistic Study. American Anthropologist 68:1418–1441.
Canaday, John
  1981 Mainstreams of Modern Art. Second edition. New York: Holt, Rinehart and Winston.
Carneiro, Robert
  1970 Scale Analysis, Evolutionary Sequences, and the Rating of Cultures. In Raoul Naroll and Ronald Cohen, eds., A Handbook of Method in Cultural Anthropology. Garden City, N.Y.: Natural History Press. Pp. 834–871.
Carpenter, Edmund
  1973 Eskimo Realities. New York: Holt, Rinehart and Winston.
Carrasco, Davíd, with Scott Sessions
  1998 Daily Life of the Aztecs: People of the Sun and Earth. Westport, Conn.: Greenwood Press.
Carroll, Noel
  1999 Philosophy of Art: A Contemporary Introduction (Routledge Contemporary Introductions to Philosophy). New York: Routledge.
Caruana, Wally
  1993 Aboriginal Art. New York: Thames and Hudson.
Chagnon, Napoleon
  1983 Yanomamo: The Fierce People. Third edition. New York: Holt, Rinehart and Winston.
Charmichael, Elizabeth and Chloë Sayer
  1991 The Skeleton at the Feast: The Day of the Dead in Mexico. Austin: University of Texas Press.
Chase, Katherine
  1982 Navajo Painting. Flagstaff: Museum of Northern Arizona.

Chenoweth, Vida
  1979   The Usarufas and Their Music. Dallas, Tex.: SIL Museum of An-
         thropology, 5.
Chernoff, John Miller
  1979   African Rhythm and African Sensibility: Aesthetics and African Mu-
         sical Idioms. Chicago: University of Chicago Press.
Cochrane, Susan
  1997   Contemporary Art in Papua New Guinea. Sydney: G+B Arts Inter-
         national.
Coe, Michael
  1962   Mexico. New York: Praeger.
Cohan, Tony
  1998   Introduction. In Melba Levick, Tony Cohan, and Masako Taka-
         hashi, Mexicolor: The Spirit of Mexican Design. New York: Chroni-
         cle Books.
Cohen, Marshall
  1983   [orig. 1962] Aesthetic Essence. In Earle J. Coleman, ed., Varieties
         of Aesthetic Experience. Lanham, Md.: University Press of America.
         Pp. 235–254. Orig. in Max Black, ed., Philosophy in America.
         Ithaca, N.Y.: Cornell University Press.
Colby, Benjamin N.
  1973   A Partial Grammar of Eskimo Folktales. American Anthropologist
         75(3):645–662.
Comfort, Alexander
  1962   Darwin and the Naked Lady: Discursive Essays on Biology and Art.
         New York: Braziller.
Coomaraswamy, Ananda
  1924   The Dance of Siva: Fourteen Indian Essays. New York: The Sunwise
         Turn.
Cooper, David, Crispin Sartwell, and Joseph Margolis, eds.
  1995   A Companion to Aesthetics (Blackwell Companions to Philosophy).
         Malden, Mass.: Blackwell.
Cordwell, Justine M.
  1953   Naturalism and Stylization of Yoruba Art. Magazine of Art, pp.
         220–225.
Covarrubias, Miguel
  1957   Indian Art of Mexico and Central America. New York: Knopf.
Cowen, Tyler
  2002   Creative Destruction: How Globalization Is Changing the World's
         Cultures. Princeton, N.J.: Princeton University Press.
Crandall, Richard C. and Susan M. Crandall
  2002   An Annotated Bibliography of Inuit Art. Jefferson, N.C.: McFarland
         & Company.

Crowley, Daniel J.
1971 An African Aesthetic. In Carol F. Jopling, ed., Art and Aesthetics in Primitive Societies. New York: Dutton. Pp. 315–327.

Csikszentmihalyi, Mihaly
1975 Beyond Boredom and Anxiety: The Experience of Play in Work and Games. San Francisco: Jossey Bass.
1978 Phylogenetic and Ontogenetic Functions of Artistic Cognition. In Stanley S. Majeda, ed., The Arts, Cognition, and Basic Skills. St. Louis, Mo.: Cemrel. Pp. 114–127.

—— and Eugene Rochberg-Halton
1981 The Meaning of Things: Domestic Symbols and the Self. New York: Cambridge University Press.

Dart, Raymond A.
1937 The Physical Characters of the I?auni— /khomani Bushmen. In J.D.R. Jones and C.M. Doke, eds., Bushmen of the Southern Kalahari. Johannesburg, South Africa: University of the Witwaterstrand Press. Pp. 117–188.

Davies, Stephen
1991 Definitions of Art. Ithaca, N.Y.: Cornell University Press, 1991.

Dawson, Thomas
1992 Rock Engravings of Southern Africa. Johannesburg, South Africa: Witwatersrand University Press.

Deregowski, J.B., H.D. Ellis, and J.W. Shepherd
1975 Descriptions of White and Black Faces by White and Black Subjects. International Journal of Psychology 10(2):1 19–123.

Deutsch, Eliot
1975 Studies in Comparative Aesthetics. (Monograph of the Society for Asian and Comparative Philosophy, No. 2). Honolulu: University Press of Hawaii.

Devereux, George
1961 Art and Mythology. In Bert Kaplan, ed., Studying Personality Cross-culturally. New York: Harper & Row. Pp. 361–404.

Dhayagude, Suresh
1981 Western and Indian Poetics: A Comparative Study. Pune, India: Bhandarkar Oriental Research Institute Press.

Downs, James F.
1972 (repr. 1984) The Navajo. Prospect Heights, Ill.: Waveland Press.

Drewal, Henry John
1973 Efe/Gelede: The Educative Role of the Arts in Traditional Yoruba Culture. Ph.D. Dissertation, Columbia University.

—— and Margaret Thompson Drewal
1983 Gelede: Art and Female Power among the Yoruba. Bloomington: Indiana University Press.

1987   Composing Time and Space in Yoruba Art. Word Image 3(3):225–251.

Eber, Dorothy, ed.
1979   Pitseolak: Pictures out of My Life. Seattle: University of Washington Press.

Elkin, A.P.
1938   Foreword to Australian Aboriginal Decorative Art, by Frederick D. McCarthy. Sydney: Australian Museum. Pp. 8–11.
1964   The Australian Aborigines: How to Understand Them. Fourth edition. Sydney: Angus and Robertson.

——, Ronald M. Berndt, and Catherine H. Berndt
1950   Art in Arnhem Land. Chicago: University of Chicago Press.

Ellis, Catherine J.
1985   Aboriginal Music: Education for Living Experiences from South Australia. New York: University of Queensland Press.

England, Nicholas
1967   Bushman Counterpoint. Journal of the International Folk Music Council 19:58–66.
1968   Music among the Zhu/wa-si of South West Africa and Botswana. Ph.D. thesis, Department of Music, Harvard University.

Enoch, Wesley
2000   Indigenous Performance. In Sylvia Kleinert and Margo Neale, eds., Oxford Companion to Aboriginal Art and Culture. New York: Oxford University Press. Pp. 349–353.

Evans, David
1982   Big Road Blues. Berkeley: University of California Press.

Farb, Peter
1978   Man's Rise to Civilization. New York: Bantam Books.

Farella, John R.
1984/1991   The Main Stalk: A Synthesis of Navajo Philosophy. Phoenix: University of Arizona Press. Reprinted 1991.

Faris, James C.
1972   Nuba Personal Art. Toronto: University of Toronto Press.
1995   The Nightway: A History and a History of Documentation of a Navajo Ceremonial. Albuquerque: University of New Mexico Press.

Feagin, Susan and Patrick Maynard, eds.
1997   Aesthetics. New York: Oxford University Press.

Ferguson, George
1954   Signs and Symbols in Christian Art. London: Oxford University Press.

Fernandez, James W.
1973   The Exposition and Imposition of Order: Artistic Expression in Fang Culture. In Warren L. d'Azevedo, ed., The Traditional Artist

in African Societies. Bloomington: Indiana University Press. Pp. 194–220.

Field, Karen L.
  1982   Artists in Liberia and the United States: A Comparative View. Journal of Modern African Studies 20(4):713–730.

Firth, Raymond
  1936   Art and Life in New Guinea. London: The Studio, Limited.

Fischer, John L.
  1971   [orig. 1961] Art Styles as Cultural Cognitive Maps. In Charlotte M. Otten, ed., Anthropology and Art. Garden City, N.Y.: Natural History Press. Pp. 141–161. Orig. in American Anthropologist 63(1):79–93.

Forge, J. Anthony W.
  1967   The Abelam Artist. In Maurice Freedman, ed., Social Organization: Essays Presented to Raymond Firth. London: Cass. Pp. 65–84.

  1970   Learning to See in New Guinea. In Philip Mayer, ed., Socialization: The Approach from Social Anthropology. ASA Monograph No. 8. London: Tavistock. Pp. 269–291.

  1971a   [orig. 1965] Art and Environment in the Sepik. In Carol F. Jopling, ed., Art and Aesthetics in Primitive Societies. New York: Dutton. Pp. 290–314.

  1979   The Problem of Meaning in Art. In Sidney M. Mead., ed., Exploring the Visual Art of Oceania. Honolulu: University of Hawaii Press. Pp. 278–286.

Forrest, John
  1988   Lord I'm Coming Home: Everyday Aesthetics in Tidewater North Carolina (Anthropology of Contemporary Issues). Ithaca, N.Y.: Cornell University Press.

Fourie, L.
  1960   [orig. 1928] The Bushmen of Southwest Africa. In Simon and Phoebe Ottenberg, eds., Cultures and Societies of Africa. New York: Random House. Pp. 87–95. Orig. in The Native Tribes of South West Africa. Cape Town, South Africa: Cape Times, Ltd.

Frances, R. and A. Tamba
  1973   Etude Interculturelle des préférence et musicales. International Journal of Psychology 8:95–108.

Fraser, Douglas
  1971   The Discovery of Primitive Art. In Charlotte M. Otten, ed., Anthropology and Art. New York: Natural History Press. Pp. 20–36.

Freud, Sigmund
  1956   [orig. 1920] A General Introduction to Psychoanalysis, trans. by Joan Riviere. New York: Permabooks.

Friedlander, Judith
 1975   Being Indian in Hueyapan: A Study of Forced Identity in Contemporary Mexico. New York: St. Martin's Press.
Frisbie, Charlotte Johnson
 1980   Ritual Drama in the Navajo House Blessing Ceremony. In Charlotte J. Frisbie, ed., Southwestern Ritual Drama. School of American Research Advanced Seminar Series. Albuquerque: University of New Mexico Press. Pp. 161–199.
 1993   Kinaalda: A Study of the Navaho Girl's Puberty Ceremony. Albuquerque: University of Utah Press.
Fry, Roger E.
 1910   Bushman Paintings. Burlington Magazine 16:334 338.
Ganguly, Anil B.
 1979   Fine Arts in Ancient India. New Delhi, India: Abhinav Publications.
Gans, Herbert J.
 1974   Popular Culture and High Culture: An Analysis and Evaluation of Taste. New York: Basic Books.
Garde, Murray
 2000   Maningrida, the Didjeridu, and the Internet. In Sylvia Kleinert and Margo Neale, eds., Oxford Companion to Aboriginal Art and Culture. New York: Oxford University Press, pp. 344–345.
Gardner, Howard
 1980   Artful Scribbles: The Significance of Children's Drawings. New York: Basic Books.
Gardner, John
 1978   On Moral Fiction. New York: Basic Books.
Gardner, Martin
 1983   The Whys of a Philosophical Scrivner. New York: Quill.
Geertz, Clifford
 1983   Local Knowledge: Further Essays in Interpretive Anthropology. New York: Basic Books.
Gerbrands, Adrian Alexander
 1957   Art as an Element of Culture, Especially in Negro Africa. Mededlingen van het Rijksmuseum voor Volkenkunde 12:110–135.
 1967   Wow-Ipits: Eight Asmat Woodcarvers in New Guinea. Trans. by Inez Seeger. The Hague: Mouton.
Getzels, Jacob W. and Mihaly Csikszentmihalyi
 1976   The Creative Vision: A Longitudinal Study of Problem-finding in Art. New York: John Wiley.
Gibson, Charles
 1964   The Aztecs under Spanish Rule. Stanford: Stanford University Press.
Gillespie, Susan D.
 1989   The Aztec Kings. Tucson: Univ. Arizona Press.

Gnoli, Raniero
    1968   The Aesthetic Experience According to Abhinavagupta. Second edition. Varanasi-1, India: Chowkhamba Sanskrit Series Office.

Golde, Peggy
    1963   Aesthetic Values and Art Styles in a Nahua Pottery Producing Village. Unpublished Ph.D. Dissertation, Harvard University.

—— and Helena C. Kraemer
    1973   Analysis of an Aesthetic Values Test: Detection of the Inter-sub-group Differences within a Pottery Producing Community in Mexico. American Anthropologist 75(5):260–275.

Goldwater, Robert
    1967   Primitivism in Modern Art. New York: Vintage.

Gombrich, E.H.
    1979   The Sense of Order. Ithaca: Cornell University Press.

Goodnow, Jacqueline J.
    1979   Children Drawing. Cambridge: Harvard University Press.

Graburn, Nelson H.H.
    1967   The Eskimo and "Airport Art." Trans-Action 4(10):28–33.
    1978   "I Like Things to Look More Different than That Stuff Did": An Experiment in Cross-Cultural Art Appreciation. In Michael Greenhalgh and Vincent Megaw, eds., Art in Society. New York: St. Martin's. Pp. 51–70.
    1999   Ethnic and Tourist Arts Revisited. *In* Unpacking Culture: Art and Commodity in the Colonial and Postcolonial Worlds. R. Phillips and C. Steiner, eds. Pp. 335–53. Berkeley: University of California Press.

Hall, John Whitney
    1959   The Confucian Teacher in Tokugawa Japan. In David S. Nivison and Arthur F. Wright, eds., Confucianism in Action. Stanford: Stanford University Press. Pp. 268–301.

Halle, David
    1993   Inside Culture: Art and Class in the American Home. Chicago: University of Chicago Press.

Hallen, Barry
    2000   The Good, the Bad, and the Beautiful: Discourse about Values in Yoruba Culture. Bloomington: Indiana University Press.

Hannerz, Ulf
    1996   Transnational Connections: Culture, People, Places. London: Routledge.

Hartman, Russell P.
    1987   Navajo Pottery: Traditions and Innovations. Flagstaff, Az.: Northland Press.

Hatterer, Lawrence J.
   1965   The Artist in Society: Problems and Treatment of the Creative Indi-
          vidual. New York: Grove Press.
Hayashiya, Tatsusaburo, Masao Nakamura, and Seizo Hayashiya
   1974   Japanese Arts and the Tea Ceremony. Trans. and adapted by Joseph
          P. Macadam. New York: Weatherhill.
Hedlund, Ann Lane
   1988   Reflections of the weaver's world: the Gloria F. Ross Collection of
          Contemporary Navajo Weaving. Denver, Colo.: Denver Art Mu-
          seum.
   1994   Contemporary Navajo Weaving: Thoughts That Count. Museum of
          Northern Arizona: Plateau, Vol 65. No 1.
Hendrickson, Elizabeth and Mary M.A. McDonald
   1983   Ceramic Form and Function: An Ethnographic Search and an Ar-
          chaeological Application. American Anthropologist 85(3):630–643.
Herbert, Jean
   1967   Shinto: At the Fountain-head of Japan. New York:
Herring, Frances Stein & Day.
   1949   Touch: The Neglected Sense. Journal of Aesthetics and Art Criti-
          cism 7:199–215.
Hessel, Ingo, Dieter Hessel (Photographer), and George Swinton
   1998   Inuit Art : An Introduction. New York: Harry N. Abrams.
Hill, Jane H.
   1987   The Flowery World of Old Uto-Aztecan. Paper read at the 86th An-
          nual Meeting of the American Anthropological Association, No-
          vember 20, 1987. Chicago, Illinois.
Hogbin, Herbert Ian
   1934/35 Native Culture of Wogeo. Oceania 5:308 337.
   1946   Puberty to Marriage: A Study of the Sexual Life of the Natives of
          Wogeo, New Guinea. Oceania 16:185–209.
   1970   The Island of Menstruating Men: Religion in Wogeo, New Guinea.
          Scranton, Pa.: Chandler.
Hori, Ichiro
   1968   Folk Religion in Japan: Continuity and Change. Chicago: Univer-
          sity of Chicago Press.
——, et al.
   1972   Japanese Religion: A Survey by the Agency of Cultural Affairs.
          Tokyo: Kodansha International.
Horton, Robin
   1965   Kalabari Sculpture. Lagos, Nigeria: Department of Antiquities.
Hrdlicka, Ales
   1975   The Anthropology of Kodiak Island. New York: AMS Press.

Hume, Nancy G., ed.
    1995   Japanese Aesthetics and Culture: A Reader. (SUNY Series on Asian
            Studies Development). Albany: State University of New York.
Hunt, Carl M.
    1979   Oyotunji Village: The Yoruba Movement in America. Washington,
            D.C.: University Press of America.
Ienaga, Saburo
    1979   Japanese Art: A Cultural Appreciation. New York: Weatherhill.
Ingalls, Daniel H. H.
    1990   The "Dhavanyāloka" of Ānandavardhana with the "Locana" of Ab-
            hinavagupta. Trans. by Daniel H. H. Ingalls, Jeffrey Moussaieff Mas-
            son, and M. V. Patwardhan. Cambridge, Mass.: Harvard University
            Press.
Irwin, Colin
    1989   Lords of the Arctic: Wards of the State. Northern Perspectives
            17(1) 1–9.
Iverson, Peter
    1981   (repr. 1983) The Navajo Nation. Westport, Conn.: Greenwood.
Izutsu, Toshihiko and Toyo Izutsu
    1981   The Theory of Beauty in the Classical Aesthetics of Japan. The
            Hague: Martinus Nijhoff Publishers.
Jacka, Lois Essary and Jerry Jacka (Photographer)
    1994   Enduring Traditions: Art of the Navajo. Flagstaff, Ariz.: Northland
            Publishing.
    1995   Navajo Jewelry: A Legacy of Silver and Stone. Flagstaff, Ariz.: North-
            land Publishing.
Jenness, Diamond
    1928   People of the Twilight. New York: Macmillan.
    1946   Material Culture of the Copper Eskimo. Canadian Arctic Expedi-
            tion 1913–18, Vol. 16. Ottawa: King's Printer.
Johnson, Vivien
    2000   Desert Art. In Sylvia Kleinert and Margo Neale, eds., Oxford Com-
            panion to Aboriginal Art and Culture. New York: Oxford University
            Press, Pp. 211–220.
Johnston, Thomas F.
    1976   Eskimo Music by Region: A Comparative Circumpolar Study. Ot-
            tawa: National Museum of Man.
Jones, Trevor
    1956/7 Arnhem Land Music, Part 2, A Musical Survey. Oceania
            26(4):252–339, 28(1):1–30.
Kaberry, Phillis M.
    1941   The Abelam Tribe, Sepik District, New Guinea: A Preliminary Re-
            port. Oceania 11:233–258, 345–367.

Kaeppler, Adrienne L.
    1971   Aesthetics of Tongan Dance. Ethnomusicology 15:175–185.
——, Christian Kaufmann, and Douglas Newton
    1997   Oceanic Art. New York: Harry N. Abrams.
Kanafani, Aida S.
    1983   Aesthetics and Ritual in the United Arab Emirates: The Anthropol-
            ogy of Food and Personal Adornment Among Arabian Women.
            Syracuse: Syracuse University Press.
Katz, Richard
    1982   Boiling Energy. Cambridge: Harvard University Press.
——, et al.
    1997   Healing makes Our Hearts Happy: Spirituality and Cultural Trans-
            formation among the Kalahari Jul'Hoansi, Rochester, VT: Inner
            Traditions International.
Kaufmann, Hans
    1910   Die/Auin. Em Beitrag zur Buschmannforshung. Trans. by Richard
            Neuse. Mitteilungen aus den Deutschen Schutzgebeiten
            23:135–160.
Kearney, Michael
    1972   Winds of Ixtepeji. New York: Holt, Rinehart and Winston.
Keene, Donald
    1958   Landscapes and Portraits: Appreciations of Japanese Culture.
            Tokyo: Kodansha.
    1971   [orig. 1958] Feminine Sensibility in the Heian Era. In D. Keene,
            ed., Landscapes and Portraits: Appreciations of Japanese Culture.
            Tokyo: Kodansha. Pp. 26–39.
    1995   Japanese Aesthetics. In Nancy G. Hume, ed., Japanese Aesthetics
            and Culture. Albany: State University of New York Press. Pp. 27–42.
Keil, Charles
    1979   Tiv Song. Chicago: University of Chicago Press.
Kellog, Rhoda
    1969   Analyzing Children's Art. Palo Alto: National Press Books. Kirby,
            P.R.
Kelly, Michael, ed.
    1998   Encyclopedia of Esthetics. New York: Oxford University Press.
Kennedy, Jean, et al.
    1992   New Currents, Ancient Rivers. Washington, D.C.: Smithsonian Insti-
            tution Press.
Kent, Kate
    1985   Navajo Weaving: Three Centuries of Change. Santa Fe, N.M.:
            School of American Research Press.
Kirby, P. R.
    1936   The Musical Practice of the /ami and /khomani Bushmen. Bantu
            Studies 10:373–431.

Kishimoto, Hideo
1967 Some Japanese Cultural Traits and Religions. In Charles A. Moore, ed., The Japanese Mind. Honolulu: University of Hawaii Press. Pp. 110–121.

Kleinert, Sylvia and Margo Neale
2000 Oxford Companion to Aboriginal Art and Culture. New York: Oxford University Press.

Kluckhohn, Clyde and Dorothea Leighton
1946 The Navaho. Cambridge: Harvard University Press.

Korsmeyer, Carolyn, ed.
1998 Aesthetics: The Big Questions. Malden, Mass.: Blackwell.

Kösaka, Masaaki
1967 The Statuses and the Role of the Individual in Japanese Society. In Charles A. Moore, ed., The Japanese Mind. Honolulu: University of Hawaii Press. Pp. 245–261.

Krishnamoorthy, K.
1979 Studies in Indian Aesthetics and Criticism. Mysore, India: D. V. Murthy.

Kupka, Karel
1965 Dawn of Art: Painting and Sculpture of Australian Aborigines. Trans. by John Ross. New York: Viking Press.

Ladd, John
1973 Conceptual Problems Relating to the Comparative Study of Art. In Warren L. d'Azevedo, ed., The Traditional Artist in African Societies. Bloomington: Indiana University Press. Pp. 417–424.

Lansing, J. Stephen
1981 A Balinese Act of Faith. In Jane E. Aaron, ed., Odyssey: The Human Adventure. Boston: Public Broadcasting Associates. Pp. 35–37.

Lawal, Babatunde
1974 Some Aspects of Yoruba Aesthetics. British Journal of Aesthetics 14:239–249.
1996 The Gelede Spectacle: Art, Gender, and Social Harmony in an African Culture. Seattle: University of Washington Press.

Leach, Edmund R.
1961 Aesthetics. In E.E. Evans-Pritchard et al., eds., The Institutions of Primitive Society. Glencoe, Ill.: The Free Press. Pp. 25–38.

Lebzelter, Viktor
1934 Eingeborenkulturen in Südwest und Süafrica, Vol. 2. Leipzig: Karl W. Hiersemann.

Lechner, Frank and John Boli
2000 General Introduction. In Frank Lechner and John Boli, eds., The Globalization Reader. Oxford, England: Blackwell.

Lee, Richard Borshay
1979 The !Kung San. New York: Cambridge University Press.

1993/2002   The Dobe Ju/íhoansi. Third edition. Belmont, CA: Wadsworth Pub Co.

LeFree, Betty
1975   Santa Clara Pottery Today. Albuquerque: University of New Mexico Press.

Leighton, Alexander and Dorothea Leighton
1944   The Navaho Door: An Introduction to Navaho Life. Cambridge, Mass.: Harvard University Press.

Leiris, Michel and Jacqueline Delange
1968   African Art. Trans. by Michael Ross. New York: Golden Books.

León-Portilla, Miguel
1963   Aztec Thought and Culture: A Study of the Ancient Nahuatl Mind. Trans. by Jack Emory. Norman: University of Oklahoma Press.

1966   Pre-Hispanic Thought. In Mario de la Cueva et al., Major Trends in Mexican Philosophy. Notre Dame, Ind.: University of Notre Dame Press. Pp. 2–56.

1971   Philosophy in Ancient Mexico, In Robert Wauchope, ed., Handbook of Middle American Indians, Vol. 10. Austin: University of Texas Press. Pp. 447–451.

1983   Three Forms of Thought in Ancient Mexico. In F. Allen Hanson, ed., Studies in Symbolism and Cultural Communication. University of Kansas Publications in Anthropology, Number 14. Lawrence: University of Kansas. Pp. 9–24.

——, and Earl Shorris, eds.
2001   In the Language of Kings: An Anthology of Mesoamerican Literature, Pre-Columbian to the Present. New York: W. W. Norton.

Lewis-Williams, David
1981   Believing and Seeing: Symbolic Meaning in Southern San Rock Paintings. New York: Academic Press

Liggett, John
1974   The Human Face. New York: Stein & Day.

Lin Yutang
1935   The Artistic Life. In Lin Yutang, My Country and My People. New York: Halcyon. Pp. 287–321.

Linton, Ralph and Paul S. Wingert
1971   Introduction, New Zealand, Sepik River, and New Ireland, from Arts of the South Seas. In Charlotte M. Otten, ed., Anthropology and Art. Garden City, N. Y.: Natural History Press. Pp. 383–404.

Lloyd, Peter C., A.L. Mabogunje, and B. Awe, eds.
1967   The City of Ibadan. London: Cambridge University Press.

Locke, Raymond Friday
1992   Book of the Navajo. Fifth edition. Los Angeles: Holloway House.

Lucie-Smith, Edward
2000   Judy Chicago: An American Vision.

Luttmann, Gail and Rick Luttmann
  1985 Aesthetics of Eskimo Dance: A Comparison Methodology. In Betty
        True Jones, ed., Dance as Cultural Heritage, Vol. 2. New York Coun-
        cil on Dance Research: Dance Research Annual XV. Pp. 53–61.
Lutz, Maija M.
  1978 The Effects of Acculturation on Eskimo Music of Cumberland
        Peninsula. Canadian Ethnology Service, Paper No. 41, a Diamond
        Jenness Memorial Volume. Ottawa: National Museums of Canada.
Magnin, André
  1996 Contemporary Art of Africa. New York: Abrams.
Maningrida Arts and Culture
  http://www.bu.aust.com/~maningrida/gallery/gallery.html
Maquet, Jacques
  1971 Introduction to Aesthetic Anthropology. Reading, Mass.: Addison-
        Wesley.
  1986 The Aesthetic Experience. New Haven: Yale University Press.
Marika, Rymattja and Nancy Williams
  2000 Marika Family. In Sylvia Kleinert and Margo Neale, eds., Oxford
        Companion to Aboriginal Art and Culture. New York: Oxford Uni-
        versity Press. Pp. 637–639.
Marra, Michele, ed.
  2000 Modern Japanese Aesthetics: A Reader. Honolulu: University of
        Hawaii Press.
—— and Michael F. Marra, eds.
  2001 A History of Modern Japanese Aesthetics. Honolulu: University of
        Hawaii Press.
Marshall, Lorna
  1959 Marriage among the !Kung Bushmen. Africa 29:335–364.
  1961 Sharing, Talking, and Giving: Relief of Social Tensions among
        !Kung Bushmen. Africa 31:231–249.
  1962 !Kung Bushman Religious Beliefs. Africa 32:221 252.
  1965 The !Kung Bushman of the Kalahari Desert. In James L. Gibbs, Jr.,
        ed., Peoples of Africa. New York: Holt, Rinehart and Winston. Pp.
        243–278.
  1976 The !Kung of Nyae Nyae. Cambridge, Mass.: Harvard University
        Press.
Marti, Samuel and Gertrude F. Kurath
  1964 Dance of Anáhuac: The Choreography and Music of Precortesian
        Dancers. Chicago: Aldine.
Martijn, Charles A.
  1964 Canadian Eskimo Carving in Historical Perspective. Anthropos
        59:546–596.

Mason, J. Alden
1927 Eskimo Pictorial Art. The Museum Journal 18(3):248–283. Philadelphia: Museum of the University of Pennsylvania.

Mason, J.W.T
1935 The Meaning of Shinto. Port Washington, N.Y.: Kennikat Press.

Mason, John
1994 Yoruba-American Art: New Rivers to Explore, in Rowland Abiodun, et al., eds., The Yoruba Artist: New Theoretical Perspectives. Washington, D.C.: Smithsonian Institution Press. Pp. 241–250.

Masson, Jeffrey L. and M. Patwardhan
1969 Sāntarasa and Abhinavagupta's Philosophy of Aesthetics. Poona, India: Bhandarkar Oriental Research Institute.
1970 Aesthetic Rapture, Vols. 1 and 2. Poona, India: Deccan College Postgraduate and Research Institute.

Maynard, Margaret
2000 Indigenous Dress. In Sylvia Kleinert and Margo Neale, eds., Oxford Companion to Aboriginal Art and Culture. New York: Oxford University Press. Pp. 384–390.

McAllester, David
1954 Enemy Way Music. Cambridge, Mass.: Peabody Museum.
1980 Shootingway, an Epic Drama of the Navajos. In Charlotte Frisbie, ed., Southwestern Indian Ritual Drama. Albuquerque: University of New Mexico Press. Pp. 199–237.

McCarthy, F.D.
1957a Australia's Aborigines, Their Life and Culture. Melbourne: Colorgravure Publication.
1957b Theoretical Considerations of Australian Aboriginal Art. Journal and Proceedings of the Royal Society of New South Wales, Vol. 9, part 1.

McChesney, Lea Stevens
1978 Man as Meaning-Seeker, Mediator, and Master: A Comparative Analysis of Hopi, Zuni, and Navajo Symbolic Systems. Unpub. MA thesis, Wesleyan University.

McCloud, Scott
1994 Understanding Comics. New York: Kitchen Sink Press.

McDannell, Colleen
1996 Material Christianity: Religion and Popular Culture in America. New Haven, Conn.: Yale University Press.

McGhee, Robert
1976 Differential Artistic Productivity in the Eskimo Cultural Tradition. Current Anthropology 17(2):203–220.

McMahon, A. Philip, trans.
1956 Leonardo Da Vinci, Treatise on Painting. Princeton: Princeton University Press.

McNaughton, Patrick R.
1979   Secret Sculptures of Komo: Art and Power in Bamana (Bambara) Initiation Associations. Working Papers in the Traditional Arts, No. 4. Philadelphia: ISHI.

McNeley, James Kale
1981   Holy Wind in Navajo Philosophy. Tucson: University of Arizona Press.

Mead, Margaret
1963   [orig. 1936] Sex and Temperament in Three Primitive Societies. New York: Morrow.
1970   [orig. 1938, 1940] The Mountain Arapesh, Vol. 2. New York: Natural History Press.

Meekison, Lisa
2000   Bangarra Dance Theatre. In Sylvia Kleinert and Margo Neale, eds., Oxford Companion to Aboriginal Art and Culture. New York: Oxford University Press. Pp. 367–369.

Megaw, V. S. and M. Ruth Megaw
2000   Painting Country: The Arrente Watercolour Artists of Hermannsburg. In Sylvia Kleinert and Margo Neale, eds., Oxford Companion to Aboriginal Art and Culture. New York: Oxford University Press. Pp. 197–204.

Meldgaard, Jorgen
1960   Eskimo Sculpture. London: Methuen.

Merriam, Alan P.
1964   The Anthropology of Music. Chicago: Northwestern University Press.
1973   The Bala Musician. In Warren L. d'Azevedo, ed., The Traditional Artist in African Societies. Bloomington: Indiana University Press. Pp. 255–277.

Messenger, John C. and Betty J. Messenger
1981   Sexuality in Folklore in a Nigerian Society. Central Issues in Anthropology 3(1):29–50.

Mitchell, William E.
1978   The Bamboo Fire. New York: Norton.

Moore, Charles A.
1967   Editor's Supplement: The Enigmatic Japanese Mind. In Charles A. Moore, ed., The Japanese Mind. Honolulu: University of Hawaii Press. Pp. 288–313.

Morphy, Howard
2000   Art and Politics: The Bark Petition and the Barunga Statement. In Sylvia Kleinert and Margo Neale, eds., Oxford Companion to Aboriginal Art and Culture. New York: Oxford University Press. Pp. 100–102.

Morris, Desmond
  1962   The Biology of Art. London: Cox and Wyman.
Morrissey, Philip
  2000   Aboriginal Writing. In Sylvia Kleinert and Margo Neale, eds., Oxford Companion to Aboriginal Art and Culture. New York: Oxford University Press. Pp. 313–319.
Morton, Eric
  2000   Comparing Yoruba and Western Aesthetics: A Philosophical View of African-American Art. Ijele: Art Journal of the African World. http://www.ijele.com/vol1.1/morton.html
Mountford, Charles Percy
  1954   Aboriginal Paintings from Australia: New York: New American Library.
  1961   The Artist and His Art in an Australian Aboriginal Society. In M.W. Smith, ed., The Artist in Tribal Society. New York: Free Press of Glencoe. Pp. 1–13.
Munn, Nancy
  1973   Walbiri Iconography: Graphic Representation and Cultural Symbolism in a Central Australian Society. Ithaca, N.Y.: Cornell University Press.
Munro, Thomas
  1965   Oriental Aesthetics. Cleveland, Ohio: Press of Western Reserve University.
Nakamura, Hajime
  1967   Basic Features of the Legal, Political, and Economic Thought of Japan. In Charles A. Moore, ed., The Japanese Mind. Honolulu: University of Hawaii Press. Pp. 143–163.
Nathan, David
  2000   The World Wide Web. In Sylvia Kleinert and Margo Neale, eds., Oxford Companion to Aboriginal Art and Culture. New York: Oxford University Press. Pp. 311–312.
Neale, Margo
  2000   United in the Struggle: Indigenous Art from Urban Areas. In Sylvia Kleinert and Margo Neale, eds., Oxford Companion to Aboriginal Art and Culture. New York: Oxford University Press. Pp. 267–278.
Nelson, Edward
  1899   The Eskimo about Bering Strait. Washington, D.C.: 18th Annual Report-Bureau of American Ethnology.
Newton, Douglas
  1971   Crocodile and Cassowary: Religious Art of the Upper Sepik River. New York: Museum of Primitive Art.
Nicholson, H.B.
  1976   Late Pre-Hispanic Central Mexican Iconographic Systems. In H.B. Nicholson, ed., Origins of Religious Art and Iconography in Pre-

classic Mesoamerica. U.C.L.A. Latin American Studies Series, 31. Los Angeles: University of California Latin American Center.

Nutini, Hugo
1988   Todos Santos in Tlaxcala: A Syncretic, Expressive, and Symbolic Analysis of the Cult of the Dead. Princeton, N.J.: Princeton University Press.

Oakes Jill E., Rick Riewe, and Roderick R. Riewe
1996   Our Boots : An Inuit Women's Art. New York: Thames & Hudson.

Oien, Kathleen
2000   Aboriginal Contemporary Music: Rockin' Into the Mainstream? In Sylvia Kleinert and Margo Neale, eds., Oxford Companion to Aboriginal Art and Culture. New York: Oxford University Press. Pp. 335–339.

Olson, Glendin
1982   Literature in Recreation in the Later Middle Ages. Ithaca, N.Y.: Cornell University Press.

O'Neale, Lila M.
1932   Yorok-Karok Basket Weavers. University of California Publications in American Archaeology and Ethnology 32(1):1–184.

Organ, Troy
1975   Indian Aesthetics—Its Techniques and Assumptions. Journal of Aesthetic Education 9(1):11–27.

Ortiz, Alfonso
1972   Ritual Drama and the Pueblo World View. In Alfonso Ortiz, ed., New Perspectives on the Pueblos. Albuquerque: University of New Mexico Press. Pp. 135–161.

Osborne, Harold
1968   Aesthetics and Art Theory: An Historical Introduction. New York: E.P. Dutton.
1974   Primitive Art and Society: Review Article. British Journal of Aesthetics 14(4):290–303.

Ottenberg, Simon
1982   Illusion, Communication, and Psychology in West African Masquerades. Ethos 10(2):149–185.

Oxford English Dictionary
1971   Compact Edition. New York: Oxford University Press.

Pager, Harold
1975   Stone Age Myth and Magic as Documented in the Rock Paintings of South Africa. Graz, Austria: Akademische Druck- und Verlagsanslalt.

Pandy, K.C.
1952   Comparative Aesthetics. Volume I, Indian Aesthetics; Volume II, Western Aesthetics. Varanasi-I, India: Chowkhambra Sanskrit Series Office.

Panofsky, Erwin
    1955   Meaning in the Visual Arts. Chicago: University of Chicago Press.
Parezo, Nancy J.
    1982   Navajo Sandpaintings: The Importance of Sex Roles in Craft Production. American Indian Quarterly 6(1–2):125–148.
    1983   Navajo Sandpainting: From Religious Act to Commercial Art. Tucson: University of Arizona Press.
Park, Edwards
    1986   Around the Mall and Beyond. Smithsonian 17(9):22–24.
Pasztory, Esther
    1983   Aztec Art. New York: Abrams.
Peckham, M.
    1965   Man's Rage for Chaos: Biology, Behavior and the Arts. Philadelphia: Chilton.
Pepper, Steven C.
    1945   The Basis of Criticism in the Arts. Cambridge: Harvard University Press.
Price, Richard and Sally Price
    1981   Afro-American Arts of the Suriname Rain Forest. Berkeley: University of California Press.
Raffe, W.G.
    1952   Ragas and Raginis: A Key to Hindu Aesthetics. Journal of Aesthetics and Art Criticism II (2):105–117.
Rasmussen, Knut
    1929   Intellectual Culture of the Iglulik Eskimos. Fifth Thule, Vol. 7(1). New York: AMS Press.
    1931   The Netsilik Eskimos: Social Life and Spiritual Culture. Fifth Thule, Vol. 8. New York: AMS Press.
    1932   Intellectual Culture of the Copper Eskimos. Fifth Thule, Vol. 9. New York: AMS Press.
Ravicz, Marilyn Ekdahl
    1976   Ephemeral Art: A Case for the Functions of Aesthetic Stimulus. Paper read at the American Anthropological Association meeting, November 19, 1976. New York City.
Rawson, Philip
    1973   The Art of Tantra. London: Thames & Hudson.
Ray, Dorothy Jean
    1961   Artists of the Tundra and Sea. Seattle: University of Washington Press.
    1977   Eskimo Art: Tradition and Innovation in North Alaska. Seattle: University of Washington Press.
    1981   Aleut and Eskimo Art: Tradition and Innovation in South Alaska. Seattle: University of Washington Press.

1996   A Legacy of Arctic Art. Seattle: University of Washington Press.

Regan, Margaret
1997   Navajo Painter, Emmi Whitehorse. Tucson Weekly, December 1, 1997.

Reichard, Gladys A.
1936   Navajo Shepherd and Weaver. New York: J.J. Augustin.
1944   Prayer: The Compulsive Word. American Ethnological Society Monograph 7. Seattle: University of Washington Press.
1970   [orig. 1950] Navajo Religion: A Study of Symbolism. Princeton: Princeton University Press.
1977   [orig. 1939] Navajo Medicine Man Sandpaintings. New York: Dover.

Rice, Prudence M.
1983   Serpents and Style in Peten Postclassic Pottery. American Anthropologist 85(4):866–880.

Rosenak, Chuck and Jan Rosenak
1994   Navajo Folk Art: the People Speak. Flagstaff, Ariz.: Northland Publishing.

Ross, Margaret Clunies and L.R. Hiatt
1978   Sand Sculptures at a Gidjingali Burial Rite. In Peter J. Ucko, ed., Form in Indigenous Art. London: Duckworth.

Ross, Stephen David, ed.
1994   Art and Its Significance: An Anthology of Aesthetic Theory. Third edition. Albany: State University of New York.

Russell, Bertrand
1967   The Autobiography of Bertrand Russell, Vol. 1. Toronto: McClelland and Steward.

Ryusaku, Tsunoda, William Theodore de Bary, and Donald Keene, eds.
1958   Sources of Japanese Tradition. New York: Columbia University Press.

Salisbury, Richard P.
1959   A Trobriand Medusa? Man 59(67):50–51.

Saraswati, S.K.
1969   Indian Art: Artist's Point of View. In S.S. Barlingay et al., Indian Aesthetics and Art Activity. Transactions of the Indian Institute of Advanced Study, No. 2. New York: International Publications Service. Pp. 89–91.

Sartwell, Crispin
1995   The Art of Living: Aesthetics of the Ordinary in World Spiritual Traditions. Albany: State University of New York Pr.

Sassouni, Viken
1981   Armenian Church Floor Plans. Hali: The International Journal of Oriental Carpets and Textiles 4(1):24–28.

Sayers, Andrew
  2001   Australian Art. New York: Oxford University Press.
Schapera, Isaac
  1930   The Khoisan Peoples of South Africa. London: Routledge.
Schmitz, Carl August
  1963   Wantoat: Art and Religion of the Northeast New Guinea Papuans.
          Trans. G.E. van Baaren-Pape. The Hague: Mouton.
Schneider, Harold K.
  1956   The Interpretation of Pakot Visual Art. Man 56:103–106.
  1966   Turu Esthetic Concepts. American Anthropologist 68:156–160.
Sculthorpe, Gaye
  2000   When Whitefellas Go Walkabout. In Sylvia Kleinert and Margo
          Neale, eds., Oxford Companion to Aboriginal Art and Culture.
          New York: Oxford University Press. Pp. 391–397.
Seidelman, Harold, James Turner, and George Swinton
  1994   [Reprint edition, 2001] The Inuit Imagination: Arctic Myth and
          Sculpture. University of Washington Press
Seizer, Richard
  1979   Confessions of a Knife. New York: Simon & Schuster.
Shostak, Marjorie
  1981   Nisa: The Life and Words of a !Kung Woman. Cambridge, Mass.:
          Harvard University Press.
  1984   The Creative Individual in the World of the !Kung San. Paper read
          at the Annual Meeting of the American Anthropological Associa-
          tion, November 15, 1984, Denver, Colorado.
  2000   Return to Nisa. Cambrige, Mass.: Harvard University Press.
Sieber, Roy
  1962   Masks as Agents of Social Control. African Studies Bulletin
          5(11):8–13.
  1971   [orig. 1958] The Aesthetics of Traditional African Art. In Carol F.
          Jopling, ed., Art and Aesthetics in Primitive Societies. New York:
          Dutton. Pp. 127–131. Orig. in Froelich Rainey, ed., Seven Metals of
          Africa. Philadelphia: University Museum, University of Pennsylva-
          nia.
Silver, Harry
  1981   Calculating Risks: The Socioeconomic Foundations of Aesthetic
          Innovation in an Ashanti Carving Community. Ethnology 20(2):
          101–114.
  1999   Tourist Art as the Crafting of Identity in the Sepik River (Papua
          New Guinea). In Unpacking Culture: Art and Commodity in Colo-
          nial and Postcolonial Worlds, Ruth B. Phillips and Christopher B.
          Steiner, eds. Berkeley: University of California Press.
Smith, Michael E.
  1996   The Aztecs. Cambridge, Mass.: Blackwell

Spencer, Baldwin and F.J. Gillan
  1938   The Native Tribes of Central Australia. London: Macmillan.
Stolnitz, Jerome
  1960   Aesthetics and Philosophy of Art Criticism: A Critical Introduction. Boston: Houghton-Mifflin.
Stewart, Gloria
  1972   Introduction to Sepik Art of Papua New Guinea. Sydney: Garrick Press.
Stow, George W.
  1905   The Native Races of South Africa. London: Sonneschein.
Strathern, Andrew and Marilyn Strathern
  1971   Self-decoration in Mount Hagen. Toronto: University of Toronto Press.
Strathern, Marilyn
  1979   The Self in Self-decoration. Oceania 48:241–257.
Suzuki, D.T.
  1983   [orig. 1959] Excerpt from Zen and Japanese Culture. In Earle J. Coleman, ed., Varieties of Aesthetic Experience. Lanham, Md.: University Press of America. Pp. 179–190.
Swinton, George
  1978   Touch and the Real: Contemporary Inuit Aesthetics-Theory, Usage, and Relevance. In Michael Greenhalgh and Vincent Megaw, eds., Art in Society. New York: St. Martins. Pp. 71–88.
  1999   Sculpture of the Inuit 3rd edition. Manitoba: McClellan & Stewart.
Sylvain, Renee
  2002   "Land, Water, and Truth": San Identity and Global Indigenism. American Anthropologist 104(4):1074–1085.
Symonds, Donald
  1995   Beauty Is in the Adaptations of the Beholder: The Evolutionary Psychology of Human Female Sexual Attractiveness. In Paul R. Abramson and Steven D. Pinkerton, eds., Sexual Nature, Sexual Culture. Chicago: University of Chicago Press.
Taçon, Paul S.C.
  1983   Dorset Art in Relation to Prehistoric Culture Stress. Etudes Inuit/Inuit Studies 7(1):41–65.
Tanaka, Sen'o
  1998   The Tea Ceremony. Tokyo: Kodansha International.
Tatarkiewicz, Wladyslaw
  1970a   History of Aesthetics. Vol. I: Ancient Aesthetics, ed. by J. Harrell, trans. by Adam and Ann Czerniawski. Warsaw: Polish Scientific Publishers.
  1970b   History of Aesthetics, Vol. II: Medieval Aesthetics, ed. by C. Barrett, trans. by R.M. Montgomery. Warsaw: Polish Scientific Publishers.

Tatarkiewicz
1974 Style and Meaning in Sepik Art. In Anthony Forge, ed., Primitive Art and Society. New York: Oxford University Press. Pp. 169–192.

Taylor, Luke
1996 Seeing the Inside: Bark Painting in Western Arnhem Land. Oxford, England: Clarendon Press.
2000 Rock Art as Inspiration in Western Arnhem Land. In Sylvia Kleinert and Margo Neale, eds., Oxford Companion to Aboriginal Art and Culture. New York: Oxford University Press. Pp. 109–117.

Theal, George McCall
1910 The Yellow and Dark-Skinned People of Africa South of the Zambesi. London: Swann Sonneschein.

Thomas, Elizabeth Marshall
1959 The Harmless People. New York: Random House.

Thompson, Robert Farris
1968 Esthetics in Traditional Africa. Art News 66(9):44–45, 63–68.
1971 [orig. 1966] An Aesthetic of the Cool: West African Dance. African Forum 2(2):85–102.
1973 Yoruba Artistic Criticism. In Warren L. d'Azevedo, ed., The Traditional Artist in African Societies. Bloomington: Indiana University Press. Pp. 19–61.
1974 African Art in Motion: Icon and Act. Berkeley: University of California Press.
1976 Black Gods and Kings. Bloomington: Indiana University Press.
1983 Flash of the Spirit: African and Afro-American Art and Philosophy. New York: Random House.
1994 The Three Warriors: Atlantic Altars of Esu, Ogun, and Osoosi. In Abiodun, Rowland, Henry J. Drewal, and John Pemberton III, eds., The Yoruba Artist: New Theoretical Perspectives on African Arts. Washington, D.C.: Smithsonian Institution Press. Pp. 225–239.

Tobias, Philip V.
1961 New Evidence and New Views on the Evolution of Man in Africa. South African Journal of Science 57(2):25–38.

Tschopik, Harry S., Jr.
1938 Taboo as a Possible Factor Involved in the Obsolescence of Navaho Pottery and Basketry. American Anthropologist 40:257–262.

Turner, Victor
1966 Colour Classification in Ndembu Ritual: A Problem in Primitive Classification. In Michael Banton, ed., Anthropological Approaches to the Study of Religion. London: Tavistock. ASA Monographs NC, 3. Pp. 47–84.

Turner, Terence S.
1980 The Social Skin. In Jeremy Cherfas and Roger Lewin, eds., Not Work Alone. London: Temple Smith. Pp. 112–140.

Tuzin, Donald F.
1980 The Voice of Tambaran: Truth and Illusion in Ilahita Arapesh Religion. Berkeley: University of California Press.

Ucko, Peter J., ed.
1977 Form in Indigenous Art. Canberra: Australian Institute of Aboriginal and Torres Strait Islander Studies.

Ueda, Makoto
1967 Literary and Art Theories in Japan. Cleveland: The Press of Western Reserve University.

Vaillant, George Clapp
1944 The Aztecs of Mexico. New York: Doubleday.

Van der Post, Laurens
1958 The Lost World of the Kalahari. New York: Harcourt, Brace, Jovanovich.

van Offelen, Marion
1983 Nomads of Niger. Photographs by Carol Beckwith. New York: Morrow.

Vatsyayan, Kapila
1968 Indian Aesthetics and Art Activity. In 5.5. Barlingay et al., Indian Aesthetics and Art Activity. Transactions of the Indian Institute of Advanced Study, No. 2. New York: International Publications Service.

Vogel, Susan M.
1979 Baule and Yoruba Art Criticism: A Comparison. In Justine M. Cordwell, ed., The Visual Arts: Plastic and Graphic. The Hague: Mouton. Pp. 309–325.
1980 Beauty in the Eyes of the Baule: Aesthetics and Cultural Values. Working Papers in the Traditional Arts, No. 6. Philadelphia: Institute for the Study of Human Issues.

Wardwell, Allen
1989 The Art of the Sepik River: An Introduction. In Leanne A. Klein, et al., People of the River, People of the Tree: Change and Continuity in Sepik and Asmat Art. Saint Paul: Minnesota Museum of Art. Pp. 5–12.

Waterman, Richard A. and Patricia Panyity Waterman
1970 Directions of Culture Change in Aboriginal Arnhem Land. In Arnold R. Pilling and Richard A. Waterman, eds., Diprotodon to Detribalization: Studies of Change among Australian Aborigines. East Lansing: Michigan State University Press. Pp. 101–115.

Watson, Christine
2000 Writing on Walls: Reflections of Rock-Art Traditions in "Urban" Aboriginal Art. In Sylvia Kleinert and Margo Neale, eds., Oxford Companion to Aboriginal Art and Culture. New York: Oxford University Press. Pp. 126–128.

Weitz, Morris
  1967 [orig. 1957] The Role of Theory in Aesthetics. In Monroe C. Beardsley and Herbert M. Schueller, eds., Aesthetic Inquiry. Belmont, Calif.: Dickenson. Pp. 3–11.

Werner, H.
  1906 Anthropologische, Ethnologische und Ethnographische Beobachtungen uber die Heihum und Kungbuschleute, nebst einern Anhang uber die Sprachen dieser Buschmannstämme. Zeitschrift für Ethnologic 38:241–268. Trans. in Human Relations Area files by Richard Neuse.

Westheim, Paul
  1965 [orig. 1950] The Art of Ancient Mexico. Trans. Ursula Bernard. New York: Doubleday.

Whiten, Andrew
  1976 Primate Perception and Aesthetics. In D. Brothwell, ed., Beyond Aesthetics. London: Thames and Hudson. Pp. 18–40.

Whiting, John W.M.
  1941 Becoming a Kwoma: Teaching and Learning in a New Guinea Tribe. New Haven, Conn.: Yale University Press.

Widlok, Thomas
  1999 Living on Mangetti: "Bushman" Autonomy and Namibian Independence (Oxford Studies in Social and Cultural Anthropology). New York: Oxford University Press.

Wilde, Oscar
  1891 The Picture of Dorian Gray. London: Oxford University Press.

Willett, Frank
  1971 African Art: An Introduction. New York: Praeger.

Witherspoon, Gary
  1977 Language and Art in the Navajo Universe. Ann Arbor: University of Michigan Press.
  1980 Language in Culture and Culture in Language. International Journal of American Linguistics 46(1):1–13.
  1981 Self-expression and Self-esteem in Navajo Weaving. Plateau 52(4):29–32.

Witherspoon, Gary and Glen Peterson
  1995 Dynamic Symmetry and Holistic Asymmetry in Navajo and Western Art and Cosmology (American Indian Studies, Vol. 5). New York: Peter Lang Publishing.

Wobst, H. Martin
  1977 Stylistic Behavior and Information Exchange. In CE. Cleland, ed., For the Director: Research Essays in Honor of James B. Griffen. Anthropological Papers NC, 61. Ann Arbor: Museum of Anthropology, University of Michigan.

Wolfe, Alvin W.
    1969   Social Structural Bases of Art. Current Anthropology 10(1):14–44.
Wolfe, Tom
    1975   The Painted Word. Harpers Magazine, April, 1975. Pp. 57–92.
Wreschner, Ernst E.
    1976   The Red Hunters: Further Thoughts on the Evolution of Speech. Current Anthropology 17(4):717–719.
    1980   Red Ochre and Human Evolution: A Case for Discussion. Current Anthropology 21(5):631–644.
Zantwijk, Rudolf A.M. Van
    1957   Aztec Hymns as the Expression of the Mexican Philosophy of Life. International Archives of Ethnography 48(1):67–118.
Zenkovsky, V.V.
    1962   Dostoevsky's Religious and Philosophical Views. In René Wellekc, ed., Dostoevsky: A Collection of Critical Essays. Englewood Cliffs, N.J.: Prentice Hall. Pp. 130–145.
Zolbrod, Paul G.
1983/1988   Dine Bahané: The Navajo Creation Story. Albuquerque: University of New Mexico Press. Reprinted 1988.

INDEX